PRAISE FOR ALI SOUFAN AND
ANATOMY OF TERROR

"Ali Soufan is our most important chronicler of the rise and spread of Islamist terror movements. A former FBI agent who identified the hijackers of 9/11, and whose interrogation of al-Qaeda members—without torture—led to innumerable breakthroughs, Soufan is a unique resource and a moral beacon. In a time when our intelligence community as well as our country seem to have lost their bearings, his clear voice guides us through the fog of war and partisanship. Anyone who wants to understand the world we live in now should read this book."   —Lawrence Wright, Pulitzer Prize–winning author of *The Looming Tower* and *The Terror Years*

"Revealing and timely. . . . Soufan writes with immense knowledge and authority. . . . *Anatomy of Terror* not only tells a gripping story but is filled with insights that put today's terror attacks by the Islamic State and Al Qaeda in perspective with the history and complicated geopolitics of the region."   —Michiko Kakutani, *New York Times*

"*Anatomy of Terror* tells the stories of the leaders of al-Qaeda and IS. . . . [F]or America, the main enemies are still the organized groups abroad."   —*Economist*

"To those inside the U.S. government, Soufan has long been something of a legend. He conducted the most effective and fruitful interrogations of Al-Qaeda suspects during the war on terrorism, and save for some inexplicable failures by the CIA, he and his team might well have prevented 9/11."   —*Harper's*

"Anyone interested in terrorism needs this book: . . . it provides a blend of history and social and political inspection that lends authority and insights."   —*Midwest Book Review*

"A concise, accessible, enormously readable account of the trajectory of al-Qaeda. . . . In a dizzying scenario of violence, Soufan provides clarity and balance."   —*Kirkus Reviews*, starred review

"Highly informative and compelling. . . . An important book for everyone who wants to understand the influence of bin Laden and al-Qaeda on today's terrorist groups."
     —Nader Entessar, *Library Journal*

"A deep look at the inner workings, ideology, internal politics, and strategies of modern Islamic terrorism. . . . Soufan reveals himself to be a true expert."   —*Publishers Weekly*

"A true insider's perspective. . . . This is an important and unsettling effort to describe and understand a threat that will continue indefinitely."   —Jay Freeman, *Booklist*

ALSO BY ALI SOUFAN

The Black Banners: The Inside Story of 9/11
and the War Against al-Qaeda

ANATOMY OF TERROR

From the Death of
bin Laden to the Rise
of the Islamic State

ALI SOUFAN

W. W. NORTON & COMPANY NEW YORK | LONDON
Independent Publishers Since 1923

To Heather

For information about permission to reproduce selections from this
book, write to Permissions, W. W. Norton & Company, Inc.,
500 Fifth Avenue, New York, NY 10110

For information about special discounts for bulk purchases, please contact
W. W. Norton Special Sales at specialsales@wwnorton.com or 800-233-4830

Manufacturing by Quad Graphics Fairfield
Book design by Dana Sloan
Production manager: Anna Oler

Library of Congress Cataloging-in-Publication Data

Names: Soufan, Ali H., author.
Title: Anatomy of terror : from the death of Bin Laden
to the rise of the Islamic State / Ali Soufan.
Description: New York : W. W. Norton & Company, 2017. |
Includes bibliographical references and index.
Identifiers: LCCN 2016055805 | ISBN 9780393241174 (hardcover)
Subjects: LCSH: Terrorism—Religious aspects—Islam. | Bin Laden,
Osama, 1957–2011. | Radicalism—Religious aspects—Islam. | Qaida
(Organization) | IS (Organization)
Classification: LCC HV6431 .S6465 2017 | DDC 363.325—dc23
LC record available at https://lccn.loc.gov/2016055805

ISBN 978-0-393-35588-8 pbk.

W. W. Norton & Company, Inc.
500 Fifth Avenue, New York, N.Y. 10110
www.wwnorton.com

W. W. Norton & Company Ltd.
15 Carlisle Street, London W1D 3BS

1 2 3 4 5 6 7 8 9 0

Now the hydra had a huge body, with nine heads, eight mortal, but the middle one immortal. . . . By pelting it with fiery shafts he forced it to come out, and in the act of doing so he seized and held it fast. But the hydra wound itself about one of his feet and clung to him. Nor could he effect anything by smashing its heads with his club, for as fast as one head was smashed there grew up two.

—PSEUDO-APOLLODORUS, *THE LIBRARY*, BOOK 2, CHAPTER 5

CONTENTS

A Note on Sources　　　ix

INTRODUCTION　Friends and Enemies　　　xi

PROLOGUE　The Old Man of the Mountain　　　1

CHAPTER 1　The Snake with Broken Teeth　　　5

CHAPTER 2　Allegience　　　43

CHAPTER 3　The Disaster　　　83

CHAPTER 4　The Emir of the Strangers　　　109

CHAPTER 5　Doctor, Wise Man, Teacher, Traitor　　　161

CHAPTER 6　The Syrian Wars　　　205

CHAPTER 7　Those Who Loose and Bind　　　233

CHAPTER 8　Steadfast Sons　　　275

CONCLUSION　Slaying the Hydra　　　289

Acknowledgments　　　305

Notes　　　307

Index　　　345

A NOTE ON SOURCES

I have spent more than two decades investigating and analyzing al-Qaeda and its offshoots. As a result, I have developed a considerable degree of familiarity with the organization's structure, methods, and narratives. With that knowledge as my guide, I consulted thousands of documents, including previously classified material and the writings, both public and private, of the terrorists themselves, alongside the best secondary sources, including research carried out by my organization, the Soufan Group. I also conducted interviews with knowledgeable individuals, many of whom bore painful witness to the events described. From this diverse array of sources, I have attempted to piece together the most comprehensive, detailed, and accurate account possible. On the few occasions where I have made assumptions in order to bridge evidential gaps, I have said as much either in the main text or in the notes that follow the text.

INTRODUCTION

FRIENDS AND ENEMIES

On a crisp morning in December of 2001, I picked up a pockmarked clay brick, one of thousands like it littering the site of what only weeks before had been a hideout for the most wanted man on earth. Perhaps, I thought, this very brick had formed part of the wall of Osama bin Laden's sleeping quarters, or the floor where he habitually sat to receive visitors. As I felt the heft and contour of that brick in my hands, I contemplated the unlikely sequence of events—some in my lifetime, others over long centuries—that had brought me to that extraordinary time and place.

I was born in Lebanon, emigrated to America, and went to college and then grad school in Pennsylvania. I took a double major in political science and international relations, with a minor in cultural anthropology, and followed that up with a master's in foreign relations. With the Cold War freshly over and America's position as the world's only superpower seemingly secure, it was tempting to conceive of the world as a complex but orderly machine, in which nation-states would set rational policies and those rational policies would dictate logical strategies.

Yet there was something fundamentally unsatisfying about this clockwork view of the world. From my graduate studies, one prominent counterexample stuck in my mind—one from 2,500 years ago. The Peloponnesian War pitted Athens's Delian League against a coalition of states led by Sparta and eventually aided by the mighty Persian Empire. After a quarter century of alarms and reversals, Athens finally surrendered. By paving the way for Alexander's unification of Greece and his subsequent conquests, the war changed the course of European and world history. But the outcome was by no means foreordained. I came to see that all the key decisions were based neither on policy nor on strategy but on personalities. Speeches and emotional appeals consistently carried the day. Half a millennium later, Cato the Younger would mark this same phenomenon in Rome's rocky transformation from republic to empire. "When Cicero spoke," he said, "people marveled. When Caesar spoke, people marched."

Theories are great tools to think with. They open your mind, broaden your perspective. But it is people who make the world go round. Individual human beings, with all their idiosyncrasies and contradictions and baggage, with their ideas sculpted by culture and belief and education and economics and family, are the agents of every grand historical force that future generations will see smoldering in the tangled wreckage of the past.

While I was still a student, I began following through the Arabic press the exploits of a dissident Saudi millionaire named Osama bin Laden and his nascent extremist organization, al-Qaeda—the Base. I marveled at this man's audacity in declaring war on America, and his charismatic ability to attract followers to his side. But my own calling could not have been more different. Fresh out of grad school, I joined the Federal Bureau of Investigation, where one of my first assignments was to write a paper on this man bin Laden and his group. My report came to the attention of John O'Neill, the legendary head of the bureau's counterterrorism section, based in Manhattan. In time, John became my mentor and a close friend. When suicide bombers murdered seventeen American sailors aboard the USS *Cole* in October 2000, John assigned me to lead the investigation. I traveled to Sanaa, Yemen's ancient capital, and began running down leads and interrogating suspects.

John O'Neill retired from the bureau in the summer of 2001. I took him out to lunch to celebrate, and told him I was getting married. He gave me his blessing. But this would prove to be our last meeting. On August 23, John became security director for the World Trade Center. Two weeks later, he died rushing back into the south tower, courageous to the very end, determined to do what he had been doing his whole career: save lives.

Three months later, standing with my colleagues in the remains of bin Laden's bombed-out Kabul compound, I felt myself overcome by a strong sense of revenge—for my country, for the thousands murdered, and especially for John. Ever since the attacks, the al-Qaeda leader had been confidently predicting America's imminent downfall. Now, bin Laden and his extremist cohorts were learning that the United States and its broad coalition of allies would not give in to terrorism so easily. For now, the sheikh still evaded capture, but the tide had turned. The piles of rubble, the lone wall that remained of a sizable residence, the twisted metal of what had once been a staircase, the smattering of air-dropped leaflets offering twenty-five million dollars for information leading to bin Laden's capture, all bore witness to the turn of fortune's wheel. Back home in the United States, some political leaders were already talking about Afghanistan as a future democratic beacon for the region.

In the decade that followed, my life changed utterly. I spent another four years with the FBI, investigating the 9/11 attacks and other terrorist crimes. I got married, left the bureau, and eventually became the father of three very energetic boys. And so it was that, on a Sunday evening in the spring of 2011, I found myself at home, assembling a pair of swing seats for our newborn twins as the television chattered away in the background. At around 9:45 pm, a special announcement broke through the babble: the president would shortly be addressing the nation. Clearly, something big had happened.

It was 11:35 p.m. by the time President Obama approached a podium in the East Room of the White House and confirmed to the world that U.S. Navy SEALs had killed Osama bin Laden. As the president spoke of the people bin Laden had murdered, of the families bereaved, of the children left fatherless, my thoughts turned again to John O'Neill and the other friends I had lost along the way. Near the end of his remarks, Obama said, "Justice has been done." That was certainly true, but the ramifications of bin Laden's demise had yet to play out. Would the jihadist edifice simply crumble without its keystone? Or would bin Laden prove more powerful as a martyr than he ever had been as a living leader? No doubt these questions were on the president's mind, too. ABC News's Martha Raddatz had reported "absolute jubilation throughout government." For my part, I could not help but feel more troubled than jubilant.

Emails began flooding my inbox, from friends and colleagues congratulating me, and from reporters seeking my take on events. An editor from the *New York Times* asked if I would put my views in an op-ed for the paper. I sat down to analyze the situation. I thought of all the dozens of al-Qaeda acolytes I had interrogated over the years, playing high-stakes games of mental chess with extremists and murderers for the sake of extracting priceless evidence. They had pledged *bayat* to bin Laden, swearing allegiance neither to the office nor the organization but to the man himself. To whom would zealots such as these now declare fealty?

Osama bin Laden had been uniquely well equipped to lead the network he founded. He had walked away from the wealth and luxury of the Saudi upper crust in order to devote himself to jihad, against the Soviets and then against America. This personal history helped him in two ways. First, his freely chosen asceticism helped inspire fanatical devotion among his followers. Secondly, at the same time, his privileged background endowed him with contacts among wealthy elites willing to bankroll terrorism. Bin Laden's death would therefore leave a gaping hole in al-Qaeda's recruitment and fund-raising efforts.

It seemed likely that bin Laden's longtime deputy, Ayman al-Zawahiri, would be named the new emir. If so, I knew that he would struggle. To be sure, Zawahiri is clever and strategic. He is, after all, a fully trained surgeon who honed his militant skills battling the Sadat and Mubarak regimes in his native Egypt. He is also a zealot of uncompromising brutality, responsible more than anyone for justifying the tactic of suicide bombing and by extension for the tragic toll it has taken on innocent Muslims. But for all his intelligence, his cunning, and his zeal, Zawahiri possesses none of the charisma bin Laden had. Indeed, his personality has alienated many people over the years. More importantly still, Zawahiri is an Egyptian. Within al-Qaeda, his appointment would inflame the already tense internecine rivalry between his countrymen and the Gulf Arabs who make up the jihadi rank and file.

As an organization, then, al-Qaeda was in deep trouble. But what of bin Ladenism as an idea? That, I felt, was a different story. I feared that some of the regional groups that bin Laden had worked so hard to keep in line—like al-Qaeda in the Arabian Peninsula (AQAP), al-Qaeda in Iraq (AQI), al-Qaeda in the Islamic Maghreb (AQIM), and al-Shabaab in the Horn of Africa—would split off. They might even intensify their ideology. No doubt they would see the nascent Arab Spring as an opportunity to impose their ideas on their fellow Muslims. In the pages of the *New York Times* I wrote:

> [W]e *cannot rest on our laurels. Most of Al Qaeda's leadership council members are still at large, and they command their own followers. They will try to carry out operations to prove Al Qaeda's continuing relevance. And with Al Qaeda on the decline,*

regional groups that had aligned themselves with the network may return to operating independently, making them harder to monitor and hence deadlier.

It brings me no pleasure to see those premonitions borne out. Al-Qaeda has indeed fractured into regional units. Zawahiri, the cold bureaucrat, has struggled to maintain control. Meanwhile, the cancer of bin Ladenism has metastasized across the Middle East and North Africa and beyond, carried by even more virulent vectors. Whereas on 9/11 al-Qaeda had around 400 members, today it has thousands upon thousands, in franchises and affiliates spread from the shores of the Pacific to Africa's Atlantic seaboard—and that is without even counting the breakaway armed group that calls itself the Islamic State. Al-Qaeda's Syrian branch alone has more members than bin Laden ever imagined for his entire network. It is striking to note that, in October of 2015, more than fourteen years after the 9/11 attacks, U.S. forces disrupted what is believed to be the largest al-Qaeda training camp ever—all thirty square miles of it—right in the organization's historic heartland of Afghanistan.

In the Middle East, the Islamic State, al-Qaeda's most vicious off-shoot to date, employs methods so savage that even hardened terrorists publicly denounce their brutality. Where bin Laden encouraged militants in his network to focus on attacking the West directly rather than hitting regimes in the Muslim world, the Islamic State has successfully done both. It has brought mass murder to the streets of Paris, airports in Brussels and Istanbul, a Russian airliner in the skies over Sinai, and a Christmas market in Berlin. It has killed worshipers at mosques in Yemen and Kuwait, attacked police, soldiers, and border guards in Egypt and Saudi Arabia, and bombed political rallies in Turkey. At the same time, it has conquered millions of acres across Iraq and Syria, aided by tens of thousands of foreign recruits. The organization's formal break with al-Qaeda in 2014 has not stopped the Islamic State from expanding to other troubled regions of the world, most notably Libya. The group has even established a beachhead in remote regions of Afghanistan, where it vies violently for control with al-Qaeda's longstanding allies, the Taliban, who governed Afghanistan until the United States removed them from power in 2001.

A video popular among Muslims living in the projects of East London, Birmingham, and elsewhere in England shows a man squatting in a Syrian field, his features covered with a ski mask, his rifle at the ready. Fighting in the Levant is "not as easy as pulling out your nine-millimeter on a back road of the streets of London and blasting a guy," he says in a forthright East London accent. "It's not as easy as putting up your feet on the couch after a hard day's work on the corner." Inspired by such bin Ladenist propaganda, as many as 38,000 foreigners had joined the fighting in Syria by the end of 2015. Compare that to the Afghan jihad against the Soviets, which attracted "only" 8,000 foreign nationals. And whereas those who made the journey to that conflict came overwhelmingly from Muslim-majority countries, the war in Syria has attracted over 5,000 foreign fighters from the United States and the European Union, as well as many hundreds from Russia. Around 20 to 30 percent of these fighters have already returned home. Not all of them are plotting violence, by any means; but the numbers are so great that even if only a small proportion of these fighters emerge from the conflict as hardened terrorists, it could spell big trouble for the West. How big? Think of it this way: the Islamic State's attacks on Paris in November of 2015, in which 130 innocent people died, were perpetrated by just 9 men.

My first book, *The Black Banners*, told the tale of al-Qaeda up to the death of its founder. In this book, I aim to take the story further. True to my conviction that personalities matter, I will focus my story through the eyes of several key individuals, notably bin Laden himself; Saif al-Adel, his wily security chief; Ayman al-Zawahiri, his deputy and successor; Abu Musab al-Zarqawi, the Jordanian militant who founded the organization that would become the Islamic State; Abu Bakr al-Baghdadi, the group's current "caliph"; and the men (and in bin Laden's case, the women) of their inner circles. Through these characters, we will trace the transformation of al-Qaeda as an organization, the simultaneous development of bin Ladenism into a far more potent and lethal force, the rise and decline of the Islamic State, and the impending resurgence of al-Qaeda.

In its landmark final report, the 9/11 Commission concluded that the tragic attacks of September 2001 were allowed to proceed in part because of a catastrophic "failure of imagination" on the part of U.S. intelligence. Analysts commonly asserted that they simply couldn't imagine someone flying a plane into a building. In a similar vein, a month before the U.S. invasion of Iraq in 2003, Deputy Secretary of Defense Paul Wolfowitz told a Senate panel, "It's hard to conceive that it would take more forces to provide stability in post-Saddam Iraq than it would take to conduct the war itself and to secure the surrender of Saddam's security forces and his army." It took less than two months, and minimal U.S. casualties, to conquer the country; yet eight years, five thousand coalition deaths, and $1.7 trillion were nowhere near enough to "provide stability in post-Saddam Iraq."

Know your enemy, Sun Tsu admonishes us across the millennia. And yet, time and again, when inquiries are held and hard questions asked, the response amounts to, "We couldn't *conceive*, we couldn't *imagine*, we couldn't *wrap our heads around* the possibility that something like this could happen." Or, just as bad, we *did* imagine some worst-case scenario and therefore it was *sure* to happen—as in the so-called One Percent Doctrine espoused by Vice President Dick Cheney, who told Americans, "If there is a one percent chance that Pakistani scientists are helping al-Qaeda build or develop a nuclear weapon, we have to treat it as a certainty in terms of our response. It's not about our analysis. It's about our response." That is the high road to an absurd and ruinous waste of finite intelligence, military, diplomatic, and law-enforcement resources.

The key to a more constructive use of our imaginations is empathy— not in the colloquial sense of sharing another person's perspective, but in the clinical sense of being able to see the world through another person's eyes. Sadly, after fifteen years of the war on terrorism, we still do not really know our enemy in this deeper sense. In this book, by delving into the personalities of men who mean us harm, I aim not to create sympathy for them—far from it—but to help point the way to a deeper understanding of their worldview, their motivations, and how best to combat the destructive ideology they represent.

I still have that battered clay brick I picked up in bin Laden's shattered hideout. A decade and a half later, it sits on a shelf in my office in Midtown Manhattan. Looking at it while I work reminds me of the progress we have made against terrorism since I first picked it up on that winter morning, but also of the missteps we have made along the way, and above all of how far we have still to go. We have killed the messenger. But the message lives.

ANATOMY OF TERROR

THE OLD MAN OF THE MOUNTAIN

Once upon a time, there was a terrorist who dwelled in the mountains. Throughout the Muslim world and beyond, his name became a byword for brutality. Tribal chieftains, great religious leaders, even sovereign rulers would take extraordinary pains to protect themselves against the terrorist and the cadre of killers he commanded. So loyal were his acolytes to their sheikh, so certain of the Paradise he promised, that they were prepared to die—horribly—on his command. His followers claimed to be the most faithful among the faithful. Their aim was twofold: to shield from its perceived enemies the religious sect to which they belonged, and to eliminate from this imperfect world the corrupting influence of apostasy and religious impurity. Their modus operandi was public murder: every death a spectacle, every spectacle a political message.

Niceties such as guilt or innocence did not trouble the terrorist or his men; they operated under a fatwa, an infallible religious ruling, commanding the murder of "infidels"—non-Muslims—and "apostates"—Muslims who failed to live up to the terrorist's own

1

austere interpretation of Islam. And, of course, the terrorist and his men arrogated to themselves the right to distinguish between faithful and faithless. It was no surprise, therefore, that the vast majority of the terrorist's victims were not Christians, Jews, or Zoroastrians but fellow Muslims.

Today, this terrorist is dead—long dead. His name was Hassan-i Sabbah. He was born sometime in the mid-eleventh century and died in 1124. The death cult he founded has long since faded away, but not before outliving its creator by more than a hundred years. Its name has passed into legend around the world—the Assassins. For Hassan-i Sabbah, the most prominent apostates were the Seljuks—the Turkish dynasty that ruled over much of the medieval Islamic world. The principal infidels were the Crusaders, who periodically rode in from western Europe to impose their disfigured version of Christian morality on the Holy Land.

Today's terrorists see the world in similar terms. Their apostates are the modern-day rulers of the Islamic world, be they secular, like Egypt's military strongmen, or allied to the West, like the House of Saud. Their infidels are the Christians, the Jews, the Americans, the West in general. They imagine themselves beset by contemporary Crusades, both literal and figurative. Some, like Boko Haram in Nigeria and the Taliban in Afghanistan, see modern, Western-style education as a conspiracy against Islam. Today's fanatic killers may use suicide bombs instead of poison-tipped daggers, but they deploy eerily similar fatwas to justify their indiscriminate murder of innocent people at the World Trade Center in New York, in neighborhoods of Beirut, on trains in London and Madrid, on a residential street in Baghdad, at a Bastille Day celebration in Nice, in a nightclub in Istanbul, and on and on.

In Hassan-i Sabbah's day, he and his followers were dismissed as wild outliers, able to execute their murderous missions only because they were stoked on drugs. The very word "Assassin" was said to derive from the Arabic *hashishin*, meaning "marijuana users." In the popular imagination, today's suicide bombers are seen as similarly brainwashed or brain-dead. In reality, many are troubled young people who discern little meaning in their own lives and view their acts as an ultimate expression of faith. Similarly, modern scholarship teaches that the word "Assassin" more likely derives not from any pharmacological association but from the Arabic *asas* (foundation of the faith). The Assassins were seen as returning to the basic principles of their religion—in other words, as fundamentalists. That is a vital difference, and one with enormous contemporary resonance. Not for nothing is the most notorious modern terrorist group known as al-Qaeda—The Base, or, in an alternate rendering, The Foundation.

It was not always thus. In fact, Islam began as a liberalizing force. It introduced racial and social equality to an Arab tribal society that had previously enjoyed neither. Islam was supposed to enlighten Arabia and deliver it from the Jahiliyyah, the Days of Ignorance. Through the new faith, women gained the right to inherit property and divorce their husbands 1,300 years before many of their Western sisters would win similar privileges. *Ijtihad*, independent thinking, was actively encouraged—one large reason why philosophy, literature, and the sciences all flourished throughout the first few hundred years of the faith. Then, around the tenth century, the political and religious establishments determined that critical thinking posed a direct challenge to their authority, which rested on dogma and ritual. The "Gate of Ijtihad" was closed. There was, these rulers said, nothing more to be learned. It was the end of history. It became impossible even to discuss whether the hijab—the head and neck scarf worn by some observant Muslim women—was ordained by law or custom, because that question and thousands of others were supposedly settled for all time centuries ago, and the state would silence anyone who dared say otherwise. In such an environment, there is little scope for constructive progress on the difficult questions of politics and society.

In 1989, the year of revolution against Soviet despotism, the *National Interest* magazine published an essay by Francis Fukuyama entitled "The End of History?" It captured the spirit of the age.

"What we may be witnessing," Fukuyama wrote, "is not just the end of the Cold War, or the passing of a particular period of post-war history, but the end of history as such: that is, the end point of mankind's ideological evolution and the universalization of Western liberal democracy as the final form of human government." In terms of governance, this was akin to saying that there was fundamentally nothing more to be learned. Western, free-market liberalism had triumphed; all that was left was for the rest of the world to catch up.

The reality was exactly the reverse. The Cold War, with its four-decade thermonuclear stalemate, did not initiate history's thrilling denouement; in fact, it functioned more like an intermission. With the fall of the Berlin Wall, the movie could begin again. Great screenwriters tell us that, stripped down to essentials, there are only so many basic plots to choose from. Real life is like that, too. Scenarios repeat; roles recur; different actors don the costumes. A Saudi millionaire dresses like an eleventh-century rebel, takes up arms, and encourages his followers to ascribe divine powers to him. In response to his atrocities, the West becomes mired in Afghanistan, a country whose highways are lined with the carcasses of Soviet tanks, and later in Iraq, a land created arbitrarily one hundred years ago by colonial fiat. After a decade of violence in that country, a shy bookworm from the sticks proclaims himself caliph of the Muslim world, puts on a black turban in imitation of the Prophet Muhammad, and demands the allegiance of all Muslims on pain of death. This false caliph's murderous movement draws sustenance from a war in neighboring Syria that bears more than passing similarities to eighteenth-century conflicts between Persian shahs, Russian tsars, and Turkish sultans. We can hope that the Islamist movement ignited by Osama bin Laden, fanned into an inferno by Abu Musab al-Zarqawi, and now fueled, like a vision of hell, by thousands of corpses, will not endure quite as long as the death cult inaugurated by bin Laden's medieval doppelgänger, Hassan-i Sabbah. But at the same time, let us also recognize that al-Qaeda's story is far from over.

CHAPTER 1

THE SNAKE WITH BROKEN TEETH

Helicopter hovering above Abbottabad at 1AM
(is a rare event).

—TWEET BY SOHAIB ATHAR, @REALLYVIRTUAL,

12.58 AM PKT, MAY 2, 2011

Go away helicopter - before I take out my giant swatter :-/
—@REALLYVIRTUAL, 1.05 AM PKT

A huge window shaking bang here in Abbottabad Cantt.
I hope its not the start of something nasty :-S

—@REALLYVIRTUAL, 1.09 AM PKT

Sohaib Athar just wanted to get away from it all. His life in the Pakistani megacity of Lahore had been a dizzying burlesque of stifling heat, filthy air, unreliable power, and the ever-present danger of terrorist attack. After a while, it had all become too much for the young software developer. So he had packed up his laptops and fled for the relative tranquillity of the mountains north of Islamabad. Abbottabad must have seemed a promising place for a new start. The city lies cupped in a high-walled valley in the foothills of what becomes, much farther to the north and east, the outer reaches of the Himalayas. At an elevation of four thousand feet— roughly comparable to that of Salt Lake City, Utah—Abbottabad is known throughout the region for its agreeable hill-station climate. The town's founder and namesake, the British Army Major James Abbott, waxed poetic about its "sweet air" and twittering birds. Its Anglican church, St. Luke's—also established by the British, and built in a style that would have been familiar to soldiers homesick for the English countryside—still ministers to parishioners on Jinnah Road in the heart of the old town. Abbottabad was founded as a garrison city, and it remains so today; since Pakistan's independence, it has been home to the prestigious Kakul Military Academy, the country's answer to West Point. The academy has trained much of the country's military leadership, including its former president, Pervez Musharraf. It is also a frequent port of call for top military brass from Pakistan's allies; General David Petraeus visited in February 2010 while serving as overall commander of U.S. forces in the Middle East, Pakistan, and Afghanistan. Abbottabad's relative isolation and strong military presence conspire to create a sense of security that is sorely lacking in so many of Pakistan's other major cities.

Unsurprisingly, therefore, Sohaib Athar was not alone in seeing Abbottabad as a place of refuge. Throughout the first decade of the twenty-first century, people had moved there from elsewhere in the country, fleeing earthquakes, flooding, and the violent war against Islamic extremists ongoing in places like Waziristan, a notoriously lawless region in the Federally Administered Tribal Areas, or FATA, two hundred miles to the southwest, along Pakistan's frontier with Afghanistan. Abbottabad had also sheltered its fair share of less welcome transplants. Umar Patek, a key conspirator in the Bali nightclub bombing that killed more than 200 people in 2002, was arrested in Abbottabad in January 2011, together with Mohammed Tahir

Shahzad, an al-Qaeda fixer who had arranged for Patek to travel to Waziristan alongside two French jihadists. It was not inconceivable, therefore, that other al-Qaeda operatives, perhaps even senior figures, could still be laying low somewhere in Abbottabad.

. . .

About a mile and a half across town from where Sohaib Athar plied his screens and keyboards, in a relatively wealthy neighborhood where a few large houses rose over gardens in which residents grew food, there stood a spacious compound of the type known locally as a "mansion." It consisted of a three-story main house, a guesthouse, and a number of outbuildings, all surrounded by uneven high walls, in places rising to twelve or eighteen feet, and crowned with a two-foot tangle of barbed wire. The compound had no cable or telephone connections, although it did have a satellite dish. It lacked regular trash pickup; evidently its inhabitants preferred to burn their refuse on site. The balcony on the third floor of the big house, added following an earthquake that occurred in October 2005, was surrounded by an unbroken seven-foot screen wall. The plans for this edifice listed the property's owner as Mohammed Arshad Naqab Khan. Khan was seldom seen, but when he did appear, he told neighbors that he was a wealthy money changer or gold merchant from the tribal regions, and that he needed high security to protect himself and his family from "enemies" he had made in that business. This seemed plausible enough. Besides, it was not uncommon for pious Pashtun families from the tribal lands to live in large, high-walled properties, to sequester their women and children indoors, and generally to keep to themselves.

But Arshad Khan and his backstory were a fiction—an alias concocted to hide the true identity of the compound's owner. Ibrahim Saeed Ahmed was an ethnic Pakistani Pashtun whose family hailed from Shangla, a rugged, sparsely populated district in the mountains northwest of Abbottabad. Ahmed, however, was born and raised in

Kuwait, and like many jihadis went by his *nisbah*, or toponym, al-Kuwaiti. Growing up in the tiny desert emirate, al-Kuwaiti had become the boyhood boon companion of a fellow Pakistani, an ethnic Baluch named Khalid Sheikh Mohammed. KSM, as he later became known to investigators, had been a jihadi since he was sixteen years old. Having fought the Soviets in the 1980s, he would go on to mastermind the 9/11 attacks in 2001 and carry out the beheading of the *Wall Street Journal* reporter Daniel Pearl the following year.

Khalid Sheikh Mohammed also served as al-Kuwaiti's mentor in jihad. He got his friend a position as emir of an al-Qaeda guesthouse in the city of Karachi, in Pakistan's deep south, and introduced him to his sheikh, a Saudi militant chieftain named Osama bin Laden. Not long after this fateful meeting, al-Kuwaiti would begin a long service to bin Laden and his family as courier, domestic servant, and bodyguard. He kept this work, along with his other jihadi duties, a grave secret, even from those closest to him. In 2001, when he was around thirty-five years old, he married a fourteen-year-old girl from his home district and brought her to live with him in Karachi. He explained his frequent absences from the marital home by saying that he often traveled back to the Gulf on business. Throughout this time, al-Kuwaiti remained close to his old friend Khalid Sheikh Mohammed; KSM's wife hosted a wedding feast for the new couple at her house. But it would be years before al-Kuwaiti would tell his bride who this mysterious friend was or admit that he, like KSM, was in reality a *mujahid* of al-Qaeda. By then, there would be no going back.

Following bin Laden's defeat at the cave complex of Tora Bora in late 2001, the al-Qaeda leader fled over the mountains into hiding in Pakistan, shaving his long beard to evade recognition. Al-Kuwaiti was once again called upon to assist the sheikh in his time of need. In the summer of 2002, he set up a house for bin Laden in Swat, not far from his ancestral homeland in the north of Pakistan. Al-Kuwaiti moved his wife and children there, too, and they were soon joined by his brother, whose name was Abrar, and Abrar's own growing family. The brothers, both olive-skinned and beardless, but with close-cropped mustaches in the traditional Pakistani style, did not look out of place in their country of origin. In exchange for their hospitality and protection, bin Laden paid the Kuwaiti brothers a salary of 9,000 rupees per month—around $100—which he supplemented from time to time with gifts and *zakat* (charity).

The Swat house nestled in a pretty stretch of countryside by the banks of a river. To Osama bin Laden, this bucolic setting may have seemed a welcome respite from the relentless pace of frontline jihad. But any feeling of serenity would prove to be short-lived. In early 2003, al-Kuwaiti's old friend Khalid Sheikh Mohammed brought his family to stay at the Swat house for two weeks. Just a month after he left, al-Kuwaiti was watching the news with his wife when KSM's face unexpectedly flashed onto the screen. The 9/11 planner had been arrested in Rawalpindi, the twin city of the Pakistani capital, Islamabad. Al-Kuwaiti flew into a panic; KSM was a tough personality and an experienced operative, but there was no telling what secrets he might divulge, knowingly or otherwise, under interrogation. Within a week, al-Kuwaiti, bin Laden, and the other residents of the Swat house had fled. Quickly, the brothers moved them to Haripur, a city to the east surrounded by squalid camps sheltering some of the millions of refugees displaced by a quarter-century of conflict in neighboring Afghanistan. Bin Laden's house in the suburbs, by contrast, was pretty and spacious, with three bedrooms, a lawn, and a roof terrace. But nobody ever visited him there. One neighbor noted that the brothers kept their gates shut, which was unusual for the area. When they needed to make phone calls, they would travel up to ninety miles away to use public call boxes.

By late 2004, al-Kuwaiti, operating under his assumed identity of Arshad Khan, had begun buying up tracts of land in Abbottabad Cantonment for what would become bin Laden's mansion. In August of 2005, with construction on the main building complete, bin Laden moved in, together with two of his wives, his son Khalid, and a number of his daughters and grandchildren. Al-Kuwaiti lived with his wife and children in the guesthouse on site, while Abrar and his family occupied the ground floor of the main house. Eventually, the screened-off third floor built after the October earthquake became bin Laden's living quarters.

Bin Laden always claimed to live in accordance with the ways of the Prophet, and few parallels between their two lives would have escaped him. So it is quite possible that he would have compared his flight from Afghanistan to Pakistan with Muhammad's Hijra, or migration, from Mecca to Yathrib, the desert settlement that would eventually become Medina. In fact, he often called on his followers to make their own hijra to Afghanistan. Since his arrival in Pakistan, bin Laden's movements, from Swat to Haripur to Abbottabad, had traced a path roughly due east, deeper and deeper into the country. Four years after 9/11, he had made it roughly two hundred miles from Tora Bora—about the same distance as the Prophet traveled from Mecca to Yathrib. Perhaps this was an auspicious sign.

. . .

Everything about the Abbottabad mansion was geared toward privacy and self-sufficiency. The brothers hired a local farmer, a man called Shamraiz, to plow an adjacent field for growing vegetables. There were animals at the site, too, including chickens and a cow. Whatever food and provisions could not be grown, raised, or made on the premises, al-Kuwaiti and Abrar would buy at the bazaar in town. Bin Laden was no stranger to spartan living conditions. Indeed, for decades, he had deliberately sought out a life of privation. Like charismatic leaders before him, including the Assassin leader Hassan-i Sabbah, he cultivated this ascetic image as an important part of his appeal. Frugality came naturally to him; indeed, it seemed to exhilarate him. When he returned to Afghanistan in 1996, he chose a grim, unkempt hideout in the mountains in preference to several much cushier residences, including a former royal palace. Later, in the compound at Kandahar, his house was among the simplest on the base, with not even a carpet on the floor. In 2005, upon his arrival in Abbottabad, bin Laden's wardrobe consisted of no more than a black jacket, a couple of sweaters, and six shalwar kameez— the traditional Pashtun dress of baggy pants and a long shirt.

In accordance with his fundamentalist reading of Islam, he had always kept the women of his household in strict *purdah*—separation from men outside their immediate family. In Abbottabad that prohibition became a matter of security as well as religious obligation. Indeed, his rules were so absolute that, from the age of three, the bin Laden women were banned from watching television, so that they would never see an unfamiliar male face. His children and grandchildren were sequestered inside the house almost twenty-four hours a day. The sheikh personally home-schooled them in the bin Laden brand of extreme religion and forbade them from playing with the children of al-Kuwaiti and Abrar, who lived just feet away within the same compound. Such was their isolation that the sheikh did not even allow them to be vaccinated for polio along with the other children. The nearest the bin Laden children came to fun was their occasional competitions to see which of them could grow the biggest vegetables in the garden.

Despite his well-known penchant for sports, hiking, and horseback riding, the sheikh's own health had taken a downturn in early adulthood from which he had never fully recovered. Forty-eight when he began living in Abbottabad, he was practically blind in one eye, the result of a childhood injury he successfully concealed from the public for many years. In his twenties and thirties, during the jihad against Afghanistan's Soviet occupiers in the 1980s, he had suffered crippling bouts of pain and paralysis, which the former surgeon Ayman al-Zawahiri had treated with a glucose drip. Having inhaled Russian napalm in Afghanistan, he frequently had trouble with his larynx. In Abbottabad he complained of pain in his heart and kidneys, but there was no question of visiting a doctor. Instead, when bin Laden felt ill, he would treat himself with *al-tibb al-nabawi*—traditional medicine based on the hadith, sayings ascribed to the Prophet. Some believe, for example, that Muhammad recommended barley broth and honey to treat an upset stomach, senna for constipation, truffle water for eye ailments, and henna for aches and wounds. "God has not made a disease without appointing a remedy for it," says one well-known hadith, "with the exception of one disease, namely old age." By his early fifties, Osama Bin Laden had become, prematurely, an old man. In videos made inside the compound, he appears hunched and frail, his face lined, his eyes tired. His beard, salt-and-pepper at the time of the 9/11 attacks, was rapidly turning white, although he was not above dyeing it jet-black in video messages meant for public consumption.

In his three-decade career of murder and mayhem, Osama bin Laden had gone by many names. His followers called him Azmaray, the sheikh, the emir, the director, Abu Abdullah. His code name at the U.S. Joint Special Operations Command was Crankshaft, reflecting his vital importance in driving the engine of al-Qaeda. But one final nickname captured the diminished circumstances of his existence in Abbottabad. In the months leading up to bin Laden's death, observing his daily walks within the bounds of a compound he never seemed to leave, analysts with the Central Intelligence Agency had taken to calling him The Pacer. But Osama bin Laden was no ordinary shut-in, and he was by no means cut off from the world. Far from it: Until the day he died, the sheikh remained in active control of the deadliest terror network in history.

• • •

Communication with the outside was difficult, to be sure. Ever since the arrest of Khalid Sheikh Mohammed so soon after his visit to the house in Swat, bin Laden had cut off face-to-face contact with other senior jihadis—or, indeed, any al-Qaeda members other than his immediate protectors. No doubt this was a wise precaution for a man with a twenty-five-million-dollar U.S. bounty on his head. Besides, house calls would be an impractical way of governing a network that bestrode much of the Islamic world. But remote means of communication were scarcely any more secure. Email was not to be trusted; bin Laden knew from past experience that the Americans were capable of intercepting such messages, even with encryption. As he himself wrote in August of 2010, "Computer science is not our science and we are not the ones who invented it. . . . Encryption systems work with ordinary people, but not against those who created email and the Internet." Cellular communication, too, was risky, because it could give away a person's location and perhaps even call forth one of the hated unmanned "spy planes" that patrolled the skies over northern Pakistan. By this time, al-Kuwaiti had evidently acquired a cellphone; but whenever he needed to place a call, he would drive out from Abbottabad for ninety minutes or more before even placing the battery in his device.

Instead, bin Laden, his deputy Ayman al-Zawahiri, and their senior jihadi associates relied upon a network of trusted couriers— among them al-Kuwaiti himself. These men would flit back and forth across Pakistan carrying thumb drives full of jihadi correspondence. Bin Laden's principal point of contact was his factotum, a veteran militant whose nom de guerre was Atiyah Abd-al-Rahman but who was better known in jihadi circles as Mahmud. Mahmud hailed from the town of Misrata, in northwestern Libya, along the coast from Tripoli and across the Gulf of Sidra from Benghazi. With his pale complexion, wispy facial hair, and boyish looks, Mahmud may not have struck many as the archetypal fundamentalist fighter; but whatever he lacked in appearance, he made up for in ability. He was a former senior member of the Libyan Islamic Fighting Group, which formally merged with al-Qaeda in 2007. While bin Laden remained cloistered in Abbottabad, Mahmud presided over a small and frequently unruly private army of militants in Waziristan. The jihadi "brothers" under Mahmud's control hailed from all over the

Islamic world and beyond that as far afield as Russia, Germany, and the Balkans.

In many cases, their level of experience and discipline fell well short of Mahmud's standards. Instead of the unquestioning obedience he demanded, Mahmud encountered insubordination, sometimes verging on mutiny. The prolonged seclusion of the great jihadi figureheads complicated matters. Some newer members insisted that they would take orders only directly from bin Laden, Zawahiri, or their nominal superior, Taliban leader Mullah Omar—certainly not from anyone as lowly as Mahmud. Others, disobeying security protocol, would hang out in the streets, gather together in large groups, or make calls on their cellphones, attracting attention and exposing themselves to American drone strikes or, even worse, arrest by Pakistani forces. Still others would grandstand through the jihadi media, puffing up their credentials as "commanders" and sowing confusion. Some of these men, in Mahmud's opinion, just needed to "grow up."

Mahmud longed for the return of experienced senior operatives, "good men" who could help "carry the burden." After 9/11, many of these old guard figures had sought secret refuge in Iran, only to find themselves arrested and imprisoned by Iranian intelligence. Some still languished in prison years later—among them a trio of seasoned commanders. Abu Mohammed al-Masri had been the leader of al-Qaeda's famous training camps and a principal architect of the 1998 bombings of U.S. embassies in East Africa; his daughter is married to bin Laden's son Hamza. Abu Khair al-Masri was once al-Qaeda's political chief, and he sheltered bin Laden at his Kabul home in the immediate aftermath of 9/11. Finally, Saif al-Adel had been al-Qaeda's stern and steadfast head of security, responsible more than anyone for keeping bin Laden safe and for developing networks in Somalia, Yemen, and elsewhere.

Bin Laden agreed with Mahmud that the release of these men would be a great benefit to jihad and to the mujahideen. Mahmud recommended that "to be safe" those returning from Iran go through a reintegration program. "They should spend six months (or even a year) getting familiar again with how things work," he wrote. "During that time, they will consult closely, and we can bring them back [into management] incrementally." Al-Qaeda had changed a great deal in the seven or eight years since their imprisonment. A new generation was moving into junior and middle management; increasingly, even bin Laden had to ask Mahmud for background on people who were unfamiliar to him. Meanwhile, al-Qaeda itself had morphed from a close-knit, intensely hierarchical battalion into something more like an umbrella organization, with a central staff overseeing a number of more or less autonomous franchises across the Muslim world. Any returnees would need time to come to grips with this new power structure. Around October of 2010, one of the former grandees was released—the enigmatic military chieftain Saif al-Adel. In Saif's case, Mahmud's recommendation of a six-month reintegration program proved prescient: Just over half a year after his release, Saif was to be called up as interim emir upon bin Laden's death.

Like their sheikh, Mahmud and his men lived continually on the brink. Alongside the rigors of a life in hiding, they had to contend with checkpoints, curfews, attacks by the Pakistani military, infiltration by spies, and above all the relentless attrition of missile strikes. "The harm is alarming," wrote a senior jihadi in 2009. "The matter is very grave. So many brave commanders have been snatched away. So many safe houses have been leveled." Names of the men Mahmud called martyrs peppered his correspondence: Khalid al-Habib, the man who replaced KSM as al-Qaeda's operations director; Abu Laith al-Libi, a senior commander and, like Mahmud, a Libyan; even Said al-Masri, who by the time of his death was functionally third in command, the man who accepted pledges of allegiance from new members on behalf of bin Laden and Zawahiri. On August 22, 2011, within half a year of bin Laden's death, Mahmud himself would be killed in a drone strike. It was the same day anti-Gaddafi forces captured Tripoli, the capital of his native Libya.

. . .

Through Mahmud, bin Laden wielded executive control over a network of extremist groups from Afghanistan to Algeria. Mahmud kept in regular contact with the leadership of franchises like al-Qaeda in the Islamic Maghreb, al-Qaeda in the Arabian Peninsula, al-Qaeda in Iraq, and al-Shabaab in the Horn of Africa. Not only did bin Laden continue to command these groups; he frequently micromanaged their operations, inserting himself into decisions on everything from hostage negotiations (if they are spies, shoot them; otherwise, negotiate for withdrawal from Afghanistan, whether or not you demand a cash ransom in addition), to which crops were best suited to the Somali climate (dates, olives, fruit trees), to the storage and rationing of wheat (the key, he told Mahmud, was to buy waterproof barrels: "You should wash them and dry them in the sun for a day. These barrels have a rubber top to make them airtight and make it possible to store fresh grain for seven years without allowing bugs to get to it").

When it came to the core group in Waziristan, the sheikh frequently involved himself in detailed personnel matters. "Please send me the résumés of all the brothers who might be nominated for high administrative positions now or in the future," he ordered Mahmud in 2010. At the same time, he advised Mahmud to appoint a deputy for himself on a one-year renewable term, and a second deputy just in case. He suggested jobs for some members, mentoring for others, and advised on matters of payroll. It would be a bad idea, he said, to pay the brothers their salaries in advance, because they would be liable to spend all the money and then come back and ask for a loan, which would put their superiors in an awkward position.

Security remained a perennial preoccupation, and bin Laden's instructions to Mahmud on the subject tended to be as detailed as they were peremptory. Keep all movements to a minimum. If you must travel, do so only on cloudy days, to avoid detection from above. Meet in groups of no more than three at a time. Carry out background checks on members with security-sensitive roles, especially the couriers. Whenever you receive ransom money, launder it twice. Exchange it for euros at one bank, then take those euros to another bank and exchange them for U.S. dollars. Family members who traveled with al-Qaeda members should learn the local language in order to blend in. Children should be kept indoors unless they need to go out for essential medical treatment, and when they play in the yard, there must be a grown-up present to keep them quiet. Finally, in the matter of appointments, the organization must be as hard-nosed as any business. Members who were not disciplined enough to keep strictly to the security protocol should be relieved of command responsibility. "Perhaps a job in the field might be best for them," the sheik said. The clunky courier system seemed preposterous to Mahmud. "How can we correspond with brothers in Algeria, Iraq, Yemen, and Somalia?" he asked, pressing for the use of email. No, Bin Laden told him. "Couriers are the only way." "Security procedures in our circumstances should be practiced at all times," he wrote. "There is no room for mistakes." Martyrdom was better than arrest, he had always said. But the ideal was to stay both alive and at liberty.

Bin Laden knew what it meant to be hunted by the United States. When the Obama administration added Anwar al-Awlaki, the Yemeni American cleric and leading al-Qaeda propagandist, to its list of "specially designated global terrorists," bin Laden sent instructions through Mahmud that Awlaki must now "change his lifestyle completely, for the enemies of Allah will be after him." Awlaki would need "instructions for his movements and directions about whom he is to see and how, and whom he is to avoid." After years of being hunted, bin Laden had developed a sixth sense for possible security breaches. When the Afghan government agreed to pay $6 million to release one of its diplomats from al-Qaeda custody, he smelled a rat. The Afghans did not usually hand over that much cash to spring their operatives. The hostage must be the relative of someone important, bin Laden speculated. Moreover, he suspected American involvement; perhaps they were tracking the money in the expectation that it might lead them to its ultimate recipient among the field commanders in Waziristan. Either way, the cash should be laundered even more carefully than usual. More than four years later, an article in the *New York Times* seemed to confirm bin Laden's instincts. According to the report, the diplomat was the son-in-law of a mentor to the Afghan president, Hamid Karzai. Part of the ransom had indeed come from American coffers, although there was apparently no program of surveillance attached.

For bin Laden and the Waziristan contingent alike, secrecy was paramount. But it is axiomatic that no terrorist organization can afford to operate completely in the shadows; they always require the oxygen of publicity. Skillful image management through the media is a must. Bin Laden therefore paid close attention to all the output of al-Sahab (the Cloud), al-Qaeda's press shop. This was the domain of Adam Gadahn, a Californian farm boy and former death metal enthusiast who in 2006 earned the dubious distinction of being the first American to be charged with treason since World War II. Until the advent of the Islamic State, Gadahn's Cloud was the gold standard in jihadi propaganda, producing exciting videos with high production values, and the outfit could boast of a strong track record of reaching mainstream news reports. In the absence of any new spectacular attacks on the West, however, al-Qaeda was finding it harder and harder to secure coverage. When Ayman al-Zawahiri released a video marking the ninth anniversary of the 9/11 attacks, bin Laden complained that Al Jazeera had shown it only in the middle of the night, and had removed it from their rolling news coverage after just a few hours. In his frustration, bin Laden suggested sending a complaint to Ahmad Zaidan, the network's Islamabad bureau chief. When it came to the rapidly approaching tenth anniversary, al-Qaeda would have to do better. Bin Laden's vision for commemorating this milestone was nothing if not grandiose. The sheikh instructed his underlings to negotiate with Arab and Western media outlets for glossy packages to commemorate the occasion, mentioning by name Al Jazeera, the British-headquartered newspapers the *Independent* and *Al Quds Al Arabi*, and the CBS television network, which he praised as "an American channel that is close to neutrality and professionalism." In the case of Al Jazeera, bin Laden's demands were particularly clear: He wanted a special program, and he wanted Ahmad Zaidan to present it. "One year for finishing it is not enough," he told Mahmud, adding that Zaidan "needs to create a vision for the program and review it several times. He will also need to interview a large number of people in various areas in the world." But, bin Laden stipulated, "ask him not to interview anyone in my family. Negotiations on this issue should continue until an agreement that will satisfy al-Sahab is reached. Please keep me posted."

Nor was the sheikh content simply to dwell on past glories. On the contrary, he had his sights set on the future. His keen interest in the appointment of deputies for Mahmud shows his concern for continuity, as does his insistence that his own number two, Ayman al-Zawahiri, be copied on all important correspondence. As always, bin Laden was thinking big. In early 2010, he gave orders to set up a new al-Qaeda research and development center, to be staffed by members with "a passion for reading" who could focus on finding and translating Western research, teaching English to their colleagues, and developing specialties like political science, computer engineering, and chemistry—especially the making of explosives. Adam Gadahn should be involved, together with other members familiar with the ways of the West.

Above all, the overlord of 9/11 was focused on preparing to strike the U.S. homeland once again. He remained characteristically clear-eyed about the rationale for this. "It is a known fact," he wrote, "that the American people, who are represented by the Congress and the White House, are the holders of the supreme power in the U.S. and they are the ultimate decision makers. Thus, we have to focus on killing and fighting the American people." One spectacular attack inside the United States, he reasoned, would have more impact on American foreign policy than any conceivable combination of coalition deaths in Iraq or Afghanistan—and he had the statistics to back up his argument. The Vietnam War, he said, took the lives of 57,000 American troops before the U.S. public forced a withdrawal. Smoking killed 400,000 Americans a year without drawing many high-profile protests against the tobacco companies. Contrast that with the country's reaction to the so-called underwear bomber, Omar Farouk Abdulmutallab, a Nigerian who had attempted to blow up a Northwest Airlines flight to Detroit on Christmas Day 2009. With a single device on board a civilian plane, Farouk had played havoc with the U.S. transportation system and the American economy— and his bomb had not even exploded. "Attacking the United States from within is of extreme importance," bin Laden told one of his senior lieutenants. Again, he turned to Mahmud, asking him to "nominate a qualified brother to be in charge of a large operation in America." Selecting the right candidate for this duty was essential, and bin Laden was prepared to be choosy; indeed, he rejected two of Mahmud's initial suggestions as unsuitable. He ordered the militants to create a training camp to prepare leaders for operations inside the United States. Again, the group should be very careful in choosing the initial cohort for this academy of terror. The students should be "pious and patient . . . apply proficiency at all times . . . [and] have a strong conviction about the importance of external work." They must also possess "intelligence, astuteness . . . knowledge," and enough stamina to see the training through. Later, the *New Yorker* was to report that at the time of his death bin Laden was overseeing the development of plots to assassinate President Obama, to attack trains, and to strike on the tenth anniversary of 9/11.

In bin Laden's mind, there was a strong strategic rationale for going after the United States first, before turning to battle ungodly regimes nearer at hand in the Islamic world. Bin Laden took frequent pains to stress this reasoning. As he explained to Mahmud in a 2009 letter, "By fighting the local enemy, we don't get the result that we deployed for, which is to reinstate the wise Caliphate and eliminate the disgrace and humiliation that our nation is suffering from. We should keep in mind that [America] still has the power to lay siege to any Islamic State, and that such a siege might force the people to overthrow their duly elected governments. We have to continue with exhausting and depleting [the United States] until they become so weak that they can't overthrow any State that we establish. That will be the time to commence forming the Islamic State."

By concentrating his ire on America, bin Laden had staked out a stark position in a doctrinal dispute with deep theological roots. It starts with the Koran's prohibition against killing Muslims, which could scarcely be any clearer—nor the penalty for transgression any graver. "It is unlawful for a believer to kill another believer," reads the injunction. "He that kills a believer by design shall burn in Hell forever." But this raises the question, What about those who profess outwardly to be Muslims but who are not believers in their hearts? Within three decades of the Prophet's death, radicals among the Kharijites—Islam's first schismatics—had declared the fourth caliph, Ali Ibn Abi Talib, to be a false Muslim. On this basis, in AD 661, some of their number had assassinated Ali inside a mosque in Kufa, Iraq, using a sword tipped with poison.

Six hundred years later, Muslims in what is now Iraq and Syria faced a problem when their land was conquered by Mongols— descendants of Genghis Khan who had since converted to Sunni Islam. A Syrian cleric named Ibn Taymiyyah, a scholar who sought to defy Mongol rule, issued religious rulings to the effect that the Mongols were not true Muslims. As proof, he cited their heretical belief that their forebear Genghis Khan was the son of God and— worse, in Ibn Taymiyyah's mind—a prophet comparable in prestige to Mohammed himself. Moreover, the Mongol rulers had placed

Genghis's man-made law, the Yasa, on a par with the Islamic Sharia, and had employed Jews and Christians in high offices of state. In short, the whole Mongol political superstructure was rotten and un-Islamic. Thus, it was not only legal to fight and kill the Mongol overlords—believers were commanded to do so.

Ibn Taymiyyah's fatwas were documents anchored firmly in their time and place, promulgated to solve a problem particular to Muslims living in Iraq and the Levant in the late thirteenth and early fourteenth centuries. But that did not stop the twentieth-century Egyptian radical Sayyid Qutb from seizing upon them to justify his own call to overthrow the secular regime of Gamal Abdel Nasser. In turn, Qutb influenced succeeding generations of jihadis, particularly in North Africa, to take up arms against their own governments. These radicals are known as *takfiris*—those who believe that the principal problem facing modern-day Muslims is their rulers' departure from the true path of Islam. The word *takfir* refers to a judgment that someone is an unbeliever (*kafir*) or an apostate (*murtad*—literally "backslider"). For obvious reasons, in mainstream Islam—and even in many relatively radical interpretations—it is extremely difficult to make such a declaration. *Takfiris*, on the other hand, apply the judgment of *takfir* with a much broader brush. They prescribe a certain way of practicing Islam, and brand as deserving of death any Muslim who fails to live up to it. This is helter-skelter logic; make your version of Islam restrictive enough, and there is no limit to how many people you can give yourself permission to murder. Thus, today, in the very same region where Ibn Taymiyyah wrote his fatwas seven centuries ago, we see a *takfiri* group that calls itself the Islamic State demanding allegiance to its so-called caliph on pain of death by decapitation.

Bin Laden would have agreed that the stain of apostasy needed to be erased; certainly there would come a time for visiting harsh judgment on *kafir* and *murtadeen*; but, as he had always maintained, it was simply a waste of time to attack local secular regimes until their puppet masters in Washington were out of the picture. *Takfiri* groups tended to dislike al-Qaeda, because it had a habit of siphoning off recruits and reprogramming them to focus on the jihad against the far enemy, the United States, rather than the local quarrels the *takfiris* wanted to pursue. But the 9/11 attacks would prove to be the high water mark for bin Laden's view of global jihad. After 9/11, with local conflicts on the rise across the Middle East and North Africa, he faced increasing difficulty keeping a lid on the *takfiri* tendency within al-Qaeda—especially following the rise to prominence of the most notorious *takfiri* in recent memory, Abu Musab al-Zarqawi.

Now, in 2009 and 2010, it fell to Mahmud to remind al-Qaeda's membership of the central importance of defeating America first. For example, through Mahmud, bin Laden instructed al-Qaeda in the Islamic Maghreb to negotiate ceasefires with local forces, because "we want the maximum number of entities to take to the sidelines as we fight our greatest enemy, the U.S." Likewise, in Yemen, al-Qaeda in the Arabian Peninsula should bear in mind that the enemy was the Americans, not the regime—even as they suffered daily from attacks by Yemeni security forces. In 2010, in the midst of Yemen's civil war, bin Laden rejected his Yemeni associates' advice that the capital, Sanaa, was al-Qaeda's for the taking. Instead, he suggested that al-Qaeda try to reach "a truce with the apostate government" of Ali Abdullah Saleh, in order to focus on fighting the United States. Bin Laden further ordered that al-Qaeda in the Arabian Peninsula must not "escalate matters . . . in Saudi Arabia" for the same reason. Even in Pakistan, bin Laden wrote, al-Qaeda should try to reach a truce with the local military. Bin Laden held fast to his view that there was no point in seeking to topple "apostate" regimes in the Muslim world, however evil they may be, and however far they had strayed from God's plan, until you had destroyed the ability of the West to protect them. But at the end of 2010, events were brewing that would bring about a sea change in bin Laden's worldview.

. . .

The sheikh had always been an eager consumer of the news. One of the few enduring essentials of his otherwise drab lifestyle was the satellite dish on the property and a monitor to pick up Al Jazeera and the BBC. In this way, while in hiding he kept on top of, and was able to comment upon, developments like the Gaza Freedom Flotilla—a Turkish-backed attempt to defy Israel's naval embargo on the Gaza Strip; the floods that devastated Pakistan in 2010, in which, typically, he saw yet another propaganda opportunity; and the release by WikiLeaks of 92,000 classified documents relating to the war in Afghanistan. In August 2010, he instructed Mahmud to assign to some capable members the herculean task of translating this potentially invaluable trove. But WikiLeaks was far from finished. Three months later, they released another tranche of documents—this time, sensitive cables from 274 U.S. diplomatic missions around the world. Many of them described in lurid detail the corruption and greed of Arab governments. A cable from the U.S. ambassador to Tunisia reported, "Whether it's cash, services, land, property, or (yes) even your yacht, the Bin Ali family is rumored to covet it, and reportedly gets what it wants." Another cable detailed how Muammar Gaddafi's son Muatassim, who served as Libya's national security adviser, paid the singer Beyoncé a substantial sum of money, perhaps as much as $1 million, to appear at his New Year's Eve party. Before he was toppled, the Libyan dictator assailed WikiLeaks as part of "a foreign plot to destabilize Arab regimes." In reality, these revelations merely added to the already familiar examples of corruption, greed, and un-Islamic behavior available to opponents of these rotten governments. By the fall of 2010, simmering anger was ready to boil over all across the Arab world.

On December 17, a Tunisian street vendor named Mohamed Bouazizi set himself on fire to protest the deep-set corruption of the Zine el-Abidine Ben Ali regime. By so doing, this otherwise unremarkable young man lit the fuse on popular protests that would spread throughout North Africa and beyond. Within a month, Tunisia's president had fled into exile in bin Laden's own native Saudi Arabia. Demonstrators in Egypt took to chanting "Ben Ali, tell Mubarak there is a plane waiting for him too." And sure enough, by the middle of February, the despised "Pharaoh" whose regime and its predecessors had spilled the blood of many Egyptian jihadists had announced his own resignation. By then, protests had erupted in Yemen, Sudan, Bahrain, Libya, Morocco, Iraq, Jordan, and beyond. There was even talk of an uprising in the Land of the Two Holy Mosques itself, although in the event it was swiftly suppressed by Saudi security, who also played a role in putting down the revolt in the neighboring island nation of Bahrain. Finally, on March 18, Syria began its long descent into barbarism when President Bashar al-Assad's security forces opened fire on activists in Daraa, near the border with Jordan.

Watching this dizzying scene unfold from his Abbottabad redoubt, bin Laden sat transfixed. In correspondence with Mahmud, and in successive drafts of a jumbled, rambling statement to the *umma*—the Islamic Nation—the sheikh's thoughts poured forth in a jubilant gush. "This is the most important point in our history," he breathlessly told Mahmud, drawing parallels with the time of Saladin, the twelfth-century sultan who retook Jerusalem after eighty-eight years of Crusader rule. Today's Arab dictators, to bin Laden's mind, embodied an even earlier figure—Abu Jahl, a powerful early opponent of the Prophet: backward, oblivious to the people's needs, soon to be hurled into the abyss by the forces of righteousness. There was a divine symmetry to be discerned in contemporary events. Whereas the twentieth century had belonged to the Americans, the twenty-first had begun with the "blessed attacks" that pierced their strongholds of New York and Washington. And now, the second decade of this still young century was set to open with the fall of the puppet regimes propped up by the far enemy. Clearly, this was a sign. America had had its day. This was the start of the Muslim century.

What was the endgame of these revolutions? The dominant view in the West at the time was that the Arab Spring could be an opening for democracy and free speech in the Middle East—a development that would have killed extremist organizations like al-Qaeda stone-dead. But that was not how Osama bin Laden saw it. Characteristically, he viewed the Arab Spring as an opportunity to impose his own fundamentalist brand of religion, using a form of government drawn from the earliest days of the Islamic empire. "These gigantic events," he told Mahmud, "will eventually engulf most of the Muslim world, will free the Muslim land from American hegemony. We hope the next stage will be the reinstating of the rule of the caliphate."

In the face of this tectonic upheaval, the role of al-Qaeda itself would have to change. Already, Mahmud was saying good-bye to militants from North Africa and the Middle East. The chaos of revolution was an opportunity to see their homes and loved ones again after so many years; and it was also a chance to wage jihad in their countries of origin, against regimes they had long despised. The departing fighters included yet another Libyan, Abu Anas al-Libi, a conspirator in the 1998 East African embassy bombings, who would be arrested in Tripoli in a daring joint FBI–Delta Force operation 2013. For bin Laden, this dispersal was all to the good. "Though the mujahideen have several duties to perform," bin Laden wrote to Mahmud following the collapse of the Tunisian regime, "their main duty now is to support the revolutions taking place." This historic task, bin Laden said, should take precedence even over the sacred struggle against the Americans in Afghanistan. "We must really mobilize," said the sheikh.

What exactly to do, and how precisely to accomplish it, were much tougher questions. Al-Qaeda could not support the uprisings too openly, because the regimes would exploit that association to paint the demonstrators as extremists. Bin Laden took his father's birthplace of Yemen as an example. If al-Qaeda openly joined the demonstrations, he wrote, the government would "tell the people that the demonstrators are al-Qaeda and that will hurt the people's cause in Yemen." Moreover, he went on, "If we select a date to call for civil disobedience and demonstrations, then the activists will think that we want to pick the fruits of their labor without them. So let them pick the fruit."

Similarly, it would not pay to be too honest about al-Qaeda's ultimate objective: "We should talk about toppling the tyrants without talking about issues related to the caliphate," bin Laden told Mahmud. Still, the revolutions needed to be kept on track somehow; otherwise "today's movements are in danger of falling into the trap of creating a system that is different from what God has ordered us to implement"—in other words, free speech and democracy. Moreover, for all his exuberance, the sheikh remained haunted by the failure of past uprisings in Algeria, Egypt, Yemen, and elsewhere.

The key, he wanted to advise those involved in the rebellions, was to be resolute and uncompromising. Bin Laden's ideas on the subject were clear. Do not present a prominent figurehead, because he can too easily be killed or co-opted. Do not be squeamish about bloodletting, because it is an inevitable part of the liberation struggle. Do not cast the security forces as "the first enemy of the people," because they can be turned onto the path of God. Above all, do not be tempted to compromise with the ruler, even if it means less bloodshed in the short term. Only if you strip away every last vestige of power can you be sure that the dictator will not simply turn around later and reimpose the tyranny that brought you to the streets in the first place. This root-and-branch approach, bin Laden observed, was one reason for the success of the ayatollahs in Iran—a rare compliment to a Shiite regime he otherwise consistently viewed as "evil" and "rejectionist."

An important part of al-Qaeda's long-term strategy, memorialized in works like the infamous jihadi handbook *The Management of Savagery*, had always been to create so-called zones of savagery—regions within the Muslim world so lawless and chaotic that the authority of the state would collapse. Al-Qaeda could then rush in to fill the vacuum left by governmental failure, providing the people with much-needed services like education, water, and electricity, and ruling in accordance with its version of Islam. For bin Laden, Zawahiri, and the rest of the al-Qaeda old guard, this was meant to be a slow and deliberate methodology, lasting perhaps as long as several generations. But the rapid collapse of regimes during the Arab Spring represented an opportunity to short-circuit the *Management of Savagery* process. Once again, bin Laden took Yemen as his principal example. "The fragmentation in the region after the fall of the regime," he wrote, "will make the area ripe for a positive response. . . . [R]eform in this environment will be strong . . . and America and Saudi Arabia will have little influence in the matter."

As prophetic as his words might prove, a man like Osama bin Laden, who had sought to sway world events for a quarter century, could never be satisfied with simply offering advice, prognostications, and encouragement from the sidelines while others made history. And yet, even with Al Jazeera's rolling coverage as a constant companion, it was hard enough just to keep up with the frantic pace of events, let alone seek to affect the outcome in any meaningful way. Clearly, these historic times would require a more considered response from al-Qaeda, and it was clear who should lead the blue-sky thinking: the omni-capable Mahmud. Around the beginning of March, bin Laden told his assistant that his work in Waziristan had come to an end: "You should work as soon as possible on arranging a safe route for getting to the Peshawar area until we find you a house in the area that I am in. This will allow you to monitor the media better and will facilitate correspondence between us to exchange opinions."

At the same time, bin Laden set about creating a brain trust. Mahmud's deputy and countryman Abu Yahya al-Libi should also leave Waziristan for a safer locale, as should "the rest of the brothers with strong capabilities. . . . Do not exclude any one of them, for each voice counts at this phase. The work is going to be a joint effort." Bin

Laden even indicated that he was open to a face-to-face meeting with Mahmud. This would break the eight-year isolation he had imposed on himself following the arrest of Khalid Sheikh Mohammed; but such was the importance of the hour. "My words contradict what I said in previous letters," he wrote. "But the magnitude of the events dictates that we implement a full mobilization."

• • •

For all the weight of historic responsibility he felt—a sense of his own importance with which al-Qaeda's membership, almost a decade after 9/11, still heartily agreed—bin Laden was also still the patriarch of a large and still growing family. Since the early 1980s, he had wed a total of five women, and was still married to three of them when he entered the Abbottabad house in 2005. Between his five wives, bin Laden fathered a minimum of twenty children, including at least four born while he was in hiding. According to ancient Arab custom, each wife was accorded a *kunya*, or nickname, honoring her for the birth of her first son: Umm Abdullah, the mother of Abdullah; Umm Ali, the mother of Ali, and so on. By the end of 2010, two of bin Laden's three remaining wives, Siham Sabar, known as Umm Khalid, and Amal al-Saddah, known as Umm Ibrahim, were living with him in Abbottabad. Amal had married bin Laden in the late 1990s, when she was only sixteen years old. The wives took turns spending the night with their husband in his third-floor quarters.

Downstairs, on the second floor, lived Osama's son by Siham, Khalid bin Laden. Khalid, around twenty-two years old in 2010, shared his father's distinctive slender nose and full lips. He served as the compound's resident handyman and plumber. He also kept a cow he had bought from a local farmer. And, like all of the men of the Abbottabad mansion, he knew his way around a Kalashnikov, and was prepared if need be to defend the sheikh with deadly force. By 2007, Khalid had reached his late teens. It was high time for him to marry. His mother, Umm Khalid, had proposed a match with a girl whose father and brother had both died for the cause. Indeed, her father was an Egyptian militant whose fame in the jihad went back to the early 1980s. During the war against the Soviets, he was rumored to have killed more Communist soldiers than any other Arab. His proficiency with the BM-12 rocket launcher earned him the nickname Abu Abdul Rahman BM. By marrying this revered man's daughter, in other words, Khalid would make a match fit for the son of Osama bin Laden.

The girl's mother, Umm Abdul Rahman, was agreeable, but the family did not live nearby, and the need for security made a meeting between the bride and groom extremely difficult—especially in light of her mother's insistence that the girl and her husband stay near them for at least four years following the wedding. Time passed by with no resolution, and by November of 2010, with Khalid now in his early twenties, his mother was beginning to worry that "losing too much time waiting may result in missing the train for both of them." She suggested a deadline of four months, after which time, if it was still impossible to arrange the wedding, they would call it off. But by April 2011, Umm Khalid judged that matters had improved enough that bride and groom could safely meet. All of a sudden, the wedding was back on, and the four-month deadline was forgotten. "I hope you will consider it completely cancelled," Umm Khalid wrote to Umm Abdul Rahman. Khalid began making arrangements to travel to the home of his new fiancée, and Umm Khalid, the proud mother of the groom, looked forward to the day when their two families would be joined. "We have been through difficult security circumstances," she wrote to the woman who would soon be her son's mother-in-law. "However, by the grace of Allah, things changed and every day that goes by our situation goes from good to better."

Bin Laden valued all his wives. In his interpretation of scripture, Muslim men were permitted to marry up to four women at a time. The Koran instructs believers to "maintain equality" among their wives. What advocates of polygamy often forget, however, is that a

few verses later the Koran also warns, "Try as you may, you cannot treat all your wives impartially." Bin Laden had fallen into this
trap; it was widely known that his favorite of all his wives had long
been Khairia Sabar, the mother of Hamza. Seven years bin Laden's
senior, Umm Hamza came from a respected family in Jeddah, his
Saudi hometown. She had a PhD in child psychology and, prior to
the bin Laden family's flight to Afghanistan in the mid-1990s, had
held an appointment as a university professor. During the family's
stay in Khartoum, Sudan, she had educated women on Islamic theology, and among bin Laden's inner circle, she was regarded as a
wise confidante, with the ability to keep people's spirits up, even in
desperate times. But for most of the past decade, bin Laden and his
most beloved wife had suffered a forced exile from each other. In
the chaos that followed the American-led invasion of Afghanistan in
2001, while bin Laden hid in Pakistan, Umm Hamza had fled along
with a number of other al-Qaeda supporters and their families west-
ward, through Iran, intending eventually to travel to Syria. But she
and her companions had been arrested by Iranian forces and imprisoned there for nine excruciating years.

Finally, in the late summer of 2010, the day before the start of
the holy month of Ramadan, Umm Hamza's bonds were broken. In
the weeks that followed, she made her way to Waziristan to meet
with Mahmud and the militants under his command. Bin Laden was
overjoyed. He instructed Mahmud to ensure that Umm Hamza was
kept safe and comfortable, and authorized use of his personal funds
for the purpose. But the sheikh's ultimate plan was for Umm Hamza
to join him in Abbottabad at the earliest possible opportunity. He
missed his wife dearly; her return, he told her, would "fill our hearts
with joy." But his desire for her presence was about much more than
the natural tug of marital affection. With the tenth anniversary of
9/11 approaching, he wanted Umm Hamza's sage and sensitive eye
on every statement to be released to the world. Of all the members of
bin Laden's inner circle, she was among the best educated and most

sensitive. Moreover, she had been with him since before al-Qaeda was even thought of—they had married in 1985, when he was still fighting the Soviet occupation of Afghanistan.

As well as holding her and their son Hamza in such high regard, bin Laden had long considered Umm Hamza one of his closest advisers. She was one of the few people he truly trusted to help him finesse his message. He therefore instructed the Waziristan contingent to buy her a computer, peripherals, and flash drives so that she could compose her thoughts and send them to him. Meanwhile, Mahmud was to proceed with making arrangements for her safe passage east to Abbottabad.

Naturally, moving Umm Hamza across Pakistan would be a delicate matter. A wife of bin Laden, particularly one who had been held in Tehran and interrogated by Iranian intelligence, would be a glittering prize for the Pakistani authorities, not to mention the Americans, especially if her movements led them to the man himself. If it was to happen at all, Umm Hamza's journey would require careful choreography, and this would take time. To start with, she would need to learn enough Urdu so as not to raise suspicions along the way. To guard against the implantation of microscopic monitoring devices, she must not bring any of the possessions the Iranian authorities had allowed her to keep while in custody. Anything a needle might puncture could conceivably be bugged—including even the filling an Iranian official dentist had put into her tooth. If the filling was done less than a year ago, bin Laden warned, the bug might still be live, and Umm Hamza should go to a doctor in Waziristan, say that the tooth was causing her pain, and have it removed. After all, "the Iranians are not to be trusted." Nor was the possibility of detection the only difficulty to deal with. With around two dozen people already under their protection, al-Kuwaiti and Abrar were becoming overwhelmed with their task, and grumbled that they were extremely reluctant to accept any more bin Laden family members.

With so many hurdles to overcome, Umm Hamza's return may

have seemed practically impossible. But bin Laden's need for her was so powerful and immediate that, by wintertime, he was even becoming desperate enough to toy with the idea of trekking across the country himself to be near her—an almost suicidally reckless mission for the world's most wanted man. One can only imagine Mahmud's reaction to that suggestion. Indeed, this proposal may have been a ploy to galvanize the membership into action; soon afterward, they were finally able to find a way to send Umm Hamza to bin Laden. She arrived at the Abbottabad compound on February 12, 2011. It was the day after the fall of Mubarak, and bin Laden must have been doubly pleased to have his wordsmith with him now that the Arab revolutions were in full swing and he was in the throes of formulating his defining message to the *umma*.

Like her husband, Umm Hamza had never been in the best of health. As a result of her frailty, while she and bin Laden were trying to conceive, she endured a number of miscarriages. But, as her *kunya* indicates, she did bear him one son. Hamza bin Laden was born in the late 1980s, around the same time as his half-brother Khalid. The last known pictures of Hamza come from jihadist propaganda videos of the late 1990s, where he can be seen, as a prepubescent boy, looking like a miniature version of his father, undergoing assault training, hanging out with the mujahideen, and preaching fiery sermons in a helium voice. After 9/11, he was taken prisoner in Iran alongside his mother. Captivity did nothing to dim Hamza's youthful militancy; his only frustration, he told his father in a letter smuggled out to Abbottabad, was that, because he had grown up largely in Iranian custody, "the mujahideen legions have marched and I have not joined them." After his marriage while in detention—to a daughter of the longtime al-Qaeda commander Abu Mohammed al-Masri—Hamza even named his firstborn son Osama and his daughter Khairia, to honor his father and mother. As he told bin Laden, "God created them to serve you."

Hamza was released from prison in Iran on the same day as his mother, August 10, 2010. Like her, he made his way to Waziristan to join with Mahmud and the other militants based there. Bin Laden briefly explored the idea of trying to persuade the Iranians to send his son elsewhere in the Gulf region, or having Mahmud's men send him there themselves, but this proved impossible, partly because Hamza would be too tempting a target for the Americans. Besides, if God permitted, the sheikh wanted his son by his side. Again, there were more than family ties in play. As a boy, Hamza had shown himself a precocious jihadi. Growing into a man in Iranian captivity, he studied scripture and became learned in Sharia, or Islamic law. Now, in Waziristan, he was eager for the al-Qaeda fighters to train him in the ways of war. Mahmud was full of praise for his young protégé. "He is very sweet and good," he told bin Laden. "I see in him wisdom and politeness. He does not want to be treated with favoritism because he is the son of 'someone'." If there was a bin Laden boy suited to carrying on his father's legacy, Hamza was his best hope.

But bin Laden had been down this road before. A few years previously, the sheikh had tried bestowing executive responsibility on another of his sons, an elder half-brother of Hamza named Saad. Saad, too, had been imprisoned in Iran, but by the middle of August 2008, he had been set free—or had escaped. Like Hamza two years later, Saad made his way to Waziristan. But Saad behaved recklessly, and sometime in the first half of 2009, he was killed by an American missile. "Saad died—peace be upon him—because he was impatient," Mahmud told bin Laden in a letter. The sheikh tried to keep his son's death quiet, but word got out. Bin Laden demanded to know how the news had leaked, and instructed his underlings to destroy photos taken of Saad after his death. His concern was not just that of a grieving father but that of a leader with his eye on the future. "We pray that God reward us for his loss and grant us a successor," he wrote to Umm Hamza.

Bin Laden was not going to allow Hamza to meet the same fate as his half-brother. The operatives in Waziristan had orders to keep

Hamza indoors, in conditions Mahmud likened to a "prison." Bin Laden even insisted on personally vetting the man assigned to guard his son. These strictures irked Hamza, who had so recently been released from captivity. But needs must; Hamza was not to leave the house unless absolutely necessary. By early April of 2011, Mahmud was close to hatching a plan for Hamza to join his father in Abbottabad. Hamza would travel directly north over mountains ruled by the Khyber tribes; or else he would go south, through the badlands of Baluchistan. This latter route was not the most direct, but it was the safest, and for that reason the one Mahmud recommended. Indeed, with this option, Hamza's wife and children could even journey with him. Once in Baluchistan, they would rendezvous with Umar Siddque Kathio Azmarai, a.k.a. Abdullah al-Sindi, one of al-Qaeda's most seasoned and trusted fixers. Al-Sindi knew Pakistan like the back of his hand and had already worked for members of the bin Laden family, including Hamza's late half-brother Saad, for many years. To get him through the checkpoints along the road, Hamza even had a fake ID, courtesy of his other half-brother, Khalid. By late April of 2011, Hamza waited in Waziristan, praying only for a cloudy sky to speed him on his way.

. . .

Osama bin Laden had always made much of dreams and visions—those of others as well as his own. He enjoyed discussing them and divining what they might mean. To him, this was no idle parlor game. Correctly interpreted, the sheikh believed, dreams could function as windows on the future. In the mid-1990s, he believed that he had foretold in his sleep the accession of Prince Abdullah to the throne of Saudi Arabia (an event that would not actually come to pass for another decade). Immediately before 9/11, his followers had recounted "prophetic" dreams of planes striking buildings and al-Qaeda pilots beating the United States at soccer. In Abbottabad, the sheikh was still dreaming, and in the second half of 2010, the portents appeared auspicious. "Good news," he wrote to his mother on August 26, in the middle of Ramadan. In a dream, he told her, "I saw that I had been chased by a huge black snake. Next thing, I was grabbing its head. I opened its mouth and I saw that all the teeth had shattered. Praise God, there were brothers close by. I told them, 'There is no harm,' or 'It won't hurt you because we smashed its teeth.' Praise God!" Indeed, a few months later, in the middle of spring 2011, things seemed to be looking up for al-Qaeda and its leader. Slowly but surely, he was bringing his family back together. The Arab Spring was sweeping away hated tyrants with breathtaking speed, possibly paving the way for the restoration of the caliphate. Bin Laden and his deputies had even begun reaching out to heal a developing rift between al-Qaeda and the splinter group that had taken to calling itself the Islamic State of Iraq (ISI).

Not all was well, however. The sheikh's security arrangements, though they had served him well for almost a decade, were far from foolproof. Much later, when they were asked to explain why bin Laden had so little visible security around him in Abbottabad, his wives would say that the sheikh "trusted in God for his protection." The reality, of course, was far more mundane: Conspicuous security would have attracted attention. As the Rhode Island senator Jack Reed put it, "If you had twenty-five eighteen-year-olds with guns, then not only would the CIA notice, but so would the Pakistani military." A low profile, therefore, was the only way to go. The downside of this was that the entire burden of protection and concealment fell upon al-Kuwaiti and Abrar, the faithful Pashtun brothers who blended in so well with the city around them. One false move from either of them could have grave consequences for the sheikh, for his family, and for global jihad itself. By 2010, the cumulative stress of concealing and providing for the most wanted terrorist in history— not to mention his ever-expanding entourage of family members— was taking its toll on al-Kuwaiti and his brother. As if to underline the point, their nerves had been tested to the breaking point by a recent scare. Watching television one night, al-Kuwaiti's nine-year-old daughter had correctly identified bin Laden from a news report on Al Jazeera. In a blind panic, al-Kuwaiti had banned his family from visiting the main house, interacting with the bin Ladens, or even watching television. Bin Laden himself was beginning to notice in his hosts the listlessness that managers of all kinds recognize among the classic symptoms of burnout. "They are getting exhausted, security-wise, from my staying with them," he wrote to Umm Hamza. In fact, "they have reached a level of exhaustion where they are shutting down. . . . I think that I have to leave them, but it will take a few months to arrange another place." Al-Kuwaiti reassured his wife that he would soon be relieved of his almost unbearable burden. Perhaps he would even be given some property in a safer locale where they could finally live out their lives in peace.

Life in seclusion cannot have been easy for the sheikh himself, an eager outdoorsman who had spent his youth—and a great deal of time since—defying his frequent bouts of ill health by playing soccer, climbing mountains, riding horses, and shooting guns. Still, he had reason to be thankful. "As far as I am concerned," he told Umm Hamza, "God Almighty has been very generous to me." Khalid would soon be wed, and to the daughter of an esteemed martyr, no less. Umm Hamza, the favored wife, was already with him, and Hamza, her golden son, was on his way, God willing. Mahmud would soon be nearby, and bin Laden looked forward to working with him to plan the next stage of jihad. His security situation remained delicate, of course. But as bin Laden had once told Mahmud, "the facts prove that the American technology and advanced systems cannot capture a mujahid if he does not make a security violation that will lead them to him." In other words, you can only get caught if you make a mistake. Besides, by late April, the family felt their situation was improving. Umm Hamza captured their mood in upbeat terms. "We consider this to be the beginning of a new era," she wrote, "especially since our security is getting better and the

signs for victory for our mujahideen have begun to be seen." Within
a week, Osama bin Laden was dead.

. . .

Amal awoke after midnight to the sound of what seemed like a
tempest barreling through the valley. This was strange, for the mon-
soon was not due to hit Abbottabad for another two months or more.
In fact, early May was meant to be among the drier times of the year.
Together with her husband, Osama, Amal crept out onto the balcony.
The air was clear, with only a light breeze brushing at their faces. Not
a drop of rain was falling. There was no lightning to crack the sky, nor
even a moon to illuminate the valley. It was neither too warm nor too
cold—a comfortable 66 degrees Fahrenheit. It was, in fact, yet another
pleasant Abbottabad evening of the kind that had drawn the British
here more than a century and a half ago. But something was wrong—
the storm noise swirled around them, louder and louder, building to a
crescendo. Back indoors, Amal reached for the light switch.

"No," said Osama. Amal drew back her hand. Her youngest
child, three-year-old Hussein, was spending the night in the same
room as Osama and his mother, while their other children slept elsewhere in the house. No doubt they, too, had heard the commotion
outside and would be frightened. Amal padded downstairs to try
to calm them. When she returned, two of Osama's older daughters,
Maryam and Sumayia, both in their late teens or early twenties, had
joined him in the master bedroom, along with some of Maryam's
own children.

"There is no God but God," they recited together. "And Muhammad is the messenger of God." Outside, the tempest's fury rose higher
and higher, until the whole fabric of the building seemed to shake.
The walls of the Abbottabad Valley formed a natural echo chamber,
so that there was no way of knowing which direction the sound was
coming from. But Osama had more than an inkling of what was happening, and of the forces behind it.

The family continued their recitation. "I bear witness that there is no god except Allah. He is one. He has no partner. And I bear witness that Muhammad is His Servant and Messenger. . . ." When they had finished reciting the confession of the faith, Osama turned to the women. "American helicopters have arrived," he told them. "All of you must leave this room at once."

They refused. They would remain, and so would Osama. Maryam took her children onto the balcony, while Amal and Sumayia struck up positions near Osama. On a shelf, within reach of Osama's slender hands, lay the Russian AK-74 assault rifle that had been his constant companion since the aftermath of the Battle of Jaji in Afghanistan almost a quarter century before. On that occasion, legend said, Osama had led a handful of mujahideen to victory against Soviet special forces two hundred strong. The gun, with its distinctive snub-nosed barrel and curving, rust-red magazine, had been awarded to him on the field of triumph. But tonight, it would remain on its shelf. Downstairs, Khalid had picked up his own weapon, a more conventional AK-47, and was patrolling from floor to floor, in and out of the family rooms, checking on the women and children of the house. "Stay away from the windows," he told them.

Almost a decade since the 9/11 attacks, the helicopters had indeed arrived, as Osama had said. They had come in low and fast from the north, skimming the treetops. Now, somewhere in the dark beyond bin Laden's walled-off third-floor balcony, two heavily modified Sikorsky UH-60 Black Hawks were disgorging their passengers—a crack team of two dozen U.S. Navy SEALs, each of them specially selected and trained for this, one of the most important missions in the five-decade history of the world's deadliest clandestine fighting force. Each stage of the raid had an assigned code word. For the climax—the encounter with Osama—the word was "Geronimo." With all the precision and coordination of a seasoned surgical team, the Americans ran through their checklist, blasting through doors, methodically sweeping room after room, floor after floor, building after building, confronting and killing the compound's defenders, cuffing women and children and holding them in a downstairs room.

In the guesthouse, al-Kuwaiti grabbed his rifle and sprayed blindly into the night in the direction of the soldiers' voices. From outside, the SEALs returned fire, and al-Kuwaiti fell dead. A short time later, over at the main house, the soldiers shot his brother Abrar in the chest as he tried to fire at them with his rifle. Blood soaked his cream shalwar kameez. Abrar's wife, Bushra, was also killed, caught in the crossfire that felled her husband.

From his position on the second floor of the main house, Khalid could hear the commotion downstairs. After the gunshots that killed Abrar and Bushra, their terrified children had begun wailing uncontrollably. Now, soldiers were attaching C-4 explosive charges to the metal door that guarded the stairwell. Khalid heard the blast, followed by an eerie calm. Then came another sound—not sharp this time, but uncanny. From out of the gloom, someone was whispering his name. Was it his father? One of the couriers? Unable to contain his curiosity, Khalid leaned out around a corner to see the source. A shot rang out, and Khalid fell dead, killed by the soldier who had breathed his name.

The Americans stepped over Khalid's corpse with its spreading penumbra of blood and made their way toward the master bedroom on the top floor. Amal heard their footsteps on the stairs. Soon she perceived a swinging beam of red light, sharp against the all-engulfing blackness. An American soldier was drawing a bead on Osama. Amal screamed. She and Sumaiya charged in the direction of the laser sight. One of the SEALs turned, shot Amal in the leg, and shoved her and Sumaiya to the floor. With a sudden pulse of pain, Amal passed out. That was when one of the Americans shot her husband in the head. "For God and country," the SEAL team commander radioed moments later. "Pass Geronimo, Geronimo, Geronimo." Not far from where Amal had collapsed lay the body of her husband, blood and tissue oozing from a v-shaped bullet hole above his eye socket. "Geronimo EKIA," the commander said. Enemy killed in action. Nearby, Amal's son Hussein was weeping.

Bin Laden had once told Mahmud that a mujahid could only be caught if he made a mistake. Did he wonder, in his final moments, how he had blundered? Perhaps he should have relieved his burned-out guards. Perhaps, after all, it had been a mistake to bring Umm Hamza to his side, so soon after her Iranian ordeal. Did he think about the martyrs whose blessed company he would soon be keeping? He had reason to believe he would be well received; before he died, his own son Saad had pledged in his will to vouch for his father before God in heaven. Did Osama feel, in those last moments, a pang of regret that he had not managed to see Hamza one last time? Or was he simply glad that the favored son was not there to meet the same fate as Khalid and the other men? Finally, as deadly darkness descended over his eyes, did this brutal man feel any remorse for the thousands of innocent lives he and his followers had stolen in the name of a religion they had twisted into an ideology of blood?

The compound's defenders, though faithful to the last, had been no match for the Americans. Apart from the exalted identity of the target and the risks of flying, stealthy and unbidden, through Pakistani airspace, the mission was, at least for the highly specialized operatives who carried it out, routine. Later, American officials would liken the raid to "mowing the lawn." It was as straightforward, they would say, as raiding a large house in suburban Virginia. That may have been true. But the consequences of that killing on a moonless mountain night would unspool on a global scale.

CHAPTER 2

ALLEGIANCE

> *God was well pleased with the faithful when they swore*
> *allegiance to you under the tree. He knew what was in*
> *their hearts. Therefore he sent down tranquillity upon*
> *them, and rewarded them with a speedy victory and*
> *with the many spoils which they have taken. Mighty is*
> *God and wise.*
>
> —HOLY KORAN, SURAH AL-FATH (VICTORY), 48:18

Amal wakes to the sound of continued commotion. She strains against the sharp plastic of her handcuffs. To her left and right, the other surviving residents watch, dazed, as the Americans busily strip their home of books, files, and hard drives. Amal flings furious curses at the *kafir* soldiers pilfering her husband's belongings, but her shouts are soon submerged beneath the hammering of a massive six-bladed Chinook helicopter putting down outside the high walls of the compound. A medic hurries out from under the thumping rotors. Gingerly he opens the nylon body bag containing Osama's disfigured remains. He injects syringes for blood and bone samples. Then he zippers the bag shut once more. The soldiers carry the body bag to a waiting Black Hawk. A huge explosion shakes the neighborhood as the Americans destroy a helicopter damaged on landing. Then, illuminated only by flames from the burning wreckage, the Americans depart, leaving Amal, inconsolable, still vainly screaming into the deep dark of a moonless morning. From out of the gloom comes the voice of a neighbor, startled from sleep by the tumult. "Sister," the voice implores. "What has happened? Why is your child crying?"

Four days after the Abbottabad raid, on May 6, 2011, al-Qaeda released a statement of felicitation.

> *Congratulations to the Islamic* umma *on the martyrdom of their beloved son Osama. Where else do men and heroes die but on the battlefield? Every end is predestined. But can the Americans kill what Sheikh Osama lived and fought for? Many more men and heroes like him will come. The soldiers of Islam will continue to plot tirelessly.*

The sheikh's body, swaddled in a white burial shroud, lay weighted down at the bottom of the Indian Ocean. His family was scattered. His wives languished in the custody of Pakistani intelligence. His sons Saad and Khalid were dead, and Hamza was in limbo somewhere in the lawless province of Waziristan, constantly menaced, like the other jihadi brothers with him, by the threat of assassination from above. Al-Qaeda's living leaders were in custody or in hiding. Some of them, having recently been released from years of captivity in Iran, were still finding their feet.

Al-Qaeda's affiliates, in Arabia, the Maghreb, Iraq, and elsewhere, remained relatively strong; but their focus lay on local struggles, not global jihad, and they had much to occupy them in their home countries. The uprisings in Libya, Yemen, and particularly Syria were entering a new and bloody phase. By the end of May, well over one thousand civilians were to die in Syria alone, including a thirteen-year-old boy, Hamza al-Khatib, tortured to death by the forces of the Assad regime, supposedly as a warning to would-be rebels. Al-Qaeda's May 6 statement had promised a posthumous "voice message of congratulations and advice" from the sheikh to the Muslim people in revolt against their governments, but the publication of that message was proving slow in coming. Partly because of the laborious communication methods that circumstances had forced upon the organization, al-Qaeda was still only beginning to formulate its response to the sequence of epochal upheavals already being referred to as the Arab Spring. To carry on the work, and to respond to the blistering pace of events, al-Qaeda would need to replace its fallen leader, and fast. There was never any real doubt as to the identity of the new emir. Six months before 9/11, al-Qaeda had formally merged with its sister organization, Egyptian Islamic Jihad. Under the terms of the merger, the Egyptian group's leader, a former surgeon by the name of Ayman al-Zawahiri, had been anointed bin Laden's deputy and heir apparent. But to step formally into the dead emir's shoes, Zawahiri would need oaths of allegiance—*bayat*—from each member of al-Qaeda's ruling council.

Bayat is a traditional system of governance dating back to pre-Islamic Arabia. It was adopted into Islam by the very earliest Muslims. The story is well known. When the polytheist rulers of Mecca were rumored to have murdered the Prophet Muhammad's herald, his followers vowed revenge. To cement their resolve, they pledged *bayat* to the Prophet in the shade of a desert tree. So poignant was this display of unity that the militarily much stronger Meccans decided not to attack the Muslims, as they had been intending, but to offer peace terms. This legend assured the place of *bayat* in traditional Islamic practice. In the ensuing centuries, the institution was to become a key source of legitimacy for the Prophet's successors, the caliphs. Today, the Islamic State, whose leader also calls himself a caliph, demands *bayat* from all its followers, from Syria to San Bernardino.

Allegiance to the emir was considered a prerequisite for formal membership in al-Qaeda, too. While bin Laden was in hiding in Pakistan, it was left to other leaders, such as Mahmud, to take *bayat* on his behalf. Having pledged *bayat* to the sheikh in person is regarded as a mark of prestige. Clasping bin Laden's hands, just as the earliest followers of the Prophet had done centuries before, al-Qaeda members would "swear before God to help and support you, putting aside my personal concerns and ideas, for better or for worse; and putting my own wellbeing behind me, I promise not to question your command." Then they would sign their names to memorialize this solemn oath. The pledge meant what it said; once sworn, a member had to do anything his superiors asked of him, no matter how taxing or humiliating. For example, a doctor might be ordered to wash cars instead of tending to patients. In the view of at least one former bin Laden acolyte, the pledge might even bind a member to do things Islam otherwise viewed as *haram*—forbidden. For many jihadis, the oath is much more than words. It is, in fact, integral to their identity, their sense of self.

The story of Ali Omran, the man who built the truck bomb that killed more than two hundred people enjoying a night out in Bali in 2002, illustrates the awesome power of *bayat*. Omran had pledged his loyalty to the Southeast Asian jihadi group Jamma Islamiya. Initially, he was proud of his vicious deed, thinking that he had fulfilled his oath by doing the bidding of his overlords. But when he discovered that the man who ordered the bombing had secretly recanted his oath to Jamma Islamiya and was, in fact, working for al-Qaeda, Omran was devastated. What caused this sea change in Omran's attitude was not a sudden realization that he had murdered scores of innocent men and women in cold blood; it was the sudden removal of the cloak of *bayat* under which this vile act had supposedly been perpetrated.

But the seriousness with which many militants took the oath could cut both ways. Bin Laden's own rather furtive *bayat* to the Taliban in 1998—an act of pragmatism rather than any deep sense of religious duty on the sheikh's part—precipitated the departure of his chief bodyguard, Abu Jandal, who saw it as compromising his master's integrity as a leader in global jihad.

If Ayman al-Zawahiri was to stand any chance of maintaining control over al-Qaeda as its new emir, he would have to show that he enjoyed the genuine, freely offered allegiance of each member of its governing *shura* council—and, thereafter, from each of al-Qaeda's affiliates around the world. Yet for the deputy to solicit his own pledges of *bayat* from al-Qaeda's leadership would be to risk calling into question the sincerity of those oaths. Al-Qaeda would need a reliable and respected pair of hands to collect the necessary pledges of fealty to the new emir. Within days of the Abbottabad raid, the organization had appointed for this task its former military chief, an Egyptian ex-soldier known as Saif al-Adel.

· · ·

Every jihadi, from the greenest recruit to the most seasoned operative, knows the name Saif al-Adel. All view him with awe; he was there at the creation. When U.S. forces swept into Kandahar in late 2001, they captured thousands of documents detailing the history, structure, and membership of al-Qaeda, including a list of the organization's first 170 charter members. On that list, Osama bin Laden is number one; Saif al-Adel is number eight. Though he did not always agree with bin Laden—and was usually unafraid to let his feelings be known—Saif's loyalty to his master was unswerving. Unlike many of the other high-ranking Egyptians in the organization—Zawahiri himself included—Saif had never owed allegiance to any other group. For years, from South Asia to East Africa and back again, he was a watchman at bin Laden's side, his narrow eyes constantly looking out for trouble, and frequently finding it. He was a trusted emissary to the rogue states and armed groups al-Qaeda courted, and to the places it sought to colonize, from Yemen to

Somalia to Iran. Osama bin Laden, who for much of his adult life was pursued across the face of the earth by assassins of many lands and allegiances, trusted Saif al-Adel more than almost anyone else. By the eve of September 11, 2001, Saif was effectively fourth in command, behind only bin Laden, Zawahiri, and the formidable military chieftain Abu Hafs al-Masri.

Saif is one of the most experienced professional soldiers in the worldwide jihadi movement, and his body bears the scars of battle: a wound under his right eye from a bursting illumination shell; a scar on his right hand; an arm injury from his time fighting America and its allies in Somalia. But this is no simpleminded thug. On the contrary, he is "highly educated and speaks good English." Former colleagues describe him as a "shrewd diplomat" with a poker face. Yet his temper, too, has become notorious. Possessed of a "caustic tongue," he is apt to threaten violence against anyone who displeases him, and is known to meet disloyalty with swift and ruthless force. Toward underlings he can be contemptuous, even brutal, in the heat of the moment; but he has also been known as a font of avuncular advice. In happier times, he even showed a talent for soccer and a penchant for practical jokes. But Saif's crimes are deadly serious. The United States has placed a $5 million bounty on his head for his role in the murder of 224 people in Nairobi and Dar es Salaam in 1998. In an organization infamous for its pitiless wholesale destruction of human lives, Saif stands out for his lack of remorse, even at times when other high-ranking terrorists have expressed doubt about the rightness of their deeds. One operative said that Saif was difficult to work with because he does not trust anyone. That is one important reason why Saif is alive and at liberty today when so many of his colleagues lie dead or in shackles.

Yet we know very little about him with any degree of certainty. Like the callow youth Pasha in Boris Pasternak's novel *Doctor Zhivago*, who uses the chaos of revolution to recast himself as the cruel Soviet commissar Strelnikov, Saif al-Adel has taken extraordinary steps to obfuscate the particulars of his apparently ordinary and blameless life before al-Qaeda. Like Strelnikov—"The Gunman"— Saif al-Adel is not a real name but a melodramatic nom de guerre that translates as Sword of Justice. There is evidence that Saif faked his own death while still in his twenties, and he may even have deliberately appropriated the identity of an entirely different man. To piece together scant details of his life and personality, we must hack through a jungle of conflicting reports, falsely attributed writings, and mistaken identity. What follows is an attempt to trace his most likely path and, in so doing, to cast new light on the origins of al-Qaeda and its possible future trajectory.

For years, analysts around the world believed that Saif was in reality an Egyptian former special forces colonel named Mohammed Makkawi; indeed, as of mid-2016, the FBI still listed that name as one of Saif's aliases. The facts seemed to fit this hypothesis. Like Saif, Makkawi hails from Egypt's Nile Delta. Both men served in their country's armed forces, and both went on to fight the Soviets in Afghanistan in the late 1980s. It is easy to draw the conclusion that Saif is Makkawi and Makkawi is Saif. The only problem with this intelligence is that it is completely false.

On February 29, 2012, Colonel Ibrahim Makkawi set foot on Egyptian soil for the first time in a quarter-century. For most, if not all, of that time, in light of the suspicions of terrorism swirling around him, Makkawi had been persona non grata in his native country. But the fall of Mubarak and the impending rise to power of the Muslim Brotherhood, a worldwide Islamist movement founded in Egypt, seemed to open the door for the return of men like Makkawi, whom the Mubarak regime had proscribed for their jihadi views. Or so Makkawi thought. Shortly after his arrival at Cairo International Airport, Egyptian security forces pounced. State media gleefully reported that the authorities had, at last, apprehended the infamous terrorist Saif al-Adel, but within hours they had admitted that the lead was a dud. Indeed, anyone who has met both men, or even com-

pared their pictures, would know this instantly. While Makkawi is
stocky and swarthy, the known images of Saif show him to be slim
and light-skinned. There is, moreover, a substantial age difference
between the two men. Indeed, Makkawi and Saif come from two
different generations of the jihad.

Mohammed Ibrahim Makkawi was born in the early 1950s. He
served in the Egyptian military during the 1973 Yom Kippur War with
Israel, became a member of a specialist anti-terrorism unit within the
Egyptian armed forces, and eventually rose to the rank of colonel. In
1987, Makkawi was briefly detained by the Mubarak regime, which
suspected him of involvement in a plot to assassinate a government
minister and a newspaper editor initiated by an underground group
calling itself Salvation from Hell. Upon his release, disgusted at the
treatment meted out to him by the government, Makkawi departed
for Afghanistan to fight the Russians as one of the "Arab Afghans"
who began pouring into the country following the Soviet invasion in
late 1979. Leaving his old life behind, Makkawi adopted a nom de
guerre—not Saif al-Adel but Abu al-Munther.

As a seasoned officer, however, he evinced little respect for the
ragtag freshman fighters around him, regarding them as reckless,
incompetent, a "generation of amateurs" fighting the "war of the
goats," hot not for victory but for slaughter. The former head of the
Libyan Islamic Fighting Group, who has met both Makkawi and Saif,
puts it succinctly: "Makkawi hates al-Qaeda." Many of the organization's operatives reciprocate his dislike, describing Makkawi as
uppity, arrogant, "short fused," "unpredictable," even "dangerously
unbalanced." Few would dare say such things about the legendary
Saif al-Adel. After the Soviet retreat from Afghanistan, Makkawi
took refuge in Islamabad, Pakistan, where he attempted to lead a
normal life, despite having attracted both the enmity of al-Qaeda
and the suspicion of domestic and foreign intelligence. Saif al-Adel,
by contrast, intoxicated by a life of permanent jihad, went on looking
for Goliaths to slay.

. . .

Of the "real" Saif al-Adel, only three images are known to exist. They show a slender-faced man with hooded almond eyes and a proud, unblinking stare—his gaze sparkling, as his future father-in-law was to note, with intelligence and cunning. We now know that his real name is Mohammed Salahuddin Zeidan. He was born in Shibin al-Kawm, a town about forty miles northwest of downtown Cairo, in the early 1960s. At that time, the Arab nationalist Gamal Abdel Nasser was one of the most respected leaders in the Arab world, pressing ahead with his pan-Arab socialist agenda of nationalizing Western-dominated industries, backing major construction projects from the Helwan Steelworks in the north to the Aswan Dam in the south, and even, for a brief time, pursuing political and economic union with Syria and North Yemen. Nasser's proxies in Yemen were Arab nationalists, fighting against the Zaidi Shia forces of Imam Ahmad Bin Yahya Hamididdin backed by Sunni Saudi Arabia—something that would be unthinkable in today's viciously sectarian climate. Indeed, the intervening five decades have seen the House of Saud switch sides in Yemen's long struggle, now supporting the government against another group of Shia rebels, the Houthis. In Nasser's day, however, the issue was not Shia versus Sunni as much as monarchy versus socialism—and for a time, socialism appeared to be succeeding. But Nasser's utopian schemes were doomed to come crashing down in the humiliation of the 1967 Six-Day War, in which Israel annihilated the bulk of Nasser's air force before Egypt could fire a shot. All over the country, terrorist cells began gaining strength, including one that had formed around a teenaged jihadi and future medical student, Ayman al-Zawahiri. Soon, a number of these cells, including the one led by Zawahiri, would coalesce to form a new organization called Egyptian Islamic Jihad.

Saif al-Adel would not join them. The sheikh of the Farjul Islam mosque, where the young Mohammed Zeidan attended prayers and lectures, recalls a quiet, studious, rather introverted young man. According to his older brother Hassan, Mohammed enjoyed good relations with all his neighbors, including even Coptic Christians, a minority who periodically became a favorite target of hardline Islamists. After graduating from high school, he earned a bachelor's degree in business from a local university, then enlisted with the Army Reserve, where he specialized in parachuting, explosives, and intelligence. In the roiling political climate of Egypt in the 1970s and 1980s, it would have been difficult, if not impossible, to avoid at least some exposure to hardline propaganda—especially on campus and in the armed forces, two institutions heavily infiltrated by Islamists. During Mohammed's formative years, moreover, events were taking place that inflamed outrage across the Arab world. He was in his teens when President Anwar Sadat signed the Camp David accords with Israel, and not much older when Sadat was assassinated by an offshoot of Zawahiri's Egyptian Islamic Jihad. And yet, while still in his home country, Mohammed Zeidan had no known connections with any extremist groups. As an Egyptian intelligence operative was to put it, he "was never part of any jihad organization . . . until he moved to Afghanistan and found his calling."

Mohammed had always told his family that he intended to leave Egypt once his military service was over. Like many young Egyptians of his generation, faced with dim economic prospects at home, he said he planned to start a new life across the Red Sea in the booming, oil-rich kingdom of Saudi Arabia. In 1987, his brother drove him to Cairo airport to board a flight to Mecca, where Mohammed intended to complete a minor pilgrimage before looking for work. It would be the last time any member of Mohammed's family would see him. A year later, a stranger arrived on his brother's doorstep, carrying a jacket that Hassan recognized as having belonged to Mohammed. The stranger told Hassan that Mohammed had indeed found work in the kingdom, as a salesman, but had been killed in a car crash. His distraught family petitioned the Saudi authorities to learn more details of how Mohammed had died, but to no avail. Consumed by grief, his mother's health declined, and she suffered a stroke from which she died. Eventually, in the absence of any contact, the Family Court of Shibin al-Kawm declared Mohammed legally dead. In a way, it was true. The person Mohammed Salahuddin Zeidan had been in Egypt, the studious youth, the loyal soldier, the decent citizen in a land increasingly gripped by violence, had indeed passed away. But Saif al-Adel was very much alive.

. . .

The life story of Osama bin Laden could scarcely have been more different. The millionaire son of a Saudi construction magnate with close ties to the royal family, by the mid-1980s bin Laden was already well on the way to becoming a hero in his own right for his central role in corralling and financing Arab Afghan brigades to fight the Soviet invasion of Afghanistan. In May of 1987, the same year Saif al-Adel left Egypt for Saudi Arabia, bin Laden had crystallized his legend by helping his mujahideen win a famous victory against Russian special forces in the mountain passes of Jaji near the Pakistani border—the battle in whose aftermath he was awarded his beloved AK-74. In short order, bin Laden became a lightning rod, attracting to his banner hundreds of Arab recruits desperate to defeat the godless Communists.

Saif al-Adel's first encounter with bin Laden may have taken place during one of the sheikh's frequent recruiting trips back to his home country. But it is equally possible that Saif never intended to stay in Saudi Arabia at all, for it was widely known across the Arab world that the kingdom was offering subsidized flights to Afghanistan for young men willing to participate in the jihad against the Soviets. Partly, this was seen as a convenient means of getting rid of Saudi Arabia's own troublesome extremist element. Either way, Saif was soon well ensconced in the Afghan jihad, and making effective use of his military background. Desperate to inflict on the Soviet Union a defeat comparable to that suffered by the United States in Vietnam a decade before, America had recently begun supplying the mujahideen with hundreds of shoulder-mounted FIM-92 Stinger missiles. One of Saif's first jobs in Afghanistan was to instruct his fellow fighters in the use of these weapons to bring down Russian Hind helicopter gunships. Years later, and thousands of miles away, he would train other fighters to use similar weapons against American Black Hawks in Mogadishu, Somalia; but that was in a future barely conceivable through the fevered late–Cold War fog of the mid-1980s.

Facing a brutal war of attrition with no end in sight, in 1988 the Soviets signed peace accords and began to withdraw from Afghanistan, and the minds of the Arab mujahideen turned to what they would do after the war was over. Some would return home to their families, but for others, this was unthinkable. For these men, jihad was not a single project but a way of life. They poured disdain on those who, in their eyes, came to the war merely for adventure or recreation—"tourism jihad," as they scornfully called it. Moreover, many jihadis—the Egyptians most of all—were unable to return home, even if they had wanted to, because they would be arrested on sight by the regimes in their countries of origin. By the late summer of 1988, this hard core of jihadis had coalesced to form a new grouping called al-Qaeda al-Askaria—the Military Base. They described themselves as "an organized Islamic faction" dedicated to "lift[ing] the word of God, to make His religion victorious." Tourist jihadis would not be welcome in this new organization; only those whose presence in the theater of war was permanent would be eligible for membership.

Al-Qaeda's first major battle would not go well. After the last Soviet soldier left Afghanistan in February of 1989, bin Laden and his fellow Arab commanders, lifted high on a wave of inflated morale, led the mujahideen in a massed assault on the city of Jalalabad. There, they took on the forces of the Marxist Najibullah regime, still backed by Russian military planning and scud missiles. Saif was among those who fought, and he was already carefully shunning the limelight; unlike many of his more publicity-hungry comrades, he refused to let himself be photographed by journalists on the scene. The Battle of Jalalabad was an unmitigated disaster for the mujahideen. Three thousand fighters died—fully one-fifth of the force that had attacked the city. Following this ignominious episode, bin Laden slunk off back home to Saudi Arabia, where he would remain for almost two years.

While bin Laden licked his wounds under virtual house arrest in his home city of Jeddah, Saif progressed up the hierarchy. His intelligence, military background, and authoritative bearing impressed his superiors, and he quickly rose to be emir of the Faruq training camp in southern Afghanistan. At Faruq and its sister facilities—where the extensive course offerings included instruction in assassination and kidnapping—Saif supervised training in explosives, intelligence gathering, and counterintelligence. His students in this period included Ramzi Yousef, who would go on to bomb the World Trade Center in 1993, Harun Fazul, later a leader of the cell that would kill scores of people at the U.S. embassies in Nairobi and Dar es Salaam, and L'Houssaine Kertchou, who would turn state's witness in the embassy bombings trial. With his tidy military mind, Saif helped transform the quality of training in the camps and establish standard operating procedures on everything from battle tactics to archiving. By 1991, he had risen into al-Qaeda's "second tier" leadership, subordinate only to bin Laden and his three closest associates. Soon, he would join them at the very top.

On graduation day in August 1990, Saif and his students planned to test their skills with explosives by staging a mock ambush. They singled out a truck pulling into the Khaldan camp and stealthily surrounded it, exploding a bomb to bring a tree down in front of the vehicle and firing their weapons as they attacked. Two Afghans who had been riding on the flatbed took shelter underneath the chassis. But the front passenger, a distinguished-looking Egyptian in his mid-forties, stepped calmly out of the vehicle and surveyed the scene. The militants recognized him at once as none other than Mustafa Hamid, a legendary figure among the Arab Afghans. Hamid had been one of the first Arabs to travel to Afghanistan, and he had become their principal ideologue and chronicler. Saif al-Adel approached Hamid, laughing heartily at the merry hell he and his men had succeeded in raising and gloating over the discomfiture of the two Afghans, who emerged from under the vehicle shaken and dripping with mud. Hamid, seeing Saif for the first time, noted his "narrow Asian eyes showing intelligence and cunning" and his "skinny strong body . . . full of energy." Over tea, Hamid and Saif discussed the news from Saudi Arabia, where American forces had just arrived to oust Saddam Hussein from Kuwait. It was the start of an enduring friendship. A year and a half later, Saif would become Hamid's son-in-law when he married his then fifteen-year-old daughter, Asma. With that, his place at the heart of the jihadi movement was assured.

· · ·

"The war in Afghanistan is winding down," Saif told a Palestinian jihadi around the end of 1992. "We are going to move the jihad to other parts of the world." In fact, the war in Afghanistan was not coming to an end but morphing from a struggle against Communist rule into a civil war between rival armed factions. There was little upside for al-Qaeda in battling fellow mujahideen. Moreover, the crushing defeat at Jalalabad, and bin Laden's subsequent retreat to Saudi Arabia, had brought about a collapse in al-Qaeda's morale and recruitment. In any event, most had already given up hope that Afghanistan could emerge from the chaos into which it was quickly descending as anything resembling al-Qaeda's idea of an Islamic state. But there was at least one regime in the world that came close to that standard: the Sudanese National Islamic Front. Almost since the moment it came to power in a 1989 coup d'état, the NIF had been trying to persuade bin Laden to move his organization to Sudan. Bin

Laden sent his own emissaries to Sudan. They told him that al-Qaeda and the NIF shared common goals. "What you are trying to do," these envoys assured bin Laden, "it is Sudan!"

During the winter of 1991–92, bin Laden took the Sudanese up on their offer. Saif helped him pack up al-Qaeda's operations and move them to Khartoum. There, Saif reestablished the training camps and continued to instruct recruits in the use of explosives. Saif's own career in al-Qaeda continued to blossom; even while he was still in Afghanistan, colleagues were describing him as "an important al-Qaeda leader." Before long, he had become a member of the organization's central military committee. Soon, Saif would be honing his deadly skills in an unlikely place: a Hezbollah training camp in Lebanon's Bekaa Valley. The sectarian divide between Sunni al-Qaeda and Shia Hezbollah was a very real one for both sides; but it was one that al-Qaeda's leadership, for their part, were willing to overlook in the name of battling their common enemy, the United States of America. At least since the start of the Gulf War, bin Laden had been spoiling for a fight with the far enemy. Behind closed doors, he had even begun to suggest that al-Qaeda should make common cause not only with a nonstate Shiite group like Hezbollah but even with their political masters in the government of Iran itself. The Islamic Republic shared this pragmatic calculus; its enemy's enemy could be considered, at least for the time being, its friend. In Khartoum, bin Laden sat down with a high representative of the Iranian regime who had access to the topmost branches of power in Tehran. The Saudi made his demand clear: He wanted al-Qaeda operatives trained to use explosives to destroy buildings, something Hezbollah had done repeatedly since its founding in 1982. Iran agreed that al-Qaeda personnel would go to Lebanon to be trained by Imad Mugniyah, one of Hezbollah's most dangerous operatives, responsible for the deaths of more Americans than any other terrorist prior to 9/11. As one of al-Qaeda's top military experts, Saif al-Adel was a natural candidate for this training; and indeed, the lessons from Mugniyah provided a terrible vision of things to come. Not long after his return from Lebanon, Saif would begin putting together the cell that would go on to kill hundreds at the U.S. embassies in Nairobi and Dar es Salaam, using methods of explosive demolition bearing striking similarities to those of Hezbollah.

Hezbollah, despite being a Shia group closely associated with the most hardline Shia government in the world, had shown itself able to work with Sunni militants like those of Hamas and Egyptian Islamic Jihad. But al-Qaeda was different. While commanders like bin Laden and Saif al-Adel were pragmatic and prepared to put aside their sectarian differences, the al-Qaeda rank and file were not. To many of them, brainwashed as they were by radical sectarian prejudice, it would almost be easier to work with the Israelis than with the Shia. So the budding relationship between al-Qaeda and Hezbollah would prove short-lived. But the contact did produce yet another vital role for Saif al-Adel: He was put in charge of managing the organization's nascent ties with elements of the Iranian regime.

. . .

From its base in Sudan, al-Qaeda extended its tentacles throughout East Africa. One of its first targets for expansion was Somalia, a fractious Muslim country on the Horn of Africa. Even before the move to Khartoum, al-Qaeda had been training militants from Somalia, and some of these alumni had since returned home to found their own radical Islamist group. By the beginning of 1992, Somalia's Marxist government—along with its whole system of governance—had irrevocably collapsed. Much of the weaponry of its Soviet-equipped military had bled out into the hands of armed nonstate groups, and a vicious civil war had broken out. All this seemed to make Somalia ripe for jihad.

Bin Laden sent Saif al-Adel to explore the possibility of expanding operations in Somalia. Initially, the outlook seemed gloomy. A shattered kaleidoscope of tribal alliances and enmities made working with any one clan impossible without alienating another. More-over, the battle-hardened leaders among the Somali Islamists did not appreciate foreign commanders bossing them around. And these leaders faced problems of their own in the shape of insubordination in the ranks and a chronic lack of public support for their activities. But these prospects were set to change, courtesy of the United States of America. Shortly after Saif's arrival, during the dying weeks of the George H. W. Bush presidency, the United Nations authorized a humanitarian intervention in Somalia. Operation Restore Hope commenced in December 1992 with the deployment of 1,800 U.S. Marines to the Somali capital, Mogadishu. Suddenly, al-Qaeda, the Somali Islamists, and the clans had a common enemy. Mustafa Hamid wrote to Saif, urging him to seize the day:

> *When you entered Somalia, the Somali arena was barren and futile. The situation changed, however, after the intervention by America and the Knights of the Cross. You most resembled a hunter aiming his rifle at the dead branch of a tree, with no leaves or birds on it. Suddenly, a bald eagle lands on the branch of the tree, directly in line with the rifle. Shouldn't the hunter pull the trigger to kill the eagle or at least bloody it? Fire at the bald eagle. Kill the Knights of the Cross. God is with you. . . . Kill them where you catch them; expand urban terror; plant mines on the roads; use all the covert weapons of war from rumor to strangulation, poisons, explosions, lightning attacks on small targets, and sniping.*

Saif traveled to the south of the country to establish a camp at Kaambooni, on the Kenyan border. This soon became the base for attacks against American-allied international forces deployed under the UN peacekeeping mandate. On one occasion, Saif's fighters ambushed a Belgian patrol, surrounded it, and shot three Belgian soldiers. "A lot of bullets were used and there was a lot of blood shed," Saif told his masters in Khartoum. Soon afterward, Belgian forces withdrew. "Thank God," Saif wrote, "we drove the Belgian contingent out of Somalia." The UN replaced the Belgians in the south with an Indian force. Saif targeted the Indians in the same way he had their predecessors. Saif's men set traps around the Indian base at Bilis Qooqaani and attacked the camp with grenades and rocket launchers, killing at least four of its defenders. The al-Qaeda commander reported that raids such as these were a great tool for recruiting local youths to the jihadi cause and suggested a concerted hearts-and-minds campaign to win further support. In his optimism, Saif even adopted a new nom de guerre—Omar al-Sumali, "Omar the Somalian."

The biggest prize, however, would be a successful attack on U.S. troops, and the best place for that would be their main base: the hot, cramped streets of Mogadishu itself. Saif took a small al-Qaeda team to the city and, as he had done in Afghanistan, proceeded to train fighters to shoot at helicopters. In an inversion of his earlier experience, however, now the weapons were Russian and the targets American. On the afternoon of October 3, 1993, two MH-60 Black Hawks participating in an antiterror operation in central Mogadishu were brought down within a few blocks of each other using Soviet-made rocket launchers. It has been reported that one of the launchers was fired by a Tunisian member of Saif's al-Qaeda squad. In the ensuing ground battle, eighteen U.S. personnel died and eighty-four were wounded. One Black Hawk crew member was taken prisoner, and the bodies of several others were dragged through the streets and pummeled by an angry mob. Saif and his men may have participated directly in the fighting on the ground; at the very least, the downing of the Black Hawks would likely not have been possible without Saif's military training. Either way, in the Battle of Mogadishu, the Sword of Justice had drawn its first American blood.

At a memorial service for the fallen, General William F. Garrison invoked Shakespeare's *Henry V*: "He which hath no stomach to this fight, let him depart. . . . We would not die in that man's company that fears his fellowship to die with us." But the steely determination of the soldiers on the ground was unmatched by political resolve in Washington, now under a new president, Bill Clinton, who had been in office less than a year. Three days after the Battle of Mogadishu, with one of the Black Hawk pilots still held hostage, President Clinton announced the staged withdrawal of U.S. forces from Somalia. To many in al-Qaeda, including its leader, the lesson was clear: Strike the United States, create some lurid images, and the serpent would soon withdraw. Mustafa Hamid again wrote to Saif and his "Africa Corps" to congratulate them on what he called their "splendid victory":

> *The Somali experience confirmed the spurious nature of American power and that it has not recovered from the Vietnam complex. It fears getting bogged down in a real war that would reveal its psychological collapse at the level of personnel and leadership. Since Vietnam America has been seeking easy battles that are completely guaranteed.*

If al-Qaeda could preserve and nurture the military expertise gained in Somalia, Hamid argued, it would prove "a successful Islamic arsenal in the severe confrontation with the pagan tyranny of the Jewish West." Moreover, Somalia itself could be a promising base for future jihad. "Plant firm pillars there," Hamid urged, "and go on working in an adjacent or nearby geographical field in preparation for a battle in which you will wrest away from the adversary additional retreats on the flanks."

This advice would go unheeded; as in Afghanistan a few years before, the invading superpower would not be the only force to cut and run. In 1995, the year after America left, bin Laden ordered the withdrawal of almost all remaining al-Qaeda forces in Somalia. Mustafa Hamid was furious, describing this emerging pattern of deployment and retreat as "stupid." But Saif al-Adel had helped inflict on America its first major defeat of the post–Cold War era.

In the process, he had cleared the way for the eventual rise of the al-Qaeda–aligned al-Shabaab militia.

. . .

For now, however, bin Laden's attention had wandered north, across the Gulf of Aden to Yemen. There, in the defeat of the Socialist faction in the 1994 civil war, bin Laden saw "clear evidence for a rejection of all secular and atheist regimes across the region," and perhaps even "a new beginning in the implementation of the Prophet's will of expelling all unbelievers from the Arabian Peninsula." Al-Qaeda had, in fact, been funding and training Yemeni operatives for combat against the Socialists since the late 1980s, and had begun shipping weapons across the straits from Somalia in the early 1990s. In 1989, bin Laden had even proposed a partnership with the Saudi government to bring about regime change in its southern neighbor, but he had been rebuffed, as he would be again a few months later when Saddam Hussein invaded Kuwait to the north. The Yemeni fight had a personal dimension for bin Laden, for he regarded the country as his ancestral home. Indeed, his own father had been born there, in a remote area that formed part of Socialist South Yemen for almost a quarter century.

Saif al-Adel traveled to Yemen in 1995, the year of al-Qaeda's withdrawal from Somalia, and set about creating a Yemeni franchise for al-Qaeda. As in Somalia, he found that things were not so simple. Once again, the complex fault lines between the various tribes were enough to confound even the best informed outsider. Moreover, with unification in 1990 and the end of Yemen's civil war in 1994, many local militants had simply lost interest in carrying on their fight by violent means; Islamic Jihad in Yemen had effectively disbanded, and two of its senior leaders had even been drafted into government posts, in exchange for their renunciation of force. Meanwhile, the North Yemeni regime of Ali Abdullah Saleh, now in control of the entire country, was in the process of rounding up and deporting foreign Arab Afghans—as many as fourteen thousand of them in 1995 and

1996 alone. But Saif did, in fact, succeed in laying the foundations for an al-Qaeda presence in Yemen that endures to the present day.

Years later, a Pakistani hothead named Khalid Sheikh Mohammed, now infamous for his role as the principal planner of the 9/11 attacks, would tell his American captors at Guantánamo Bay that he had linked up with Saif al-Adel during the latter's mid-1990s mission to Yemen. These claims are, of course, difficult to verify. KSM was not, at the time, a member of al-Qaeda, although the group had shown itself prepared to work with trusted independent jihadis who shared its agenda; only later, when he was once again firmly established in Afghanistan, did bin Laden begin to insist on formal allegiance to al-Qaeda as a condition of collaborating on missions. But whenever and wherever Saif and KSM first met, their ideas would go on to shape the next phase of al-Qaeda's existence; the occasionally stormy relationship between these two powerful personalities—one a careful soldier, the other a wild-eyed killer—would expose veins of conflict that ran right to the heart of the organization.

. . .

During al-Qaeda's sojourn in Khartoum, attacks linked to the group increasingly came to target Americans. In December 1992, bombs exploded at two hotels in Yemen used by U.S. Marines on their way to their deployment in Mogadishu at the start of Operation Restore Hope. The Americans had already left by the time the devices exploded, but one of the blasts killed a tourist and a hotel worker. Two months later, a much larger device in the parking garage under the south tower of the World Trade Center killed six people, including a pregnant secretary, and wounded around a thousand. The bomber was KSM's nephew, a Pakistani named Ramzi Yousef, and although the attack was not an official al-Qaeda operation, Yousef had trained at al-Qaeda camps in Afghanistan. On the day of the bombing, in February 1993, Yousef was just twenty-four years old; like his uncle, he had grown up in Kuwait and studied in the West, in Yousef's case in the United Kingdom. Yousef had expected the buildings to topple, but despite the fact that his device had carved a six-story crater through the parking decks and the floors above, the towers failed to fall; evidently that would take far greater force. Later the same year, the Battle of Mogadishu shocked U.S. public opinion and precipitated American and United Nations withdrawal from Somalia. Then, in November 1995, a car bomb exploded at a facility in Saudi Arabia where the U.S. military was training Saudi National Guardsmen. Five Americans and two Indian government officials were killed.

As al-Qaeda's murderous reach expanded, so did the danger to its leader. Attempts to assassinate bin Laden multiplied. In one of the most serious incidents, in February 1994, a gunman killed three of the sheikh's guards in the grounds of his Khartoum home, sending bin Laden scurrying into the basement with bullets whistling past his ears. Bin Laden himself blamed Egyptian intelligence, although there is some evidence that the assassination attempt was the product of an internal dispute within al-Qaeda's Sudanese operation. There was even talk of rival *takfiris* having carried out the effort, supposedly in retaliation for al-Qaeda's perceived poaching of *takfiri* recruits. Whoever was responsible, this and other dangerous incidents showed clearly bin Laden's need for enhanced security and counterintelligence. Saif al-Adel, with his suspicious mind and military training, was just the man for the job. His star within al-Qaeda continued to rise.

Among the additional bodyguards assigned to bin Laden following the assassination attempt was a Sudanese militant, Ibrahim Qosi, whose long and varied terrorist career has also included stints as bin Laden's accountant and personal cook, as well as a mission to deliver $5,000 to fund a 1995 assassination attempt against Egyptian President Hosni Mubarak. As late as December 2001, Qosi was still defending the emir at the climactic Battle of Tora Bora, in whose aftermath he was arrested and transferred to Guantánamo Bay. In exchange for pleading guilty before a military commission,

Qosi was released in 2012 to his home country of Sudan. In short order, he crossed the Red Sea to Yemen and joined al-Qaeda in the Arabian Peninsula. By 2015, Qosi, now gray-bearded and wrinkled, was being presented in AQAP's propaganda as one of its elders, his reputation among jihadis immeasurably bolstered by his long history of personal contact with bin Laden. And Qosi's story is by no means unique; in fact, it is typical of al-Qaeda's current leadership. While the organization's form may have changed, many of its senior personnel are the same determined, experienced terrorist leaders the West has been fighting for decades.

. . .

In 1996, Sudan reluctantly gave in to growing international pressure and expelled bin Laden and al-Qaeda. On May 18, he left in the company of a handful of his closest associates, including Saif al-Adel; the others would follow later. To display their continued respect for the terrorist leader, the Sudanese government chartered a plush Learjet for the occasion and sent an official minder along for the ride. Bin Laden and the other al-Qaeda leaders were even allowed to keep their loaded Kalashnikovs with them on the plane. Saif sat next to his master in the front row, a mark of his own growing stature in the organization. Behind them, another senior operative peered out of the window, frantically folding and refolding his map in an attempt to figure out where they were going. Saif himself was in perpetual motion, shuttling between his seat and the cockpit to check the aircraft's progress. His apprehension must have mounted as the plane left the Red Sea behind and began flying over Saudi Arabia somewhere near bin Laden's boyhood home, the merchant city of Jeddah. Far below, Muslims of many lands prayed at the sacred mosques of Mecca, while the House of Saud ran affairs of state from the palaces of Riyadh. If the Saudis got wind of who was on the plane, they might send their American-made F-15s to intercept the aircraft and shoot it down. Even worse, they might force it to land inside the kingdom and take its passengers prisoner. Nervous chatter began filling the cabin, until bin Laden, in his reedy yet authoritative voice, admonished his fellow travelers to "pray to God in silence until we leave Saudi airspace." Finally, the golden desert terminated in the blue-black of the Persian Gulf, but this was not the end of the danger, for on the opposite shore, they were rapidly approaching the mountains of Iran. Despite Saif's cordial relations with certain elements in the Islamic Republic, the Shia ayatollahs could scarcely be counted upon to confer a warm welcome to a beleaguered band of Sunni extremists dropping suddenly into their homeland from a clear blue sky. Yet as the Learjet crossed into Iranian airspace, they seemed to be descending. They needed to refuel, the pilots said, and Shiraz in the southwest of the country was the place. Almost as soon as the plane's wheels touched tarmac, Iranian customs officials hurried over, demanding access to the cabin. Expecting to be boarded at any moment, bin Laden, Saif, Abu Hafs al-Masri, and bin Laden's fifteen-year-old son, Omar, sat with their weapons trained on the aircraft's door. But the Sudanese official ran out and held the Iranians back with oily charm and, in all probability, greased palms. He assured them this was a Sudanese diplomatic plane and that there was no cause for alarm. The Iranians backed off. The door closed. The plane gathered speed and lifted off once more. Saif and the others relaxed their grip on their weapons. Soon, they were passing once more over mountains, then deserts, and finally the Sistan Basin, marking the westernmost reaches of the Islamic State of Afghanistan.

In that late spring of 1996, an uneasy calm seemed to have settled over much of the Muslim world. In the Balkans, the Dayton Accords had brought an end to the Bosnian War, and the Kosovo conflict was not yet aflame. Chechen rebels, still reeling from the assassination of their president, Dzhokhar Dudayev, were days away from signing a cease-fire with Moscow. In the heartland of the Levant, a fresh Israeli-Palestinian truce held for the time being, though punctuated by fiery attacks from the Iranian- and Saudi-backed militant group

Hamas. In the United States, meanwhile, public attention had turned to the upcoming presidential election and the unfolding trial involving President Clinton's purchase of real estate through the Whitewater Development Corporation. It was, in many places and in many ways, the eye of the storm.

. . .

While al-Qaeda had been away from Afghanistan, the Islamist Taliban movement had come to dominate much of the country, and it was now encroaching on the capital, Kabul. Its leader, a village preacher named Mullah Mohammed Omar, had donned the alleged Cloak of the Prophet kept at a shrine in Kandahar and proclaimed himself Emir al-Muminin—Commander of the Faithful—a title adopted by Islamic rulers since the seventh century. One month later, bin Laden's plane touched down in Jalalabad, eighty miles east of Kabul, the same city he had so spectacularly failed to capture in 1989. Jalalabad was not yet under Taliban control, but al-Qaeda enjoyed the protection of local warlords—largely thanks to the foresight of Saif al-Adel, who had dispatched his own personal secretary, Harun Fazul, a jihadi from the Comoros Islands, to strike up a relationship with them several years before. These men now offered bin Laden the use of a former royal palace, gave him a spacious tract of land on which to build a compound, and even, in an act of symbolic Pashtun hospitality, transferred title to his old hideout in the mountains of Tora Bora. Characteristically, bin Laden eschewed the more salubrious alternatives and chose the mountain. He ordered al-Qaeda's senior leadership and their families to move to a squalid base lacking electricity, running water, or even doors on many of the buildings. On their first visit to the dusty, trash-strewn site, the sheikh enthused about the rugged life in store for them at Tora Bora. As bin Laden's teenaged son Omar surveyed the scene in disbelieving horror, Saif maintained the stony composure that had become his hallmark.

Just three days after bin Laden, Saif al-Adel, and the rest of the leadership touched down in Jalalabad, Abu Ubaidah al-Banshiri, al-Qaeda's second-in-command, who was also the head of its operations in Africa, was killed in a ferry disaster on Lake Victoria. Saif led an investigation into his death, dispatching his personal secretary and a future leader of al-Shabaab, Harun Fazul, to carry out the groundwork. The investigation concluded that al-Banshiri's death had indeed been an accident. Al-Banshiri was well liked and deeply mourned; al-Qaeda named a training camp in his honor, and to this day its leaders still quote poetry written about him. But al-Banshiri's death did mean another sudden promotion for Saif al-Adel. Functionally, he was now al-Qaeda's number three, behind bin Laden and the military chief, Abu Hafs al-Masri.

In the second half of 1996, the Afghan civil war was approaching its bestial peak. By September, Taliban forces had taken Jalalabad. Two weeks later, they overran Kabul. Young Taliban fighters entered the United Nations compound in the city where the Russian-aligned former president Mohammed Najibullah was sheltering. They beat him, castrated him, dragged him to his death behind a truck, then strung his body from a traffic control tower, a cigarette and a ruble banknote between his fingers to symbolize the decadence and corruption of his regime. Soon, Taliban religious police were out in force on the streets of the capital, chasing down unveiled women and clean-shaven men, beating miscreants with pipes and cables, amputating the hands of thieves, publicly executing those who failed to live up to their medieval code of morality.

Shortly after the fall of Jalalabad, the Taliban sent a high-level representative out to Tora Bora. At this point, it was by no means certain that the new government would be friendly toward al-Qaeda, particularly as the organization had thrown in its lot with local leaders who made a point of operating independently of the Taliban. One of these warlords had told bin Laden ominously, "There is little I can do after they reach you." But at their meeting in the mountains the Taliban emissary greeted bin Laden warmly, telling him, "We do not say that you are our guests, and we do not say that we are your servants. But we say that we serve the ground upon which you walk."

In part, this welcome reflected the Pashto tribal tradition of hospitality, as well as an Afghan respect for native Arabic speakers, who can read the Koran proficiently in its original language, and especially for those who hail from the holy land of Saudi Arabia. At the same time, the emissary's embrace of bin Laden also marked the beginning of what would remain, despite the trouble it caused for the Taliban, a remarkably durable relationship. Two years later, in the wake of the East African embassy bombings, even as international condemnation and American cruise missiles rained down on his country, the Taliban's own deputy foreign minister would tell bin Laden, "Our protection to you is a matter of religious duty." The sheikh obliged his new hosts by issuing a fatwa declaring jihad on their archrivals for control of Afghanistan, a loose military conglomerate called the Northern Alliance that would later attract American backing during the 2001 U.S. invasion. Bin Laden also complied with the Taliban's request that he move from Tora Bora to a proper compound. This must have come as a relief to many, not least his put-upon wives and children. But there were two further quid pro quos. To secure Mullah Omar's support, bin Laden had to pledge to refrain from giving media interviews and, more importantly, to stop antagonizing the United States, whose Pakistani allies had repeatedly threatened military action against the Taliban if al-Qaeda attacked America, and Saudi Arabia, which, along with the United Arab Emirates and Pakistan, was one of only three countries in the world to recognize the Taliban as the government of Afghanistan. Bin Laden made both promises. But, as we shall see, he would keep neither.

On August 23, 1996, a mere fourteen weeks after his return to Afghanistan, bin Laden publicly declared jihad against America. At first glance, this vendetta against the world's only superpower may have seemed irrational, even perverse. Had America not supported, with decisive results, the jihad in Afghanistan? Had it not ejected the "apostate" Saddam Hussein from Kuwait and stopped him from threatening the Land of the Two Holy Mosques? Had it not helped oppressed Muslims in Bosnia and condemned Russian brutality in Chechnya? In anyone's interpretation, the United States had never sought confrontation with al-Qaeda, whether in Mogadishu or Lower Manhattan.

But for Osama bin Laden, this new feud was personal. When Saddam Hussein had invaded Kuwait, bin Laden had offered to put together a task force of mujahideen to drive him out. He put the size of the army he could muster at 100,000. Even that wildly optimistic promise would have amounted to barely one-tenth the estimated strength of Iraq's armed forces, the world's fifth largest at the time. "We will fight him with faith," bin Laden had promised the Saudi defense minister. Unsurprisingly, the pragmatic House of Saud rejected bin Laden's proposal in favor of a more technologically and militarily developed plan put forward by the American General H. Norman Schwarzkopf. This rebuff mortified bin Laden, who saw himself as having been denied an opportunity to "save Kuwait and Saudi Arabia" and thereby further burnish his reputation as "the greatest Arab hero of all time." Moreover, he blamed the United States for various attempts on his life, for the Saudi government's decision to revoke his citizenship, and for his expulsion from Sudan. But personal offense is not enough for a holy war; bin Laden would have to come up with a religious justification. Ironically, he found it in a novel interpretation of scripture that now formed part of Saudi official doctrine: the entirely unsupported idea that, according to Islam, only Muslims were allowed to inhabit the Arabian Peninsula. This clearly did not come from the Prophet Muhammad, who was quite content to have Jews as his own neighbors. But both the Saudi establishment and bin Laden himself believed it. King Fahd had gotten around the prohibition by having his own clerics write a fatwa to the effect that American troops were permitted on Saudi soil because they were to be used against an enemy that threatened the kingdom. Bin Laden rejected this ruling. The Americans were not permitted, he said. Period.

In any event, King Fahd had promised the Saudi people that U.S. forces would stay only temporarily, until Iraqi troops were driven out of Kuwait. Yet five years after the end of the Gulf War, the Americans were still there, giving rise to the suspicion that they were intended as much to prop up the House of Saud as to eject the forces of Saddam. Again, religion and politics collided with explosive results. In his declaration, bin Laden called the Saudi regime an "agent" of the "Israeli-American alliance" and wrote that, besides faith in God, there was no greater duty than "warding off the American enemy."

Bin Laden datelined this manifesto "Khorasan"—the ancient name for a broad province of the pre-Islamic Persian Empire spanning parts of modern-day Iran, Afghanistan, and Pakistan, among other countries. But the location was symbolic rather than geographical. According to al-Qaeda, the Prophet had predicted that before the ending of the world an army from Khorasan—one bearing black banners—would rage west across the mountains and the deserts. This army would capture Jerusalem, and, when it did, it would bring on the apocalypse.

Bin Laden's new message of global confrontation with the United States appealed to many jihadis but by no means all. In late 1996, a few months after bin Laden's declaration of war, a band of around forty fighters, mainly Gulf Arabs, veterans of the war in Bosnia, arrived in the north of Afghanistan to battle the Soviets in nearby Tajikistan. When this plan failed to materialize, the fighters were taken to Kabul, where they met with Osama bin Laden, Saif al-Adel, and other al-Qaeda leaders. Bin Laden laid out his case for jihad against the Americans, in terms redolent of his August declaration of war. When he was done, around half of the fighters decided to stay and pledge *bayat* to him, while the other half opted to depart. As one of their number later explained, "The Brothers from the Northern Group are fighters who fight the enemy face-to-face. They don't understand Bin Laden's war and the new jihad, so they went home." Of those who remained, some made their pledges of allegiance conditional; if another jihad with a clearer justification opened up else-where, they would be at liberty to depart and fight that war instead. But the presence of more Gulf Arabs in al-Qaeda lent legitimacy to bin Laden's claim that he was engaged in liberating the Arabian Peninsula from infidel occupation. Many of the Northern Group operatives who stayed with him would prove critical to future attacks against American interests, including 9/11 itself.

· · ·

Saif al-Adel would play an ever more central role as al-Qaeda found its feet in the new Afghanistan and focused on the global jihad against the United States. At the ever-shifting war front between the Taliban and the Northern Alliance, Saif coordinated al-Qaeda fighters supporting the Islamists. On the rare occasions when the sheikh insisted on venturing near to the fighting, Saif would oversee his security. Training was still part of his portfolio, but increasingly only for the most advanced recruits; having been instructed by Saif al-Adel was now a sign that a member was destined for special operations. Saif handpicked students for courses covering target selection, information gathering, kidnapping, and assassination, favoring those exhibiting dedication, discipline, and high moral character. His methods remained as brutal as ever; one practical exercise he assigned would involve kidnapping fellow trainees in the dead of night and, in the words of one al-Adel alumnus, "beat[ing] them into submission." Apparently, Saif considered this harsh treatment of their colleagues justified in the name of giving his protégés the necessary experience.

Graduates of the Afghan camps in these days would go on to rule over al-Qaeda franchises as far afield as Yemen, the Maghreb, and Syria. For a select few, Saif also taught an "advanced commando course" at the Mes Aynak camp near Kabul, where promising recruits learned to maneuver in the dark, fight at close quarters, and shoot targets while riding a motorcycle. Alumni of these courses subsequently transferred to Karachi, Pakistan, where Saif's old acquaintance Khalid Sheikh Mohammed, who had gone to college in North Carolina, instructed them in how to blend in with Western cultures. Late in 1999, KSM even tentatively began overseeing the training of a handful of recruits in the hijacking and flying of civilian airliners.

Yet Saif's most significant role in al-Qaeda in this period was to provide security for the organization and its emir. The Egyptian was now a permanent fixture of bin Laden's close entourage, and he commanded, as well as trained, the sheikh's corps of personal bodyguards—called the Black Guard for the scarves they wore masking all but their eyes. The need for such protection had never been more acute; the sheikh was in danger of his life more so than ever. Threats emanated from the Northern Alliance, from foreign intelligence agencies, and especially from the adversaries al-Qaeda had always feared the most—rival jihadis, particularly those of the *takfiri* school, who laid heavy emphasis on declaring fellow Muslims "apostates." Saif trained bin Laden's guards to be hypervigilant in spotting such men. On one occasion, the head of bin Laden's security detail burst in on a meeting with a local *takfiri* and beat the man bloody because he had seen him through the keyhole gesticulating for emphasis as he made a point and assumed the man meant to lunge at bin Laden.

Within a year of bin Laden's arrival in Afghanistan, the Taliban had foiled yet another assassination attempt against him—but not until the assassins had come within earshot of the place where bin Laden and his guards were sleeping. Taliban fighters killed a number of the attackers, and Saif personally interrogated the survivors, who claimed to have been sent by Saudi intelligence. A few weeks later, in March 1997, with Jalalabad once again threatened by a Northern Alliance advance, al-Qaeda moved to the firmly Taliban-controlled southwest. Saif coordinated and led the convoy. They occupied Tarnak Farm, a disused agricultural cooperative near the decaying remains of a Soviet airbase. The compound was large, with some eighty family homes, an office block, and its own mosque, wheat silo, water tank, general store, and medical clinic. In an emergency, the buildings could be evacuated via underground tunnels, something that must have pleased the meticulous security chief, although Saif's frugality seems to have precluded him from following the fashion on the base of installing a private bomb shelter at his own home.

To protect al-Qaeda's communications, Saif used his cryptographic training to devise the ingenious "Salahuddin" code system, a grid with more than a quarter of a million possible combinations. He drafted public service flyers urging the members to adopt basic counterintelligence precautions like keeping official business on a need-to-know basis, having their hair and beards cut before traveling, and moving their watches to the left wrist—rather than the right as was traditional for the mujahideen. Saif instituted security screening for new recruits, and reserved the right to expel members based on little besides his own feelings of suspicion.

He also established a cadre of intelligence operatives, some fifty in number. This intelligence service claimed to have succeeded in unmasking a great many spies, including one who purportedly confessed to a plot to assassinate bin Laden with so-called dirty bombs containing nuclear waste. On another occasion, it was noted that a certain Jordanian recruit possessed a suspiciously large amount of cash, seemed to know little about war-fighting, and had in his passport a valid Afghan visa—a formality on which few self-respecting mujahideen would waste their time. When this Jordanian was overheard talking in code to his handler in Jordan, the game was up. Abu Mohammed al-Masri, al-Qaeda's head of training, drove the Jordanian to a camp south of Kabul to bring him before bin Laden.

Furious at this breach of security, Saif al-Adel rounded up a posse of militants and brought them to the camp, thirsting for vengeance. But al-Masri appealed to Saif's pragmatic side. It would be better, he said, to hand over the Jordanian to the Taliban authorities. Al-Qaeda did not want a repeat of ugly incidents in the past when an accused spy had been beaten to death and another had been summarily executed. This was the Taliban's country, and al-Qaeda must live under their laws. "Al-Qaeda does not want to be accused of taking the law into its own hands," al-Masri said. Saif agreed to hand over the spy but continued his own investigation into the breach. The Taliban allowed him to interrogate the Jordanian. Saif brought along bin Laden's chief bodyguard, Abu Jandal—"The Father of Death"—who repeatedly hit the prisoner. He also procured an intelligence dossier on the Jordanian from a well-known compatriot who had also recently arrived in Afghanistan, a petty criminal turned Islamic radical named Abu Musab al-Zarqawi.

Since his declaration calling out the United States, bin Laden had been attracting increased attention from the U.S. and international news media. In direct contravention of his promise to the Taliban to avoid courting publicity, he was granting more and more interviews. On occasion, Saif would appear in the B-roll footage recorded to accompany television pieces, standing menacingly behind bin Laden or performing military exercises, but always masked. His most important role, as ever, was security. Before interviews, he would have reporters blindfolded and driven around the countryside for hours in confusing patterns. When CNN's Peter Arnett came to sit down with bin Laden, Saif swept him and his team for bugs using a sophisticated-looking electronic scanner; only later did he confide to colleagues that the scanner, little more than a plastic box, did not actually work. During the interview, Arnett asked bin Laden whether he would target American civilians as well as military personnel. "It is not permissible for any non-Muslim to stay in Arabia," the sheikh replied. "Therefore, even though American civilians are not targeted in our plan, they must leave. We do not guarantee their safety."

. . .

"Fix the car," Saif told bin Laden's driver, Salim Ahmed Hamdan, one day in early August 1998. Hamdan was taken aback. "The car's fine," he said. "Get it fixed anyway," Saif replied, "and tune it up. We'll be on the move soon." A few days later, Saif ordered Tarnak Farm evacuated. Hamdan drove bin Laden away, while Saif took his family to another compound in his own truck. Later, he returned and ordered defensive trenches dug around the perimeter, especially near the guard posts. "Preventative measures," he told the fighters. "The Americans are going to bomb us soon."

Hours later, on the morning of August 7, 1998, two massive truck bombs exploded outside the U.S. embassies in Nairobi, Kenya, and Dar es Salaam, killing 224 people and wounding nearly five thousand. The die was cast. Al-Qaeda was no longer simply sponsoring acts of terror carried out by others; it was committing them itself. The seeds Saif had planted during his time in East Africa had germinated and borne fruit. Harun Fazul, who, as we have seen, had been Saif's personal secretary before going on to lead the cell that carried out the bombings, called his vicious handiwork "[t]he first act in the war against the Americans." Saif himself was evidently pleased with the carnage his protégés had wrought—according to those who saw him shortly after the bombings, he allowed a rare smile to creep across his face.

Saif was prudent to evacuate Tarnak in anticipation of American retaliation. On August 20, al-Qaeda compounds in Afghanistan were hit by Tomahawk cruise missiles fired from U.S. naval vessels in the Indian Ocean. Some twenty militants died in the onslaught. Saif, bin Laden, and the other al-Qaeda leaders survived unscathed. Nevertheless, Saif bolstered bin Laden's security detail. His bodyguard was now composed almost entirely of Yemenis, chosen in part for what was seen as their ingrained "culture of revenge." Shortly after the attacks, while he was holed up in a safe house in Kabul, bin Laden gave his chief bodyguard a pistol and two bullets. "If one day the enemy traps us, and we are certain to be arrested," the sheikh said, "I want to be shot twice in the head rather than be taken prisoner. I must never, ever, be taken alive by the Americans. I want to die a martyr and above all never end up in prison."

After the bombings and the retaliatory strikes, many leaders among the Taliban, and even within the Arab Afghan contingent itself, began to voice disquiet. Why provoke the United States? Why risk everything they had built in Afghanistan? Factions began to develop within the Arab community and the Taliban leadership—those for and against bin Laden—representing a severe problem for al-Qaeda. It was easy to imagine ill-feeling developing into an existential danger to the group and a mortal risk to its sheikh. To placate his critics among the Taliban, bin Laden pledged *bayat* to Mullah Omar as Commander of the Faithful—a title traditionally held by the caliphs of old. Evidently, however, bin Laden was aware that this was unlikely to prove popular among many in the al-Qaeda rank and file, who were keen to maintain the organization's independence. He kept the pledge secret from most members outside the top leadership, including Abu Jandal, the head of his security detail, for several months. After the attack on the USS *Cole*, the al-Qaeda leader further placated his host by doubling down on his pledge of loyalty; in a speech at the wedding of his son Mohammed bin Laden, he explicitly referred to Mullah Omar as the Caliph of the Muslims. Over the years his allegiance to the Taliban would not only hold; it would go on to play a central role in disputes over a decade later between al-Qaeda and the Islamic State.

Despite the extravagant flattery he bestowed on Mullah Omar, it seems likely that bin Laden pledged fealty to the Taliban not because he felt it was right but because he had to. For some traditionalists, however, such a utilitarian view of *bayat* ran counter to the sacred nature of the institution. Abu Jandal was distraught when he eventually found out about his master's pledge to the Taliban, believing that it made al-Qaeda little better than a wholly owned subsidiary of the Afghan regime. He confided in Saif al-Adel his fear that "al-Qaeda would be absorbed into the Taliban and that would be the end of [bin Laden's] independent jihad against the Americans." Ever the pragmatist, Saif reassured Jandal that bin Laden had merely been "constrained by circumstances." This explanation did not satisfy the bodyguard. *Bayat* was a matter of religion, he said, and religion cannot be changed. This perceived betrayal of principle became a major factor in Jandal's decision to leave al-Qaeda temporarily in 1999, and in his permanent break with the organization a year later.

Despite the resultant political and security headaches, the embassy attacks had shown what external operations could achieve in this new, highly disciplined al-Qaeda that Saif al-Adel had done so much to create. Saif continued his outreach efforts, working to establish contacts in the more fractious parts of the Islamic world—particularly the Levant, where tensions were once again brewing between Israel and the Palestinians. So when the Jordanian terrorist Abu Musab al-Zarqawi arrived in Afghanistan in the second half of 1999, talking grandly of his ambitions to create a militant franchise in the Middle East, Saif viewed it as essential to pull him into al-Qaeda's orbit. Saif argued that Zarqawi's plans could be just what al-Qaeda needed to plant its flag in the Levant.

Zarqawi was a fiercely independent operator. At least for now, he had no intention of giving *bayat* to al-Qaeda. But Saif convinced bin Laden to give Zarqawi five thousand dollars in seed capital and help him set up a training camp inside Afghanistan. Zarqawi and his associates spent a month and a half training with al-Qaeda while Saif made arrangements for his group to occupy a base near Herat in the far west of the country beside the Iranian border. Saif reportedly used his long-standing connections with certain elements of the Republican Guard and Quds Force to smooth the passage of recruits from the Middle East through Iran. Soon the camp was teeming with recruits and their families, and Saif's protégé was making plans for jihad far beyond Afghanistan.

Meanwhile, a new millennium of the Common Era was approaching, and with it tempting new opportunities for symbolic strikes on America and its allies. Plots were afoot. In Amman, Jordan, a cell operated under a *bayat* to bin Laden with this chilling motto: "The season is coming, and bodies will pile up in stacks." The group had amassed 2.6 tons of nitric acid to make explosives for use against the Radisson Hotel and three other sites. In Vancouver, Canada, a jihadi who had trained in Afghanistan was getting ready to bomb Los Angeles International Airport on New Year's Day. And in the port city of Aden, Yemen, another cell was packing explosives onto a small boat in preparation for a suicide attack on an American warship. Each of these plots would fail, through a combination of smart law enforcement and dumb luck. Jordanian intelligence broke up the Amman cell after intercepting its handler's phone call giving the order to proceed. The bomb intended for LAX was discovered by U.S. officials at Port Angeles, Washington, and the bomber taken into American custody. In Aden, the boat carrying the explosives sank well before it reached the target; but the Aden plotters, unlike their counterparts in Jordan and the United States, remained undetected, and most of their equipment proved salvageable. Soon there would be another day and another ship.

. . .

Ever since its return to Afghanistan, al-Qaeda had been rapidly developing into a much more sophisticated organism. Now, at the beginning of the new millennium, it had its own guesthouses, its own training camps, its own administration. It was planning its own missions against the United States. From its earliest days, the group had been governed by a Majlis al-Shura, or consultative council, a common governance structure in the Islamic world based upon the Koranic injunction for believers to "conduct their affairs by mutual consent." Now, in Kandahar, a more complex committee structure was taking shape, in which members of the senior leadership were assigned detailed, differentiated portfolios of responsibility: military, training, security, administration, religious affairs, and so on.

In the summer of 2001, after months, if not years, of deliberation, al-Qaeda finally merged with Ayman al-Zawahiri's Egyptian Islamic Jihad, forming a new organization officially called al-Qaedat al-Jihad (Base of Jihad). This arrangement gave Egyptian Islamic Jihad personnel, at a stroke, three of the top spots in the al-Qaeda leadership, including that of deputy emir, which, of course, went to Zawahiri. Although himself an Egyptian, Saif had strongly opposed the merger. It was, as he was not afraid to point out, a woefully lopsided arrangement. Al-Qaeda had around 400 pledged members, at least 250 of them in Afghanistan, of whom around 100 were actively engaged in fighting the Northern Alliance in the civil war still raging near Kabul. Zawahiri's group had just ten members, and these men did little more than create propaganda. In any case, only half of them, just five individuals, were willing to go along with the merger. Why allow such a minuscule group to hijack much of the leadership of al-Qaeda? Bin Laden would not be dissuaded. The matter had a personal dimension: Zawahiri had long served, in effect, as bin Laden's personal physician, treating him for his frequent bouts of fainting and kidney pain since his days fighting the Soviets in the 1980s. Seeing that the decision had been made, Saif fell into line. The merger was consummated, and Ayman al-Zawahiri became bin Laden's deputy.

Saif al-Adel's own central role in the organization had been formalized as head of the Security Committee; in effect, he served as al-Qaeda's Secret Service chief, Secretary of Homeland Security, and FBI and CIA director, rolled into one. Together, Saif al-Adel and the military chief, Abu Hafs al-Masri, oversaw the External Operations Committee, which had overall responsibility for planning acts of terror, picking the operatives to carry them out, and providing them with equipment and training. Saif would put cells together, vet their members, insulate them from penetration by foreign intelligence, and stop them from spinning apart before they could complete their deadly missions.

The other departments included Administration, run by Sheikh Said al-Masri; Religious Affairs, whose head was Abu Hafs al-Mauritani, al-Qaeda's only theologically trained senior leader; and Political

Affairs, led by Abu Khair al-Masri, an Egyptian who came with Zawahiri. Military training, another vital aspect of the organization's activities, was the domain of Abu Mohammed al-Masri. These last two top leaders, Abu Khair and Abu Mohammed, were the two with whom Saif al-Adel would later be imprisoned in Iran. More junior militants, such as bin Laden's bodyguard, Abu Jandal, affectionately called Saif and his fellow members of the *shura* council al-Shiba— the Old Men. At al-Qaeda's Kandahar base, you knew when a big operation was afoot, because you could see these grandees gathering. "Al-Shiba are meeting," Jandal would tell his colleagues. "May God help us." He was only half-joking; whenever the United States retaliated militarily in the wake of an attack, al-Qaeda foot soldiers were the most likely to be killed.

. . .

Less than a week after the turn of the new millennium, on Eid al-Fitr, the feast marking the end of Ramadan, Osama bin Laden summoned dozens of senior al-Qaeda members and other Arab Afghans to hear him preach a sermon at his compound of Tarnak Farm. The emir rallied the troops. "We are like mountains of stone against anti-Muslim aggression," he told them, assuredly prophesying the imminent downfall and dismemberment of the United States, just as the Soviet Union had fallen and broken apart after the Afghan jihad. A cameraman was on hand to record the proceedings, and among those in attendance, we can make out several of the men who would go on to plan and execute the 9/11 attacks. In the days after the summit, at the same compound, and on the same video tape, two of the eventual hijackers would record themselves reading their last wills.

The video also gives us our first brief glimpse in years of the security chief Saif al-Adel. We see him grin as he playfully jostles the camera. His hooded almond eyes are bracketed now by a black beard and a white turban. After a few seconds of raising hell, he is gone, a face in the crowd once more. And this, indeed, reflects his preferred modus operandi on a larger scale: He emerges sporadically from the shadows to raise hell before disappearing once more. To paraphrase the Gospel of Matthew, "You shall know him by his fruits."

Around this time, too, Saif al-Adel could be seen leafing through an encyclopedia of warships, and lingering over the pages dealing with American destroyers. For those with eyes to see, this was an indication of al-Qaeda's next target. From the point of view of the inhabitants of Tarnak Farm, the organization's attacks were by now falling into a familiar pattern: Bin Laden and the military chief Abu Hafs al-Masri would develop the overall strategy and general target selection, while personnel, training, and execution were the responsibility of Saif al-Adel and the head of training, Abu Mohammed Al-Masri. Having failed in its initial attempt shortly after the millennium, the Yemen cell tried again on October 12, 2000. This time, the boat found its target, the Arleigh Burke–class destroyer the USS *Cole*, which had docked to fill its fuel tanks. The suicide bomb tore a forty-foot gash in the ship's hull, killing seventeen crew members and wounding more than three dozen. Only the swift and sustained action of their comrades averted a fuel explosion that would almost certainly have sunk the vessel.

Following the standard procedure established by Saif al-Adel, bin Laden's security was tightened again, and the Afghan compounds were evacuated. But this time, there would be no military retaliation, partly because America was then in the white heat of a bitterly fought and long drawn out election campaign that was destined, within weeks, to wind up in the Supreme Court. The lack of a response did not please Osama bin Laden. In the weeks following the attacks, he could be heard complaining bitterly, despite the boost to al-Qaeda's fund-raising and recruitment efforts the Cole attack provided. As the 9/11 Commission would later write, "Bin Laden wanted the United States to attack, and if it did not he would launch something bigger."

CHAPTER 3

THE DISASTER

The guesthouse is clean and plainly decorated; this is how the sheikh likes it. Bin Laden sits on the floor with a group of followers in turbans and military fatigues. The topic of their conversation is the same one still preoccupying newsrooms and dinner tables around the globe: the tumultuous events of the past few weeks in New York, in Washington, DC, in Shanksville, Pennsylvania, and now here in Afghanistan. A former mujahid, a man who fought the Russians in the 1980s and the Serbs in the 1990s, addresses bin Laden. "Everybody praises what you did," he says. "This is the guidance of God and the blessed fruit of jihad."

The man is paralyzed from the waist down, the result, he says, of wounds suffered in Bosnia. This, rather than any superiority of rank, explains why he did not get up when the sheikh entered the room. But his disability has not stopped him from traveling more than fifteen hundred miles from Saudi Arabia to be among the mujahideen at this crucial time. Nor is he the only one to have made the journey. "Few only would follow you until this huge event happened," the paraplegic veteran goes on, warming to his theme. "Now, hundreds of people are coming out to join you. The only ones who stay behind will be the mentally impotent and the hypocrites. God has bestowed honor on us, and he will give us blessing and more victory during this holy month of Ramadan."

In New York, rescuers are pulling human remains from wreckage strewn over several city blocks. Lower Manhattan is still wreathed in wraiths of acrid smoke. All over America—all over the world—families, communities, even whole countries are in mourning. The sheikh grins. "Thanks be to God," he says.

. . .

Terrorists have long viewed civilian airliners as tempting targets. Indeed, the first fatal terrorist hijacking took place as early as 1947, and the first clearly politically motivated airline bombing—an unsuccessful attempt to assassinate the Chinese premier Zhou Enlai—was in 1955. Various groups used such tactics to deadly effect in the 1970s and 1980s, from the tarmac in Beirut, Entebbe, and Teheran to the skies over Lockerbie, Scotland. In June 1985, the Hezbollah hijackers of TWA Flight 847 even claimed to be "suicide terrorists" and threatened to crash the jet into the airport's control tower or Lebanon's presidential palace—but in their case it was just a ploy to get permission to land. Deliberately using a plane as a weapon—a guided missile in all but name—would be something new and terrifying under the sun.

The idea had crossed the minds of al-Qaeda–linked operatives long before September 2001. Before leaving Egypt for the Soviet jihad, Colonel Ibrahim Makkawi, the man so frequently mistaken for Saif al-Adel, had mused about the possibility of crashing aircraft into the Egyptian House of Representatives in Cairo. Many of Makkawi's jihadi colleagues from this period dismissed him as a dangerous crackpot. A few years later, Ramzi Yousef, disappointed by his own failure to destroy the twin towers in the 1993 bombing, would consider aiming a private plane at CIA headquarters outside Washington, DC. But the 9/11 attacks began in the fevered imagination of Yousef's uncle, the Pakistani terrorist facilitator Khalid Sheikh Mohammed.

KSM had long been interested in attacking the United States, and his plots and fantasies often involved airliners. As a teenager growing up in Kuwait, he had reportedly written a play about bringing down American planes. Later, after obtaining his bachelor's degree in North Carolina, KSM joined his nephew, Ramzi Yousef, in the failed plot against CIA headquarters, another facet of which was to involve blowing up passenger aircraft en route from Asia to the United States. Following stints in the Philippines, Bosnia, and Qatar, KSM moved to Afghanistan at the beginning of 1996, a few months ahead of al-Qaeda. Shortly after bin Laden's declaration of jihad against the United States that August, KSM described for the sheikh his fiery vision of jetliners plowing into American skyscrapers and smashing the neoclassical palaces of the U.S. federal government. He called it "the Planes Operation." In its complexity and brutality, the plot far outstripped anything yet attempted by any terrorist organization. If al-Qaeda could pull it off, it would put even the devastating East Africa embassy bombings in the shade. In fact, the Planes Operation would become, overnight, the new yardstick by which all future terror attacks would be judged.

"It is not feasible," bin Laden told Khalid Sheikh Mohammed when he first raised the Planes Operation in the fall of 1996. Nevertheless, he invited the Pakistani to join al-Qaeda; the organization could make use of a member with his diabolical imagination. KSM politely declined, but between about 1996 and 1999 he continued to curry favor with the al-Qaeda leadership, deploying his technical skills to help his old contact Saif al-Adel with certain "computer and media projects" and other tasks. As the latter half of the 1990s wore on, KSM's nightmare vision grew steadily more vivid in the mind of the sheikh. Ideologically, bin Laden reasoned, it was right and proper to take any opportunity to strike his main enemy, the United States—the harder the better. American troops still lingered on the Arabian Peninsula. Moreover, an attack on Israel's principal backer would show support for the Palestinian cause—something that became especially pressing with the start of the second intifada, in September 2000, seven years after the first such period of violent Israeli-Palestinian conflict had ended. As with the Soviet invasion of Afghanistan twenty years before, the sound and fury of the attacks would draw hundreds of fresh fighters to bin Laden's banners. In the mind of the sheikh, these unprecedented atrocities would make al-Qaeda unquestionably the premier Islamist group in the world.

But the plan still faced powerful resistance. The Taliban's Commander of the Faithful, Mullah Omar, had made known his opposition to major attacks directly against the United States. Such operations, he feared, would risk drawing the superpower into Afghanistan's civil war—something the Taliban could do without, especially while they were making tentative headway against their Northern Alliance antagonists. Many among bin Laden's senior lieutenants were sympathetic toward this point of view and wanted to defer to the wishes of their hosts. Afghanistan was, after all, the Taliban's country—however much they might express admiration for bin Laden and solidarity with the aims of his organization. And for better or worse, the sheikh had pledged his allegiance to their leader, Mullah Omar.

Bin Laden was unpersuaded. He countered that there was no need to defer to the Taliban on this matter. Surely his pledge of *bayat* extended only as far as Afghanistan's borders; it could not hamper actions halfway around the world on a different continent. Moreover, there was nothing for the Taliban to object to. In fact, they ought to be grateful. The attacks, like previous operations, would attract more recruits, larger donations, and greater assistance from sympathetic foreigners. Al-Qaeda would continue assisting their hosts by sending fighters to the war front and, it had recently been decided, by carrying out a plot to assassinate the Northern Alliance's supreme commander, Ahmed Shah Massoud.

Besides, the sheikh said, the Americans were *not* coming. They would never put an invasion force in Afghanistan. They would do what they always did—lob a few cruise missiles at a few camps, maybe carry out a couple of air strikes, then retreat. A handful of militants might die, but they would perish as martyrs—the better to drum up fresh recruits seeking paths of glory. At the very most, bin Laden thought, the United States might send a commando detachment to capture or kill him. If that happened, he had a plan to thwart the raid, and humiliate the great enemy, by luring the Americans to their deaths in the mountains of Tora Bora—just as he had done with Soviet special forces at Jaji fourteen years before. Even if, by some twist of fate, the United States did come in force, what had the mujahideen to fear? Were not the roads of Afghanistan lined to this day with dead Soviet tanks? Had not bin Laden's own cherished Kalashnikov been stripped from the corpse of a Russian officer? The mujahideen would crush the Americans, just as they defeated the Russians, and as the forebears of today's Afghans had seen off the British, the Mongols, the Persians, the Greeks. Not for nothing has Afghanistan been called the Graveyard of Empires. The sheikh knew from experience just how much damage one could inflict on a superpower among the high places of the Hindu Kush; he had inflicted no small portion of that damage himself. In any case, the American soldier, as bin Laden had always said, was weak, unfit for real combat. In fact, the United States, a democracy whose people had shown little appetite for wars of attrition, might fold even faster than the Russians, and Osama bin Laden, vanquisher of empires, would in that moment become a saint.

It must be acknowledged that in light of America's record in the years preceding 9/11, this view was not without justification. As bin Laden himself had pointed out in his 1996 declaration of jihad, U.S. forces had withdrawn from Lebanon within four months of the

1983 barracks bombing. A decade later, they had followed more or less the same timetable in getting out of Somalia in the aftermath of the Battle of Mogadishu. The bombing of the World Trade Center that same year, masterminded by KSM's nephew—a man who had trained in the Afghan camps—had produced criminal investigations but no real retaliation. Subsequent experience seemed to confirm, in the minds of many jihadis, America's fecklessness. In response to the East Africa bombings, in which a dozen Americans died, the United States had launched Operation Infinite Reach. Cruise missiles rained down on targets in Sudan and Afghanistan but failed to inflict any lasting harm on al-Qaeda. And even these minimal strikes had cost the Clinton administration disproportionate political capital: They had doubtful military merit and had occurred just three days after President Clinton had admitted "inappropriate intimate contact" with White House intern Monica Lewinsky.

Two years later, following the USS *Cole* attack, many in al-Qaeda, including Saif al-Adel, had expected, and prepared for, tougher reprisals; but none came. By the time it became clear that bin Laden had been behind the suicide bombing, America's attention was on the recent presidential election, which was hurrying toward resolution in the Supreme Court. Neither the outgoing Clinton administration nor its successor harbored much appetite for a retaliatory strike against al-Qaeda at anything like the level of intensity that would be necessary to disrupt the organization. Al-Qaeda could survive indefinitely this pattern of American action—or, more frequently, inaction. In fact, in terms of propaganda, fund-raising, and especially recruitment, the biggest attacks on America had so far raked in the biggest benefits.

It is also worth noting that, prior to the attacks themselves, nobody in al-Qaeda believed that they would cause the twin towers to collapse. Bin Laden would later say that he was the most "optimistic" of all when it came to the predicted level of destruction. But even he, drawing upon his experience in the construction industry, only expected the top few floors to fall. The level of destruction eventually visited upon New York City exceeded even the wildest of KSM's warped dreams.

Even so, the old soldier Saif al-Adel viewed the matter differently. It was not that he cared deeply about civilian casualties; in fact, Abu Jandal was to note that, among all of al-Qaeda's senior leaders, Saif "seemed least affected by the deaths of innocent civilians." But Saif could see that KSM's hellish vision would be qualitatively different from hitting an embassy in a foreign capital or a warship in a faraway harbor. A strike on the U.S. homeland on the scale of the Planes Operation would represent a provocation orders of magnitude greater than either of these strikes. If ever there was an intervention that could cure America of Vietnam syndrome, this was it.

With his military experience and his pragmatic frame of mind, Saif was perhaps better placed than any of his colleagues in al-Qaeda's upper echelons to foresee the disaster that would befall the organization if the Americans were to put their full might into the response. As Saif's father-in-law, Mustafa Hamid, told bin Laden, "The problem is not how to start the war but how to win the war." If the Americans invaded, Saif knew, al-Qaeda would face ruin, not just in Afghanistan but around the world. There was no viable plan for defending the Islamic emirate against a concerted American onslaught. If the Taliban fell, what other government would step in to harbor the jihadists? And in any event, why risk destroying what al-Qaeda regarded as the only true Islamic state on earth? As for bin Laden's plan to lure U.S. troops to destruction at his mountain lair, to Saif's mind this was sheer insanity. Tora Bora was not Jaji, and the United States was not the Soviet Union. Far from being a good place to spring a clever trap, any tactician worth his salt could see that the isolated cave complex would be acutely vulnerable to heavy aerial bombardment and a protracted siege—a strategy that would massively favor the Americans, with their unbridgeable advantages in manpower, technology, and logistics. If the *kafir* soldiers did not seal up the passes, sooner or later the winter snows would take care of that for them. Surely starvation in the mountains—or, for that matter, incineration from above—was not the kind of glorious martyrdom Osama bin Laden had in mind.

A majority of al-Qaeda's *shura* council sided with Saif al-Adel against the Planes Operation. In fact, besides bin Laden himself, only Zawahiri and his new Egyptians came down in favor of the strikes. Abu Hafs al-Mauritani, the religious head of al-Qaeda, wrote bin Laden a letter couching his opposition in Koranic terms. Even Abu Hafs al-Masri, Al-Qaeda's military chief, came out in opposition. But bin Laden had convinced himself of the righteousness of KSM's wild plan, and that was all that mattered. "I will make it happen," the sheikh told his followers, "even if I do it by myself." In March or April 1999, bin Laden gave KSM the green light to proceed with the Planes Operation. A few months later, another event fired the sheikh's imagination still further—the October 1999 EgyptAir disaster, in which a suicidal copilot deliberately downed his plane in the Atlantic Ocean, killing himself and 216 others en route from New York to Cairo. According to the Yemeni al-Qaeda leader Nasser al-Wuhayshi, bin Laden felt that the copilot should have crashed into a building instead.

Privately, bin Laden's obstinacy in the face of sensible counsel frustrated Saif al-Adel. "If someone opposes him," Saif wrote, "he immediately puts forward another person to render an opinion in his support, clinging to his opinion and totally disregarding those around him, so there is no advice nor anything." Once the decision was made, however, the doubters as usual fell into line. Saif, like the good soldier he was, now helped plan the very attacks he had opposed. At the same time, anticipating the rain of fire that 9/11 would call down, Saif began scouting for locations in which to shelter al-Qaeda's leaders in the aftermath. He soon concluded that their safest hiding place would be the Pakistani tribal stronghold of Waziristan.

. . .

In the run-up to the attacks, in August of 2001, Saif was appointed to lead the defense of the al-Qaeda and Taliban citadel of Kandahar, together with its nearby airport and training camps. He began his preparations around two weeks before the attacks, with seventy-five fighters under his command—a number that would soon swell exponentially. Saif ordered trenches dug along a four-mile front around the airport and the Farouq camp and set traps to ensnare approaching enemy vehicles and men. He split the city into five sectors—one in the center and four around the outskirts. In addition, he created a rapid deployment force mounted on Toyota pickup trucks. The Toyotas, Saif found, were stealthy and highly maneuverable, whether in the mountains or on the flat plains. "If the Japanese had seen the vehicles in action," Saif said, "they would have used them for marketing advertisements."

Not every item in al-Qaeda's arsenal was as impressive, however. Much of the militants' weaponry, like most of the matériel in Afghanistan, dated back to the Soviet era. Alongside the ubiquitous grenade belts and AK-47 assault rifles in various states of repair, Saif's men possessed shoulder-fired Strela-2 surface-to-air missiles, a tank nicknamed The Elephant, and an ancient Chinese-made twelve-tube BM rocket launcher of the kind that had earned Abdul Rahman BM, the father of the girl who would become Khalid bin Laden's fiancée, his nickname. In place of field radios or the useful but easily traceable satellite phones, Saif created lines of communication using human couriers mounted on motorcycles or even on horseback. When it came to zeal, his men wanted for nothing, and a commitment born of absolute faith goes a long way. Even so, Saif al-Adel the military realist might not have liked his chances against American air superiority and Special Forces prowess.

At the beginning of September, bin Laden gathered all the residents of Tarnak Farm at the mosque. "An operation is about to happen," he told them. "We will be evacuating this compound." This much was, by now, familiar protocol. As with previous attacks, bin Laden got into a car, this time heading north, accompanied by his son Uthman and a laptop bag full of U.S. dollars. To minimize the very real threat of a decapitation strike, Saif al-Adel had instructed bin Laden's bodyguards to keep him on the move between safe houses in Kabul and Jalalabad. Saif said farewell to his sheikh and got back to firming up the defenses for the coming war.

. . .

In order to appease Mullah Omar and the Taliban leadership, Saif and others had hatched a plan to kill the Northern Alliance supreme commander Ahmed Shah Massoud. It was hoped that Massoud's death would disorient the enemy and pave the way for a final Taliban takeover of all territory still held by the alliance. The killers were to enter Massoud's camp posing as documentary filmmakers seeking to interview the commander. As part of their cover, the attackers would claim to be Belgians of Moroccan origin; in fact, they were Tunisians, but had spent some time in Molenbeek, the Brussels neighborhood that was home to many of the Islamic State terrorists who attacked Paris in November 2015 and Brussels in March 2016. When they sat down for the interview, the assassins would explode a suicide belt and a booby-trapped battery pack, with the intention of killing themselves and Massoud. Saif arranged for the assassins to be trained for this mission by the man who had built the two East Africa truck bombs, while bin Laden's deputy Ayman al-Zawahiri forged letters of intro-duction in clumsy French—a language Massoud knew from having been educated at an elite French-run school in Kabul—to get the phony journalists admitted to Massoud's presence. Around the same time Saif al-Adel began sinking trenches at the Kandahar airport, the assassins were entering the Northern Alliance camp four hundred miles away to the northeast. Two weeks later, on September 9, they finally sat down with Massoud. One of the men told the translator his three opening questions, each of which concerned Massoud's assumed enmity for bin Laden. Before the first question could be translated, the assassins exploded their devices with a burst of blue flame, piercing Massoud's heart with shards of metal. The blast blew one of the assassins apart; the other escaped, only to be captured and killed by Massoud's bodyguards. Within minutes, in the back of a car sent to speed him to the nearest field hospital, Massoud himself was dead.

Two days later, at airports in the northeastern United States, nineteen hijackers boarded their final flights. Together, they murdered nearly three thousand civilians and first responders. "Those young men," bin Laden told his followers, "said in deeds, in New York and Washington, speeches that overshadowed all other speeches made everywhere else in the world." At a stroke, Osama bin Laden, Khalid Sheikh Mohammed, Saif al-Adel, and all who had participated in planning and carrying out the Planes Operation took their places among the most prolific mass murderers in global terrorism.

· · ·

Saif al-Adel estimated that, in the aftermath of 9/11, more than two thousand fighters rallied to Afghanistan from all over the world, equivalent to five times al-Qaeda's total strength worldwide at that time. These men did not necessarily become formal al-Qaeda members, but they gathered under bin Laden's standard nonetheless. Most of the new recruits probably came looking for yet another "tourist jihad." Like bin Laden, they would have expected the United States, as in the past, to make a show of force with some missiles and then move on. The tourists would get to feel the heat of explosions, maybe take a few potshots at some planes, then return home to tell their war stories and bask in the adulation of their friends. Lists began circulating for volunteers to register their interest in al-Qaeda's "martyrdom brigades," those to be used as suicide bombers against the enemy. By the end of October, 120 men had signed up, around the same number that al-Qaeda had fighting the Northern Alliance before 9/11.

But this was not going to be like previous attacks. In Washington, President Bush had been granted congressional authority for "all necessary and appropriate" military force to bring justice to the perpetrators. In Brussels, for the first time in its history, the powerful NATO alliance invoked Article 5 of its founding treaty, obliging all members to assist the United States. Across the world, public opinion rallied behind America. A military coalition was taking shape, the likes of which had not been seen in decades. Soon, Afghan towns from Kabul to Herat would start falling to the Northern Alliance, backed up by the United States and its allies. In a matter of weeks, the enemy would be at the gates of Kandahar itself. This was no tourist jihad. The serpent had emerged from its burrow. Now it was baring its fangs.

Knowing only too well what lay over the horizon, Saif al-Adel set about evacuating Kandahar. He ordered one of his fighters, an alumnus of the East African attacks, to take some Arab families across the border to safety in Iran, where Saif had arranged for their arrival and protection with his contacts among the Quds Force. "Get in your truck right away and take the families," he told the man. The fighter was incredulous. "Why are you sending me?" he protested. In his hand, the man brandished a copy of *Time* magazine showing his own face, beside those of Saif al-Adel, Osama bin Laden, and nineteen others America had named on its first-ever public list of Most Wanted Terrorists. "I'm wanted by the Americans!" the man protested. "I have millions of dollars on my head because of the embassy bombings." He pleaded to be sent to safety in Pakistan instead. But Saif had no time for special pleading. "I am ordering you," he said. "Go."

On October 7, 2001, the first night of coalition aerial bombardment, explosions rocked al-Qaeda camps near Kandahar and Kabul. Later, Saif drove to Tarnak Farm to survey the damage. Over the course of just a few hours of bombing, fully one-quarter of the eighty family homes had been reduced to rubble. Soon, the compound would be for practical purposes completely destroyed. Raids on targets in and around Kandahar intensified still further after U.S. Marines seized a landing strip around eighty miles distant. Saif watched as the skies above the city filled with fast jets, B-52 high-altitude bombers, Apache helicopter gunships, cruise missiles, and—perhaps most worryingly of all—C-130 Hercules heavy lifters, of the type used to mount airborne howitzer cannons and to deliver the U.S. military's heaviest ordnance. These war machines waged, in Saif's words, "a stormy campaign." He could identify them all, and he knew what they meant for him and his men.

Nor was there much encouragement to be gleaned out of news from elsewhere in Afghanistan. On November 9, U.S. precision bombs hit Taliban positions in the northern town of Mazar-i-Sharif. From out of the smoke of these explosions, there came galloping, almost incredibly, the first massed cavalry charge of the twenty-first century. Hundreds of Northern Alliance horsemen, riding alongside American special operators, soon overran the city. Within a day, it had fallen to the coalition. Four days later, the Northern Alliance took the Afghan capital, Kabul. Herat, the city where Saif al-Adel had helped create a camp for the Jordanian militant Abu Musab al-Zarqawi, fell the same day, forcing Saif's father-in-law, Mustafa Hamid, to flee over the border into Iran. Zarqawi himself also fled, eventually to link up with his mentor once more in Kandahar. Barely two months since the Planes Operation, al-Qaeda and its Taliban allies had already lost functional control of the entire northern half of Afghanistan.

At this moment of crisis, Saif al-Adel was suddenly thrust even further to the fore. On the night of November 15, coalition missiles hit the home of al-Qaeda's military chief, Abu Hafs al-Masri, crumpling it into a pile of stones at the bottom of a deep crater. While most al-Qaeda commanders had evacuated, Abu Hafs had been unable to do so because of a slipped disk in his back. He was crushed beneath the concrete of his own house. Nearby lay the corpse of another erstwhile colleague of Saif al-Adel's—the Tunisian who had shot down a Black Hawk helicopter over Mogadishu eight years before.

With Abu Hafs gone, Saif al-Adel was next in line to be al-Qaeda's military commander. Once again, the unlooked-for death of an al-Qaeda leader had spelled advancement for the Egyptian. But this battlefield promotion had come in the worst possible circumstances. In Kandahar, which was facing a ground war within weeks, there was no time to grieve. Saif convened an emergency meeting of senior Arab Afghans and Taliban leaders to firm up the city's defenses. Khalid Sheikh Mohammed attended, as did Abu Musab al-Zarqawi, fresh from the destruction of his camp at Herat. A number of senior figures from the other Arab groups operating out of Afghanistan also joined the gathering. Collectively, they appointed Saif al-Adel commander over all the Arab fighters in Kandahar, and for this limited purpose, they all gave *bayat* to al-Qaeda. Ironically, by creating an emergency on an unprecedented scale, 9/11 had, albeit indirectly, accomplished bin Laden's dream of uniting all the Arab groups under his banner; but this state of affairs would prove short-lived, for Kandahar was almost lost.

. . .

Beneath a sky ablaze with bullets, bombs, shells, and missiles, Saif found it hard to sleep. It was the beginning of Ramadan, when observant Muslims abstain from eating and drinking during daylight hours. Little by little, the November days grew shorter. That was a mercy for the fighters' fasting stomachs, but it also meant more and more time between nightfall and sunrise, when the heaviest bombardment would happen. On November 19, the third night of the fasting month, Saif woke after 1:00 a.m. in a state of anxiety. Fearing a direct hit was on the way, he swiftly ordered the fighters with him out of the house, but before they could leave they heard an explosion far away across town. A cruise missile had struck the offices of al-Wafa al-Igatha al-Islamia, a terrorist front charity that had arranged for a number of militants, including the paraplegic mullah, to travel to Afghanistan following the attacks on America. Still shaken, Saif and the fighters sat down for *suhur*, the predawn breakfast. Toward the end of their meal, Saif heard another missile tear across the sky above; and this time, judging by the sound, it was much closer. The missile exploded just 300 feet from their door, shattering two houses at the end of the street. Saif and his companions ran out to see the smoking ruins. The aircraft that had fired the rocket lingered overhead, looking for further targets. Suddenly, it let loose a second trail of smoke and flame. Saif and the fighters dove for cover as the missile smashed into the middle of the street where they had been standing.

Once the early morning sky was clear, the fighters picked themselves up and tramped over to one of Saif al-Adel's defensive positions. "Stay here," Saif told the fighters. He drove across town to the hospital to check on the casualties, then paid a visit to an al-Qaeda forward operating base. All over Kandahar, buildings lay in ruins or in flames. Warplanes swarmed overhead, hunting for fresh targets. Jets and rotors beat the air. Someone told Saif that the strike on al-Wafa had slain one of his trainers from the Farouq camp. In a separate incident, two young children of an al-Qaeda fighter had been killed. Saif tried to comfort the grieving father. "Your children," he told the man, "will be brought to Paradise on the Day of Resurrection, God willing." He then went to check on his own wife, Asma Hamid, and their five children, whom he had not seen in some time. They were unharmed.

Worse was to come. Behind the ridgeline to the north of the city, U.S. special operators had already linked up with fighters loyal to a Pashtun politician and former mujahideen fund-raiser named Hamid Karzai. To the south, the forces of Gul Agha Sherzai, Kandahar's once and future governor, encroached on the traps and trenches around the airport. Since September, Saif's defense force had swelled more than tenfold; eight hundred jihadi fighters now awaited his command, some at the airport, others in the city itself. But it was still by no means certain that the Taliban would back them up. On November 29, with the two battle fronts rapidly approaching, Saif demanded an audience with Mullah Omar's private secretary. His question could not have been more urgent: Would the Taliban stand and fight? Or would they withdraw, as they had done in Kabul and Herat? In the middle of the meeting, a missile exploded nearby. Without warning, the entire ceiling came crashing down on Saif, his companions, and the Taliban representatives. Astonishingly, all escaped serious injury. Shaken, bruised, and covered in dust, Saif and his companions pulled a number of al-Qaeda and Taliban militants out of the rubble and brought them to safety. But the other news from the meeting was not as positive, for it was becoming increasingly apparent that the Taliban intended not to fight to keep Kandahar but to negotiate for its surrender.

Around the first day of December, halfway through Ramadan, one of Saif's men noticed a scout vehicle on a broken bridge near the airport. The man opened fire on the vehicle, and its occupants responded with a few volleys of their own before speeding away. It was then, as Saif would write later, that "hell broke out in the area."

Airplanes came from every direction and in all kinds. C-130s attacked, jets attacked with missiles, helicopters attacked with missiles and guns. The area was transformed into a ball of fire for more than an hour. Gul Agha's [Northern Alliance] forces began to advance again, assured that there were no breathing souls left in the area other than their forces. As soon as they entered the killing field, bombs of the youngsters [al-Qaeda fighters] rained on them from every direction, and they [Gul Agha's men] were gunned down with machine guns. Calls of "God is great" and "victory" were screamed aloud. The brothers killed many of them and captured two. The rest fled. It was a success by the will of God Almighty.

There followed five relentless days and nights of what Saif termed "wild combat," alternating between coalition air strikes and Northern Alliance ground offensives. Saif commandeered the Kandahar Religious Institute and had it set up as a field kitchen for al-Qaeda fighters, serving three meals a day. The Egyptian commander could be seen speeding up and down the front lines, barking orders at the Arabs under his command who surrounded the city. Saif's strategy emphasized the need to confound the airborne enemy with small targets, constantly in motion; he had therefore divided his forces into many tight-knit, mobile units. These cells roamed the city and the airport in trucks with missile and rocket launchers bolted to their flatbeds. B-52 bombers sailed overhead. Three days into the fighting, a guided bomb destroyed the Chinese BM rocket launcher. Then the tank called The Elephant took a direct hit from a missile. A number of fighters were killed in a fierce, close-quarters battle on the roads around the airport, in which one al-Qaeda commander could be seen, in Saif's words, "harvesting the souls of the enemy." At times, however, Saif had difficulty controlling the militants under his command, who would get excited in the white heat of combat and abandon their assigned positions, or else waste scarce ammunition by shooting at aircraft wildly out of range of their weapons.

Around the same time, speaking by satellite phone from his position with U.S. Special Forces north of Kandahar, Hamid Karzai addressed delegates at the Bonn Conference deciding the future of Afghanistan. On December 5, even as Karzai continued his advance on the city, the conference named him the interim president of his country. Buoyed by this vote of confidence, Karzai demanded the unconditional surrender of Kandahar. In the days that ensued, many Taliban leaders, including Mullah Omar himself, bowed to the inevitable and fled to avoid capture or death. Al-Qaeda's senior leaders, too, began pouring out of the city; reportedly some two dozen of them left together one day in a single convoy. On December 9, Gul Agha's troops finally took the city, scattering its defenders and their commanders. Like his comrades and underlings, Saif al-Adel took to the hills.

In the meantime, Osama bin Laden had done exactly what Saif

al-Adel had warned him not to do: He had fled to the mountain enclave of Tora Bora. Still acting on the flawed theory that he could prime a trap there for Western forces to blunder into, the sheikh even took a radio with him, in an effort to give away his position on purpose. On top of all this, the base was woefully lacking in provisions: Instead of ordering its resupply in good time, bin Laden had, not uncharacteristically, prevaricated until the last moment. Day after day, the U.S. Air Force pounded Tora Bora with a relentless bombardment. On one occasion, the strikes lasted for seventeen consecutive hours. On another, a C-130 Hercules, one of the largest planes in the U.S. arsenal, dropped a 7.5-ton "daisy cutter" bomb on the site, causing the mountains to tremble for miles around. Meanwhile, moving during the gaps between bombing raids, American Special Forces on the ground closed in. Before the battle was over, they had killed perhaps 250 Taliban, al-Qaeda, and other Arab fighters. On December 17, barely three months after 9/11, Tora Bora fell. But bin Laden was neither captured nor discovered broken beneath the rubble, as the Americans had hoped, for by then the sheikh was long gone.

. . .

Knowing defeat when he saw it, Saif al-Adel left the fires of Kandahar blazing behind him and fled. On December 8 he reached Zurmat, close to the border with Waziristan, the Pakistani tribal region he had recommended as a place to lie low. A number of senior al-Qaeda and Taliban leaders gathered in the town, including Abu Mohammed al-Masri, who would later be Saif's prison-mate in Iran. Over the next few days, Saif made his way through the mountains and over the border into Pakistan, where he was to spend the next few months in hiding. After the chaos of Kandahar in the days before its fall, Saif's stay in Pakistan must have come as a welcome respite. There, he enjoyed breathing space and even some time to relax. A fellow militant who visited him in this period remembers playing soccer with him one day before lunch. "He was a really good player," the man observed. "Sharp and fast."

But Pakistan would not remain a safe haven for long. The United States was putting the country's government under unprecedented pressure to round up al-Qaeda suspects seeking sanctuary on its soil. Over the course of 2002, the authorities began closing in, snatching militants from the streets of Pakistan's cities. In March, Abu Zubaydah, a conspirator in the Millennium plots who had fought alongside Saif al-Adel in the twilight days of Kandahar, was arrested after a shootout in Faisalabad. Six months later, and one year after 9/11, a key facilitator in the Planes Operation, Ramzi Bin al-Shibh, was captured following another gun battle in a house with "There Is No God but Allah" scrawled on the walls in blood. The following March, Khalid Sheikh Mohammed himself was picked up in Rawalpindi after someone in the building texted authorities to tell them he was there.

Before being taken into custody, KSM had established a relationship between al-Qaeda and the gangs of smugglers who haunted his ancestral homeland of Baluchistan in southwestern Pakistan. In the wake of 9/11, these groups formed a pipeline to transport militants from their hiding places in Pakistan through Baluchistan and into Iran. To begin with, the Iranian National Guard had turned a blind eye to the Arabs fleeing over the border. However, after an understandable outcry from the local population, Iranian intelligence had rounded up the militants and their families and deported them, either back to Pakistan or onward to their home countries.

Clearly Iran was not the safe haven some in al-Qaeda had thought. But the militants still hiding in Pakistan, hunted and harried by the authorities, were out of options. In the months that followed the first wave of mass deportations, a second group of al-Qaeda members and families moved into Iran and spread out between a number of cities. As part of this second wave, Saif hid out in Shiraz in the southwest with his old jihadi brothers-in-arms, Abu Khair and Abu

Mohammed al-Masri, under the protection of local al-Qaeda sympathizers. At first, Saif and his Arab colleagues were allowed to live in Iran, free but closely monitored; the authorities even helped some of the new arrivals get settled in the country. But Mustafa Hamid, who had been in Iran himself since having been forced out of Afghanistan after the fall of Herat, correctly speculated that the Iranians were simply biding their time, using the hiatus to gather as much intelligence as possible about the Arabs newly arrived on their soil. Sooner or later, the authorities would have to clamp down.

Around the close of 2002, operating out of an al-Qaeda safe house in Iran, Saif al-Adel received word that al-Qaeda's cell in Saudi Arabia was negotiating to buy three Russian nuclear weapons. For the United States and its allies, this was the nightmare scenario; in terms of its capacity for destruction and horror, a nuclear atrocity would outdo even 9/11. For al-Qaeda, however, this lead on a clutch of "loose nukes" represented an opportunity to prove its enduring strength following the Afghan debacle. "If you can obtain such a weapon," Saif told the cell's leadership, "no price is too high to pay." Still, he counseled caution; al-Qaeda had been fooled by fakes before. Saif therefore advised his operatives in the kingdom to fly in a Pakistani nuclear scientist to check that the devices were genuine. Western intelligence, eavesdropping on these communications, took the potential threat seriously enough to share it not only with their Saudi counterparts but also, exceptionally, with the Iranians themselves.

Around the same time, the Saudi cell was preparing plans of a more traditional terrorist nature. In an encrypted phone call in early March of 2003, around the time Khalid Sheikh Mohammed was being taken into American custody in Rawalpindi and the U.S. invasion of Iraq was getting under way, Saif reportedly gave the cell's leaders the order to proceed with a campaign of conventional bombings inside Saudi Arabia. It has been reported that the Saudi authorities intercepted Saif's encrypted phone call and furiously demanded that Iran take action to stop the al-Qaeda leadership now operating from Iranian territory. Whatever steps were taken, they were not enough to prevent the deaths of more than three dozen people in suicide attacks on residential compounds in Riyadh used by foreign workers. And although al-Qaeda has never officially claimed responsibility, these strikes certainly bore the organization's grimly familiar fingerprints.

Finally, around April of 2003, the al-Qaeda members in Iran realized that they were being watched and began taking steps to evade Iranian monitoring. This discovery, at last, forced the authorities' hand; fearing that al-Qaeda might slip through their fingers, Iranian intelligence moved in. According to Mustafa Hamid, the ensuing dragnet pulled in practically every al-Qaeda operative in the country, together with many of their families. Saif al-Adel was arrested on April 23 along with the companions who were living with him in the Shiraz safe house, Abu Khair and Abu Mohammed. Al-Qaeda's military commander was to spend almost the next seven years in captivity.

. . .

Saif al-Adel had served in the Egyptian armed forces. He had battled the Soviets as one of the Arab Afghan mujahideen, fought United Nations troops in Somalia, and commanded the defense of Kandahar against the combined might of NATO and the Northern Alliance. For more than a decade, he had helped lead one of the most feared terrorist groups in the world, training militants, protecting the sheikh, organizing terror cells, planning assassinations. From such a seasoned operative, there could be no hiding the scale of the disaster that had befallen al-Qaeda in the wake of the 9/11 attacks. Abu Hafs al-Masri, its supreme military commander, lay dead. By Saif's own reckoning, more than five hundred Arab Afghans, including many al-Qaeda members, had either been killed or had fled. Others had been captured, in Afghanistan or over the border in Pakistan; some of them now languished in American custody at Guantánamo Bay,

Cuba. The surviving members of the *shura* council were scattered. Bin Laden and his deputy, Ayman al-Zawahiri, had gone on the run. The immediate aftermath of the fall of the Taliban was, to a practical man like Saif al-Adel, a time to regroup, assess the damage, and start rebuilding the organization from the ground up. Yet, to Saif's lasting horror and amazement, some operatives, even now, hastened to carry on the fight as if nothing had happened. Foremost among them was the man whose demented vision had spawned 9/11 in the first place—Khalid Sheikh Mohammed.

In January of 2002, Saif al-Adel had received word that a British Islamist, Omar Sheikh, together with a crew of foot soldiers from various extremist groups, had kidnapped the *Wall Street Journal*'s Islamabad bureau chief, Daniel Pearl, in Karachi. Saif called KSM, who was then hiding out in the city, and told him the news. "These people don't know what to do with him," Saif told KSM. "They want to know if we want him." Saif ordered KSM to take custody of Pearl on behalf of al-Qaeda. But he also instructed him that it would be a bad idea to kill the hostage. KSM simply disregarded this order. Within days of the kidnapping, he had taken the journalist to an al-Qaeda safe house, slit his throat, and beheaded him on camera in the kind of snuff video that was shortly to become a fixture of the insurgency in Iraq, under the influence of another protégé of Saif al-Adel's, Abu Musab al-Zarqawi. So eager was KSM to be about his bloody business that he acted before the camera operator had put a tape into the machine; the video failed to capture the initial butchery, recording only the decapitation of Daniel Pearl's mutilated corpse. After the killing, KSM dismembered Pearl's body, buried the pieces in a shallow grave, and had the tape delivered to the Western media.

Saif al-Adel was incandescent with rage. On June 13, he sent Khalid Sheikh Mohammed the second of two vituperative letters containing an extraordinary indictment, not just of KSM, but of bin Laden himself and the blind zealotry that had dragged al-Qaeda to the brink of the abyss. He wrote:

Today we are experiencing one setback after another and have gone from misfortune to disaster. There is a new hand that is managing affairs and that is driving forcefully; every time it falters, it gets up and rushes again, without understanding or awareness. It rushes to move without vision, and it is in a hurry to accomplish actions that now require patience because of the security activity throughout the whole world. This hand does not pay attention to what is happening, as if we will not be summoned to account before God for all these souls, this blood, and this money. The consequences that you see are nothing but an outcome of this onrush. Had I spoken before the disasters occurred—and speak I did—I would have been considered proud, but now that the matter has become a reality, I have absolved my conscience. You are the person solely responsible for all this because you undertook the mission, and in six months we have lost what took years to build.

Bin Laden, Saif told the Pakistani, "pushes you relentlessly and without consideration, as if he has not heard the news and does not comprehend events." In light of the damage already done, al-Qaeda "must completely halt all external actions until we sit down and consider the disaster we caused," lest the organization "become a joke for all the intelligence agencies in the world." Saif ordered KSM to "[s]top all foreign actions. Stop sending people to captivity. Stop devising new operations, *regardless of whether orders come or do not come from Abu Abdullah.*" Abu Abdullah, as KSM knew very well, meant Osama bin Laden. Saif's letter was eventually made public, having been intercepted by U.S. forces. No doubt bin Laden took umbrage at the letter's explicit call for insubordination; it may be for this reason that he later disparaged Saif, who had played a pivotal role in al-Qaeda's history, as of secondary importance to Abu Mohammed al-Masri, who as head of training was below Saif in the hierarchy, and Abu Khair al-Masri, a Zawahiri loyalist who had only been promoted to the *shura* council when the merger with Egyptian Islamic Jihad was finalized.

By any standard, the letter marks a singular moment for Saif al-Adel. The steadfast Egyptian, who for so many years had played the loyal, sensible soldier struggling to corral the savage beasts filling out al-Qaeda's rank and file, had reached his breaking point. With this extraordinary letter, he had openly countermanded not just a superior officer but the commander in chief himself. It was an indication of just how seriously Saif took the unfolding emergency—and of just how deep was the abyss into which he felt al-Qaeda had stumbled.

. . .

In public, however, al-Qaeda's 9/11 skeptics had all fallen into line with bin Laden's exultant interpretation of events. Even Abu Hafs al-Mauritani, al-Qaeda's religious chief, whose original objection had been based on the Koran, changed his tune. At the end of November 2001, with the Taliban ousted from Kabul and the mountains set to quiver under Tora Bora, al-Mauritani told the TV station Al Jazeera that he could not contain his "joy" over the attacks, as a result of which he confidently foresaw "the beginning of the end" for America.

Saif al-Adel maintained a similar mask of defiance. Shortly before his arrest in Iran, he published two articles in which he lauded the 9/11 hijackers as "heroes" whose "blessed operation" had ignited a "spark in the hearts of the youth of the *umma*." Saif lionized the heroism of those killed in the Battle of Kandahar—so-called martyrs like "Hamza the Qatari. . . . I personally felt the wonderful scent that was covering him . . . his face was wearing a beautiful smile, and what a smile that was . . . as well as Samir the Najdi who seemed very gracious and beautiful in death despite the blood covering his body." Saif claimed victory in the ground battle for Kandahar—implicitly suggesting that the city would never have fallen were it not for the Taliban's craven unwillingness to defend it. In describing his experience of warfare against the Americans in Afghanistan, he cited a verse from the Koran: "If they harm you, they can cause you but a slight hurt; and if they fight against you they will turn their backs and run away."

American soldiers, Saif still insisted, were "not fit for combat." They were "phonies," puffed up by "Hollywood promotions," able to take territory in Afghanistan only thanks to the Northern Alliance mercenaries in their pay. "The American soldier is qualified to perform cinematic roles only," Saif assured his audience. "The mujahideen are still in the battlefield," he went on, "and the fight continues, and will not end, God willing, until Afghanistan returns to Sharia and Islam once more." This narrative, of course, conveniently eschews all mention of al-Qaeda and the Taliban's ignominious abandonment of Kandahar in December 2001.

As he makes clear, Saif wrote principally to encourage those preparing to fight the same foe in an altogether different part of the Muslim world:

> We do not, by the will of God, doubt the final defeat of the American empire. What happened in Afghanistan is only one battle. The war is still going on and the victory is leaning towards the Army of Allah. This empire of Crusaders and Jews is walking to its destruction in the blessed region of the Gulf.

America's invasion of Iraq came as little surprise to many members of al-Qaeda. As far as they were concerned, apocalyptic hadith had predicted it, just as they had foretold the army of the black banners rising out of Khorasan. One of these hadith promised that Armageddon would not come until "the Euphrates lays bare a mountain of gold. The people will fight over it, and ninety-nine out of every hundred will be slain." For al-Qaeda's true believers, the meaning was clear. The gold under the earth was the oil that gave the United States its reason to meddle in the Middle East time and again. By starting a war in Iraq, therefore, America was not only creating a military and diplomatic quagmire for itself and diverting much-needed resources from the unfinished conflict in Afghanistan; it was playing directly into the ideological hands of its sworn enemies.

· · ·

It is the night of March 20, 2003, and the mosques and monuments of Baghdad are floodlit by the light from hundreds of explosions. American military planners have taken to terming this weaponized supernova "shock and awe." In less than a month's time, U.S. forces will patrol these streets, the dictator Saddam Hussein will have been driven from power, and President George W. Bush will have declared "Mission Accomplished" from the deck of the USS *Abraham Lincoln*. But Iraq's decade and more of violence is just getting started.

By the end of August, terrorist bombs will have killed 124 people across the country, including the head of the United Nations Assistance Mission, Sergio Vieira de Mello, and dozens of Shia Muslims deliberately targeted for their faith. Soon, the names Fallujah and Abu Ghraib will be on the lips of millions of people around the world, heaping yet more fuel on the wildfire of a violent insurgency. Partly in response, terrorists will release videos showing them gloating over the beheaded bodies of Western workers. Much of this carnage will be perpetrated by an organization that will pledge allegiance to Osama bin Laden and rename itself al-Qaeda in Iraq. Its leader will be a particularly brutal pupil of Saif al-Adel—the Jordanian ex-convict Abu Musab al-Zarqawi.

CHAPTER 4

THE EMIR OF THE STRANGERS

Jordan, the mid-1990s. The evidence against the accused was clear. For several months, following his return from the jihad in Afghanistan, he had been an active member of a banned terrorist organization, Bayat Al-Imam, or Allegiance to the Imam. In March 1994, a cache of grenades had been discovered hidden in the basement of the home he shared with his family. When police raided the building, he had tried to shoot the arresting officers, then himself; both times, he had missed.

Now he was on trial for his crimes before Jordan's feared, quasi-military State Security Court. A more rational man might have fallen on the court's mercy, pleaded for leniency. Instead, he submitted an absurd defense, claiming that he had found the grenades on the street. He refused even to recognize the legitimacy of the court or the government it represented. At one point during his trial, the accused handed the judge his own alternative indictment, implicating two defendants: King Hussein of Jordan and the trial judge himself. "I was expected to inform the first defendant of the charges," the judge

recalled ten years later. Unsurprisingly, Zarqawi's obviously fabri-
cated defense and mocking alternative indictment failed to impress
the State Security Court. Its sentence was fifteen years' hard labor, to
be served in the desert prison of al-Sawwaqa.

In the dozen years between his arrest in 1994 and his death in 2006,
Abu Musab al-Zarqawi transformed himself into one of the most
notorious terrorists in the world. As leader of what became al-Qaeda
in Iraq, he was responsible for the deaths of dozens of American soldiers and hundreds of Iraqi civilians. His organization carried out the
videotaped beheadings of several Western hostages, with Zarqawi
decapitating one of the victims himself. His men murdered, tortured,
and brutalized the inhabitants of Iraqi towns under their control. And
they precipitated a sectarian civil conflict in Iraq that would claim the
lives of thousands, Sunni and Shia Muslims alike. For these crimes,
courts in his native Jordan sentenced him to death in absentia no fewer
than four times over. But perhaps Zarqawi's most consequential and
destructive legacy is one with which we are still grappling today: He
is responsible, more than anyone else, for al-Qaeda in Iraq's mutation
into the armed cult that calls itself the Islamic State.

Before his conversion to radical Islam, Zarqawi had served time in
prison for sexual assault and drug possession. In 2004, while he was
quickly making a name for himself as Iraq's top terrorist, King Abdullah dismissively told the Italian daily newspaper *Corriere della Sera*:

> *As far as I know, he was some sort of a street thug in the town
> of Zarqa. Definitely, he was not known for his intellect or bril-
> liance. Unexpectedly, he ended up in al-Qaeda's network after
> his past as a common criminal and drunkard. Zarqawi has now
> become a problematical element in Iraq, where in my opinion he
> is given undeserved merit.*

Zarqawi, who died in June 2006 in a U.S. air strike, was certainly
a brutal and despicable man. But his journey from "street thug" to

violent extremist is, in fact, not at all uncommon. Indeed, while ideology has a part to play in radicalizing and motivating terrorists, the opportunity to engage in criminal violence for its own sake appears to be just as significant a draw. A study by German intelligence found that around two-thirds of foreign fighters traveling from Germany to Syria had prior criminal records. Similarly, the backgrounds of the terrorists who attacked Paris in 2015 and Brussels in 2016 included convictions for theft, carjacking, assault, burglary, and drug dealing.

Time spent as a criminal may actually enhance the résumé of an aspiring jihadi—extremist networks often bankroll their activities with drug smuggling, human trafficking, forgery, and other crimes; the Taliban funded their operations in part through opium trafficking. Zarqawi may have pioneered an especially brutal brand of terrorism. He may have risen to become leader of Iraq's foreign jihadis and, in effect, America's public enemy number one. But in terms of his background, he was not at all exceptional. Indeed, as the seemingly limitless flow of recruits to the Islamic State attests, Zarqawi and men like him seem to constitute an endlessly renewable resource.

This should come as no surprise. Conditions in the Middle East are perfect for creating an abundance of angry young men acutely vulnerable to terrorist ideology. For decades, Arab governments have exhibited a cavalier disregard for education, with catastrophic consequences. Arabs aged twenty-five and older have an average of just six years of schooling—roughly equivalent, in American terms, to having completed elementary school. According to a 2012 report by the Arab Thought Foundation, the average Western child spends around 200 hours per year reading, while his or her Arab counterpart spends six *minutes*. Adults do even worse. In the West, adults read an average of eleven books each year; in Arab countries they read one-quarter of one page. Almost one hundred million Arabs cannot read or write at all. The Arab world displays relatively little intellectual openness to the wider world. Greece, with a population of eleven million, translates five times as many books annually as every Arab country put together.

Even these statistics do not begin to tell the full story: Even at its highest levels, Arab education is a backward affair. Egypt, historically the center of Arab learning, is home to the region's leading universities; but its top graduate students are mostly learning how to memorize exactly what their professors tell them. Refuse to parrot back what you have been fed and you are apt to fail. Think for yourself, critically weigh what you have been taught, express yourself originally, and you are sure to. Over the centuries, this perpetual drilling and memorization has forcibly stunted the imagination and hobbled the critical thinking of generation after generation. The result is a region not only ill-prepared for modernity but also shockingly removed from it.

The Arab world holds itself back in other ways. Women are systematically shut out of the workplace; only about a third are employed. Many Arab countries have developed monoculture economies, built around oil or natural gas, that richly reward the few while denying a living wage to the many. Corruption is rampant. So is unemployment, particularly among the young. The striking absence of educational and economic opportunity, compounded by the lack of political accountability and a hopelessly distorted sense of history, has made Arab countries fertile soil for extremists. Even in Western countries, the neighborhoods that have churned out the most recruits for the Islamic State—such as Molenbeek, in Brussels—look, from the point of view of a lower-class young man, like miniatures of the Arab world: low employment, dim prospects, and a government apparently uninterested in addressing the root causes of these problems. From Minneapolis to Mosul, this sorry state of affairs has produced legions of young men confused about their identity, angered by the hobbling of their prospects, and incapable of critical thought—the kind of people most acutely vulnerable to demagogues like Osama bin Laden and Abu Musab al-Zarqawi. Not for nothing did H. G. Wells call history "a race between education and catastrophe."

. . .

King Abdullah was surely correct to grumble, as he did in his *Corriere* interview in 2004, that Zarqawi's status as a terrorist mastermind was exaggerated by the media; in fact, although His Majesty refrained from saying so, certain governments were equally culpable in talking up his importance. But to take the opposite course and dismiss him as a petty criminal is much too simplistic. Whatever else he may have been, Zarqawi was a prolific terrorist in his own right and a ruthless manipulator of public opinion. During his lifetime, his actions helped ignite a murderous conflict between Sunni and Shia at the center of the Arab heartland. Today, his angry ghost inhabits an armed group that, with its thousands of recruits, has conquered vast swathes of territory in Iraq and Syria.

The record shows Zarqawi to have been more than a ruthless, emotionless brute. He apparently succeeded in memorizing the Koran and was deeply affected by the experience. He was also an avid student of the twelfth-century ruler Nur ad-Din Zangi, a Mesopotamian commander famous for his battles against European Crusaders. Zarqawi perceived that he and Nur ad-Din lived in similar times. Then as now, power in the Middle East was splintered. The central government of the Abbasid caliphs was in decay, and local warlords—like Nur ad-Din's own family, the rulers of Mosul in modern-day northern Iraq—were taking over. Meanwhile, powers from outside the region took advantage of the chaos to set up bases in Syria, Iraq, and Egypt. When Crusaders assassinated his father, Nur ad-Din strove to unite his fellow Muslims across Iraq and Syria against the Western invaders and drive them back into the sea—a dream that would eventually be realized a generation later by his Kurdish rival, Saladin.

In 1149, after defeating and capturing the Crusader Prince of

Antioch, Nur ad-Din had his enemy decapitated and the head sent as a trophy to the Caliph al-Muqtafi—nominally still Nur ad-Din's overlord. Then, in a grand gesture calculated to suggest the sweep of land he controlled, Nur ad-Din marched his army across the Syrian desert and symbolically bathed in the Mediterranean. Just as in Nur ad-Din's day, Arab civilization stands divided against itself, and the region is in palpable decline, spiritually, culturally, and economically. Once again, latent feelings of humiliation and rage spew forth like oil gushing from the desert floor. Then and now, Western invaders occupied areas of the Middle East—a new Crusade, in Zarqawi's mind. Ethnically, Nur ad-Din was not Arab but Turkic—a characteristic he shares with many top Islamic State leaders. And if there is one event that sealed that group's murderous reputation, it was its 2014 capture of Nur ad-Din's old family seat, the city of Mosul. History repeats, Karl Marx wrote—first as tragedy, then as farce.

. . .

The man who would become Abu Musab al-Zarqawi was born Ahmed Fadl Nazal al-Khalaya in the blue-collar town of Zarqa, a few miles northeast of the Jordanian capital, Amman, in October 1966. He was raised in al-Masoum, a poor neighborhood that blends into the outskirts of the al-Ruseifah Palestinian refugee camp, where Zarqawi was to become attuned to radical ideas for the first time. Ethnically, however, Zarqawi was not a Palestinian like millions of his countrymen but a member of the Bani Hassan tribe of Bedouin. This cultural identity gave him a special place in the esteem of some Jordanians—an advantage that he would later use to full effect.

Since at least the 1960s, Zarqa had been the epicenter, in Jordan, of the intensely puritanical Salafi school of Islam, and in particular an even more virulent substrain known as the Salafi-jihadi movement, a violent and intolerant creed to which both al-Qaeda and the Islamic State adhere. Hundreds of young men from Zarqa and its twin town of Ruseifah fought in Afghanistan in the 1980s,

Chechnya in the 1990s, and Iraq in the 2000s. To this day, Zarqa still seethes with extremism and discontent. Even Jordanian intelligence officers—who rank among the boldest and most effective such operatives in the world—are fearful of the area.

In September of 1970, when Zarqawi was three years old, the leader of the Palestine Liberation Organization, Yasser Arafat, called for the overthrow of what he called the "fascist" government of King Hussein of Jordan. Thousands of disenfranchised Palestinians living in Jordan joined an armed uprising called Black September. Jordanian security services routed the insurgents. In towns like Zarqa, the unrest sent yet more young people into the arms of radical fundamentalists. And it had another damaging effect, this one longer-term; as a quid pro quo for its cooperation in putting down the revolt, King Hussein handed control of Jordan's education ministry over to the Muslim Brotherhood, which promotes adherence to dogma above intellectual curiosity.

When Zarqawi was seventeen years old, his father died. He was forced to drop out of high school a year early to help his mother take care of the household. But the young man's slide into depravity had already begun. Two years earlier, when he was just fifteen, he had reportedly participated in a robbery at the home of a relative, in the course of which the relative had been killed. Now, in his late teens and early twenties, he became a full-blown dropout. For a time, he worked in a video store, but he was soon fired. He began getting tattoos, eventually covering so much of his body that he acquired the nickname The Green Man. He drank heavily, took drugs, became involved in gang crime and perhaps pimping. Within a few years, he was serving his first jail time, for sexual assault and drug possession.

Following his release under the terms of one of Jordan's periodic royal amnesties, Zarqawi began attending radical lectures and sermons in Zarqa and at the neighboring Ruseifah Palestinian refugee camp. He would later say that he "returned" to Islam around September of 1989, at the minute and modest al-Falah mosque in his home neighborhood of al-Masoum. Three months later, at the age of twenty-three, he was on a plane to Afghanistan. Zarqawi's trip, like those of many others, was facilitated by the Jordanian cleric Abu Qatada—later notorious for his extremist preaching at London's Finsbury Park Mosque—and financed by the Office of Mujahideen Services, a group set up by Osama bin Laden's mentor, Abdullah Azzam. By the time Zarqawi arrived in Afghanistan, bin Laden had already slunk off to Saudi Arabia in disgrace following the disastrous mujahideen attack on Jalalabad. The Soviets and the CIA had pulled out, leaving behind a conflict grotesquely morphing from a freedom struggle against an aggressive outside power into a vicious intertribal war.

Zarqawi trained under al-Qaeda's military chief, Abu Hafs al-Masri, and gave himself the nom de guerre al-Gharib, or The Stranger. Abdullah Azzam's son, who knew Zarqawi during this first tour in Afghanistan, remembered a man of few words, "an ordinary guy," but one who did not "know the meaning of fear," and who "intentionally place[d] himself in the middle of the most dangerous situations." Over the course of a number of battles, Zarqawi witnessed the colossal Muslim-on-Muslim violence that characterized this new and horrifying phase of the Afghan conflict. When not fighting, he worked as a correspondent for the jihadist magazine *al-Bunyan al-Marsous* (The Solid Edifice), which also counted among its alumni Khalid Sheikh Mohammed, the architect of 9/11; and Wadi al-Hage, one of the principal co-conspirators in the 1998 embassy bombings.

When Zarqawi returned to Jordan in the early 1990s, it was to a country even more vexed by extremism than it had been when he had left. King Hussein, having given up Jordan's territorial claim to the West Bank in the late 1980s, was making further peace overtures to Israel, a move that had Jordanian radicals seething with anger. In the aftermath of the 1990–1991 Gulf War, Kuwait had expelled its Palestinian population en masse, perceiving them as supporters of Saddam Hussein. Many of the refugees had come to Jordan, and around 160,000 of them had settled in Zarqa. Among them was one of the most influential scholars in the Salafi-jihadi movement, the cleric Abu Mohammed al-Maqdisi. Zarqawi had first encountered Maqdisi in Peshawar, a way station for those bound for the fighting in Afghanistan. In short order, the young Zarqawi, still in his midtwenties, fell under the spell of Maqdisi's fiery teachings.

Maqdisi had been born in the West Bank, at the time under Jordanian control, but while he was still a child his family had emigrated to Kuwait. There, and in neighboring Saudi Arabia, he came into contact with scholars promoting the radical jihadi form of Salafism. Maqdisi has risen to become one of the principal exponents of the fundamentalist Salafi-jihadi movement, revered by his followers as a charismatic preacher and a brilliant scholar and writer. In the mid-1980s, he wrote in his first and most influential book, *The Creed of Abraham*, that anyone who even so much as obeyed laws made by secular rulers (as opposed to the Sharia, made by God) was practicing a form of polytheism and was therefore not a real Muslim. In Maqdisi's view, apostates—those who turned away from the true faith—were far worse than infidels: those who were never Muslim in the first place. Therefore, Maqdisi reasoned, the more important jihad was not the one against the far enemy—the Americans, whom Maqdisi saw as mere infidels—but the one targeting the near enemy: secular regimes of the Muslim world itself, which he painted as apostates. This was the diametric opposite of the worldview that Osama bin Laden would come to espouse a decade later in his declaration of war against America.

In the fevered atmosphere of early 1990s Jordan, extremist groups began popping up all over the country, especially in historically rebellious Zarqa. One of these groups, Bayat al-Imam, coalesced around Maqdisi in about 1993. Zarqawi joined Bayat al-Imam soon after its formation and lost no time in reaching out to Jordanian militants with experience of fighting in the ongoing civil wars in Afghanistan, Yugoslavia, or elsewhere. In keeping with Maqdisi's sermons,

Zarqawi's pitch to these men revolved around overthrowing the near enemy—starting with Jordan's own Hashemite monarchy. But Bayat al-Imam's first terrorist operation was a shambles. The group sent an operative to blow up a local movie theater in Zarqa. But the man assigned to the job, apparently unable to wrench his eyes away from the screen, forgot about his mission, stayed too long in the theater, and wound up blowing his own legs off. Soon, Zarqawi and Maqdisi found themselves imprisoned together. At first, they operated in partnership. Maqdisi preached his religious justifications for jihad and wrote books and articles on fundamentalist theology, which he published online. Meanwhile, Zarqawi governed his fellow inmates with an iron fist. One of them later recalled:

> *Zarqawi was the muscle, and Maqdisi the thinker. Zarqawi basically controlled the prison ward. He decided who would cook, who would do the laundry, who would lead the readings of the Koran. He was extremely protective of his followers, and extremely tough with prisoners outside his group. He didn't trust them. He considered them infidels. . . . He could order his followers to do things just by moving his eyes.*

Zarqawi exercised rigorous control over his followers, down to their attire, facial hair, reading material, and contact with inmates outside the group. He waged open warfare against the prison's other gangs and became known for his violent attacks on guards and inmates alike. On one occasion, he was placed in solitary confinement for participating in a brawl, and when he returned to the main ward, his followers spontaneously broke into a triumphant chant of "*Allahu Akbar*." It was not long before Zarqawi had pushed aside his former mentor to assume sole command of Bayat al-Imam, with Maqdisi demoted to the status of a mere adviser.

"Jail was very good for the movement," one member said. "Jail enhanced the personalities of prisoners and let them know how large was the cause they believed in. Inside jail is a good environment to get supporters and proselytize." It was not the first time prison would galvanize a jihadi movement, and nor would it be the last. In the 1980s, imprisonment in Mubarak's Egypt strengthened the resolve of terrorist leaders like Ayman al-Zawahiri. Twenty years later, in Iraq, American prisons like Camp Bucca would bring jihadis into contact with former servants of the Saddam regime, thereby helping to revivify the organization that would become the Islamic State. Jail was very good for Abu Musab al-Zarqawi, too. His network of criminal and extremist contacts grew wider and stronger than ever. At the same time, his presence became ever more commanding; a jihadi who knew him both before and after said, "When I heard Zarqawi speak, I didn't believe this is the same Zarqawi." Behind bars, he had acquired the swagger for which he was to become notorious during his brief, murderous career in Iraq. He was still prepared to use dogma as a tool of persuasion, but whatever patience he once had for religious argument had now evaporated. Doctrinal disputes of the kind that bin Laden and Maqdisi were apt to enter into—discussions about the near enemy and the far enemy, the permissibility of spilling Muslim blood, whether and when to declare an enemy an unbeliever—meant little to him now. As far as Zarqawi was concerned, his enemy was anyone who failed to live by his own backward concept of Islam and morality—a category that includes almost all Muslims, as well as almost all of humankind. Zarqawi's world was full of foes, and he was interested in fighting as many of them as he could lay blows upon as quickly as possible.

. . .

On February 7, 1999, King Hussein died, and his thirty-seven-year-old son ascended the throne as Abdullah II. To commemorate the occasion, as was traditional, the new monarch declared a general amnesty. Once again, Zarqawi was released from prison—ironically, given his avowed aim of overthrowing the Hashemite monarchy. In

Amman, he involved himself in directing the preparations for the failed Millennium bomb plots, for which the Jordanian authorities would later indict him. But he was hungry for jihad on a grander scale. In the company of some of his closest Jordanian companions, he made his way once more to the extremist entrepôt of Peshawar. His mother was by now gravely ill with leukemia, and he brought her with him, in hopes that the climate might help her condition. Zarqawi was in the process of arranging to travel to Chechnya—then the world's hottest theater of jihad—when he was abruptly informed that he was about to be thrown out of Pakistan for visa irregularities. Hurriedly, he and his companions made their way across the border to Afghanistan.

In his pocket was a letter of introduction from a respected Jordanian jihadi who had won fame fighting the Soviets in the 1980s. Apparently this was enough to secure Zarqawi an audience with the sheikh. In December 1999, Abu Musab al-Zarqawi and Osama bin Laden met face-to-face, for the first and quite probably only time, at a Taliban guesthouse in Kandahar. Bin Laden, as always, would have sat cross-legged on the floor of a drab, sparsely decorated room. Dressed in his usual plain shalwar kameez, the sheikh would have spoken softly and would have expected the young Jordanian to show the same hushed reverence almost every visitor afforded him. But Zarqawi, still skinny in those days and perennially full of nervous energy, would have found difficulty sitting still or keeping his voice down—something that was sure to antagonize the sheikh.

The meeting did not go well; as an Israeli intelligence official would later say, it was a case of "loathing at first sight." Bin Laden was already predisposed to be suspicious of Jordanian operatives, having learned through bitter experience how comprehensively Jordanian intelligence had infiltrated their networks. The al-Qaeda leader, soft-spoken, reserved, and used to being treated with the utmost respect, bridled at the younger man's braggadocio. And Zarqawi did not hold back. He lambasted al-Qaeda's Taliban hosts for what he branded their insufficient zeal in applying Sharia, and for recognizing the United Nations, which Zarqawi saw as a "council of infidels." He even had the gall to criticize bin Laden himself, for associating with the Taliban and for failing to denounce other supposedly insufficiently Islamic regimes. Needless to say, Zarqawi would not be pledging *bayat* to Osama bin Laden any time soon. He also made a show of his own deep hatred of those Muslims who did not conform to his own ideas of the faith, starting with the other main sect of Islam. "Shiites should be executed," Zarqawi declared—a death sentence that would have included the families of the sheikh's own mother and first wife. At the same time, Zarqawi said, he would not fight the Northern Alliance, because that would involve "real" Muslims killing their fellow believers.

In the midst of his tirade, Zarqawi demanded al-Qaeda's support in developing a terror network with the aim of overthrowing the Jordanian monarchy. Given how deeply his words alienated the sheikh, this was like Jefferson asking George III to finance the construction of Monticello. Unsurprisingly, bin Laden initially demurred. But after lengthy discussion, Saif al-Adel persuaded bin Laden that assisting Zarqawi and his group would be in al-Qaeda's best interests. This was partly because al-Qaeda felt the need for a foothold in the Levant, but it was also to thwart an independent jihadi, Abu Musab al-Suri, who had recently set up camp in Afghanistan. Al-Suri was siphoning off Levantine recruits who otherwise might have joined al-Qaeda. Ironically, Zarqawi's group, having morphed into the Islamic State of Iraq and the Levant (ISIL), would eventually turn on al-Qaeda, whereas followers of al-Suri would go on to form al-Qaeda's own loyal franchise in Syria, a group called al-Nusra.

As a result of Saif's intervention, Zarqawi and his companions were sent for forty-five days' training at one of al-Qaeda's camps near Kandahar. Then, with real estate and seed capital provided by al-Qaeda, Zarqawi established his own camp at Herat, in Afghanistan's far west. The location was chosen in part to keep his group at arm's length, in case of infiltration by Jordanian intelligence. This suited Zarqawi, too. From his point of view, the distance from Kandahar served to emphasize the ideological gap between himself and al-Qaeda, and to attract some of the many Arab jihadis who preferred not to fight under bin Laden's banner. Herat's proximity to the Iranian border, moreover, helped facilitate the smuggling of recruits into Afghanistan through Turkey and Iran. This was not only a more convenient pipeline for recruits from the Levant and Mesopotamia; it also freed Zarqawi from reliance on the al-Qaeda fixers in Peshawar. To reflect his territorial ambitions, Zarqawi initially called this new group Jund al-Sham (Soldiers of the Levant). As a Jordanian official would put it shortly before Zarqawi's death:

> Herat was the beginning of what he is now. He had command responsibilities for the first time; he had a battle plan. And even though he and bin Laden never got on, he was important to them. Herat was the only training camp in Afghanistan that was actively recruiting volunteers specifically from the Sham [Levant]. . . . In Herat, he called himself "Emir of the Sham."

The al-Qaeda high command furnished the camp with supplies and held monthly meetings to keep tabs on Zarqawi and his followers, whose numbers quickly mushroomed until he had dozens of men under his command. Many of the major operatives at the camp were Syrians, some of whom would later show their faces on the battlefields of Syria and Iraq. Many jihadis even brought their families to live with them at the camp, leading Zarqawi to boast that he presided over an ideal Islamic society in miniature. During his time at Herat, he married again, taking as his second wife the fourteen-year-old daughter of one of his Palestinian followers.

Zarqawi doggedly maintained the autonomy of his group, which he soon renamed Tawhid wal Jihad (Monotheism and Jihad). Despite repeated overtures, he declined to pledge bayat to al-Qaeda or indeed to any of the other Arab groups operating in Afghanistan. He stubbornly "refused to march under the banner of another individual or group," as a fellow Islamist would later put it. At the same time, he was stretching his tentacles further and further from Afghanistan. He dispatched emissaries as far afield as Turkey and Germany to seek cash and recruits. His fund-raising efforts in Europe even competed with those of al-Qaeda.

Naturally, al-Qaeda did not make Zarqawi, a nonmember with whom it had, to say the least, a fraught relationship, privy to its plans. The attacks on New York and Washington in September of 2001 therefore came as a complete surprise to him and his group. But they would have tremendous consequences for them nonetheless. In their immediate aftermath, his "miniature society" at Herat would be shattered. But the extended American response to 9/11 would ultimately bring Zarqawi's terrorist career to its apotheosis.

. . .

When the U.S. invasion of Afghanistan began, Zarqawi was in Kandahar, consulting with the powers that be in al-Qaeda and the Taliban. Upon hearing news of the invasion, he raced back to Herat to command his followers. Under intense ground and aerial assault, Herat's Taliban defenders quickly folded, and the Northern Alliance took the city on November 12. Zarqawi and Tawhid wal Jihad fled Herat in a long convoy, bound for Kandahar. There, they took part in the defense of the city under the command of Saif al-Adel. In the course of one bombardment, Zarqawi reportedly suffered broken ribs when a ceiling collapsed on him, but he refused to leave the fighting. In the end, however, he was forced to bow to the inevitable. Along with the other Taliban and Arab Afghan leaders, he fled Kandahar and Afghanistan. Long after the fact, Zarqawi's propaganda would claim that his intention in leaving Afghanistan was not to flee but to "open several new battlefronts with the Americans to disperse their forces and deny them the chance to focus on one region."

Around the close of 2001, Zarqawi crossed into Iran with a group of perhaps three hundred fighters. Some followers of the Afghan warlord Gulbuddin Hekmatyar, a former CIA protégé who had taken refuge in Teheran following the Taliban victory in 1996, helped Zarqawi and his group establish a presence in Iran. But this sojourn in the land of the ayatollahs would prove limited in duration, partly because, as a side effect of the conflict in Afghanistan, Iranian and American objectives in the region had suddenly come into alignment. It was in the best interests of both powers to tackle Sunni extremism and weaken any potential allies of the Taliban. In furtherance of this policy, Iran started to crack down on the many Arab militants who had taken up refuge on its soil. As much as 80 percent of Tawhid wal Jihad was caught up in the ensuing purges.

Iran was not the only government taking a hard line with such groups. In February and April of 2002, around a dozen Tawhid wal Jihad members were detained in Turkey and Germany. They made Zarqawi's presence in Iran known to the authorities, and within weeks of the second set of arrests, Zarqawi was forced to relocate over the border to northern Iraq. Once again, his propaganda arm would later paint this move in a much more flattering light, claiming that his departure was the result of a premeditated and farsighted decision made in order to "prepare for confrontations to face the U.S. invasion and defeat the Americans."

In April 2002, he took refuge with Ansar al-Islam, one of the Kurdish Islamist groups camped out in the mountains of Iraqi Kurdistan. There is evidence that Saddam Hussein's intelligence operation was, on some level, coordinating with Ansar al-Islam and similar groups in the region. There was no love lost between Islamist militants and secular Baathists; but both sides expected war with the United States and recognized their mutual interest in fighting the Americans. Besides, Saddam's government already had a long history of sponsoring global terrorists. To many such groups, the regime offered not only safe haven but also weapons, training, and logistical assistance.

The beneficiaries of Iraqi hospitality included armed groups that aimed to attack Iran, Israel, and the United States. While sheltering in Iraq, Palestinian and leftist terrorist groups carried out bombings, assassinations, and hijackings—including that of the *Achille Lauro* cruise ship, in which an elderly, disabled American passenger was murdered and his body dumped overboard. Around the same time as the 1990–91 Gulf War, the Iraqi regime itself attempted several terrorist attacks, using its own intelligence operatives and various Palestinian factions, although each of these efforts ended in failure. Later, during the second Palestinian intifada of 2000 to 2005, Saddam used the Arab Liberation Front—his own personal pawn in the Israeli-Palestinian conflict—to offer $25,000 to the family of each Palestinian killed in an Israeli attack.

Like other Islamist groups, al-Qaeda was certainly no friend to secular Muslim rulers like Saddam; in 1990, bin Laden had even offered to help eject the regime's armed forces from Kuwait. On the other hand, once the Gulf War was over, Saddam and al-Qaeda had a common enemy in the shape of the United States, and both sides had shown themselves pragmatic enough to make deals with their natural adversaries. During the 1990s, according to the CIA, Saddam's intelligence service had made contact with al-Qaeda on a number of occasions, both in Sudan and in Afghanistan, although these links "did not add up to an established formal relationship." In the course of their discussions, there had been some mention of safe haven in Iraq for bin Laden, although it is by no means clear that such protection was ever actually offered.

By the beginning of the Iraq War, between one hundred and two hundred al-Qaeda members and associates had moved into Iraqi Kurdistan, anticipating an opportunity to take on America on Muslim soil. Like Zarqawi, these fighters were hosted by Ansar al-Islam, a group founded in December 2001 as the product of a merger between several Kurdish Sunni extremist groups. From its inception, Ansar al-Islam had enjoyed strong links with al-Qaeda. Al-Qaeda helped to train at least one of its predecessor groups, and its charter members may have included a contingent of al-Qaeda operatives fresh from the fighting in Afghanistan. However, the Iraqi group's own main focus was, at least in the beginning, more localized: It aimed to battle its more secular Kurdish rivals, with the goal of eventually turning the Kurdistan region into an independent Islamic emirate.

Zarqawi himself was, of course, not a member of al-Qaeda— at least not yet. Almost from the moment of his arrival in Iraq, he set about building his own independent web of militant cells, putting in place the network he would need to exploit the chaos to come. Jihadis entering Iraq were inspired in part by a dubious hadith allegedly prophesying an apocalyptic battle for Mesopotamia. Zarqawi helped construct an infrastructure to smuggle recruits into the country through Syria. This pipeline soon included recruitment centers where would-be fighters could sign up at a registration desk in the morning and cross into Iraq by bus a few hours later. The Assad regime not only allowed this to take place; it happily assisted Zarqawi and his peers. Syrian officials ferried jihadists from Damascus International Airport to the Iraqi border. With an invasion of its neighbor clearly in the cards, the regime feared that it might be next on America's list. When it came to Iraq, therefore, Assad calculated that his best chance of survival lay not in cooperating with the United States but in ejecting American troops from Syria's back yard before it was too late. In March 2003, days before the U.S. aerial assault on Baghdad began, Assad told his close ally, Ayatollah Khamenei, "If we cannot defeat the Americans, then we need to ensure the situation remains volatile and suicide operations carry on unabated." Assad would make sure that the insurgent pipeline through Damascus remained open throughout the Iraq War; in 2009, Iraqi prime minister Nuri al-Maliki—though closely aligned with Assad's most important patron, Iran—complained that "90 percent" of the foreign terrorists in Iraq had entered the country by crossing the Syrian border. Syria also harbored exiled Iraqi Baathists, whom Assad's intelligence services helped plan several deadly attacks, including one of the war's bloodiest, a truck bombing at the Finance Ministry in 2009 that killed over 100 people, in response to which the Maliki regime recalled its ambassador from Damascus.

Using the Syrian pipeline, Zarqawi built up a network of perhaps hundreds of foreign fighters. Naturally enough, many of them, particularly in these early days, were Syrians, who likely wanted to escape the prying eyes of the Assad regime. On one occasion, three dozen Syrians pledged *bayat* to Zarqawi en masse; it was a group that included, among others, Abu Mohammed al-Adnani, who would eventually become the principal spokesman for the Islamic State. Soon, Zarqawi would be importing Libyans, Moroccans, Algerians, Yemenis, Tunisians, and a particularly sizable contingent of Saudis. Zarqawi's Syrian pipeline became so efficient that, by the start of the invasion, Saif al-Adel was asking if he could use it to bring al-Qaeda operatives into Iraq. Zarqawi traveled the country and the region, distributing his terror cells around Baghdad, Fallujah, and Iraq's other cities. By the beginning of 2003, he was almost ready to begin operations. Yet despite his high profile among foreign fighters traveling to Iraq, he and his group were still practically unknown to the American public. That was set to change dramatically.

• • •

On February 5, 2003, U.S. Secretary of State Colin Powell, who had been the Chairman of the Joint Chiefs of Staff at the time of the Gulf War, took his seat at the vast, circular table of the United Nations Security Council to deliver a presentation meant to make the case for renewed military action against Iraq. The main focus of the speech was the Saddam regime's alleged pursuit or possession of chemical, biological, and nuclear weapons. But toward the end of his hour-long address, he included a passage meant to substantiate a link between Saddam and al-Qaeda. In terms of U.S. public opinion, this was an important part of the argument for war. It suggested that

Saddam might put his doomsday weapons into the hands of terrorists. It also tacitly hinted at a connection, however obscure, between
his regime and 9/11. The attacks had taken place less than eighteen
months before.

Powell described a "sinister nexus between Iraq and the al-Qaeda
terrorist network." And at that nexus, according to the Bush administration, was Abu Musab al-Zarqawi. The secretary of state painted
Zarqawi's Herat camp, as well as certain facilities of Ansar al-Islam,
Zarqawi's onetime hosts in Kurdistan, as virtual poison factories,
specializing in the manufacture of ricin, a toxin that can be lethal
even in comparatively minute doses. Powell claimed that an Iraqi
agent embedded in Ansar al-Islam had invited Zarqawi into northern Iraq in 2002, and said that the agent had said that Zarqawi was
planning attacks in Europe and Russia. The picture of Zarqawi as
the crucial link between Saddam and bin Laden was, at best, something of a stretch, not least because Zarqawi was still fiercely independent of al-Qaeda. But the impression of Abu Musab al-Zarqawi
as the premier foreign terrorist in Iraq had now become indelible. It
was an image that would serve him well.

With terrible irony, much of the erroneous information in Powell's
speech was extracted using methods of the kind that would in time
prove an even more potent recruiting sergeant for terrorism than the
war itself. Ibn al-Sheikh al-Libi, once head of the Khaldan camp in
Afghanistan through which so many jihadis passed on their way to a
terrorist career, was arrested in Afghanistan, removed from FBI custody before his interrogation could be completed, rendered to a third
country, and repeatedly tortured at the behest of the CIA. Hoping to
stop the torture and avoid transfer to an even less sympathetic intelligence service, al-Libi told his captors just what they wanted to hear:
that Saddam Hussein had trained al-Qaeda in the use of chemical
and biological weapons. This was the lie that helped open the door
for an invasion of Iraq. But torture's trail of destruction did not end
with faulty intelligence. Harsh treatment of detainees in U.S. cus-

tody, particularly when documented on film, fed directly into the terrorists' own lie that the United States was waging war against Islam and would stop at nothing in its determination to humiliate Muslims. As the former general counsel of the U.S. Navy, Alberto Mora, would tell the Senate Armed Services Committee in June 2008:

> *There are serving U.S. flag-rank officers [that is, those ranked rear admiral and above] who maintain that the first and second identifiable causes of U.S. combat deaths in Iraq—as judged by their effectiveness in recruiting insurgent fighters into combat— are, respectively, the symbols of Abu Ghraib and Guantánamo.*

Nor did the power of these symbols dissipate when the United States left Iraq. Years later, militant hostage-takers still dress their Western captives in orange jumpsuits in symbolic revenge for the Guantánamo Bay detainees; and images from Abu Ghraib still help radicalize young men around the world, including the French-born terrorists who murdered a dozen people at the offices of *Charlie Hebdo* in January 2015.

In private, Powell expressed reservations about the administration's case for war, but he was led to believe that the intelligence was accurate, and his presentation made clear the Bush White House's determination to use force in Iraq, with or without a Security Council resolution explicitly authorizing an invasion. About a week after the speech, with the war drums beating louder and louder, bin Laden himself released an audio message, addressed "To Our Muslim Brothers in Iraq," in which he emphasized the need for unity in the face of what he called a "Crusade." The forthcoming battle, he said, "should be for the sake of the one God. It should not be for championing ethnic groups." In such circumstances, he said, it was permissible to make common cause with elements of the Saddam regime. Tactically, he recommended guerrilla warfare and "martyrdom operations"—suicide bombings. In due time, he even envisaged the exporting of the conflict to neighboring states. Zarqawi would eventually deliver on all of these agenda items, with one glaring exception: Far from unifying Muslims, he would seek to tear the Islamic community apart with unprecedented ferocity.

. . .

Even by the nihilistic standards of contemporary jihadi terrorism, Zarqawi's methods were especially vicious. His statements of this period make for chilling reading. In one audio message he sanctioned the indiscriminate murder of innocents:

> There is no doubt that God has commanded us to target the unbelievers, and to kill them and fight them with every means that can accomplish this goal. Even if the means does not distinguish between the intended warring unbelievers and unintended women and children, as well as those among the unbelievers whose intentional killing is not permitted.

In another message, he countenanced the killing even of "real" Muslims, if that was necessary to keep his jihad going. "The shedding of Muslim blood is allowed," he said, "in order to avoid the greater evil of disrupting jihad. . . . Islamic law states that the Islamic faith is more important than life, honor, and property. . . . [W]e cannot kill infidels without killing some Muslims." Perhaps most disturbingly of all, Zarqawi told Osama bin Laden and Ayman al-Zawahiri simply, "blood will be spilled. This is exactly what we want, since right and wrong no longer have any place in our current situation."

His years away from Jordan had done nothing to blunt his hatred for the government of his home country. In the summer of 2002, months before the U.S. invasion began, he set up a base in Syria to train operatives for attacks on Jews and Americans inside Jordan. Quietly, he set up at least one cell in Amman, and provided it with weapons, finance, and direction. In late October 2002, his operatives struck for the first time. They ambushed Laurence Foley, a senior diplomat with the U.S. Agency for International Development, as he got into his car on his way to work, and shot him dead. Two of the murderers, a Jordanian and a Libyan, were captured and confessed that Zarqawi had sent them. This was the first of the four crimes for which Jordan would sentence Zarqawi to death in absentia.

Around a year later, he was planning another strike in Amman, this time a mass-casualty attack, possibly involving chemical weapons. The plot was foiled by the Jordanian security services. Undeterred by the unraveling of his plan, Zarqawi threatened further attacks against the Hashemite Kingdom, saying in a statement: "[W]ar has ups and downs, and as the days go by, we will have more fierce confrontations with the Jordanian government. The chapters of some these confrontations have ended, but what is coming is more vicious and bitter, God willing."

In the summer of 2003, when his campaign of murder inside Iraq began in earnest, Zarqawi's first major target was, again, Jordanian. On August 7, a vehicle exploded outside the Jordanian embassy in Baghdad, just as dozens of locals were lining up outside, waiting to have their visas processed. There were reports of a rocket having been fired at the vehicle to ignite the explosives inside. The force of the blast propelled a car that had been parked outside the building onto a neighboring rooftop. Seventeen people died, all of them Iraqis.

Less than two weeks later, a twenty-six-year-old Moroccan, a young father who just that morning had been told that the baby his wife was carrying was a boy, crashed a cement mixer full of explosives through the wall around the United Nations compound in Baghdad. It exploded as a press conference about landmine removal efforts was under way, and struck the building just under the office of the Secretary General's Special Representative in Iraq, Sergio Vieira de Mello, who was killed along with sixteen others. The young bomber could be identified only by his severed feet and hands, which the authorities found 150 yards from the scene of the explosion. Apart from the loss of life, the bombing also had another tragic consequence: the with-drawal of the United Nations and other international agencies from Iraq, just when they were most sorely needed to aid efforts toward reconstruction and reconciliation.

From the start of U.S. operations, Zarqawi's operatives rained rocket fire on American forces. But overall, more than three-quarters of his targets were Iraqi. And the so-called enemies for whom Zarqawi reserved his most venomous hatred were Shia Muslims. Zarqa-wi's black animus toward the Shia ran deep. He called them "rejec-tionists," "the enemy," and "liars" and accused them of harboring "hidden rancor toward the Sunnis." He blamed them for the Mon-gol conquest of Iraq in the thirteenth century and for sabotaging the Ottoman attempt to take over Western Europe three hundred years later; he professed to believe that Shia Muslims were the servants of the Antichrist. Lost in his own black-and-white, sectarian moral universe, Zarqawi rejected calls for all Muslims to unite against the Americans; in fact, he viewed the divide between Sunnis and Shia in much starker terms than that between Sunnis and Americans. As he asked rhetorically:

> Why is it permissible to strike the enemy when he has blonde hair and blue eyes, but it is not permissible to strike him when he has dark hair and black eyes? A Muslim American is our dear brother: an infidel Arab is our hated enemy, even if we both come from the same womb. We have revived the jurisprudence of our good ancestors in fighting heretics and enforcing God's law on them. Jihad will be continuous and will not distinguish between Western infidels and heretic Arabs until the rule of the caliphate is restored or we die in the process.

Mesopotamia has always been one of the stages on which Islam's great schism has played out. Two of the most revered figures in Shia Islam, Imam Ali ibn Abi Talib (the fourth caliph) and his son Imam

Hussein, were each killed (martyred, according to Shia tradition) within about a hundred miles of Baghdad. The Imam Ali Mosque in Najaf is built around a shrine Shias believe houses Ali's tomb. It is the third holiest site in Shia Islam, after Mecca and Medina. There, on Friday, August 29, 2003, just as prayers were breaking up, a suicide car bomb struck the departing motorcade of Ayatollah Mohammed Baqral-Hakim, engulfing several vehicles in a ball of flame. Ayatollah Hakim was killed, together with more than 100 other worshippers. The suicide bomber whose device caused the carnage was Zarqawi's own father-in-law; his daughter was the Palestinian teenager Zarqawi had married back in Herat. It was the bloodiest attack of the Iraq War so far, although its death toll would soon be surpassed. The pattern of attacks on international and Shia targets continued for the rest of 2003 and into 2004. In March, Zarqawi's group helped stage multiple coordinated attacks on Shia sites in Karbala—sacred to Shia Muslims as the place where Hussein, the son of the fourth caliph, Ali, was beheaded—on Ashura, the day of mourning for Hussein's death. In those attacks and simultaneous atrocities in Baghdad, around 180 worshippers and bystanders were killed.

. . .

Zarqawi and his followers still did not control any appreciable territory from which to launch attacks, however, and this boded ill for their avowed aim of reestablishing the caliphate, a vast empire that once stretched from Pakistan to the Pyrenees. One senior Zarqawi lieutenant wrote a report lamenting this state of affairs:

> [A]fter one year of jihad, we have not accomplished anything on the ground. None of us could find a piece of land to use as a shelter or a place to retire to safety amongst some members of [our] group. . . . We would hide in daylight and sneak like a cat at night. . . . Homes were raided and the heroes were chased. It was a dark picture and everyone felt a sense of terrible failure.

The insurgency needed a base, a safe haven, a beachhead they could control. One of the clearest candidates was Fallujah, an ancient city on the east bank of the Euphrates, around forty miles east of Baghdad and known locally as the City of Mosques for its many sacred buildings. Located inside the area west and northwest of Baghdad known as the Sunni Triangle, Fallujah had been a bastion of support for the Sunni regime of Saddam Hussein. Beginning just after the U.S. invasion, American forces had helped foment unrest in the city with their heavy-handed tactics. In April 2003, American soldiers opened fire on peaceful protesters, killing seventeen civilians. Insurgents retaliated for this and similar incidents by murdering four Blackwater security contractors and publicly displaying their blackened corpses, hung from a bridge on the city's western approaches. Al-Qaeda and its allies saw an opportunity to turn Fallujah into a focal point of resistance against the occupation and a secure beachhead for the insurgency, and fought the Americans hard for control of the city. By the beginning of May 2004, the U.S. had withdrawn, leaving Fallujah in the hands of al-Qaeda. The militants were to hold the city for more than half a year.

The next month, June 2004, Zarqawi reportedly presided over a ceremony in Fallujah in which some of the local insurgent leaders pledged *bayat* to him. His foreign fighters set about turning Fallujah into what his deputies called the Republic of al-Zarqawi. In so doing, they transformed the City of Mosques into a vision of hell comparable in its ferocity to the nightmare the Taliban had made of Kabul eight years before. According to local residents, men who failed to grow beards were publicly whipped, as was anyone suspected of drinking alcohol. Women wearing makeup or displaying their hair were publicly humiliated. Suspected spies could be summarily shot. It was a pattern of repression that would repeat itself years later in the areas of Iraq and Syria controlled by the Islamic State. Fallujah anticipated the Islamic State in other ways as well. Prominent among the foreign fighters ruling the city was a contingent of Tunisians, many of them from the small city of Ben Gardane, on the Libyan border. Zarqawi was so impressed with these militants that he reportedly said, "If Ben Gardane had been located next to Fallujah, we would have liberated Iraq." Tunisians would later become the largest foreign contingent fighting in Syria—more than 1,000 of them from Ben Gardane alone.

Fallujah's traumatized residents might have turned Zarqawi and his crew out of their city had Zarqawi not enjoyed the support of a respected and feared local fundamentalist, Omar Hadid. A decade earlier, Hadid had tried to impose puritanism on his home town using violence, by intimidating business owners, bombing the city's only movie theater, and assassinating a Baath Party official. It was Hadid who had led the anti-American insurgency in Fallujah, months before Zarqawi decided to make the city a hub for his own operation. Now, Hadid pledged fealty to the Jordanian, although he claims to have participated only in fighting the Americans, not in bombings or beheadings of civilians, which he says he left to the foreigners.

During his reign of terror in Fallujah, Zarqawi began to articulate more forcefully his plan to export this stygian vision to the rest of Iraq and the region. Toward the start of the occupation, he stated that he saw his role in Iraq as "waging jihad with my brothers to establish for Islam a homeland and for the Koran a state." And as the occupation of Fallujah wore on, he came increasingly to see that outcome as a genuine possibility. Around this time, too, Zarqawi began stepping up his campaign against the United States and its allies in the new government of Iraq. His group was blamed for the assassination, on May 17, 2004, of the Shia president of the Iraqi Governing Council, killed by a suicide car bomb. In June, Zarqawi's fighters blew up a Western convoy, killing thirteen people, including three employees of General Electric. In mid-September, they attacked a market in west Baghdad, killing at least forty-seven people. At the end of the month, a bombing at the inauguration of a new water treatment facility took the lives of thirty-five children who were running to accept sweets being handed out by American troops. A second blast was timed to kill rescuers trying to help those injured in the first explosion. Characteristically, a statement from Tawhid wal Jihad lauded these callous acts of mass murder as "heroic operations."

. . .

Soon after the militants took over Fallujah, the videotaped beheadings began. One week after the U.S. withdrawal from the city, the body of Nick Berg, a twenty-six-year-old telecommunications engineer from Pennsylvania, was discovered dangling upside down beneath a highway overpass between Fallujah and Baghdad. His head was found discarded on the ground nearby, blood matting his hair and beard. Days later, a video surfaced showing his beheading, in which it was later confirmed that Zarqawi had personally wielded the knife. A statement read out immediately before the murder made specific reference to the recent revelation that U.S. troops in Iraq had tortured and otherwise abused insurgent prisoners in their custody. "[T]he dignity of the Muslim men and women in Abu Ghraib is not redeemed except by blood and souls," the masked militant intoned. Until the West withdrew from Iraq, he said, "You will receive nothing from us but coffin after coffin slaughtered in this way."

By the end of the insurgent occupation of Fallujah, in November 2004, at least eight more foreign hostages had been decapitated. Many of their deaths, like that of Nick Berg, were broadcast online. The body of one Japanese hostage was discovered wrapped in an American flag. It is a depressing fact that these videos have become as commonplace as they are programmatic, as predictable as a bad horror story but incomparably worse for being real. A row of jihadists, masked or hooded like assassins, lines up before a black banner. In front of them another figure, kneeling, quaking, in an orange jumpsuit—a deliberate visual reference, as we have seen, to the conditions of detention at Abu Ghraib and Guantánamo Bay. The victim makes a brief statement identifying himself—name, nationality, place of birth, religion. A militant reads a longer, bloodier, more apocalyptic speech. Then another pulls a knife. Methodically he saws off the victim's head and holds it up for the camera. In the final frames, the head is seen resting on the corpse's back. Somewhere nearby lies the instrument of death, often displayed propped up on the body itself.

Zarqawi's bloodthirsty admirers reveled in these displays of depravity, which soon earned him the nickname Sheikh of the Slaughterers. When the videos dried up in late 2004, following the liberation of Fallujah, jihadists took to online forums to complain. One anonymous user lamented:

> *We used to start our day by watching a slaughter scene, for it is no secret to the knowledgeable that it stimulates and appeases the contents of the chest.... [M]any of those who suffer from high blood pressure and diabetes have complained about the cease of these operations, for they were tranquilizing them.... Someone told me, and I believe he speaks the truth, that he does not eat his food until he has watched a beheading scene, even if it were replayed or old.*

However, not everyone who shared Zarqawi's goals was so enamored of his methods. Local insurgent leaders complained bitterly that his brutality was alienating international sympathy for their cause. In July 2004, the third month of the Republic of al-Zarqawi in Fallujah, reports surfaced that some Iraqi resistance factions had cut their ties with Zarqawi because of the unacceptable level of civilian casualties. The Sunni Association of Muslim Scholars in Iraq—vocal supporters of the anti-American insurgency—condemned the beheadings of foreign hostages as violations of Sharia. The Egyptian Sunni cleric Yusuf al-Qaradawi, who once described Palestinian suicide bombings as "evidence of God's justice," likened Zarqawi to the Kharijites, an early Islamic sect infamous for a simplistic and faulty reading of scripture that led some of their number to murder the Caliph Ali.

Even Zarqawi's old Jordanian mentor, Abu Mohammed al-

Maqdisi, soon became critical of his actions. In July 2004, Maqdisi posted on his website an article entitled "Al-Zarqawi—Aid and Advice." In it, he accused Zarqawi of "defil[ing] the jihad and its honorable image" with attacks that killed Muslim civilians who were not engaged in "aid[ing] the infidels." This article came out shortly before Maqdisi was moved from prison to house arrest, which in the view of at least one commentator implies that it may have been published as part of a secret deal with the Jordanian authorities. But, as we shall see, Maqdisi was far from done criticizing his former protégé.

· · ·

Despite his efforts to create a pipeline through Syria, and despite the outpouring of admiration for his efforts on jihadist social media, the inflow of foreign fighters into Zarqawi's organization was still not enough to satisfy his grandiose vision of an apocalyptic battle for control of the Middle East. In a statement published in January 2004, he questioned the masculinity of those who would not join him. "[T]he gates of heaven are open," he said. "If you are unwilling to be one of the knights of war, make way for the women so they can run the war, and you take the cooking utensils and makeup in their stead. If you are not women in turbans and beards, go to the horses and seize their harnesses and their reins." In September, in the midst of Fallujah's Republic of al-Zarqawi phase, he continued in a more explicitly apocalyptic vein:

My nation, the nation of the sword and the pen, why is it that your sword is now broken and your pen has been laid down? You used to be prouder than the stars, and have now become downtrodden under the feet of the invaders and under the hooves of the usurpers' horses. My dear nation, my words to you today are laden with sorrow. Don't you hear the serpents, hissing as they wind their way in the darkness of your apathy in order to assassinate your dawn?

Far more severe, however—and far more dangerous to Zarqawi's image in Iraq—was his failure to attract local recruits. Besides their natural revulsion for his methods, Zarqawi's naked sectarianism alienated many Iraqi Sunnis. In contrast to Zarqawi's native Jordan, where practically everyone belongs to the Sunni tradition, around half of Iraqi Muslims—and a clear majority of Iraqi Arabs—are Shia. By the standards of the Arab world, there is strikingly little animosity between the groups. Even in 2012, after years of sectarian attacks and a Shia-led government that was itself widely criticized for being divisive, only 14 percent of Iraqi Sunnis said that Shias were not Muslims, compared with 43 percent in Jordan and 53 percent in Egypt. Indeed, in Iraq the two communities are to an extent intermingled. Few Iraqis wanted to attack people who for centuries had been their neighbors—let alone their friends, wives, fathers, and mothers. Of course, this was not how Zarqawi saw things. He preferred to blame the dearth of Iraqis in his organization on their lack of "expertise or experience [or] farsightedness" and on what he saw as their timidity. "The Iraqi brothers still prefer safety," he told Osama bin Laden in a letter. "Sometimes the groups have boasted among themselves that not one of them has been killed or captured. We have told them . . . that safety and victory are incompatible."

Nonetheless, among Iraq's contingent of foreign terrorists, Zarqawi fashioned a leading role for himself. Fighters trying to reach the country depended upon his Syrian pipeline. Once in Iraq, they relied upon his network's superior contacts and intelligence-gathering capability. In effect, then, Zarqawi had made himself an Emir of the Strangers. By the fall of 2004, Jordanian intelligence called him "the head of the pyramid of terrorism in Iraq" and spoke of him as a potential rival to bin Laden.

Yet Zarqawi remained deeply frustrated by what he saw as his lack of progress. Fallujah was not turning out to be the secure foothold the militants had hoped for; throughout the summer and into the fall of 2004, the city came under increasing pressure from U.S. forces, eager for revenge for the dramatic reversals they had suffered there earlier in the year. He continued to be unsatisfied with the pace of recruitment, and his fund-raising efforts, too, remained rudimentary, if admittedly ingenious—involving, for example, having associates with clean records buy ordinary cars in Jordan and drive them over the border to be sold for cash in Iraq. By mid-2004, Tawhid wal Jihad's coffers were running low. It was a far cry from the millions of dollars al-Qaeda was capable of raising from wealthy Saudis and other donors—and the hundreds of recruits the al-Qaeda name drew in. With that kind of backing, Zarqawi must have thought, he could solve his recruitment woes and intensify still further his battle against the Americans, the emerging Iraqi government, and the Shia. Unfortunately for him, al-Qaeda appeared to be ignoring his advances.

Around the beginning of 2004, just over four years after he had first met Osama bin Laden and declined to pledge allegiance to him, Zarqawi had once again reached out to the al-Qaeda leader and Ayman al-Zawahiri. In a letter to them, he painted a bleak picture of the insurgency's future if drastic action were not taken soon. Iraq's Sunnis, he said, were rudderless and lost. Their clerics were interested only in ceremonies, while the Muslim Brotherhood had forsworn jihad in order to grub for subordinate political power in a Shia-dominated government. Iraqi fighters were inexperienced and overly cautious; foreign fighters were too few in number "compared to the enormity of the expected battle." All the while, the United States was tightening its "grip around the throats of the mujahideen."

Worst of all, Zarqawi claimed, the Shia were on the march. "The unhurried observer and inquiring onlooker will realize that Shiism is the looming danger and the true challenge," he wrote. "People without exception know that most of the mujahideen who have fallen in war have done so at the hands of these people." The Shia were already fighting on the side of the Americans, he told the al-Qaeda leadership. Sooner or later, they would take over the running of the country for good. Together with the hated regimes of Iran and Syria, they would form a "Shia Crescent" from the Gulf to the Mediterranean—a danger against which even secular rulers like King Abdullah of Jordan and Egypt's Hosni Mubarak had warned, albeit for security rather than sectarian reasons. When that happened, the mujahideen would have to give up and find another theater of jihad, just as they had done in Afghanistan.

Zarqawi proposed a full-blooded sectarian holy war against the Shia. Declaring such a jihad would not only strike a blow for so-called true Islam; it would galvanize the Sunnis themselves and propel them into the fight. Al-Qaeda need not be squeamish about the probable consequences. "God's religion is more precious than lives and souls," Zarqawi wrote. "There has to be some sacrifice for this religion. Let blood be spilled, and we will soothe and speed those who are good to their paradise." Once again, this was the old *takfiri* claim, traceable to Ibn Taymiyyah and the Mongols: It doesn't matter whom we kill, or in what numbers, because God will send the good dead to Heaven and the bad to Hell.

Finally, Zarqawi told bin Laden and Zawahiri his true demand—to unite his own organization with al-Qaeda:

> *This is our vision, and we have explained it. This is our path, and we have made it clear. If you agree with us on it, if you adopt it as a program and road, and if you are convinced of the idea of fighting the sects of apostasy, we will be your readied soldiers, working under your banner, complying with your orders, and indeed swearing fealty to you publicly and in the news media, vexing the infidels and gladdening those who preach the oneness of God. On that day, the believers will rejoice in God's victory. If things appear otherwise to you, we are brothers, and the disagreement will not spoil [our] friendship. [This is] a cause [in which] we are cooperating for the good and supporting jihad. Awaiting your response, may God preserve you as keys to good and reserves for Islam and its people.*

American intelligence sources told the media that they believed al-Qaeda had rejected Zarqawi's proposal. That decision would have made a lot of sense: The al-Qaeda leader had rejected Zarqawi's expressions of violent *takfirism* four years before at their meeting in Kandahar; it is hard to believe that he would have been any more receptive now that the Jordanian was proposing a full-scale sectarian civil war.

But that was not the only consideration in play. Al-Qaeda as a whole faced tough challenges by 2004. Many of its senior leaders had been killed in Afghanistan or arrested in Pakistan or Iran. Its affiliates had recently carried out bloody attacks in Bali, Spain, and Saudi Arabia, but the organization possessed barely a toehold in Iraq, which was quickly becoming the center of gravity for the global jihad. More alarmingly still, Zarqawi was now being spoken of as a potential rival to bin Laden—a threat that al-Qaeda would need to neutralize quickly. The surest way of doing that might be to make him a subordinate, which is exactly what Zarqawi was proposing.

On October 17, 2004, Zarqawi announced that he had pledged *bayat* to bin Laden. Tawhid wal Jihad would henceforward be called Qaedat al-Jihad fi Bilad al-Rafidayn—The Base of Jihad in the Land of Two Rivers, better known in the West as al-Qaeda in Iraq. In his statement announcing the allegiance, Zarqawi struck a triumphant tone. "Hold fast to the rope of God and you shall not be divided," he wrote, quoting the Koran. "This is undoubtedly an indication that victory is approaching, God willing, and that it represents a return to the glorious past . . . a caliphate that follows the guidance of prophethood."

Initially, the authenticity of this statement was called into question. Iraqis were bound to view the insurgency less sympathetically if, instead of a "legitimate" struggle against an occupier, it was seen as merely another battlefield in bin Laden's terror campaign against the West. Some militants therefore dismissed reports of Zarqawi's pledge of allegiance to al-Qaeda as American propaganda designed to discredit their cause. But the *bayat* was real. Bin Laden confirmed it in an adulatory audio message two months later:

> The warrior commander [and] honored comrade Abu Musab al-Zarqawi and the groups who joined him are the best of the community that is fighting for the sake of the word of God. Their courageous operations against the Americans and against the apostate Allawi government [a reference to the Iraqi prime minister Ayad Allawi] have gladdened us.... We in the al-Qaeda organization very much welcome their union with us. This is a tremendous step on the path to the unification of the efforts fighting for the establishment of a State of Truth and for the uprooting of the State of the Lie.... Know that the warrior comrade Abu Musab al-Zarqawi is the emir of al-Qaeda in the Land of the Tigris and the Euphrates, and the comrades in the organization there must obey him.

At a stroke, Abu Musab al-Zarqawi had stamped his organization with the most feared and revered brand in contemporary global jihad and secured access to deeper pockets and wider pools of volunteers than his group had ever had before. For himself, he had gained still greater personal notoriety and global reach and cemented his authority as emir of all foreign jihadis in Iraq. But there was a crucial difference between al-Qaeda in Afghanistan and al-Qaeda in Iraq. However much bin Laden might from time to time have antagonized the Taliban during his second Afghan sojourn, he remained their honored guest. Zarqawi did not enjoy anything like that level of esteem among the leaders of Iraq's insurgency. His methods showed little consideration for the Iraqi people on whose behalf the local insurgents claimed to be fighting. As 2004 drew to a close, the Jordanian's welcome in Iraq was wearing thin.

. . .

In November, some twelve thousand American troops, alongside British and Iraqi forces, descended on Fallujah and began clearing the city of militants, house by house, in the bloodiest single battle of the entire Iraq War. Hundreds of insurgents were killed or captured in the fighting. In the south of the city, U.S. Marines raiding al-Qaeda's headquarters captured page after page of written instructions from Zarqawi himself. The liberation of Fallujah left the insurgency once again without a secure base for its operations. The debacle also dealt a heavy blow to the foreign fighters' already tarnished image among ordinary Iraqis. Not only had these men brutalized the local population with beheadings and summary violence; many of them had simply fled before the U.S. advance, deserting the people they had promised to defend. In keeping with his sectarian worldview, Zarqawi blamed the Shia fighters who had participated in the battle on the same side as the Americans. In his mind, this was yet more proof that Iraq's Shia Muslims were out for Sunni blood.

Shia political leaders, for their part, were about to consolidate their power in dramatic fashion. Elections for national and regional parliaments had been scheduled for January 30, 2005. Support for the elections fractured largely along ethnic and sectarian lines. Grand Ayatollah Ali al-Sistani, the most senior Shia theologian in Iraq, told his followers that it was their "religious duty" to participate, and he set about organizing a big tent coalition of Shia parties: the United Iraqi Alliance. Kurdish parties, who also stood to benefit, joined Shia leaders in endorsing the elections. By contrast, prominent Sunni Arab groups, including the Association of Muslim Scholars, called for a boycott. Osama bin Laden also condemned the elections, maintaining that they were ordained under man-made laws that permitted nonfundamentalist candidates to run for office. Zarqawi went further. His organization—curiously, using its old name of Tawhid wal Jihad—issued a specific death threat against all election officials and their families. One week before the elections, he published an audio message denouncing democracy as a system in which "man is deified, worshipped, and obeyed, not God[;] a person has the right to believe whatever he pleases [and] nothing is sacred." His mentor, Maqdisi, had published a book, *Democracy Is a Religion*, making much the same argument. Lovers of democracy, Zarqawi insisted, were just as ignorant and sinful as the Children of Israel who worshipped the Golden Calf before Moses set them straight.

The Sunni Arab boycott skewed the election results dramatically; in Anbar Province, for example, turnout languished at just 2 percent. Mass nonparticipation left Sunni parties with just 6 seats in the National Assembly, compared to 140 for Ayatollah Sistani's United Iraqi Alliance bloc and 75 for the Kurdistan Alliance. On the other hand, Shia participation was apparently little influenced by threats from Zarqawi and others. Even without the bulk of the Arab Sunni population, turnout across the country, at 58 percent, compared favorably with the 61 percent Americans had achieved in their most recent presidential election three months before—itself a thirty-six-year record. Insurgent attacks did take place; but thanks in part to an unprecedented security operation, with 130,000 Iraqi troops deployed to guard the country's 5,200 polling stations, the militants failed to disrupt the vote in any meaningful way. The result was a government in which most of the major posts, including president and prime minister, were occupied by Kurds or Shia, and a constitutional drafting process in which Sunnis would have disproportionately little input. Sunnis quickly came to rue their decision to boycott the vote; they would not make the same mistake next time, no matter what Zarqawi or anyone might say.

At the same time, the pressure on Zarqawi personally was beginning to ramp up. It emerged that in late 2004, in the aftermath of the recapture of Fallujah by coalition forces, he had actually been arrested in the city by Iraqi police, held for two or three hours, and interrogated. Then, apparently failing to recognize the most wanted terrorist in Iraq, and satisfied with whatever story he had spun for them, the Iraqis had let him go. It was a frustrating moment. But a more sophisticated manhunt was already under way. Following the arrest of Saddam Hussein in December 2003, and the capture or killing of many of the regime henchmen depicted on the notorious deck of playing cards handed out to coalition troops, many of the special operators, intelligence agents, and other assets previously engaged in that pursuit were free to focus on tracking down Zarqawi.

On February 20, 2005, someone in Zarqawi's organization tipped off U.S. forces that the emir was due to attend a meeting in Ramadi and would be getting there by pickup truck along a particular stretch of riverside highway. As they got into their vehicle, Zarqawi and his driver must have missed the tiny speck of an RQ-7 Shadow reconnaissance drone, high above, recording their every move. Somewhere along the highway, Delta Force operators threw up a roadblock in his path, but the pickup charged through. With the Deltas in hot pursuit, Zarqawi's vehicle now approached a second checkpoint, manned by Army Rangers. One of the Americans trained a heavy machine gun on the rapidly approaching truck. The gunner requested permission to open fire, but his commanding officer, no doubt haunted by the possibility of yet more civilian casualties, wanted a positive ID. It was too late. The pickup sped past this second group of Americans, close enough for them to note Zarqawi's Blackhawk tactical vest, his American assault weapon, and the look of panic on his face. The Deltas were now only a few seconds behind. Zarqawi could be heard screaming at his driver to exit the highway onto a side road, then to stop the truck. He leapt out of the pickup and fled on foot into a town. Out of the vehicle, the Americans seized the driver, a laptop with a "treasure trove" of information, and $100,000 in cash. But the Emir of the Strangers was gone.

Three months later, in Qaim, a desert town in Anbar Province a stone's throw from the Syrian border, his hideout took a hit from a U.S. air strike. Zarqawi was wounded, apparently seriously enough to require hospitalization. An al-Qaeda in Iraq spokesman urged followers to "[p]ray for the healing of our Sheikh Abu Musab al-Zarqawi for an injury he suffered in the path of God." Later, Iraqi and U.S. forces reportedly stormed the hospital in Ramadi where he was being treated. Once again, however, Zarqawi disappeared. A week after the air strike, in a public audio message addressed to bin Laden, he brushed off rumors that he had been critically wounded or even killed, assuring supporters that, "[m]y wounds were light." He signed off with unusual subservience: "From a private to a commander."

In reality, his relationship with the al-Qaeda leadership was far from supplicatory—or stable. While Zarqawi crisscrossed Iraq by road, meeting with local commanders, recording vitriolic audio statements, furtively avoiding detection by airborne or ground-level spies, bin Laden and Zawahiri crouched impassively in their Pakistani safe houses, brooding over the news delivered by al-Qaeda's network of couriers and growing more agitated by the day. Never had the contrast in temperament between bin Laden and Zarqawi been clearer or more consequential. Al-Qaeda had no use for a sectarian bloodbath, still less an insurgency that appeared to go out of its way to alienate the Iraqi public with its brutalizing methods; Zarqawi's reckless conduct threatened to create both. And yet he still represented al-Qaeda's only foothold in what by 2005 had become one of the most important theaters of jihad worldwide. The rank and file adored him, and his swagger and fury, however antagonizing to the top brass, were good for recruitment. Dealing with him was a delicate matter for al-Qaeda. Bin Laden had become so vexed with the issue that he had created a committee of senior operatives to figure out how to handle it. Sometime during 2005, he assigned Abdul Hadi al-Iraqi, the only Iraqi on al-Qaeda's *shura* council, as a liaison who might talk some sense into Zarqawi.

It surprised virtually no one that al-Iraqi failed to make much progress. In July 2005, Ayman al-Zawahiri sent Zarqawi a cease and desist letter. Missives among the upper echelon, still hand-delivered by courier, had become an art from of their own. With Edwardian politesse, Zawahiri began by propitiating Zarqawi with praise for his historic and God-given mission. Then he got down to brass tacks. He could only observe from afar, he wrote. But that did give him the advantage of perspective. In contrast to Zarqawi's reckless approach of lashing out in all directions at once, Zawahiri offered a chillingly intricate sequential analysis of the conflict:

> The jihad in Iraq requires several incremental goals. The first stage: Expel the Americans from Iraq.... The second stage: Establish an Islamic authority or emirate.... The third stage: Extend the jihad wave to the secular countries neighboring Iraq. The fourth stage (it may coincide with what came before): The clash with Israel.

Based on this analysis, clearly Iraq was still in the first stage. What was needed was a leader who could unite all Muslims against the American occupation. The mujahideen must maintain popular support and "avoid any action that the masses do not understand or approve." There was a salutary lesson, Zawahiri wrote, in the fate of the Taliban, who had systematically alienated most of the Afghan population and then found that they had few supporters when the Americans invaded. Zarqawi should not dwell on arcane theological differences with mainstream Sunni clerics. He would do well to remember that his own hero, Nur ad-Din Zangi, followed the Ashari school—a relatively tolerant and broadminded creed, much criticized by the more rigid Salafis and Wahhabis. Moreover, he should stop releasing those gruesome beheading videos—"scenes of slaughter," Zawahiri called them—because the people would never find these "palatable." Besides, it would be just as easy to "kill the captives by bullet."

Above all, Zawahiri told Zarqawi, he should stop attacking the Shia, however wrongheaded and dangerous they may be. These actions served only to alienate the majority of Sunnis and distract attention from the main task of defeating the Americans. Whatever guilt Shia clerics and leaders might bear, scholars agreed that ordinary Shia were forgiven because of their "ignorance." Moreover, there was no practical way of meting out death to every Shia in Iraq, so sectarian killings would merely alienate a powerful plurality of Iraqis. Besides, al-Qaeda needed to keep the Iranian regime on-side if they were to stand any chance of releasing their comrades held prisoner there. In short, there was little to be lost in refraining from attacking the Shia, and much to be gained.

Considering the scope of Zarqawi's transgressions, this was a very mild rebuke indeed. But it had been a long time in coming. Zawahiri was not the only senior figure to complain. Around the same time, Abu Mohammed al-Maqdisi gave an interview to Al Jazeera in which he pointed out that even Zarqawi's fiery, fundamentalist idol, the medieval scholar Ibn Taymiyyah, had stopped short of declaring every Shia Muslim an unbeliever. "Even if our Sunni brothers in Iraq have many justifications," Maqdisi told Al Jazeera, "this does not justify blowing up mosques. . . . Permitting the blood of the Shiites is a mistake in which jihad fighters had best not become entangled." Around a week later, Maqdisi gave another interview, this time to the pan-Arab daily newspaper *Al Hayat*, in which he added that suicide bombings were not permissible "if the jihad fighter could kill the enemy with a Kalashnikov or a pistol."

These rebukes stung Zarqawi but failed to induce the hoped-for repentance. He described Maqdisi's renewed criticism as "a new arrow aimed at our hearts." On suicide bombings, he averred that he had agreed "when I was in Afghanistan during the Communist invasion" but had changed his mind during his second tour in 1999. "Not only did I adopt the idea that [suicide bombings] are permissible," he said, "but I see fit to advocate them as commendable." To the warnings about fighting the Shia, Zarqawi paid even less heed. In fact, he was about to double down on his call for sectarian warfare.

. . .

In the spring of 2005, al-Qaeda in Iraq seemed to have found itself a new Fallujah: Tal Afar, a largely Turkmen town in the far north of the country, about one-quarter Shia and the rest Sunni; natives of the city would later fill some of the top leadership spots in the Islamic State of Iraq. AQI took advantage of the sectarian divide to carve Tal Afar into what one American commander called two "armed camps in direct military competition with one another." Al-Qaeda terrorists would abduct and behead Shia, leaving their bodies outside the Ottoman castle where the town's entirely Shia police force had taken shelter. The police, for their part, reciprocated in kind, dispatching what have been called "death squads" to cut down Sunnis. By late summer, the spiraling violence had become intolerable. On September 3, U.S. troops entered the old city—al-Qaeda's stronghold—with overwhelming force. American ground forces crept across rooftops so as not to set off explosive traps left for them in the streets below, while Apache gunships rained rocket fire on the al-Qaeda positions from above. At the height of the battle, which he monitored from a safe house well clear of the front lines, Zarqawi issued a face-saving statement: "Martyrdom operations are ongoing at Tal-Afar; in addition to planting explosive devices, and luring the enemy into street fights[,] [we are] avoiding civilian casualties between Muslim women and children. We withdrew from some neighborhoods just for this purpose alone."

In truth, what al-Qaeda was facing in Tal Afar was nothing less than a rout. American commanders put the number of dead fighters at 151; the rest, as in Fallujah one year before, had fled. Once again, Zarqawi blamed the defeat on the Shia, whom he accused of declaring war on Sunnis and of carrying out atrocities including the rape of Sunni women. He used the defeat at Tal Afar as an excuse for his own public declaration of "all-out warfare against all Shiites in Iraq." He warned his adversaries, "Take care, for we swear that we shall offer you no mercy."

The response was swift and damning—even from vocally pro-insurgent Sunni clerics. The Association of Muslim Scholars in Iraq called Zarqawi's declaration "dangerous" and demanded that he retract his threats, lest they "damage the image of jihad . . . and lead to further bloodshed of innocent Iraqis." The jihadi theorist Abu Basir al-Tartusi, echoing Zawahiri and Maqdisi, said that he knew of no "highly regarded *ulama* [clerics] of Islam who have issued a fatwa permitting the killing of any Shiite merely because he is a Shiite." Some Iraqi Sunnis now openly defied Zarqawi. When al-Qaeda in Iraq put up posters threatening to behead anyone who voted in the upcoming constitutional referendum, imams in Dhuluiya, north of Baghdad, went around the town tearing the notices down and ripping them into shreds.

Still, Zarqawi refused to repent. An al-Qaeda in Iraq statement published on October 21 said, "We do not understand why this ferocious campaign against mujahideen is occurring at the present time. This is exactly what the cross worshippers and their collaborators [a reference to the Americans and the Iraqis who worked with them] want to see." Within a month, al-Qaeda suicide bombers had struck two Shia mosques in Khanaqin, a town northeast of Baghdad close to the Iranian frontier, killing at least seventy-four worshippers as they knelt for Friday prayers. Attacks like these infuriated the al-Qaeda establishment. But in a sense, Zarqawi was merely giving his backers what they demanded. On the one hand, the Assad regime, which facilitated al-Qaeda in Iraq operationally, was delighted with the chaos Zarqawi was able to create using fighters supplied through the Syrian pipeline. On the other, the wealthy Saudis and others who lined Zarqawi's pockets were desperate to ensure that Iraq did not fall into the hands of the Shia, who were sure to align themselves with Iran and against Saudi Arabia. Such donors evidently saw horrific violence against innocent Shia Muslims as the way to ensure that this outcome did not materialize.

. . .

At the same time, Zarqawi continued to nurse his hatred against his oldest enemy, the Jordanian state. In August, his operatives in the port of Aqaba in the southwest of the country had fired a number of missiles from a World War Two–era Soviet Katyusha truck-mounted rocket launcher. One had killed a Jordanian soldier and narrowly missed two U.S. Navy ships in the harbor; another had landed over the border on a road in Israel, wounding a taxi driver. But this paled in comparison to what was to come. On November 9, suicide bombers sent by Zarqawi staged a far bigger assault in Amman, blowing themselves up at three hotels and killing sixty people—the vast majority of them Jordanian Sunni Arabs. The deadliest blast, at the Radisson—the same hotel that would have been targeted in the failed Millennium plot—tore through a wedding reception, killing almost forty guests, including the fathers of the bride and groom. The two suicide bombers assigned to the Radisson were themselves a married couple from Fallujah. In a room full of joyous singing and dancing, the male terrorist unleashed a deadly burst of fire and shrapnel. "Everything was white at our wedding," the groom later recalled. "But it all turned red because of the blood."

Within twenty-four hours, al-Qaeda in Iraq had claimed responsibility for the Amman atrocities. The group said the attacks had been aimed at "some of the dens that have been implanted in the land of the Muslims . . . some of the hotels that the tyrant of Jordan had converted into a back yard for the enemies of the religion." What Zarqawi seemed to be alleging was that the hotels had been targeted because they accommodated Western officials. It was a claim that fooled almost no one; instead, Jordanians immediately recognized the attacks for what they really were: a savage, cowardly assault on the softest of targets. A few days after the bombings, 100,000 people took to the streets of Amman in protest. Jordanians shouted that Zarqawi was a "coward" who deserved to "burn in Hell." Once again, Abu Mohammed al-Maqdisi gave an interview to Al Jazeera condemning his former protégé.

Evidently alarmed at the scale of the revulsion, Zarqawi went into full public relations damage-control mode. In a written statement issued a day later, he asserted that the hotels were "centers for waging war against Islam and for supporting the Crusader presence in Mesopotamia and the Arabian Peninsula, and supporting the presence of the Jews in Palestine [and] the favorite work locations for [foreign] intelligence services." Later, he claimed that the deaths of Jordanian Sunnis were "an unintended and unexpected occurrence." Addressing his fellow Jordanians directly, he added: "If we wanted to spill your blood, God forbid, it would have been simpler by far to have those martyrs blow themselves up in public places where hundreds of people congregate and present such easy targets, such as the Hashimiyah Square, the al-Abdali complex, or commercial centers, such as the Safeway, etc."

Osama bin Laden, for his part, is said to have been "furious" about the bombings. But given Zarqawi's importance to the jihad in Iraq, it was still too risky to allow this frustration to show in al-Qaeda's public pronouncements. On November 18, the very day tens of thousands of Jordanians marched in protest, an al-Qaeda mouthpiece, the Global Islamic Media Front, characterized Zarqawi as one of the "commanders of the global jihad," standing alongside Ayman al-Zawahiri, Mullah Omar, and bin Laden.

In private, al-Qaeda severely rebuked its wayward commander. Mahmud, the former senior member of the Libyan Islamic Fighting Group who was subsequently to serve as bin Laden's factotum, wrote to Zarqawi in December expressing concerns similar to those Zawahiri had raised a few months earlier. Mahmud was an old acquaintance of Zarqawi's from his Herat days, and unlike Zawahiri, he did not seem concerned with wounding Zarqawi's pride. Zarqawi's "perilous and ruinous" conduct, Mahmud wrote, was producing "corruption and havoc." He bluntly "commanded" the Jordanian to "remedy the deficiency." As a subordinate, Zarqawi must consult the leadership before making big decisions, by which Mahmud meant

declaring war against the Shia and expanding the jihad to neighboring countries like Jordan. He must forthwith send emissaries
to Waziristan to meet with al-Qaeda's leaders. This was, Mahmud
wrote, "more important than preparing and sending the brothers for
some operations like the recent operation of the hotels in Amman!
Truly, I am not joking." Once again, this dispute prefigured later
conflicts within al-Qaeda; eight years later, Zawahiri was to order
Zarqawi's successor, Abu Bakr al-Baghdadi, to keep his own operations within Iraq and let al-Nusra take care of Syria. His wishes
would largely be ignored.

In his desperation to rein in Zarqawi's damaging conduct, Mahmud seemed out of his depth, his demands taking on an almost far-
cical tone. He ordered Zarqawi to stop killing and alienating Sunni
tribal leaders and scholars who did not agree with him. Instead,
Zarqawi must consult with them, "win them over . . . say nice
things." It was supremely important that the people view the mujahideen with affection, not "merely [as] people of killing, slaughter,
blood, cursing, insult, and harshness." Mahmud urged Zarqawi to
"leave the path of excuses" and take steps to rein in his behavior.
Finally, he issued a threat:

> [A]nyone who commits tyranny and aggression upon the people,
> and causes corruption within the land and drives people away
> from us and our faith and our jihad and from the religion and
> the message that we carry, then he must be taken to task, and we
> must direct him to what is right, just, and for the best. Other-
> wise, we would have to push him aside and keep him away from
> the sphere of influence and replace him and so forth, for this is
> an important matter.

The considered, consultative approach Mahmud advocated was
laughably far removed from the intentions of al-Qaeda's most unruly
operative. Two months later, massive explosions ripped apart the

gilded dome of the Golden Mosque in Samarra—one of Shia Islam's holiest places—killing dozens of people and setting off a tidal wave of reprisals that would claim thousands more lives across the country.

As Iraq stared into the abyss, Zarqawi's status in the insurgency became less and less clear. In January of 2006, one month before the golden dome fell, al-Qaeda in Iraq joined five other insurgent groups to form an entity called the Mujahideen Shura Council. Leadership of the council was placed in the hands of an Iraqi, Abdullah bin Rashid al-Baghdadi—said to be the same man who, as Omar al-Baghdadi, was to become the first emir of the Islamic State of Iraq. Formally at least, Zarqawi was excluded from the council's top table. But al-Qaeda in Iraq was still the council's most powerful member group; indeed, some of the council's statements were still issued on al-Qaeda in Iraq letterhead. Among foreign terrorists in Iraq, the Emir of the Strangers remained the most respected jihadist in the country. One veteran jihadi would later claim that Zarqawi had been forced to step down as leader of the foreign fighters sometime in March. But the next month, Zarqawi issued a video, the first in which he is known to have appeared, announcing that the council would be "the starting point for establishing an Islamic State": "We hope to God that within three months from now the environment will be favorable for us to announce an Islamic emirate."

· · ·

Abu Musab al-Zarqawi made many enemies with his reckless campaign to pit Sunni against Shia in Iraq. But in the end, his most potent enemy would prove to be the Sunnis themselves. To an outside observer, Zarqawi seemed to go out of his way to alienate Sunni leaders, particularly tribal sheikhs. In February of 2005, he openly accused tribal elders of "stand[ing] as a stumbling block in the path of jihad" and threatened reprisals. Later, he made good on these threats, assassinating dozens of leaders and moderate Sunni clerics. Over the course of that year, Sunnis began to retaliate. The murder of one local sheikh prompted his tribe to round up, try, and publicly execute several foreign members of al-Qaeda in Iraq. An Iraqi intelligence official told the *New York Times*, "The tribes are fed up with al-Qaeda and they will not tolerate any more."

Meanwhile, AQI had also begun assassinating more moderate Sunni religious figures, in a campaign known as the Culture of the Silencers for the weapons typically used to carry out the killings. In Anbar Province between 2005 and 2007, the group murdered around 250 scholars, clerics, and *khatibs* (preachers who deliver Friday sermons). Hamza al-Isawi, the grand imam of Fallujah, a scholar well known throughout Iraq for his religious writings, spoke out against extremism during his Friday sermon. The same day, he was shot dead. In Ramadi, gunmen killed a local imam, Abdul Alim al-Saadi, the brother of the grand mufti of Iraq. Militants attempted to assassinate Dr. Khalid Sulaiman al-Fahdawi, a popular member of parliament formerly in charge of Sunni religious endowments in Anbar, and succeeded in killing two of his bodyguards. (Fahdawi himself would later be assassinated in a suicide bombing at a Sunni mosque in Baghdad in 2011.)

Sunnis of all persuasions, as well as a number of fellow militants, grew appalled at AQI's excesses. Groups including Ansar al-Sunna wrote repeatedly to bin Laden himself, warning the emir of the damage being done to his cause. These groups would eventually join together in the Jihad and Reform Front, with the express purpose of opposing the Islamic State of Iraq. From the latter half of 2005 onward, in a movement later known as the Sunni Awakening, Sunni tribes began cooperating with the Iraqi government and even the Americans to rid their territories of foreign fighters, including al-Qaeda in Iraq. By the end of January 2006, the movement had led to the arrest of some 270 foreigners in Anbar Province alone. So traumatized was AQI by this experience that to this day, its successors in the Islamic State justify killing opposition Sunnis by branding them as agents of al-Sahwa—Arabic for "awakening."

During the first few months of 2006, the coalition task force hunting Zarqawi carried out dozens of further raids, killing or arresting hundreds more suspects, including many of Zarqawi's closest lieutenants. On April 16, the Jordanian was reportedly within a couple of blocks of a safe house in Yusufiyah, south of Baghdad, when U.S. Special Forces attacked in the small hours of the morning. The Americans fought room by room, killing five al-Qaeda operatives and arresting five more. Once again, Zarqawi escaped. But one of those detained was familiar with the elaborate security protocol around meetings between Zarqawi and his "spiritual adviser," a man known as Sheikh al-Rahman. After a few days of questioning, the prisoner divulged what would prove to be a critical piece of intelligence. Whenever he went to see Zarqawi, the man said, Rahman would change cars a number of times. But when he climbed into a "small blue car," his next stop would be with the Jordanian.

As the noose tightened, Zarqawi's behavior became increasingly neurotic. He spouted hadith nonstop and followed more and more closely what he took to be the personal habits of Muhammad, down to cleaning his teeth with a twig, scenting his body with musk, and keeping to what he believed were the same waking and sleeping hours as the Prophet. Zarqawi's carefully cultivated tough-guy pose was beginning to wear thin. After the Yusufiyah raid, the United States released a captured "blooper reel" from his April video message, showing him wearing black pajamas with white New Balance sneakers and a black do-rag, amateurishly swinging a loaded machine gun around, and requiring the assistance of a masked helper to perform the elementary operation of clearing the weapon's chamber.

On June 7, the coalition's eyes in the sky spotted Rahman getting into a small blue car, just as the man captured in Yusufiyah had said he would. Rahman was driven to Hibhib, a village north of Baghdad, where he went into a steel-frame concrete house in the middle of a date palm plantation. A satellite phone trace confirmed that the Jordanian was there. As there was no time to lose, American F-16s, already patrolling above, were scrambled to deliver the killing blow. One of them dropped laser- and satellite-guided bombs collectively weighing half a ton, reducing the building to dust almost instanta- neously. Zarqawi and Rahman, coalition sources told the media, would have had no warning of the strike. Yet incredibly, when Delta Force commandos reached the site, Zarqawi was still alive and semi- conscious. Feebly, he struggled to escape, but the soldiers strapped him to a gurney. Inside his battered body, the tissue of his lungs had been fatally bruised and ripped in the blast. Blood sputtered from his mouth. Then his heart gave out. Zarqawi's fresh corpse was taken to the nearby Balad Airbase for identification and postmortem exam- ination. An American commander delivered an epitaph of sorts over the blasted body, saying laconically, "That's one dead son of a bitch."

. . .

"The Wedding of the Martyr and Hero Abu Musab al-Zarqawi," read a white banner above a tent sheltering several dozen gray plas- tic patio chairs. The "wedding" in question, on a street in Zarqa, Jordan, was between the dead terrorist and the several "dark-eyed companions, chaste as virgin pearls" whose company he was, even now, supposedly enjoying in the afterlife. In truth, even in Zarqawi's native city, opinion on him was divided; while some residents did indeed regard him as a hero, others castigated him as a thug who brought shame on their town. "May God burn him in hell," one of them told an American reporter.

No doubt the feelings of the al-Qaeda leadership were similarly mixed. Zarqawi's own wife had described her husband as "nothing more than a soldier in the ranks of bin Laden's armies," while Osama bin Laden pronounced himself "deeply saddened," calling Zarqawi "a lion in Islam" and a "role model for future generations." In real- ity, given all the trouble he had caused, al-Qaeda probably hoped never to see an operative like him again. They could have wished for more biddable underlings.

Shortly before Zarqawi died, a Jordanian official had predicted, "There is no such thing as Zarqawism. What Zarqawi is will die with him." Unfortunately, this proved false. As distasteful and brutal as it may be, there was such a thing as Zarqawism, and it endured long after its author sputtered his last breath on a stretcher in Hibhib. Zarqawi had wanted to foment sectarian violence, and by the time of his death, he had succeeded in doing so on a massive scale; the years 2006 and 2007 would prove the bloodiest since the conflict began, a record that has not been surpassed, despite the excesses of the Islamic State. In particular, Zarqawi's wanton destruction of the Golden Mosque had triggered a chain reaction of revenge and counter-revenge that claimed the lives of thousands of people. As the then-commander of U.S. Special Forces, General Stanley McChrystal, lamented, "We had killed Zarqawi too late."

And what of the other component of Zarqawi's agenda, the creation of a new caliphate? That would take longer, to be sure. But the form, if not the reality, was in place soon after his death. In October 2006, al-Qaeda in Iraq again joined with other jihadi groups to form the Islamic State of Iraq and pledge *bayat* to Emir Abu Omar al-Baghdadi. This was the same group that would become the Islamic State of Iraq and the Levant in 2013 and simply the Islamic State in 2014, when it proclaimed itself the reborn caliphate. Through every stage in its life cycle, Zarqawi's ideology of murderous rage and blind hatred has been the organization's lifeblood. Its magazine, *Dabiq*, takes its name from a saying attributed to Zarqawi that is reproduced on the masthead of every issue. The Islamic State's official spokesman, Abu Mohammed al-Adnani, a Syrian who pledged *bayat* to Zarqawi in the very earliest days of the conflict, describes his mentor's pronouncements as the definitive word on Shia Muslims. Abu Bakr al-Baghdadi, the Islamic State's second leader and first "caliph," traces a direct line from Tawhid wal Jihad through al-Qaeda in Iraq and the Mujahideen Shura Council to the Islamic State. "The path that [Zarqawi] trod," he has written, "those who came after him followed its course.

And we, God willing, are following in their footsteps. . . . [T]hey have drawn for us a way that doesn't recognize borders and sketched for us a methodology that doesn't belong to a nation or race[,] and its journey of ascent does not stop."

"This is the story of the whole war," said one of the U.S. intelligence operators responsible for hunting down Zarqawi. "Kill this one guy, and it will make things all better. I still don't understand where this notion comes from."

CHAPTER 5

DOCTOR, WISE MAN, TEACHER, TRAITOR

While Abu Musab al-Zarqawi sowed chaos in Iraq, and later, as the posthumous consequences of his reign played out, the al-Qaeda organization at large was undergoing a transformation of historic proportions. It was changing from a single, centralized, hierarchical institution into a web of affiliates, each enjoying a level of autonomy bin Laden would never have tolerated before 9/11. As to the upshot of this phase shift, opinions vary, even within the organization itself. "We have become an idea and we are no longer a group," was one senior militant's skeptical appraisal; but that assessment does not account for the network's continuing ability to work together to wreak destruction. Ayman al-Zawahiri probably came closer to the mark when he said that, following the changes in its structure, "al-Qaeda is a message before it is an organization." The message is both potent and dangerous; but so, even today, is the organization.

Zawahiri was in a position to know. When American bullets finally found Osama bin Laden in May 2011, Zawahiri, previously bin Laden's deputy, suddenly became the ringmaster, charged with taming al-Qaeda's menagerie of far-flung and exotic affiliates. His complex personality is one of the keys to understanding the huge changes and challenges al-Qaeda has faced since bin Laden's death. Like many prominent jihadis, Zawahiri possesses a character riddled with apparent contradictions. Having been a pious, eager student who abhorred violence, Zawahiri wound up ordering suicide bombings and justifying the wanton destruction of innocent lives, including those of children. Trained as a surgeon, he traveled halfway around the world out of compassion for desperate Afghan refugees, only to begin plotting to use their country as a base for violent jihad. So fervent is he about the practice of *sujud*—bowing to the floor in worship—that a dark, irregular callus has developed on his forehead; yet his long history of murder and betrayal in the service of his own political interests could scarcely be further from this image of prostrate piety. To his family, he is a doting father. Former underlings remember him as approachable, good-humored, and easygoing, with a winning smile. But to those who defy him, including his fellow jihadis, he can be lethal. Despite his carefully cultivated reputation as a grand strategist, much of his fifty-year militant career has been a story of dismal failure. In al-Qaeda, he has been known as doctor, wise man, and teacher; the Islamic State simply calls him a traitor.

Above all, Ayman al-Zawahiri is unshakably committed to violence in preference to politics as a means to achieving his ends. "There is no solution without jihad," he has argued, describing "all other methods" as having failed. "If I fall as a martyr in the defense of Islam," he reasoned, "my son Mohammed will avenge me. But if I am finished politically and I spend my time arguing with governments about some partial solutions, what will motivate my son to take up my weapons after I have sold them in the bargains market?" Compromise, according to Zawahiri, leaves nothing but "a legacy of despair." Ironically, Zawahiri's son would himself become a victim of his father's violent intransigence when he was killed in a coalition air strike in Afghanistan.

To other points of view, Zawahiri is simply closed; he is fond of quoting Sayyid Qutb, one of the leading Muslim Brotherhood theorists, as saying, "Brother, push ahead, for your path is soaked in blood. Do not turn your head right or left but look only up to heaven." At the same time, he has condemned the Brotherhood for renouncing violence and accepting the people, alongside God, as a possible source of authority in a modern state; in Zawahiri's world-view, everyone fights either under God's banner or that of Satan. Through a hopelessly distorted interpretation of U.S. foreign policy and of democracy itself, he makes every citizen of the West into a legitimate terrorist target:

> *Regardless of the method by which [Western] governments obtain the votes of the people, voters in the Western countries ultimately cast their votes willingly. These peoples have willingly called for, supported, and backed the establishment and survival of the State of Israel . . . the fruit of a tree watered by hatred of Islam and the Muslims for several centuries. . . . [T]he West, led by the United States . . . does not know the language of ethics, morality, and legitimate rights. They only know the language of interests backed by brute military force. Therefore, if we wish to have a dialogue with them and make them aware of our rights, we must talk to them in the language that they understand.*

This wording closely mirrors a statement Zawahiri made in 1998, promising to respond to the arrest of his followers in Albania "in the only language [the United States] will understand." The next day, truck bombs exploded at two U.S. embassies in East Africa, killing more than two hundred people.

For all his fire-and-brimstone rhetoric, however, Zawahiri enjoys none of the charisma of his predecessor. On the contrary, with his intransigence and rudeness, he reliably alienates almost everyone he comes into contact with. A close associate of Zawahiri's back in Egypt, noticing "something missing" in his friend, reportedly told him, "No matter what group you belong to, you cannot be its leader."

. . .

On the social ladder, Ayman al-Zawahiri started high. His great-grandfather came from Saudi Arabia. Eventually settling in Tanta, Egypt's fifth largest city, he founded a mosque there that is named after him to this day. Ayman was the product of not one but two families of great distinction. His maternal grandfather served as president of Cairo University and Egypt's ambassador to Pakistan, Yemen, and Saudi Arabia. A great-uncle on his father's side was imam of the tenth-century Fatimid al-Azhar mosque and rector of its affiliated university. Another, on his mother's side, was the founding secretary general of the Arab League. Ayman's father, a university professor, had a reputation for being charmingly absentminded.

Ayman al-Zawahiri was born in June 1951. He and a twin sister grew up in a well-to-do suburb of Cairo called Maadi. As a child, he spent a brief period in Pakistan while his grandfather was ambassador there. His uncle Mahfouz was a student of the founder of modern Salafism, the dissident author Sayyid Qutb, and later served as Qutb's legal counsel. The young Zawahiri learned a great deal about Qutb and his uncompromising philosophy from the stories Uncle Mahfouz told of the great man. In school, Zawahiri was a gifted student and showed his piety from a young age by reading the works of Qutb and other Islamist scholars. Reportedly, he refused to participate in roughhousing with the other boys and regarded contact sports as "inhumane." According to a former classmate, he displayed a level of shrewdness well beyond his years: "He was extremely intelligent, and all the teachers respected him. He had a very systematic way of thinking, like that of an older guy. He could understand in five minutes what it would take other students an hour to understand. I would call him a genius."

When Zawahiri was in his mid-teens, the secular socialist government of Gamal Abdel Nasser began a crackdown on Islamists, especially the Muslim Brotherhood, of whose membership some seventeen thousand were arrested. The crackdown culminated in 1966 with the execution of Uncle Mahfouz's mentor, Sayyid Qutb. That same year, at the age of only fifteen, Zawahiri formed his first jihadist cell at his high school with his brother Mohammed. Both would eventually find their way into the terrorist organization that became Egyptian Islamic Jihad, or EIJ.

In September 1970, President Nasser, his reputation shattered by Egypt's humiliation in the Six-Day War, died of a heart attack at the age of fifty-two. He was succeeded by his vice president, Anwar Sadat. The new regime was inclined to much greater tolerance toward Islamists; Sadat seems to have assumed that by striking a deal with the weary old guard of Muslim Brothers, he could pacify the entire Islamist movement. In this he was mistaken; whatever the old-timers might have said or advised, the younger generation was still out for blood. Thus, as Zawahiri would later recall, Sadat's misguided policy "let the genie out of the bottle." As if to antagonize militant Islamists still further, within a few years of his accession Sadat began aligning Egyptian foreign policy with that of the United States and making peace overtures to Israel. These moves were to exert a profound influence on the thinking of young radicals like Ayman al-Zawahiri.

Outwardly, the future emir of al-Qaeda seemed to be living the sort of charmed life his intelligence and social privilege opened up for him. In 1974, he graduated cum laude from Cairo University's Medical School. Following three years of military service as an army surgeon, he obtained a master's degree in surgery in 1978 and set up his own general surgery clinic on a floor of his parents' duplex in Cairo. Beneath the surface, however, Zawahiri pursued violence. In 1975, while serving in the Egyptian Army, he seized control of his

EIJ cell after its former leader fled to Germany. Around the same time, he made contact with bin Laden's future mentor, the Palestinian theologian Abdullah Azzam, who had come to Cairo to pursue a PhD in Islamic studies at al-Azhar, the university of which Zawahiri's great-uncle had once been rector. Azzam's theology helped shape Zawahiri's own rapidly developing extremism. Though still only twenty-four years old, Zawahiri was no young man in a hurry; he was prepared to bide his time until conditions were right for a successful and sustainable Islamist takeover of Egypt's government. But within a few years, history would show that not every EIJ cell was capable of such patience.

In 1980, Zawahiri was doing locum work in a Muslim Brotherhood clinic in Cairo. One day, the clinic's director asked him if he would like to go to Pakistan to assist refugees from the fighting in neighboring Afghanistan, which the Red Army had invaded months before. Zawahiri duly traveled to Peshawar, a city a few dozen miles from the Khyber Pass that was already becoming a hub for those displaced by the conflict and a way station for fighters heading in the opposite direction. Joining Zawahiri in Peshawar were an anesthetist and a plastic surgeon; they claimed to be the first three Arabs to participate in the Afghan relief efforts. Conditions in the clinic where they served were terrible, and the facility was so poorly equipped that Zawahiri occasionally found himself dressing wounds with honey instead of modern disinfectant—a technique he learned from *al-tibb al-nabawi*, the "prophetic medicine" used by many jihadis, including, as we have seen, bin Laden. On at least one occasion, he ventured across the border with Afghan tribesmen to see firsthand the heroism of the mujahideen, desperately battling the Soviet juggernaut with no air support and rifles that had been obsolete for decades; not for another five years would the CIA's shoulder-mounted missiles arrive to turn the tables on the Russians.

While he was in Peshawar, Zawahiri had another insight: The lawless mountains of Pakistan and Afghanistan might serve as a staging ground for jihad elsewhere. As he wrote in his 2001 memoir, *Knights Under the Prophet's Banner*:

> *I saw this [trip] as an opportunity to get to know one of the arenas of jihad that might be a tributary and base for jihad in Egypt.... The problem of finding a secure base for jihad activity in Egypt used to occupy me a lot, in view of the pursuits to which we were subjected by the security forces and because of Egypt's flat terrain which made government control easy, for the River Nile runs in its narrow valley between two deserts that have no vegetation or water.... When I came into contact with the arena of Afghan jihad in 1980, I became aware of its rich potential and realized how much benefit it would bring to the Muslim nation in general, and the jihadi movement in particular.*

A year after his first visit, Zawahiri returned to Peshawar for another tour of duty, all the while taking careful note of the ways in which this jagged region might offer safe haven for Egyptian Islamic Jihad.

. . .

On March 26, 1979, Anwar Sadat stood on the north lawn of the White House to clasp hands on an Egyptian-Israeli peace treaty with Prime Minister Menachem Begin of Israel and U.S. president Jimmy Carter. It was an event that, predictably, sparked outrage among Egypt's Islamists. Determined, as he saw it, to break the insidious link between Islam and politics, Sadat cracked down on Islamic student associations and banned the wearing of the veil on campus. Not long afterward, Ayman al-Zawahiri began helping another member of his cell, Issam al-Qamari, a major in the Egyptian army's armored division, to stockpile weapons for a possible coup attempt. Zawahiri hid some of the guns in his own medical clinic. But he was not interested in quixotic gestures. His vision for Egypt was a Sunni version of Ayatollah Khomeini's recent achievement in Iran—a root-

and-branch replacement of the secular political order with a religious one. He was prepared to wait until the time was right for such a revolution; and as objectionable as Sadat might be, that time had patently not yet arrived. Killing Sadat would be futile at this stage. Not everyone in EIJ shared his view. On June 10, 1981, around a month after Zawahiri returned from his second stint at the clinic in Peshawar, an EIJ cell led by a serving artillery officer, Khalid Islambouli, assassinated Sadat in broad daylight during a military parade. Zawahiri would later claim that he had had no knowledge of the plot until a few hours before Sadat was shot, and that when he found out about it he had voiced his objection, rhetorically asking the member who briefed him on the operation, "Do they want us to shoot up the streets and let the police detain us?" But as a prominent member of EIJ, Zawahiri was rounded up in the ensuing dragnet anyway. In prison, he faced harsh treatment. As he wrote: "The treadmill of torture and repression turned at full speed. . . . [It] broke bones, stripped off skins, shocked nerves, and killed souls. . . . It detained women, committed sexual assaults, and called men feminine names, starved prisoners, gave them bad food, cut off water, and prevented visits to humiliate the detainees."

To save himself from further torment, Zawahiri sold out Major Qamari, the man with whom he had been stockpiling weapons, and turned witness against him. Eventually, Zawahiri was put on trial alongside 301 other defendants. Early on, during a lull in proceedings, he addressed the international television cameras trained on the defendants' thick-barred cage. In fluent English, with an impassioned voice that occasionally cracked into something approaching a scream, he announced that the defendants had been arrested simply for trying to establish an "Islamic state and Islamic society" to take the place of the "dictatorship, corruption, [and] dirty business" of the Sadat regime. Zawahiri and his fellow EIJ operatives, he told the reporters, "are the real Islamic front against Zionism, Communism, and imperialism." He went on to detail the "inhuman treatment" to which he said he and his fellow prisoners had been subjected, even reenacting one of the torture positions in which he said they had been hung over cell doors. At another point in the proceedings, the defendants lifted their garments to show the marks of torture on their bodies—something Sayyid Qutb had done in court twenty years before. "We are not sorry about [what] we have offered for our religion," Zawahiri declaimed. "We have sacrificed, and we are still ready for more sacrifices, until the victory of Islam."

Convicted of the charges against him, Zawahiri was sentenced to three years in prison, most of which he had served by the time the trial finally lumbered to a close. Toward the end of 1984, he was released. He had been a committed jihadist before his arrest; but his experience of prison made his determination as clear and hard as a diamond, and he became more and more convinced of the need for violence as a vector for political change. And he had apparently decided something else in the dungeons of Mubarak's Egypt: that the "real enemy"—as he told an American acquaintance who had converted to Islam—was the United States. Sooner or later, Zawahiri said, a showdown was on the way.

. . .

By 1986, Zawahiri was back in Peshawar, once again treating Afghan refugees. At the same time, he was still looking for a way to rebuild EIJ following the disaster of the Sadat assassination by fulfilling his vision of using Afghanistan and Pakistan as a jihadi base. Occasionally, a famous mujahid financier and recruiter named Osama bin Laden would deliver talks at the hospital where Zawahiri worked. Among other things, bin Laden lectured on the need for a boycott of U.S. goods to show support for the Palestinians. In response, Zawahiri offered the Saudi some free advice: If he intended to take on the United States, bin Laden would need to beef up his personal security. "As of now," cautioned Zawahiri, "you should change the way in which you are guarded. You should alter your entire security system, because your head is now wanted by the Americans and the Jews." This may just have been a ploy to get closer to a potential wealthy benefactor; at any rate, the United States was, as yet, paying little attention to bin Laden. But Zawahiri's warning evidently rattled the Saudi. The trouble was, bin Laden's own organization was not yet equipped to provide the requisite level of security. So Zawahiri helpfully offered the use of his own Egyptian operatives to fill the gap, and as a result, the close cadre of followers around bin Laden soon became predominantly Egyptian.

The meeting between Zawahiri and bin Laden was the beginning of a very dangerous friendship. The two men soon found that their strengths and weaknesses dovetailed neatly—while Zawahiri's organization was full of grizzled veterans but chronically strapped for cash, bin Laden's was firmly in the black financially but still green when it came to fighting. In due time, Zawahiri became not only an important strategic adviser to bin Laden but also, in effect, his personal physician; an important position given the sheikh's repeated bouts of low blood pressure and other ailments, some of them possibly warning signs of the endocrine disorder known as Addison's disease. In the late 1980s, during the Battle of Jalalabad, Zawahiri would come to bin Laden's bedside in his mountain lair to treat him for various debilitating symptoms. Zawahiri continued to supervise aspects of bin Laden's medical care right up until the eve of 9/11.

Yet Zawahiri was not the only one vying for access to bin Laden and his seemingly bottomless coffers. Ever since his prison days, Zawahiri had carried on a war of words with the "Blind Sheikh," Omar Abdul Rahman, who was the leader of Gamaa al-Islamiya, or GI, a rival Egyptian jihadi group. Rahman and Zawahiri had been put on trial and imprisoned alongside each other in the aftermath of Sadat's assassination, but the two leaders' intense enmity had prevented EIJ and GI from becoming allies in the fight against Egypt's secular government. Behind bars, the two emirs vied for overall con-

trol of the movement. In a notorious exchange, Zawahiri told Rahman, blind since childhood, that "the emir cannot be a blind man,"
to which Rahman responded with a phrase that in Arabic sounds
almost identical: "the emir cannot be a prisoner." This exchange
encapsulated an armed standoff between the two organizations that
was to last well over a decade.

Now, both groups had relocated to Pakistan and found themselves competing with each other for bin Laden's largesse. Their feud
escalated, first to scurrilous pamphlets, then to open accusations
of apostasy—a virtual death warrant in the jihadi worldview—and
finally, to outright murder of each other's followers. Zawahiri would
claim victory against the Blind Sheikh, netting far more assistance
from bin Laden than GI ever did. He is also rumored to have van-
quished another of bin Laden's suitors: Abdullah Azzam, the Palestinian scholar whom Zawahiri had encountered in Cairo in the
1970s. Rather than fight Muslim rulers, Azzam wanted to focus
the jihad exclusively on infidel powers like the Soviet Union, and he
worked to persuade bin Laden of the wisdom of his position. At the
time, this was anathema to EIJ, which was still training its fire on
fighting the Mubarak regime. Zawahiri worked to discredit Azzam,
even spreading a rumor that the Palestinian was an American agent.
When Azzam was assassinated by a car bomb in 1989, Ayman al-
Zawahiri, among others, fell under the cloud of suspicion.

By the early 1990s, Zawahiri was firmly in charge of EIJ. At
the same time, he was becoming deeply frustrated at the Islamists'
apparent inability to make any inroads in Egypt. Even the most violent tactics seemed utterly ineffectual. In one typical blunder, EIJ had
planned to assassinate the interior minister in retaliation for government raids on extremist hideouts and radical mosques. The bomb
failed to go off, and the would-be bomber was arrested. In the midst
of his frustration, Zawahiri began his journey away from *takfirism*,
with its concentration on local fights, and toward the more global
brand of jihad advocated by Azzam and bin Laden. In his despera-

tion to rationalize EIJ's failure in Egypt, a new picture began to come into view: an unbroken chain of foreign manipulation of the Muslim world, from revolutionary France through the 1916 Sykes-Picot Agreement—the treaty by which colonial powers set the arbitrary national borders of the modern Middle East—to the establishment of Israel and its alliance with the United States, from the Yom Kippur War of 1973 to the intifada begun in 1987. In the Gulf War of 1990–91 Zawahiri came to see "the transformation of the United States from a mover of events from behind a veil to a direct opponent in its battle against the Muslims." This revelation was to widen the focus of his jihad by an order of magnitude.

. . .

During the early 1990s, just like his Saudi benefactor, Zawahiri moved his organization's base of operations to Islamist-ruled Sudan. Bin Laden gave him a quarter of a million dollars to set up a camp north of Khartoum. This and several other donations from the Saudi notwithstanding, EIJ still struggled with money. In 1993, traveling under an assumed name, Zawahiri made a brief fund-raising tour of mosques in California, but the proceeds of this trip were disappointing, amounting to perhaps no more than a few hundred dollars. With EIJ in constant danger of financial collapse, Zawahiri despairingly confided in one of his lieutenants that the only option was ever closer union with bin Laden's organization. Indeed, as time went on, more and more of EIJ's members found themselves being paid not by EIJ itself but out of al-Qaeda coffers. Not everyone in EIJ saw this as a wholly beneficent arrangement. As one disgruntled member of the organization's governing *shura* council would tell Zawahiri, "He who owns my food owns my decisions." But it seemed that the two groups' galaxies were fated to collide, and Zawahiri, whose attention was in any case shifting to the global jihad espoused by bin Laden, was increasingly content to let it happen.

Operationally, too, EIJ faced setbacks. One of the biggest came in

1993, when the Egyptian authorities arrested the group's membership director, along with a computer that contained a database of every EIJ member in the world. As a result, eight hundred suspects were arrested, decimating EIJ's capacity to operate inside its own home country. EIJ's response, a second attempt to assassinate the interior minister, flopped again when shrapnel from the blast was absorbed by a large stack of files on the car seat next to the minister—possibly one of the few occasions on which overwork has actually saved a person's life.

Three months later, EIJ operatives tried again, this time attempting to assassinate Egypt's prime minister, Atef Sidqi, as his convoy drove past a girls' school in Cairo. Not only did the prime minister survive unscathed; the bomb killed a schoolgirl, who was crushed beneath a door thrown by the force of the explosion. Facing a public relations catastrophe, Zawahiri tried to pay blood money to the girl's family. He proffered the lame excuse that the militants sent to survey the site thought that the school was under construction, when in fact it was only undergoing repairs. In a clear echo of Ibn Taymiyyah's fourteenth-century justification of indiscriminate attacks against the Mongol rulers of Iraq and Syria, Zawahiri wrote:

> *The unintended death of this innocent child pained us all, but we were helpless and we had to fight the government. . . . We had warned the people several times before . . . to stay away from the pillars of the regime, their homes, and the routes they used. . . . [T]hese officials are mixed with the public and they take cover behind them. So we have no choice but to hit them while cautioning the general public. . . . If we want to put the issue of [the deceased girl] in perspective, we must weigh her on one scale of the balance and put on the other scale our daughters and women who have lost their fathers and husbands for no reason other than that their fathers and husbands were performing the most honorable duty, the duty of jihad for the sake of God.*

The Egyptian public was scandalized. Protests erupted at the girl's funeral, with mourners chanting, "Terrorism is the enemy of God."

It may be a mark of the desperation EIJ felt following this series of hammer blows that, in April of 1995, Zawahiri agreed to work with his former archrivals, Gamaa al-Islamiya, on a plot to assassinate President Mubarak. On June 26, as Mubarak was being driven from the airport into Addis Ababa, Ethiopia, for a meeting of the Organization of African Unity, a number of Arab men blocked the street and opened fire with assault weapons from the ground and from rooftops. Bullets peppered Mubarak's car, but its armor held, and the well-trained driver performed a lightning U-turn and sped back to the airport. When he arrived back in Egypt's capital, the president gave a press conference at which he struck a defiant tone, vowing to continue the fight against terrorism. In the weeks that followed, Egyptian forces stepped up their efforts to round up EIJ members.

By now, the growing crackdown was affecting the group not just in Egypt but around the world. In particular, those members who had stayed on in Pakistan after the Afghan jihad were being targeted by Egyptian intelligence, with help from local and Western security forces. In revenge, EIJ decided to plan an assault inside Pakistan. Zawahiri's original intent was to attack the U.S. embassy or another Western diplomatic mission, but it seemed that was now beyond EIJ's capacity to pull off, so the Islamabad cell turned its attention to the Egyptian embassy instead. On November 19, two huge truck bombs tore the front off the embassy building, killing fifteen people and wounding fifty-nine. Zawahiri would later write that this attack "left the embassy's ruined building as an eloquent and clear message." It also marked the advent of a new phenomenon in Sunni extremist terrorism—the use of suicide bombers.

In its desperation to rid itself of EIJ for good, the regime's tactics reached levels of brutality comparable to those of the jihadists themselves. In Khartoum, Egyptian operatives captured the thirteen-year-old son of an EIJ associate, drugged him, raped him on camera, and used this leverage to blackmail the boy and one of his friends into spying on Zawahiri and planting a bomb to kill the EIJ leader. Sudanese agents captured the boys before they could go through with their plans. When Zawahiri discovered the plot, he persuaded the Sudanese regime to hand the boys over to him "for questioning," then promptly had them shot, and issued a video of their execution as a warning to anyone else who might be considering betrayal. Even for the extreme Islamist Sudanese government, this was beyond the pale; the regime ordered Zawahiri and his associates to leave the country, reportedly without giving them time to pack. Zawahiri protested, complaining that "[a]ll we did was to apply God's Sharia."

· · ·

With his organization now diminished to fewer than 100 members, Zawahiri became a nomad in search of a new safe haven. The stamps in his Sudanese passport—issued under a false name— revealed multiple trips during 1995 and 1996 to Yemen, Malaysia, Singapore, and Taiwan. Other reports from the period place him in Hong Kong, Bulgaria, Bosnia, Denmark, the Netherlands, and Switzerland, although at least one scholar suggests that some of these alleged trips may have been an elaborate smoke screen thrown up in an effort to confound the various intelligence services looking for Zawahiri.

One potential base on Zawahiri's shortlist was Chechnya, where Islamist militants were locked in a murderous insurgency against Moscow. Near the end of 1996, he traveled to Azerbaijan, where EIJ still had a cell, and at four o'clock in the morning of December 1, he was driven over the border into Russia in a minivan with two EIJ operatives, a Chechen fixer, and $6,400 denominated in seven different currencies. Less than thirty miles from the Azeri frontier, and still several hours' drive from Grozny, Russian security forces stopped the van at a checkpoint. Finding no valid visas in their passports, the Russians promptly arrested the van's occupants. Zawahiri and his companions said that they were "merchants" looking to buy leather and pharmaceuticals. Almost incredibly, this lie held, even after Zawahiri's laptop was sent to Moscow for analysis; Zawahiri would later claim that he and his fellow militants had been saved by divine intervention. They were, nevertheless, convicted of Russian immigration violations and sentenced to six months, five of which they had already served by the conclusion of the trial. On his release in May 1997, Zawahiri returned to Azerbaijan, but not before successfully making contact with elements in the Chechen jihad, as he had intended all along. This small victory did little to salve the rage of those among Zawahiri's followers who had not endorsed his probe into Chechnya. The organization's Yemeni branch condemned Zawahiri's ill-conceived Russian adventure as "a disaster that almost destroyed the group." By this point, the strain on the EIJ leader had become so intense that he had developed a peptic ulcer. With his leadership, his organization, and even his health in severe jeopardy, Zawahiri was left with little choice but to throw himself back upon the mercy of his old benefactor, Osama bin Laden.

From Azerbaijan, Zawahiri made his way to Kandahar to link up once more with al-Qaeda. Yet again, bin Laden took him in. For a few years, Zawahiri was finally able to lead a relatively tranquil family life; his wife gave birth to a child, Aisha, whom Zawahiri diagnosed right away as suffering from Down syndrome. Though its strength was at a low ebb, EIJ still maintained cells in Yemen, Italy, Albania, and Azerbaijan. Back home in Egypt, however, the picture was bleak. Many imprisoned EIJ and GI operatives, worn down by years of brutal incarceration, were giving up the fight, taking advantage of a deal proposed by the Mubarak government under which they would renounce militancy in exchange for freedom. Zawahiri, safely at liberty two thousand miles away in another country, publicly opposed this deal and urged his followers to continue their struggle against the Egyptian government. Many paid him no heed, and the jihad in Egypt continued to decline.

At the same time, Zawahiri realized that, in order to secure EIJ's line of credit from al-Qaeda, he would have to commit his organization once and for all to bin Laden's globalized brand of jihad. By January 1998, negotiations were under way for a joint declaration against the United States, to be signed by the leaders of both groups, as well as those of Gamaa al-Islamiya and two Pakistan-based groups. The fatwa, finally issued on February 23, restated the familiar anti-American gripes: The United States, it claimed, was "occupying" the Arabian Peninsula, oppressing Muslims, interfering in the Arab region, and supporting Israel against the Palestinians: "All these crimes and sins committed by the Americans are a clear declaration of war on God, his messenger, and Muslims. . . . The ruling to kill the Americans and their allies—civilians and military—is an individual duty for every Muslim who can do it in any country in which it is possible to do it."

Reviewing the fatwa's signature block brings yet another reminder that, when it comes to the global jihad, the past is never quite dead and buried. Rifai Ahmad Taha, the Egyptian jihadi leader whose signature appeared alongside those of bin Laden and Zawahiri, was arrested at the airport in Damascus a month after 9/11 and extradited to Egypt. By 2012, however, Taha was free and helping to organize protests in Cairo against the United States. In the years that followed, he traveled to Syria to help lead Jabhat al-Nusra, al-Qaeda's Levantine franchise, until he was finally killed in an air strike near Idlib in April 2016. Many more old-guard figures like him are still at large.

Zawahiri would justify his own shift to global jihad on the basis that "the forces of the disbelievers have united against the mujahideen. . . . The battle today cannot be fought on a regional level without taking into account the global hostility towards [Muslims]." America, he said, would desist from supporting apostate Arab regimes "only if the shrapnel from the battle reaches their own homes and bodies." But there was no use denying that the fatwa directly contradicted the principle on which EIJ had been founded—namely, jihad against the near enemy, the government of Egypt. For many in EIJ, Zawahiri's signature on the fatwa was tantamount to heresy. In April, Zawahiri called an emergency meeting of the group in Afghanistan. Tensions were so high that one attendee feared that the twenty-five-year-old organization was seconds from dissolution, and "expected some members to start wrestling each other." Zawahiri, though, was unrepentant. "Stop digging problems from the grave," he told his irate membership. "Gathering together is a pillar of our success." But many still felt betrayed. In the aftermath of the disastrous Afghanistan meeting, even Zawahiri's brother Mohammed, who had been with him ever since he founded his very first jihadi cell in the mid-1960s, finally quit the group.

Still Zawahiri would not be deterred. Even before the fatwa was published, negotiations were already under way for a full-scale merger between EIJ and al-Qaeda. The merger was at last announced at a luncheon in June 2001. Zawahiri gave an intransigent speech, denouncing the Egyptian government and calling for Sharia law in Egypt. But in reality, EIJ's Egyptian dreams had now been subsumed into bin Laden's much grander global project. "We must admit," Zawahiri wrote around this time, "that the Islamist movement's goal of establishing an Islamic government in Egypt is yet to be achieved. The Islamic Jihad movement, however, had not set a specific date for achieving this goal. [It] could take several generations." He pointed out that eleventh-century European Crusaders occupied parts of the Levant for two hundred years before being driven out, while the British Empire later occupied Egypt for seventy years, and the French colonized Algeria for over a century. "Thus," he concluded, "we could affirm that the Jihad movement is growing and making progress in general. It may retreat or relax for a while, but this happens because of the campaigns of brutality or during the periods of siege."

. . .

Following the merger, bin Laden and Zawahiri conducted a joint tour of al-Qaeda facilities in Afghanistan to cement the new arrangement. It was probably their last opportunity to do so, for those same facilities were about to be obliterated in a hail of American and coalition bombs. Among the members of al-Qaeda's *shura* council, those who had recently arrived from EIJ had been the only strong proponents of the Planes Operation. But the 9/11 attacks would cost each of them dearly, and Zawahiri would suffer more than most. During the U.S. invasion that followed, an air strike flattened the house in which members of his family were staying. Zawahiri's wife and one of his sons were crushed to death under the rubble, while his daughter Aisha, the baby who had been born in Kandahar with Down syndrome, died a day later from a burst artery in her brain. Zawahiri himself escaped on horseback, through the Khyber Pass to Pakistan and into hiding. Some reports suggest he may have spent time in Iran, but it is likely that his permanent base, as with other senior al-Qaeda figures, has been in the Pakistani tribal areas; in 2010, Mahmud, himself almost certainly writing from Waziristan, was able to tell bin Laden that the deputy emir was well and "his family is with him."

In the aftermath of the Taliban's fall, Zawahiri's statements remained characteristically strident. At one point, he threatened to follow up the New York and Washington attacks with an equally devastating strike against Tel Aviv. Despite heavy losses from the fighting in Afghanistan, he insisted that "an Islamist coalition is taking shape." On the other hand, he accepted that the movement would have to make tactical retreats to avoid further deaths and arrests, and that he would have to lie low until the time was right for it to reestablish itself. In the meantime, he thought, much could be accomplished by using the carnage of 9/11 and al-Qaeda's other atrocities to inspire lone wolves and small independent cells. He wrote:

Tracking down the Americans and the Jews is not impossible. Killing them with a single bullet, a stab, or a device made up of a

popular mix of explosives or hitting them with an iron rod is not
impossible. Burning down their property with Molotov cocktails
is not difficult. With the available means, small groups could
prove to be a frightening horror for the Americans and the Jews.

In the long term, the objective remained the same: to establish an
Islamic state to serve as a base of operations "in the heart of the Arab
region." However, Zawahiri cautioned that this was "not an easy or
close target. . . . The jihad movement must patiently build its structure until it is well established. It must pool enough resources and
supporters and devise enough plans to fight the battle at the time and
[in the] arena that it chooses." In the meantime, "We must seek to
move the battlefront to the heart of the Islamic world."

In the years that followed, as it became clear that al-Qaeda's leaders would have to endure a protracted period in hiding, bin Laden
continued to insist that his deputy be copied on all important correspondence, and frequently solicited Zawahiri's opinion on various
matters. In addition, Zawahiri became one of al-Qaeda's principal
spokesmen, delivering statements in a leaden, hectoring tone worlds
away from bin Laden's thrilling, enigmatic half-whisper. In the tapes,
Zawahiri gloated over militant advances in Iraq, threatened further
strikes against the United States, and eulogized dead al-Qaeda terrorists; but as the flow of successful new attacks against the West
seemed to dry up, global interest in these statements dwindled, to the
point where Al Jazeera and many other outlets that had previously
run them in their entirety now paid them scant heed. When antigov-
ernment protests erupted in Egypt in 2011, bin Laden toyed briefly
with giving Zawahiri some kind of role in formulating al-Qaeda's
response. Other than that, it is not entirely clear what Zawahiri's
specific role was within al-Qaeda. It is possible that, like deputies in
many large organizations, he simply struggled for relevance.

. . .

Clearly, al-Qaeda's ideology, its *-ism*, remained strong after 9/11; indeed, it gained many more adherents, especially after the Arab Spring turned into cold and bloody winter. But the real-world organization called al-Qaeda had not simply sublimated into a scattering fog of dogma and theory; there was, and is, still such a thing as al-Qaeda. To be sure, it has changed radically. Before 9/11, if you wanted to work with al-Qaeda, to enjoy its largesse, train in its camps, benefit from its capabilities, you not only had to join the organization and pledge fealty to its emir; bin Laden demanded that you physically travel to Afghanistan. He called this practice "making hijra," after the Prophet Muhammad's legendary "migration" into exile in Medina—the event from which the Islamic Hijri calendar dates all subsequent events. This was not only a matter of vanity; when Abu Musab al-Suri, the media fixer and author of a number of tracts on jihadi theory and strategy, asked to be let in on al-Qaeda's future plans while he was living in Madrid and London in the late 1990s, bin Laden rebuffed him, saying, "I can't share this with you as you are in the enemy's belly." After the fall of the Taliban, however, gathering together in large groups became all but impossible. Thus, power in the organization began to diffuse, flowing out from the central hub to affiliates in Yemen, Somalia, the Maghreb, and beyond.

It would be wrong to view this dynamic as heralding the defeat or near-defeat of al-Qaeda. To assert that al-Qaeda is finished, as various Western officials have done, is to ignore not only the grip of its message on the minds of thousands of disenfranchised young people around the Muslim world but also the all-too-real power that still resides with al-Qaeda's affiliates today. Today's terrorist recruiters prey on young men who harbor a sense of grievance that usually stems, naturally enough, from the humiliating circumstances of their individual lives. But these same recruiters are adept at taking those resentments and twisting them, via disfigured theology and grotesque conspiracy theories, into boiling anger against the United States and the West. Ayman al-Zawahiri himself started out fighting the Egyptian regime but wound up firmly in the global jihadi camp; and even Osama bin Laden once focused narrowly on expelling U.S. forces from his own country of Saudi Arabia. By redirecting local anger toward a supposed global threat, al-Qaeda has been able to spread its countercultural message and anti-Western narrative to recruits all over the world.

Moreover, al-Qaeda central—the modern equivalent of Hassan-i Sabbah's Assassin castle in the mountains—remains important. Within the organization, members refer to the central command as Khorasan—a reference to the hadith about an army with black banners coming to conquer Jerusalem. Al-Qaeda operatives on the ground refer to Khorasan the way FBI agents in a field office might say "Washington," meaning headquarters. Orders come down from Khorasan in much the same way as they do in the FBI or any such organization, and some field offices are better than others when it comes to following these directives. Khorasan plays an important organizing role; but it lacks the capacity to carry out attacks by itself, much to the frustration of many of its leaders. While he was still in charge, Osama bin Laden continually pushed for more attacks against U.S. and other Western interests—a desperation for action that sometimes assumed tragicomic proportions, as in the search for a new manager of global terrorism, in which the sheikh, like the human resources department of a small business looking to expand into new markets, solicited from each applicant a résumé and cover letter outlining his plans for developing al-Qaeda's capabilities.

By the time of bin Laden's death, there was no getting away from the fact that power had become decentralized. In order to strike its enemies, whether near or far, al-Qaeda had become increasingly reliant on affiliates and lone wolves. It is telling that the two biggest attacks in the West in the years immediately following 9/11, the train bombings in Madrid and London, were carried out by tiny, independent cells with little, if any, connection to Khorasan or its affiliates. In corporate terms, we might say that al-Qaeda was no longer Starbucks, with multiple branches all managed centrally; instead, it was now McDonald's, with a proliferation of independent franchises receiving guidance from headquarters that could be more specific or less so, depending on the situation. In fact, bin Laden increasingly encouraged franchises to drop the name al-Qaeda lest they draw unwanted Western attention. Several affiliates followed this advice; for example, al-Qaeda in the Arabian Peninsula rebranded itself as Ansar al-Sharia (Partisans of Islamic Law) to gain acceptance among Yemenis. Like any diligent CEO facing a public relations crisis, at one point bin Laden had even considered rebranding al-Qaeda as a whole with a new name—something more inclusive and more recognizably Islamic than simply The Base. Zawahiri would continue this tradition by advising al-Nusra, al-Qaeda's Syrian franchise, to split off from the parent organization, in hopes of making al-Nusra more acceptable both to Syrians themselves and to foreign governments looking for an effective proxy through which to end the Syrian civil war. In July, 2016, al-Nusra did, in fact, announce that it was leaving al-Qaeda and renaming itself Jabhat Fateh al-Sham, or the Levantine Conquest Front. But this "split," like AQAP's rebranding exercise, was no more than window dressing: The organization's commitment to the ideology of bin Ladenism remained, as did its individual members' bayats to al-Qaeda.

Al-Qaeda's franchisees shared a common ultimate goal: the establishment of an Islamic state. But they had radically different ideas about how, and in particular how quickly, to go about achieving that goal. For his part, bin Laden counseled patience. He continued to believe that there was no point in seeking to establish an Islamic state while America still had the military muscle and political sway over local governments to smother such a state in the cradle. Until such time as it could be declawed, therefore, the United States remained the primary adversary. In fact, al-Qaeda's standard playbook for establishing the Islamic state was well known in jihadi circles. It had been discussed at great length in two extremely influential works, both published in 2004. The first of these, entitled *The Management of Savagery: The Most Critical Stage Through Which the Umma Will Pass*, appeared in the online al-Qaeda magazine *Sawt al-Jihad* under the pseudonym Abu Bakr Naji. Whoever wrote it—and many theories have been propounded—the book sets out a strategy that is closely aligned with official al-Qaeda doctrine. The problem, Naji insists, is not with the use of violence itself; indeed, he claims that the most extreme forms of terrorist brutality are necessary to create "regions of savagery" in which the writ of traditional nation-states does not run. The term "savagery" refers to something like the Latin concept of barbarianism, which imperial Rome used to describe areas and people outside its zone of control, such as the Germanic tribes that rebelled against Roman rule and would eventually topple the Western Empire in the fifth century. *The Management of Savagery* proposed the creation of similar "savage" power vacuums, into which Islamist armies could march. The next stage, according to Naji, is "justifying [jihadi rule] rationally and through the Sharia"—not to the West, nor to any governmental authority, but directly to Muslims themselves, in a way that makes the cause seem right, even inevitable, and draws in more and more recruits. One of the keys to this process of justification, Naji tells his readers, is to provide the people under the state's jurisdiction with fair, efficient governance based on the precepts of Sharia law. Once the people's support is assured, permanent governmental structures can be established. The *Management of Savagery* playbook therefore proceeds in three phases. Phase one involves creating and exploiting chaos, or "savagery." Phase two entails building popular support for Salafijihadi rule. Not until phase three do we reach the establishment of a permanent Islamic state.

Around the same time, a veteran Syrian jihadist, Abu Musab al-Suri, was publishing his own work on the same subject, a magisterial tome of 1,600 pages entitled *The Call of the Global Islamic*

Resistance. The work is profoundly shaped by al-Suri's personal history. After having fought in the failed Muslim Brotherhood revolt against Bashir Assad's father Hafez in the early 1980s, he sought asylum in Europe, where he became increasingly critical of jihadi strategy, particularly in Algeria, where he witnessed, from afar, an insurgency alienating public support by imposing policies that were simply too extreme for the local population. From exile, al-Suri wrote prolifically on jihadi theory. Ayman al-Zawahiri called him "the professor of the mujahideen." His most influential book, *The Call of the Global Islamic Resistance* stresses the importance of having local populations on board. "The Islamic movement," al-Suri writes, "can only establish the Muslim society through a popular jihad." In line with bin Laden's own thinking, he also emphasizes the need to rid the Muslim world of the United States before taking on local leaders: "The old strategic goal of confronting governments has changed. . . . Establishing the rule of the law of God . . . will result from the success of the resistance in . . . bringing about the downfall of the greatest power, America."

Both *The Management of Savagery* and *The Call of the Global Islamic Resistance* remain popular playbooks among today's jihadis. But over the past two decades, actual attempts to create Islamic states have hewed much more closely to the timetable set out in a third work from the same period, a book called *Al-Zarqawi: The Second Generation of al-Qaeda*, published in 2005 by the Jordanian Islamist writer Fouad Hussein. As its title suggests, the book bills itself as a biography of the founder of al-Qaeda in Iraq. In fact, it presents an ambitious, seven-stage, two-decade strategy for reestablishing the caliphate and ushering in the End of Days, in the process of which the forces of righteous Islam will finally vanquish the apostates and infidels. Part One, "The Awakening," which involves shocking the Islamic world out of its long dormancy, had already occurred when the book was published, in the shape of 9/11 and the U.S. invasion of Iraq. Part Two, "Eye-Opening," was also well under way, with the

Iraq War functioning as a magnet drawing young Muslims eager to die for the cause and kill Americans. Part Three, "Arising and Standing Up," scheduled for 2007–2010, was to involve jihadis turning their attention to, among other places, Syria. Part Four, concluding in 2013, would see the fall of existing governments throughout the Arab world, in a process much like the real-life Arab Spring. Part Five would culminate in the declaration of a new caliphate in 2016— something the Islamic State managed a good two years ahead of schedule. Part Six was to witness a "Total Confrontation" between true believers and their apostate and infidel opponents. The final stage would be the worldwide rule of the refounded caliphate.

It goes without saying that this accelerated timetable—from drowsy indolence to world domination in under twenty years— is wildly out of line with the gradualism typically advocated by bin Laden and other top-echelon al-Qaeda commanders and theoreticians. Yet in the decade following the 2003 invasion of Iraq, a number of al-Qaeda offshoots would try to establish Islamic states, and they would do so on a schedule much closer to this one than to those of either Naji or al-Suri. Each of these attempts would ignore bin Laden's advice to exercise prudent restraint and avoid attracting foreign attention; on the contrary, they would seek to impose an extreme conception of Sharia with medieval harshness, and draw interventions from powerful outside forces. Each of them would fail.

. . .

It began in Iraq. Just over four months after Zarqawi's death in a U.S. air strike, his acolytes proclaimed themselves the Islamic State of Iraq. Initially, to curry support from Iraqi Sunnis, ISI pretended that its goal was merely to establish a safe haven for their sect—a necessary counterweight to the regime of Prime Minister Nuri al-Maliki's Shia-dominated government in the south and the Kurdish zone of control in the north. But behind the scenes, and occasionally in public, its backers would articulate a much grander vision. They called the Islamic State of Iraq's titular ruler Commander of the Faithful, a title traditionally held by caliphs, and they sought to establish his descent from the Prophet Muhammad, another traditional sine qua non for anyone aspiring to rule as caliph.

Khorasan had repeatedly shown its inability to control Abu Musab al-Zarqawi. But now Zarqawi was dead, no doubt much to the relief of the al-Qaeda brass. Perhaps, they might have thought, they would have better luck with the new leadership. On paper, the leader of the Islamic State of Iraq was an Iraqi going by the nom de guerre Abu Omar al-Baghdadi. But Abu Omar was a nobody. Even his *kunya*, al-Baghdadi, was a lie. It was meant to suggest that he hailed from the Iraqi capital—a fitting background, ISI believed, for the successor to the Abbasid royal family, which had ruled from Baghdad for over half a millennium. In fact, Abu Omar was from a small town out in the sticks, 130 miles from the big city. He had served as a police officer in his home town, until he was dismissed when his religious extremism became too vocal for his superiors to stomach. For a while, he became an electronics repair man, before joining the insurgency in the run-up to the invasion. One ISI operative described Abu Omar as "nothing but a regular militant" with questionable qualifications and no right to the allegiance of anyone, much less the top leaders of ISI's constituent groups.

The real leader, and the true successor to Zarqawi, was an Egyptian by the name of Abu Hamza al-Muhajir (his *kunya*, which translates as "The Immigrant," suggests why ISI felt it necessary to mask him with a local figurehead). Officially, Muhajir was war minister in Abu Omar's cabinet; in reality, he was the one pulling the strings. Muhajir had an incomparably longer history in the jihad than Abu Omar, and had been much closer to the al-Qaeda leadership than Zarqawi ever was. In 1982, he had joined Egyptian Islamic Jihad, the organization in which Ayman al-Zawahiri had made his name, and which he would later come to lead. Muhajir traveled to Afghanistan alongside Zawahiri and trained in al-Qaeda's camps there. In early 2003, Zawahiri sent Muhajir to Iraq. A year and a half later, with Zarqawi's merger into al-Qaeda, Muhajir began working for the Jordanian.

Initial signs were encouraging for Khorasan. Within a few days of Zarqawi's death, Muhajir had issued a statement reiterating his loyalty to bin Laden and to al-Qaeda. "We are an arrow in your quiver," he told the sheikh. "Shoot us where you wish." Yet just four months later, Muhajir had signed off on the creation of the Islamic State of Iraq, and a month after that, he had unilaterally disbanded al-Qaeda in Iraq, dissolved his forces into the Islamic State of Iraq, and pledged *bayat* to Abu Omar on behalf of himself and all his followers. Khorasan had authorized none of these developments, and cannot have been pleased with any of them. But Muhajir had presented the al-Qaeda brass with a fait accompli that they were forced to accept. Bin Laden, Zawahiri, and the other leaders remained as mindful as ever of the need to keep a toehold in Iraq. Publicly, therefore, they issued statement after statement in support of ISI. Privately, however, they continued to be irritated, if not outright alarmed, by the excesses of Muhajir and his cronies. Zawahiri continually demanded that Muhajir explain what was going on, but these requests went unheeded. Relations became so strained that some senior members even began to counsel bin Laden to cut ties with ISI, believing that the association was now doing al-Qaeda more harm than good. But in public, al-Qaeda maintained the charade that it approved of what its Iraqi arm was doing.

The Islamic State of Iraq remained a potent terrorist force. Well over a year after his death, Zarqawi's erstwhile followers remained capable of violence on a mass scale, such as the string of coordinated truck bombs that killed more than five hundred people in August 2007 in the deadliest day of the entire Iraq War. The group crushed dissent with an iron fist, frequently murdering jihadis and others who refused to bend the knee to Abu Omar. But as a governing political entity, the Islamic State of Iraq was, like its cardboard emir, no more than a tenuous fiction. Many of its operatives, and even its senior leadership, were too drunk on heady talk of the impending End of Days to function effectively as anything other than a killing machine. Some rank-and-file al-Qaeda members like Abu Jandal were fond of spouting supposed end times hadith, and the organization happily fed their obsession with its own symbolism—for example, referring to its high command as Khorasan based, as we have seen, on the black banners hadith, and calling al-Nusra's house magazine after the white minaret in Damascus where Jesus was supposed to appear immediately before the apocalypse. But official al-Qaeda doctrine saw these events as happening far in the future, decades or generations hence. Khorasan had repeatedly warned Muhajir against indulging in apocalyptic rhetoric implying that the end was nigh, telling him such talk was "very dangerous and corrupts policy and leadership." For al-Qaeda, the *Management of Savagery* playbook had to be followed: Build public support first, then a state, then think about what comes next. But Muhajir insisted again and again, apparently without irony or conscious exaggeration, that he expected the arrival of the Mahdi—the Islamic Messiah—"any day."

Meanwhile, the Islamic State of Iraq under Muhajir shamelessly exaggerated its achievements, even to the extent of faking operations in its propaganda films by splicing together old footage. It was an open secret that Abu Omar was a paper tiger; but even his real boss, Abu Hamza al-Muhajir, was said to have isolated himself from the battlefield. The former chief judge of the Islamic State of Iraq, who was so concerned about Muhajir's shaky leadership that he fled to Pakistan to seek Khorasan's intercession, told al-Qaeda leaders that Muhajir was "totally isolated, barely seeing or seen by anyone" and that he was too weak to deal with corruption among his own lieutenants. Muhajir routinely sent fighters to their deaths on absurdly dangerous missions with no real chance of success, such as an ill-timed assault on the city of Ramadi. Worst of all, the Islamic State of Iraq, supposedly the successor to one of the greatest land empires in history, controlled no territory worthy of the name. Its leaders cowered in the wastes of Anbar Province in an effort to evade the attention of the Americans and the Sunni Awakening groups. Muhajir's own wife is said to have chided him about this, on at least one occasion screaming, "Where is this Islamic State of Iraq you're talking about? We live in the desert!"

Bin Laden, al-Suri, and the pseudonymous author of *The Management of Savagery* had warned again and again of the danger of proceeding without public support. But ISI not only did not enjoy such support; it had seemingly gone out of its way to alienate vast swathes of the Iraqi population. Its leaders were obviously corrupt, and the local populace grew understandably enraged at being pushed around by foreign thugs fighting for ISI. Nor did the group's slate of policies do much to endear it to many Iraqis. In a March 2007 audio statement entitled "Some of Our Fundamentals," Abu Omar called for bans on statues, tombs, and satellite television; demanded that women be veiled and refrain from "mixing" with men; called Shia Muslims idolaters and apostates; condemned anyone who helped the Americans, worked for the Iraqi government, or in any way "participate[d] in the political process"; and demanded that Christians and Jews pay a protection tax on pain of death. In areas temporarily under its control, ISI imposed beheadings, amputations, and deadly stonings— reportedly even against children. Anyone who dared to resist would be pronounced an infidel or apostate and risked being killed. Almost the only people Muhajir bothered to avoid alienating were other militants; when another al-Qaeda–aligned group complained about his conduct, he issued a groveling apology, saying that he "would carry your shoes on my head and kiss them a thousand times."

Even by the standards of terrorist fanatics, the diabolical levels of violence visited on Iraq by the Islamic State of Iraq went way beyond what was acceptable. A reckoning for its crimes was long overdue. When the Islamic State of Iraq was proclaimed, its leaders had said they enjoyed the backing of at least 60 percent of Sunni tribal elders within its sphere of influence. Even at the time, that was probably a gross exaggeration, if not an outright lie. Since then, its relentless brutality had eroded that natural support base so comprehensively that local Sunni armed groups had started working with the Shia-led government, and the Americans themselves, to destroy the Islamic State of Iraq once and for all. At its height, the Sunni Awakening co-opted more than 100,000 Sunni fighters to battle ISI. Meanwhile, the U.S. "surge" put 30,000 additional American boots on the ground. As a result, the State was pummeled—indeed, it was almost extinguished altogether—by a relentless series of defeats, deaths, and arrests. By the close of 2007, it was facing what one high-level internal analysis called "an extraordinary crisis." Bin Laden issued a backs-to-the-wall audio statement in which he admitted that "the malice has increased and the darkness has become pitch-black," and called for more recruits from elsewhere in the Muslim world, attempting to entice them with the dubious inducement that "being stabbed in the throat is more honorable than being stabbed in the back."

.   .   .

Other affiliates, it is fair to say, presented less of a headache for Khorasan. In Yemen, his family's ancestral homeland, bin Laden had long seen a potential battleground, recruiting station, and safe house for the global jihad. In addition, of course, he harbored a long-standing grudge against the regime in the neighboring country to the north, his homeland of Saudi Arabia. So it is perhaps unsurprising that al-Qaeda in the Arabian Peninsula, or AQAP, the organization's affiliate in Yemen and Saudi Arabia, has long been the closest to al-Qaeda central, in terms both of ideology and organization. In sharp contrast to that of ISI, all of AQAP's main leaders were at one point or another members of al-Qaeda's Islamist model society in Afghanistan. Having been steeped in bin Laden's conception of the global jihad, these veterans understood his philosophy in a way that those recruited after the fall of the Taliban never would.

AQAP was headed by Nasser al-Wuhayshi, a Yemeni and a confirmed member of the al-Qaeda establishment. Twenty years younger than bin Laden, like many jihadis of his generation Wuhayshi had been inspired by the Saudi's anti-American statements of the 1990s and had traveled to Afghanistan to join his hero. With conspicuous intelligence and aptitude, and no small measure of self-deprecating humor, Wuhayshi rose quickly to become a member of bin Laden's inner circle, eventually serving as the emir's chief of staff. Wuhayshi recruited into al-Qaeda a number of his fellow Yemenis, including Fahd al-Quso, who would go on to participate in the 2000 bombing of the USS *Cole* while it lay at anchor in the Yemeni port of Aden. Wuhayshi stuck with bin Laden through the U.S. invasion of Afghanistan and fought against American Special Forces at the Battle of Tora Bora in late 2001. After fleeing to Iran, he was apprehended and deported to face terrorism charges back home in Yemen, but in February 2006, he helped lead two dozen jihadis in an audacious escape in the course of which they tunneled into the women's bathroom of a mosque across the street from the jail. His storied background made Wuhayshi a legendary figure within al-Qaeda. After breaking jail, he set about rebuilding al-Qaeda's operation in Yemen, becoming its leader in mid-2007. Meanwhile, following a series of bombings, kidnappings, and assassinations across the kingdom, al-Qaeda's Saudi branch faltered and almost collapsed under an onslaught from the Saudi security forces. In 2009, the Yemeni and Saudi Arabian branches officially merged. Wuhayshi was the natural choice to lead the resulting jihadi conglomerate, al-Qaeda in the Arabian Peninsula.

Another prominent figure in AQAP was a Yemeni-American cleric, Anwar al-Awlaki. Born in New Mexico and educated at Colorado State University, by his midtwenties Awlaki had married, started a family, and become a popular and, at first, relatively moderate preacher, first in southern California and then in northern Virginia. But unbeknownst to his family, Awlaki led a double life; he frequented prostitutes and, on at least two occasions while living in San Diego, had been arrested for attempted solicitation. By September 11, 2001, Awlaki had risen to the position of imam at a prominent mosque in the suburbs of Washington, DC, in which role he gave lectures at the U.S. Capitol building and the Pentagon. In the broad investigation that followed 9/11, FBI agents learned that two of the hijackers who crashed American Airlines Flight 77 into the Pentagon had once worshipped at the San Diego mosque where Awlaki preached. The agents interviewed Awlaki and put him under surveillance. The investigation uncovered no links to terrorism but did reveal Awlaki's habit of visiting DC-area prostitutes. In early 2002, another witness interviewed by the FBI tipped Awlaki off that the agents knew of his activities. Fearing arrest and humiliation, Awlaki fled the country, first to the United Kingdom and then to Yemen, where his preaching became increasingly inflammatory and anti-American. After a year and a half of imprisonment without charge in Yemen, Awlaki joined AQAP, becoming, in effect, the group's chief propagandist, as well as a mainstay of its recruitment efforts, especially when it came to recruits living in the West. His ability to speak flawless, colloquial American English represented a huge asset in enlisting English-speaking Muslims like the 2009 Fort Hood shooter, the 2013 Boston Marathon bombers, and the twenty-four-year-old Kuwaiti-American who killed five military personnel in Chattanooga in 2015. All were either recruited directly by Awlaki or inspired by his preaching. Even today, years after his death in a U.S. drone strike, his message—delivered via CDs, DVDs, and YouTube videos—continues to prompt young Americans, Brits, and others to join the Islamic State.

Awlaki's influence and Wuhayshi's connections, together with a prodigious talent for making millions of dollars from hostage ransoms—which Wuhayshi described as "an easy spoil. . . a profitable trade and a precious treasure"—all played a major role in making AQAP by far al-Qaeda's most dangerous offshoot in terms of global terrorism. Among all of the organization's affiliates, AQAP was the only one that Osama bin Laden truly trusted with missions against Western interests. In the five years preceding bin Laden's death, most major attacks and plots against the United States could be tied back to AQAP or its forerunners—including the September 2008 bombing of the U.S. embassy in Sanaa, the failed "underwear bomb" plot against a Northwest Airlines plane in December 2009, and the plan to blow up U.S. cargo planes that was foiled in 2010.

Yet even AQAP struggled at times to slake bin Laden's prodigious thirst for more attacks against America and its allies. In June 2010, AQAP began publishing its online English-language magazine *Inspire*—cofounded, like its older Arabic cousin, *Echo of Battles,* by an eager millennial with an appetite for social media. Samir Khan was born in Saudi Arabia to Pakistani parents but grew up largely in New York City and North Carolina, where he ran a jihadist blog under the screen name Revolution. Khan would later die in the same drone strike as Anwar al-Awlaki. His creation, *Inspire* magazine, was designed to do just what its name suggests: to motivate and instruct wannabe terrorists to take matters into their own hands— preferably lone wolves capable of traveling freely and avoiding detection. Thus, in the first edition, alongside an "exclusive interview" with Wuhayshi, readers could enjoy an article by the cryptonymous "al-Qaeda Chef" entitled "Make a Bomb in the Kitchen of Your Mom." It seems to have worked; *Inspire* would go on to play a role in radicalizing and instructing, among others, the Chechen-American terrorists Dzhokhar and Tamerlan Tsarnaev, whose pressure-cooker bombs killed three people and maimed more than two hundred others in Boston.

At the same time, AQAP was also focusing some of its efforts locally, with attacks and assassination attempts in Yemen and Saudi Arabia. Like many jihadis, Wuhayshi harbored territorial ambitions. In 2010, in the midst of Yemeni tribal unrest bordering on civil war, he wrote to bin Laden saying, "If you want Sanaa, today is the day." Bin Laden replied, with his trademark caution, "We want Sanaa to establish an Islamic State, but first, we want to make sure we have the capability to control it." Again, the emir set out at length his long-held doctrine that America must be defeated first; otherwise, "the enemy continues to possess the ability to topple any state we establish." The Yemeni regime, though secular and incompetent, was "less dangerous to us than the one America wants to exchange it with." Moreover, he said, patience in this regard might soon pay off; the United States would "have to withdraw during the next few years for many reasons," bin Laden wrote, "the most important of which is America's high deficit."

The following year, when the Arab Spring reached Sanaa, AQAP took advantage of the ensuing chaos to occupy a swathe of poorly defended territory in southern Yemen, around the historic port town of Zinjibar. They did not formally declare an Islamic State; but in practice, they were governing, albeit branded as Ansar al-Sharia rather than al-Qaeda. AQAP did make an effort to provide services, like education and clean water, to southern populations historically neglected by the northern-dominated government; one tribal elder reported that, whereas the government in Sanaa had reluctantly promised his people half a dozen teachers, Ansar al-Sharia had provided sixteen. Nevertheless, these ministrations were still accompanied by the usual round of beheadings, stonings, and amputations, sadly familiar from previous jihadi occupations elsewhere in the world. Bin Laden, as usual, had advised Wuhayshi to avoid antagonizing the local population, in particular the tribes. For now, it seemed, as with the Islamic State of Iraq, that his advice had fallen on deaf ears. But AQAP would soon prove much more adaptable in this regard than al-Qaeda's wayward Iraqi offshoot.

. . .

Across the Gulf of Aden in Somalia, there lay another longstanding theater of jihad. In 2006—Somalia's fifteenth year without a functioning central government—an Islamist group called the Islamic

Courts Union, or ICU, conquered most of Somalia's southern arm, and briefly held Mogadishu, before being ousted from the capital by Ethiopian forces a few months later. The ICU's brutal private army was a group euphemistically referred to as its "mujahideen youth movement"—Harakat al Shabaab al-Mujahidin. Al-Shabaab, as the group came to be known for short, would soon find itself galvanized by the Ethiopian presence on Somali soil into the most dangerous militant organization in the entire region. Al-Shabaab is a complex organism. Many members are nationalistically inclined and locally focused, while some prominent voices hew more closely to the bin Ladenist brand of global jihad. For the most part, al-Shabaab does indeed keep its focus on domestic issues within Somalia, battling the embryonic Somali government as well as regional forces and United Nations peacekeepers; but the group also enjoyed strong ties to Khorasan through one of its leaders, Harun Fazul.

Fazul had been a member of the notorious Mogadishu team of Saif al-Adel's that precipitated the Black Hawk Down incident in 1993. Five years later, he was part of the cell that carried out the 1998 East Africa embassy bombings. Within al-Shabaab, Fazul led a globally minded faction that was eager to give the group's *bayat* to al-Qaeda. In 2008, al-Shabaab did indeed pledge allegiance to bin Laden, but the sheikh urged the group, as he had done with others, to play down its links to global jihad to avoid losing local support and attracting foreign intervention. Nevertheless, the following year, al-Shabaab announced that bin Laden was its emir, and bin Laden in turn appointed Fazul as the overall leader of al-Qaeda in East Africa.

Al-Shabaab enjoyed particularly close links to its al-Qaeda brethren in nearby Yemen, a country with a large Somali diaspora. A number of attacks inside Yemen claimed by AQAP and its predecessors, including the September 2008 bombing of the U.S. embassy compound in Sanaa and the March 2009 murder of Korean tourists posing for photographs at the desert city of Shibam, were carried out or facilitated by operatives trained in Somalia. And AQAP scratched al-Shabaab's back in return. One edition of *Inspire* carried a story inciting readers to violence against member countries of AMISOM, the African Union peacekeeping mission in Somalia.

At the same time, al-Shabaab was becoming more internationally minded. In 2010, the group threatened to "connect the Horn of Africa jihad to the one led by al-Qaeda and its leader Sheikh Osama bin Laden"; and in June of that year, it began its campaign of attacks outside Somalia with a series of suicide bombings that killed seventy-four people watching the World Cup final at parties in Kampala, Uganda, a leading AMISOM member state. Like many local jihadi groups, al-Shabaab's narrative of grievance extended beyond Somalia and its neighbors to encompass the West in general and the United States in particular. Al-Shabaab's propaganda twisted U.S. air strikes targeting al-Qaeda terrorists operating in Somalia into evidence of an American war on Muslims. The group began recruiting in Somali diaspora communities in the Middle East, Europe, and the United States, promising disillusioned young men "victory or martyrdom." In October 2008 it deployed the first known American suicide bomber, a twenty-six-year-old community college dropout from Minneapolis, who killed twenty-four people at a government compound in Puntland in northern Somalia.

But al-Shabaab's ultimate grand vision was of an ethnic Somali emirate, stretching from Kenya in the south to Djibouti in the north. By 2009, the group had conquered one of the largest jihadi territories since the Taliban, an area of southern and central Somalia that included the important port towns of Kismayo and Marka. Like the Taliban before them, al-Shabaab ruled without mercy or moderation. They banned movies, music, smoking, the shaving of beards, and the cherished local custom of chewing the natural stimulant known as khat; and they enforced their rulings with executions, beatings, amputations, torture, and suicide bombings. Reportedly, al-Shabaab fighters once stoned to death a thirteen-year-old girl for the "crime" of having been raped. Like the new al-Qaeda itself, al-Shabaab organized its roughly 7,000 fighters loosely into companies of 100 or so capable of operating autonomously, a decentralized structure that made the group extremely difficult to pin down. Even if senior leaders were killed, surviving commanders could easily continue to operate. Once again, however, al-Shabaab had made the mistake of alienating the local tribal population with its repressive policies, something that evidently frustrated bin Laden, who gave instructions for al-Shabaab "to be compassionate with the people" lest the citizens turn on the group and "become an instrument for the enemy to use against us." The group ignored bin Laden's protests and continued its repression—a mistake for which, in time, it would pay dearly.

. . .

On the opposite side of the Sahara, another of al-Qaeda's regional affiliates was wreaking havoc. Like its Somali adoptive cousin, al-Qaeda in the Land of the Islamic Maghreb, or AQIM, did not start out as an al-Qaeda franchise. It began life as the Salafi Group for Preaching and Combat, an insurgent organization formed to fight the Algerian government in that country's bloody civil war. The group's military leader, Mokhtar Belmokhtar, had fought in Afghanistan following the Soviet withdrawal, before returning to Algeria. Like the Algerian insurgency as a whole, the Salafi Group suffered many setbacks. In an effort to shore up its fortunes, it declared *bayat* to bin Laden in 2003, formally affiliated with al-Qaeda in 2006, and renamed itself al-Qaeda in the Land of the Islamic Maghreb the following year. To this day, AQIM's leaders, including its emir, Abdelmalek Droukdal, are largely Algerian in origin, and are thought to be headquartered in mountain holdfasts east of the capital, Algiers. But the group's association with al-Qaeda brought with it a new global focus. While continuing to pursue longstanding local struggles, AQIM began targeting Western interests in its zone of operations. In 2007, it attacked the United Nations office in Algiers. The following year, it staged a gun assault on the Israeli embassy in Nouakchott, the capital of Mauritania. And in 2011, it bombed the French embassy in Bamako, Mali, and kidnapped French nationals in Niger. But AQIM's own experiment in state building would have to wait until the violent aftermath of Libya's Arab Spring.

Besides its major affiliates in Africa, the Middle East, and the Arabian Peninsula, al-Qaeda also enjoyed ties with a clutch of smaller or less closely affiliated groups. In Chechnya, for example, the Caucasus Emirate, originally an outgrowth of the ethnonationalist Chechen independence struggle, received funding from Khorasan and announced its relationship with al-Qaeda central. Its fighters formed a small but powerful contingent in Syria, and a sizable chunk of the group would eventually peel off and pledge allegiance to the Islamic State, forming the caliphate's "Caucasus Province." In its hub region of Waziristan, al-Qaeda central worked together with a number of tribal entities to keep its people safe and fend off the Pakistani military. Tehrik-i Taliban Pakistan—more often known as the Pakistani Taliban—a broad group that had come together in December 2007, while not formally affiliated with al-Qaeda, also helped shelter Khorasan's operatives in Pakistan's tribal north. Al-Qaeda and the Pakistani Taliban worked together to pull off attacks like the December 2009 suicide bombing of Camp Chapman, a U.S. base in Khost Province, Afghanistan, which killed seven CIA personnel, a Jordanian intelligence operative, and the base's Afghan security director. In addition to these affiliates and allies, by the time of bin Laden's death, the broader al-Qaeda "family" also included groups of varying size and strength as far afield as Indonesia, Uzbekistan, and the Philippines. The organization was a far cry from al-Qaeda as it existed before 9/11; but it was still a potent and dangerous force.

. . .

That was how things stood on May 1, 2011. Then, all of a sudden, bin Laden was dead, and Zawahiri was in charge. The interim emir, Saif al-Adel, did his duty—he secured *bayat* from all *shura* council members—and Zawahiri officially assumed the post of permanent emir in mid-June. Now, Zawahiri was faced with a task that was at once more difficult and—in the new, decentralized al-Qaeda—more important: corralling the organization's smorgasbord of global affiliates. Obtaining their formal allegiance, it seemed, would be the easy part; almost before bin Laden's corpse hit the continental shelf, the troublesome Islamic State of Iraq had recognized Zawahiri as his successor. Abu Bakr al-Baghdadi, who succeeded Abu Omar al-Baghdadi as the leader of the Islamic State of Iraq, said in a public statement, "I tell our brothers in al-Qaeda led by Ayman al-Zawahiri, go on with God's blessing and be glad that you have faithful brothers in the Islamic State of Iraq who are marching on the path of right." Baghdadi stopped short of pledging allegiance, but it appears that his organization did offer to renew its *bayat* secretly, studiously following bin Laden's edict to avoid overt association with the tarnished al-Qaeda brand.

Obtaining al-Shabaab's *bayat* may have seemed a more difficult task. Harun Fazul, a leading member, as we have seen, of both al-Qaeda and al-Shabaab whom bin Laden had appointed to head up al-Qaeda operations across the Horn of Africa, had publicly drawn a distinction between the "mother al-Qaeda organization" and mere "collaborators" like EIJ. Fazul had made clear that, in his view, Zawahiri was not entitled to succeed bin Laden. This animosity might have posed a serious barrier to any pledge of allegiance from al-Shabaab; but on June 7, just five weeks after bin Laden's death, Fazul himself was suddenly gunned down, reportedly when his car tried to blow through a Somali government checkpoint. Given the suspicious timing, and the fact that Fazul had historically also been a frequent gadfly to the leadership of al-Shabaab, at least one scholar has suggested the possibility that Fazul might have been assassinated by the al-Shabaab leadership at Zawahiri's behest. At any rate, within two weeks of Fazul's death, al-Shabaab had issued a statement pledging allegiance to Zawahiri. "We await your instructions," they told their new emir. Eight months later, al-Shabaab and al-Qaeda went further still in announcing their formal merger. By the end of July, AQIM, the Pakistani Taliban, and AQAP had all publicly pledged *bayat*. In his statement on behalf of AQAP, Nasser al-Wuhayshi reflected the dual focus of many al-Qaeda affiliates, swearing to continue the battle against the Yemeni government but also pledging that "[o]ur war against the Zionist Crusaders remains. . . . It is as if we were only created to fight them and vex them."

Zawahiri now had the official backing of the *shura* council and each of the most powerful affiliates; in formal terms, he was firmly established as emir of al-Qaeda. But his worries were far from over: He faced an uphill battle for acceptance and relevance among al-Qaeda's membership at large. The first strike against him was his nationality. Al-Qaeda's upper echelons had long been dominated by Egyptians. They were the ones who had stuck by Bin Laden most reliably since al-Qaeda's formation, partly because political conditions in Mubarak's Egypt meant that they simply could not go home. These men needed a means of support, and the wealthy Saudi was the best available. Moreover, Egyptians tended to be valuable recruits for al-Qaeda because, as even Harun Fazul had to admit, many of them came with valuable experience serving in their country's well-equipped, finely drilled armed forces. As well as the senior leadership, therefore, Egyptians made up a disproportionate share of al-Qaeda's trainers, senior terrorists, and military commanders. At the same time, many non-Egyptian members resented what they saw as the undue influence these men exerted over bin Laden. This was especially true among Arabs from the Persian Gulf; back home in their oil-rich kingdoms, poor Egyptians worked for them. Inside al-Qaeda, this pattern was reversed: the Gulf Arabs in the rank and file tended to serve under the command of Egyptian officers. Even intramural soccer matches would often pit teams of Egyptians against teams of everyone else.

To make matters worse, many old-guard al-Qaeda members,

like Harun Fazul, viewed Zawahiri as an interloper and a freeloader who had more or less conned bin Laden into giving him a sweetheart deal to save his own skin. Moreover, on a personal level, Zawahiri himself was not particularly well liked. It was perfectly obvious to anyone who met him that he had none of bin Laden's personal magnetism. In conversation, his style was rigid and confrontational, and he had an unfortunate habit of trash-talking other members when he thought they were not listening. Writing before bin Laden's death, Abu Jandal, the sheikh's bodyguard, predicted trouble ahead should Zawahiri become emir:

> Bin Laden was a born leader, he operated with a transparency that made everyone accept him, he was open to discussion, and had a historical legitimacy. Zawahiri, on the other hand, operates in secrecy. Many members of al-Qaeda will refuse to accept Zawahiri's leadership. His behavior, and that of the Egyptians, aroused a lot of concern and sometimes very lively criticism. All of this leaves its mark. Sometimes his ideas were rejected by other leaders and I doubt he can command the necessary authority for the post, even though he is known for his authoritarian and controlling attitude.

From early on in his tenure, events did not seem to be going Zawahiri's way. Just three months after bin Laden was killed in May 2011, Mahmud, the assistant of bin Laden's who had done so much on a day-to-day basis to help keep the organization humming, died in a drone strike in Waziristan. In September, Pakistani forces captured Younis al-Mauritani, the man whom bin Laden had put in charge of waging a new terror campaign against Western interests. The same month, Anwar al-Awlaki, AQAP's Yemeni-American propagandist and recruiter, was also killed, although his sermons would enjoy an indefinite afterlife on the internet. For a while, it seemed as if al-Qaeda might have been dealt a mortal blow.

Not for the first or last time, however, the tempo of attacks and plots picked up once more. In January 2013, Mokhtar Belmokhtar, who had split from AQIM the previous year, led a new al-Qaeda–aligned group to attack the Tigantourine natural gas complex, a British, Norwegian, and Algerian joint venture in the Algerian desert. During the raid, Belmokhtar's men took more than eight hundred workers hostage and killed thirty-nine of them. In September, al-Shabaab kicked its deadly campaign against the citizens of AMISOM countries into high gear with an assault and siege at the Westgate Mall in Nairobi in which at least sixty-seven people died. But it was AQAP that remained al-Qaeda's most dangerous global affiliate, especially when it came to plots against Western interests. In July 2013, Zawahiri further cemented the Yemeni group's privileged position within al-Qaeda by appointing its leader, Nasser al-Wuhayshi, general manager of the whole worldwide network, and empowering him to call on resources from any affiliate. Wuhayshi was now, in effect, al-Qaeda's chief operating officer; all communications with Khorasan were to pass through him. At the same time, Zawahiri commissioned Wuhayshi to carry out attacks on the West, and the AQAP leader promised his emir an assault that would "change the face of history." AQAP set to work on two plots: a program of coordinated attacks against U.S. diplomatic missions across the Muslim world, and a plan to seize major ports and destroy oil pipelines in order to cripple the Yemeni economy. Fortunately for the United States and for Yemen's government, Western intelligence had been listening in on communications between Zawahiri and his COO. In response, the United States temporarily closed twenty of its diplomatic missions and bolstered their security, while Yemeni forces, with close support from American drones, moved in to foil the ports and pipelines plot. This time, the United States had been lucky. But the scale of the conspiracy, and the economic and diplomatic disruption it caused, served as a clear indication that reports of al-Qaeda's death had once again been greatly exaggerated.

CHAPTER 6

THE SYRIAN WARS

Within a few months of bin Laden's demise, the Arab world had changed utterly. The governments of Tunisia, Egypt, and Libya had fallen; that of Yemen was teetering on the brink; and the Assad regime in Syria was locked in an increasingly bitter struggle for survival. By the close of 2011, the arc of unrest stretched from Morocco to Iran. Across the region and beyond, the protests engendered a sense of hope. Citizens of the Arab Spring nations began to feel more empowered than they had in decades. Capturing the mood of the moment, an Al Jazeera commentator said: "Now the Arabs have found their voice, and are out in their millions in the streets in the Arab world. So, in a sense, the whole idea of al-Qaeda, even if it had any merits in the eyes of very few, it simply has absolutely no role in today's Arab world."

Zawahiri and others like him reject such optimism. On an ideological level, those who preach the al-Qaeda brand of Salafist extremism despise genuine representative government as little better than a form of polytheism, putting the law of men above that of God.

More importantly still, hope represents an existential threat to their movement; feelings of personal empowerment can act as a powerful antidote to all the toxins of despair, grievance, and humiliation that poison the minds of disillusioned young men and propel them toward lives of terrorism. In the face of the Arab Spring, with its peaceful shift from despondency and despotism to democracy and aspiration, it seemed that groups such as al-Qaeda, which trumpet nihilistic violence as the only viable path to dignity and self-determination, risked obsolescence and decline.

But Ayman al-Zawahiri, ever the attentive student, knew his history too well to believe for one moment that the Arab Spring would give birth to a democratic Middle East. As he was well aware, the Arab world had seen it all before. In the 1950s, millions of people had taken to the streets in Syria, Iraq, Jordan, Lebanon, and beyond, denouncing the existing regimes and calling for change. In Jordan, revolutionaries forced the king to give up significant power to a pan-Arabist prime minister, while in Lebanon, the situation became so volatile that President Eisenhower dispatched U.S. Marines to stabilize the country. In the wake of the general upheaval, autocratic regimes came to power in Iraq, Egypt, and Tunisia. When asked about his country's political system, Tunisia's new ruler, Habib Bourguiba, channeled Louis XIV, quipping, "I am the system." Barely three decades later, during the 1980s, protests once again erupted in the Arab world. Again, they went viral. Riots swept across Egypt, Jordan, Yemen, and Morocco. Algeria descended into the abyss of civil war. Sudan's president was toppled by a military coup. Tunisia's was overthrown by a slick former soldier and diplomat, Zine el-Abidine Ben Ali, who came to power promising democratic reforms. This was the same Ben Ali whose widespread and barely concealed theft from his own people would ignite the Arab Spring and see him, in his turn, deposed by new leaders; it remains to be seen whether, this time, the democratic dream will be fulfilled.

The plain truth is that mass protests in North Africa and the

Middle East are common enough; and when they occur, they are likely to spread to neighboring countries with the same language and religion and similar histories and cultures. Decades before the first tweet or Facebook post, Gamal Abdel Nasser was using the power of radio to foster pan-Arab sentiment. Even in 2011, Qatar used the thirty-year-old phenomenon of cable news—in the guise of the Al Jazeera network—to ensure blanket coverage of the Arab Spring and the escalating violence in Syria. Whatever the year, and whatever the medium, the Arab world's tribal patriarchies, with zero history of liberalism, let alone participatory democracy, are simply not going to become Madisonian utopias any time soon. Arab leaders—many of them, like Ben Ali and Assad, partly educated in the West—have rarely shown even the smallest appetite for surrendering power once they have a hold on it. Instead, one corrupt autocrat is replaced, often bloodily, by another corrupt autocrat. And whether they arrive in office sporting a general's epaulets, a cleric's robe, or a lawyer's pinstripes, these men soon take on the trappings of dictatorship. "Meet the new boss," as Pete Townshend wrote. "Same as the old boss."

Bin Laden sought to break the never-ending cycle from one corrupt autocrat to the next by creating chaos. "Freedom is not achieved without a heavy price," he wrote in reference to the Arab Spring. "And blood is a component that cannot be separated from the other components to achieve it . . . [E]xposing the people of the Islamic nation to death is a very difficult matter, but there is no other way to save them. No other way." The genius of al-Qaeda's plan lies in its recognition that, in an important sense, dictators like Tunisia's Bourguiba, who claimed they *were* the system, had been right all along: Take away the pharaoh without immediately replacing him with another strongman, and the whole polity fractures along atavistic lines, into its component sects, tribes, and so on. What follows is not liberal democracy but chaos, bloodshed, and broken dreams. Al-Qaeda has long recognized that such societal collapse—"savagery," in jihadi jargon—is an indispensable part of strategy: "the most critical phase through which the *umma* will pass," as the subtitle to *The Management of Savagery* puts it. This worldview sees violence and political turmoil as the wrecking balls necessary to smash the institutions of central government and clear the way for fundamentalist rule.

Those jihadists who adhered to this basic playbook, from bin Laden in his high-walled mansion in Abbottabad and Zawahiri in his South Asian hideout to the Islamic State of Iraq in its desert foxholes, therefore heard in the tumult of the Arab Spring not a death knell but a call to action. Properly exploited, they realized, the uprisings would leave behind a void—much like the vacuums described in *The Management of Savagery*—ready to be filled with extremist ideology. When the dictators were gone, for good this time, their pompous nationalism would evaporate, the phony colonialist nation-states would crumble, and religion would once again be the one unifying factor—just as in the storied days of the original Rashidun Caliphate.

Reality, of course, would conform neither to the democratic nor to the jihadist vision. Some Arab Spring revolutions, like those of Bahrain, Algeria, and Saudi Arabia, would simply fizzle out without changing much. Egypt would follow the established pattern and exchange one autocrat for another. In Syria, Libya, and Yemen, however, al-Qaeda and other extremist groups would indeed manage to manipulate the uprisings to create upheaval and grab territory; and in each case, they would be assisted, wittingly or unwittingly, directly or indirectly, by foreign powers eager for influence. Nowhere has this pattern been more evident than in Syria.

For Zawahiri and the Islamic State of Iraq, Syria's precipitous descent from relative urbanity to abject barbarism helped create the greatest bonanza of the whole Arab Spring: an arc of state failure across northern Iraq and Syria, ripe for jihadi exploitation—precisely in line with the course outlined in *The Management of Savagery*. The ensuing war can seem like a confusing tangle of militias and terrorist groups with agendas now parallel, now competing. But, as with an Old Master painting in a museum, take a step back and the chaos of tiny brushstrokes begins to resolve itself into a more meaningful picture. With sufficient distance, we begin to see a remarkably traditional set of interests driving the conflict: those of nation-states with regional and global axes to grind. Clearly, al-Qaeda and its panoply of peers are by no means the only actors seeking advantage in Syria's misfortune.

When I was a schoolkid growing up in Lebanon, I was taught that every sect, every political group, every minute subdivision of my country's intricately variegated gene pool, was somehow in thrall to some international power. In the mistrustful Middle East, this kind of thinking is hardly unique. But in Lebanon, we raised such theories to an art form. The Sunnis? No question: The Ottoman Turks were their masters. The Maronites took orders from the French, the Druze from the British; the Orthodox answered to Moscow and the Shia to Tehran. So it went, all the way down the line; every gradation belonged to someone. And this was no mere street-corner speculation or tea-house gossip. This was written down, in newspapers and school history textbooks, and thus ratified in the permanency of print: one more example of the crazed conspiracy obsessions that bedevil every country in the Arab world. And yet, there was an essential kernel of truth to what we were taught in our history classes. True, the alliances we learned about were nowhere near so firm as we were given to believe, but on the geopolitical stage, you are nobody until you have at least one dog in the perpetual mêlée that is the Middle East.

The Syrian civil war is a particularly ugly example of this phenomenon. It is a conflict in whose outcome myriad powers hold equity, both within the region and beyond: Iran, Turkey, Saudi Arabia, the Gulf states, Russia, China, the United States, Europe, and on and on. Most of those doing the fighting and dying in Syria are essentially little more than pawns. Assad's most effective defenders have little personal attachment or emotional commitment to him, and those who oppose him do not do so out of any deep-seated personal animus. Whether they know it or not, they fight on behalf of the interests in the shadows that have chosen to move them to this particular place, at this particular time, in the pursuit of goals having little to do with local concerns; as is often the case, the people actually waging the war, like those suffering its consequences, are the ones with the least to gain.

· · ·

With only U.S. media coverage as a guide, one could be forgiven for thinking that, aside from the Assad regime itself, the Islamic State is the only game that matters in Syria. Nothing could be further from the truth. On the contrary, the Islamic State is merely the largest and most brutal of a bewildering array of opposition groups, with agendas that seem to clash more than they overlap; indeed, from a jihadist's point of view, the history of the Syrian conflict has been at least as much about rival groups fighting each other as it has been about any of them battling Assad or the secular opposition. In 2013, faced with a simmering dispute between Jabahat al-Nusra and the newly renamed Islamic State of Iraq and the Levant—then nominally al-Qaeda's franchises in Syria and Iraq, respectively—Ayman al-Zawahiri appointed a "personal representative" in the hopes of breaking the logjam. The man he chose, Abu Khalid al-Suri, belonged neither to al-Nusra nor to ISIL but to a third group, Ahrar al-Sham. Yet Abu Khalid's ties to al-Qaeda stretched back almost to the organization's founding.

As his toponym suggests, Abu Khalid al-Suri was Syrian. He was born Mohammed Bahaiah in Aleppo in 1963, the year Assad's Syrian Baath Party seized power in a coup d'état. As a young man, he became a close associate of Abu Musab al-Suri, who would go on to pen the influential tract *The Call of the Global Islamic Resistance*, in which he called Abu Khalid "[m]y brother and friend, my companion throughout my life." As members of the Fighting Vanguard, a militant splinter of the Syrian Muslim Brotherhood, both men fought in the uprisings against Hafez al-Assad, Bashar's father and predecessor, that took place during the late 1970s and early 1980s. That unrest culminated in 1982 in Hama, a city on the main highway between Damascus and Aleppo. In an effort to reassert control, twelve thousand regime troops laid siege to rebels holed up in Hama. Between ten thousand and forty thousand people reportedly died in the fighting—one survivor recalled having to step over corpses in the streets—and many more were abducted, imprisoned, or tortured in the reprisals that followed. The regime's terror tactics worked; Hama would prove to be the last major uprising in Syria until the Arab Spring nearly thirty years later, by which time a different Assad would be in control. To anyone familiar with images of the current violence in Syria, the pictures of Hama's burned-out buildings and ash-strewn streets look disturbingly familiar. As one Syrian activist's tweet mordantly declared, "Homs 2011 = Hama 1982, but slowly, slowly."

Like many Syrian jihadis who survived the devastation of Hama, Abu Khalid quickly fled the country. By the early 1990s, he had found a place in Afghanistan where he helped run media operations for various jihadi groups, met Ayman al-Zawahiri for the first time, and attended al-Qaeda's infamous Faruq training camp, then under the leadership of a contemporary of Abu Khalid's, the young Saif al-Adel. Later, Abu Khalid relocated to Spain and became bin Laden's chief courier in Europe. In 1997—around the time KSM was pushing his "Planes Operation"—an employee of Abu Khalid's brother-in-law made surveillance tapes of the World Trade Center and other U.S. landmarks. The following year, Abu Khalid ferried the tapes to bin Laden in Afghanistan. By September 11, 2001, Abu Khalid had become an important al-Qaeda fixer, helping to arrange funding and logistics for a number of plots, including the 9/11 attacks themselves.

Following 9/11, according to some reports, Abu Khalid fought U.S. troops in Iraq and Afghanistan. At any rate, he appears to have been apprehended in Pakistan in 2005 and transferred first to CIA custody, then to Syria, where he was interned at Sednaya, a prison in the mountains north of Damascus known for its population of political and jihadi inmates. Abu Khalid thus became a member of the "Sednaya Generation," a group of influential jihadis who came together behind bars—much as imprisonment at the U.S. facility Camp Bucca brought together the hotchpotch of religious militants and Saddam loyalists who would go on to lead the Islamic State. Many of Abu Khalid's contemporaries at Sednaya have played outsized roles in the Syrian conflict; one, Abu Atheer al-Absi, became the Islamic State governor of Aleppo province and mentored Mohammed Emwazi—the British executioner more commonly known as "Jihadi John"—and members of the cells that attacked Paris in November 2015 and Brussels in March 2016. It goes without saying that men of the Sednaya Generation like Abu Atheer and Abu Khalid pose a significant threat to secular Arab regimes like that of Bashar al-Assad. Yet in 2011, with the rebellion against his rule boiling over into civil war, Assad voluntarily released these two men and many others like them. This may seem puzzling, even paradoxical. But it was all part of a conscious strategy on Assad's part—one that had served him well in the past.

. . .

Bashar al-Assad was never meant to be president. Since childhood, his older brother Bassel had been groomed for the role. As a cavalry major in the Syrian army, a gifted horseman, and the head of his father Hafez Assad's personal security detail, Bassel cut a figure around Damascus, where his photograph—dark aviator sunglasses, neat black beard, red army beret—stared confidently from shop walls and car windows. Meanwhile, Hafez's younger son was left largely to his own devices. Bashar trained in medicine, became an ophthalmologist, and furthered his studies for a while in London. In January 1994, however, Bassel was killed when he crashed his car at high speed on the way to Damascus airport in heavy fog. Bashar, suddenly the heir apparent, was called back to Syria, rebranded as a military officer, and swiftly elevated to the rank of colonel in the armored corps.

When the old dictator himself died six years later in June 2000, it was Bashar who took up the reins of power, touting himself as a reformer. But despite his youth, his time abroad, and his glamorous Syrian-British wife (a Sunni, unlike the Alawite Assad family), Bashar's regime produced no meaningful changes. It announced hundreds of pieces of modernizing legislation but never followed up with implementation orders. It made no effort to reform Syria's antiquated court system, leaving most legal matters to a minority-dominated bureaucracy. Nor was there any palpable attempt at political reform. Instead, like his father before him, Bashar al-Assad kept political, administrative, economic, and military power concentrated within his own extended family. Corruption skyrocketed, even as human development flatlined. As part of a campaign of economic "modernization," Assad cut subsidies to rural areas, historically the heartland of Baathist support. Not coincidentally, these same areas would later become hotbeds of opposition to Assad during the Arab Spring. Even before the civil war, almost the only countries willing to risk money in Syria were its political allies, especially Iran; and the Islamic Republic's motives often had less to do with economic investment than with currying influence in a strategically significant region.

Bashar had been in power for little more than a year when al-Qaeda terrorists crashed their stolen planes into the World Trade Center and the Pentagon. Syria had no direct connection to the attacks, but in their immediate aftermath, Assad became alarmed at the sweeping antiterror powers the Bush administration was able to amass and act upon. Less than two weeks after the fall of the twin towers, the United States had procured Security Council Resolution 1373, which obliged every country in the world to cooperate to defeat terrorism. Assad's vice president expressed the fear that 1373 was in reality "an international emergency law that will limit countries' sov-

ereignty and place them under the Security Council's tutelage, thus
paving the way . . . for a conflict of civilizations instead of dialogue."
This was an ironic enough statement, one might think, coming from
a regime that had itself governed under an official state of emergency
for over thirty years; but it reflected Assad's trepidation in the face of
this new peak of American power.

Initially, hoping to placate the United States during one of its
strongest moments on the international stage, Assad cooperated with
the Bush administration, helping the CIA to round up and interrogate terrorist suspects. But if the United States appreciated this assistance, it chose a strange way of showing its gratitude. In May 2002,
Undersecretary of State John R. Bolton publicly added Syria to President Bush's ill-conceived "Axis of Evil" list, citing its chemical and
biological warfare program. By then it had already become clear that
the Bush administration's overall policy in the region was to carry
out, as one well-placed analyst put it, "an overhaul of the Arab and
Islamic world, rather than dealing with it as it is." The centerpiece
of the remodeling effort was, of course, to be an invasion of Syria's
neighbor and fellow Baathist state, Iraq. Saddam and the Assads had
ended diplomatic ties after Syria joined the coalition to end Iraq's
occupation Kuwait in 1991, and had not restored them since; but
the Syrian tyrant realized that once his Iraqi counterpart was gone,
he might well be next on America's hit list. So Assad resolved to
make life as difficult as possible for the Americans, in order to eject
them from the region before they could press on to Damascus. Hence
Assad's assistance to Abu Musab al-Zarqawi and others in setting up
a corridor through Syria for jihadi recruits heading for Iraq. Hence,
also, after a decade of hostility, his regime's sudden overtures to
Saddam. Immediately before the 2003 U.S. invasion, Syria's prime
minister traveled to Baghdad, where he presented the Iraqi president
with a ceremonial sword and reportedly told him that Assad would
consider any invasion of Iraq an attack against Syria.

Assad also reached out to Syria's long-standing ally, Iran. Just

days before "shock and awe" hit Baghdad, he traveled in person to
Tehran for a meeting with Supreme Leader Ayatollah Khamenei.
According to leaked minutes of that meeting, Assad told Khamenei:

> *We are the only leaders in the region who are masters of their
> own fate—as you are well aware—and we believe the best course
> of action for us is to draw out the war to exhaust the Americans
> and push them deeper into the Iraqi quagmire. And while it's
> true that the people of Iraq are not fond of Saddam Hussein, they
> will not tolerate a U.S. occupation of their territory. Therefore,
> we are all but certain that resistance will erupt against the occu-
> pation, and we need to coordinate before war breaks out. . . .
> We must thwart U.S. efforts in Iraq; and, if we cannot defeat the
> Americans, then we need to ensure the situation remains volatile
> and suicide operations carry on unabated. After all, the thing
> that frightens Americans the most is telling them their sons will
> be killed in Iraq.*

Despite the shocking scale and speed of Saddam's collapse, Assad's
strategy ultimately prevailed, at least in the medium term. As Assad
had predicted, the U.S. public proved unwilling to absorb a flood
of body bags, especially from a conflict whose raison d'être many
Americans perceived as paper-thin. In 2008, after half a decade of
bloodshed, the United States elected a new president on a platform
of ending the war posthaste—something that Obama eventually did
three years later.

Bashar al-Assad, however, was not done pouring gasoline on the
fires of jihadism. When the revolt against his rule broke out in 2011,
protesters clamored for the release of "political prisoners." Assad saw
in this demand an opportunity both to quell immediate criticism and
undermine the legitimacy of the revolution. In May and June 2011,
he issued an amnesty for dangerous jihadis, including many members
of the "Sednaya Generation"—among them, Abu Khalid al-Suri—

hoping that they would hijack the uprising in the name of jihad and thus give Assad a palatable excuse for crushing the opposition.

. . .

Abu Khalid's post-Sednaya activities seemed to confirm Assad's thinking. Within a few months of their release, Abu Khalid and a group of fellow Sednaya alumni had cofounded a new militant group, Ahrar al-Sham—Free Men of the Levant. The name was intended to burnish the group's credentials as legitimate local "freedom fighters"; they were not to be seen as foreign jihadi extremists. In many ways, Abu Khalid's group has come to embody the complexities of the Syrian conflict. On the one hand, Ahrar's goals are unabashedly Islamist—indeed, they explicitly include bringing Syria under fundamentalist rule. While Ahrar does not always agree with the al-Qaeda franchise in Syria, Jabhat al-Nusra (indeed, the two groups have sometimes come to violent blows), more often than not Ahrar's agenda aligns with that of al-Nusra, and the two factions' militants frequently fight alongside one another against Assad's forces. On the other hand, Ahrar has explicitly rejected the sectarianism and brutality espoused by some of its rivals. It has also disavowed any international agenda—unlike al-Qaeda, which sees America as the main enemy—and has gone out of its way to distance itself from al-Qaeda central.

Despite his seniority and his centrality to the group's creation, Khalid al-Suri was never made Emir of Ahrar al-Sham; partly, no doubt, because of the negative publicity he would bring as someone who had once been close to bin Laden. Instead, the top job went initially to another Sednaya alumnus, Hassan Abboud. By 2013, Abboud, Abu Khalid, and their colleagues had built Ahrar al-Sham into one of the most effective militias fighting Assad—and, with perhaps 20,000 members, one of the largest, behind only al-Nusra and the Islamic State. Together with a rotating cast of allied groups, Ahrar has made broad territorial gains in the northwestern provinces of Idlib and Latakia, in the process defeating and stripping weapons from Free Syrian Army groups, including at least one backed by the United States. Apparently conscious of the popular antipathy that helped bring down the first Iraqi insurgency shortly after Zarqawi's death, Ahrar has held back from imposing its harsh conception of Sharia right away. Instead, it has tried to maintain public support in the region under its control by feeding its inhabitants, supplying them with fuel, and rebuilding roads, bridges, and water pumps.

For much the same reason, the group's official communications repeatedly emphasize its ideological differences with al-Qaeda, especially its avowed rejection of global jihad in favor of a focus on Syria alone. In contrast to the naked sectarianism peddled by the heirs of Zarqawi, Abu Khalid's group has mostly shied away from discriminatory rhetoric, and has even promised to allow members of religious minorities to hold posts in any future government it may form. In late 2013 or early 2014, asked about the group's ties to al-Qaeda, a spokesman said, "There is neither a secret nor a public link," emphasizing that Ahrar al-Sham included "no-one who belongs to al-Qaeda." This was disingenuous at best, since at the time Ahrar was at the height of its cooperation with al-Nusra. Moreover, the statement was made while Abu Khalid was serving as Zawahiri's personal representative in Syria—in which capacity he was not only attempting to resolve disputes in Khorasan's favor but also siphoning off donations to the Syrian opposition from wealthy Gulf donors and redirecting the funds to al-Qaeda central. "He was to me and my brothers such a great advisor," Zawahiri said of Abu Khalid in this period. However, as bin Laden himself had been acutely aware, there was mileage in disavowing any connection with al-Qaeda, especially for a group interested in attracting aid from foreign governments and in nurturing goodwill among locals with a view to future participation in politics. This approach has paid off for Ahrar al-Sham; as more secular-minded projects like the Free Syrian Army have seemed to run out of steam, Western allies in the region, such as Saudi Arabia and Turkey, have increasingly come to rely on relatively moderate Islamist groups like Ahrar as a means of carrying on the fight against Assad. But these countries' motivations go much deeper than the elimination of a regional rival.

. . .

Prince Mohammed bin Nayyif, Saudi Arabia's Crown Prince and Interior Minister, knows the dangers of terrorism firsthand, having survived at least three assassination attempts. In the closest of these attacks, in August 2009, an al-Qaeda militant detonated a concealed suicide bomb at a reception in the Prince's home. The explosion tore the bomber apart—footage of the aftermath showed the walls, floor and ceiling spattered with blood and body parts—but bin Nayyif, astonishingly, escaped with only minor wounds, and was discharged from the hospital the same day. Experiences like this helped forge in bin Nayyif a determination to reverse his government's longstanding policy of tolerance toward the thousands of young Saudi men who have been traveling abroad for jihad ever since the Soviet invasion of Afghanistan. For bin Nayyif, the Syrian conflict has made plain the dangers inherent in such a policy. The roughly 2,500 Saudis fighting for extremist groups in Syria make them the second most prevalent nationality among Sunni foreign fighters (after Tunisians), and the Saudi combatants are known for being peculiarly zealous—a trait that shows in their disproportionate propensity to volunteer as suicide bombers. Someday, these radicals will return, and many will still have murder in mind. It is even possible that the Islamic State's so-called caliph, Abu Bakr al-Baghdadi, may seek to make good his improbable claim to be the leader of all the world's Muslims by seizing the two holiest places in Islam, Mecca and Medina, both of which are in Saudi Arabia. Indeed, in July 2016, Islamic State suicide bombers struck the Prophet's Mosque in Medina, hoping to damage the legitimacy of the Saudi regime as custodian of the holy sites. But even that threat pales in comparison to the danger posed by radicalized young men who choose to stay at home. Tight-knit local cells are already pursuing a terror campaign across the kingdom that has featured assassinations of police and suicide bombings of mosques. These men are more difficult to detect than fighters abroad, precisely because they do not cross international borders and do not need to communicate electronically over long distances.

Bin Nayyif's influence on high-level decisionmaking in the Kingdom signals a shift away from those Saudi figures who preach radicalism. He engineered a major reshuffling of the former king's closest advisers, including the removal of several foreign policy hawks from his inner circle, among them Prince Bandar bin Sultan, a former ambassador to the United States and the ex–deputy minister of defense. Under bin Nayyif's guidance, in February 2014, the late King Abdullah issued a royal decree forbidding Saudi involvement in extremist groups and participation in foreign wars, including those raging in Syria, Iraq, and Yemen. The following month, Saudi Arabia designated ISI and the al-Qaeda franchise al-Nusra as terrorist organizations, which had the effect of formally outlawing donations and assistance to those groups. Shortly after taking office at the beginning of 2015, the new king, Salman bin Abdelaziz, made bin Nayyif first in line to the throne, in addition to his position as interior minister.

But bin Nayyif's influence is far from absolute. The crown prince must compete for attention with the man who stands to inherit the throne after him: King Salman's own son, Prince Mohammed bin Salman. In his early thirties, bin Salman is a generation younger than bin Nayyif, but he holds similarly powerful offices, serving as deputy crown prince and defense minister. President Obama has called the millennial prince "wise beyond his years"; but in private other commentators more commonly accuse him of impulsiveness, arrogance, and naïveté. In contrast to bin Nayyif's caution, bin Salman has urged a more interventionist policy toward Syria. The kingdom has stepped up supplies of American-made TOW anti-tank missiles to moderate Free Syrian Army groups; this support has been credited with halting government gains in the strategic Ghab Valley south-west of Idlib. But not all recipients of bin Salman's assistance have been as benign. In 2015, Saudi Arabia helped create, fund, and arm the Army of Conquest, the coalition of militant groups of which Abu Khalid's organization, Ahrar al-Sham, is a leading member, as is the al-Qaeda franchise, al-Nusra (and its successor organization, Jabhat Fateh al-Sham). Bin Salman is thought to be the architect of both these initiatives. In February 2016, he appeared to go further, speak-ing publicly about contributing ground forces to fight the Islamic State; but this announcement forced a swift "clarification" from the Saudi government to the effect that the kingdom would only offer a largely symbolic contingent of special forces, and even then only as part of a future American-led ground intervention—a prospect that seems remote, to say the least.

The influence of bin Salman has greatly contributed to what Ger-man intelligence has publicly called "an impulsive policy of inter-vention" in Syria, as well as in Yemen, where Saudi forces face a quagmire largely of the kingdom's own making. In both cases, the goal has been to stave off the one terrible vision that looms over all Saudi policy-making: an ascendant Iran at the jeweled hilt of a vast Shia scimitar, slicing through the Middle East from the Arabian Sea to the Eastern Mediterranean. With a Shia-dominated government in Baghdad, a resurgent Hezbollah in Lebanon, and an Iranian cli-ent clinging to power in Damascus, this nightmare seems closer than ever to reality. This makes the Syrian issue an existential one for the House of Saud. But the kingdom is not the only Sunni power to turn to proxies like Ahrar al-Sham in hopes of bolstering its influence in the region.

. . .

"Democracy is like a tram. You ride it until you arrive at your destination, then you step off." So said Recep Tayyip Erdogan, then mayor of Istanbul, in the mid-1990s. In his eleven years as prime minister of Turkey from 2003 to 2014, Erdogan sought to put that maxim into practice, striving to centralize as much power as possible in his own hands. Since moving to the presidency in August 2014, he has embarked upon a project whose aim is no less than the transformation of Turkish government from a parliamentary system into a presidential one—the "Executive Presidency," as he has termed it. And there could be no more potent symbol of Erdogan's ambitions than the thousand-room, six-hundred-million-dollar White Palace he has built in Ankara for himself and his successors—that is, should he ever decide to step aside and let someone else ride the democracy tram.

Erdogan's staying power shows few signs of flagging. In July 2016, his government faced down an attempted military coup. Within days of the rebellion's failure, Erdogan had arrested or removed thousands of soldiers, judges, prosecutors, teachers, and academics. The crackdown was so sudden and so severe that one in three Turks believed the outlandish theory that the uprising had been staged by Erdogan himself, in order to justify a further consolidation of his power. While there is no evidence that Erdogan was behind the coup, it certainly seems that he had a long list of opponents ready to be purged should the opportunity arise.

Erdogan combines his authoritarianism with a strong Islamist streak. His party, AKP, emerged from the Islamist Welfare Party, founded in the 1980s and long exiled from Turkish politics for its nakedly religious ideology. After four years as mayor of Istanbul, Erdogan served jail time for "religious incitement," partly for reciting in public a poem that included the words, "The mosques are our barracks." The military banned Erdogan, as well as his former party, from Turkish politics, until AKP reversed that decision in 2003 and made him prime minister. Since then, he has presided over a full-scale revival in Islamist policies—pushing, among other measures, legislation to restrict the sale of alcohol and outlaw adultery.

As he has grown more authoritarian domestically, Erdogan has become increasingly hawkish on the international scene. In 2009 he notoriously stormed out of a panel discussion in Davos after an angry exchange with Israel's then-president Shimon Peres. The following year, he backed a Freedom Flotilla to help ease the plight of Palestinians in the Gaza Strip. He has paired his growing independence of the United States and NATO with increasing hostility toward Israel and support for the pro-Islamist agenda championed by the Muslim Brotherhood. Erdogan threw his support enthusiastically behind Egypt's Muslim Brotherhood president, Mohammed Morsi, then became enraged when Morsi was overthrown, and alienated Egypt's new president, Abdel Fattah al-Sisi, by accusing his regime of "tyranny" and "state terrorism." But if Turkey is to live up to its president's international ambitions, it must have a card of some kind to play in the Syrian conflict. Only by influencing the course of events there will Turkey be able to check regional rivals like Iran and Saudi Arabia, tamp down Kurdish separatism in the south, and position itself to host a pipeline transporting natural gas from reserves under the Mediterranean to Eastern Europe and beyond. None of this is likely if Syria remains in the hands of a regime whose biggest allies are Iran and Russia.

Like that of the other major Sunni power in the region, Saudi Arabia, Turkey's policy toward the Islamic State (IS) is complicated. On the one hand, Erdogan's government has allowed the United States to launch strikes against Islamic State positions from Incirlik Air Base, just over 100 miles from Aleppo as the F-16 flies. In late 2015, Turkish forces even began training Iraqi Kurds—whose brethren in Turkey battle Ankara for independence—for operations to retake Mosul from IS. Indeed, Turkey has good reason to set itself against the Islamic State: IS has subjected Turkish cities to a campaign of suicide bombings that have killed scores of people. Yet Turkish officials have reportedly turned a blind eye to Sunni foreign fighters crossing into Syria, including those bound for the ranks of the Islamic State, even when they proffer obviously phony passports. Turkey's southern border has become known as the "new jihadi highway"—the entry point of choice for such fighters, avoiding more perilous routes across the desert or through Shia-controlled areas of Lebanon or Iraq. Just as significantly, Erdogan's government has tolerated cross-border shipments of stolen oil worth over a million dollars a day—the Islamic State's main source of funds.

Erdogan has openly backed opposition to Assad from groups sharing the Turkic ethnicity of a majority of Turks. It is no coincidence that the Russian plane shot down by Turkish forces in November 2015 was in the area in order to bomb Turkic militants backed by Ankara. These groups bring another benefit to Ankara, in that they fight their Kurdish counterparts, staving off Turkey's recurring nightmare of a breakaway Kurdish state.

Erdogan has also joined Saudi Arabia in supporting the al-Nusra and Ahrar al-Sham–led Army of Conquest—the Islamist coalition that has fought U.S.-backed groups and captured territory in northwest Syria. Indeed, Turkey's participation has been essential to ensuring that arms and supplies reach the group across the border. A Turkish official told the Associated Press that this support was intended to strengthen Ahrar al-Sham at the expense of al-Nusra, but it was not clear how this could possibly work, as the two groups were at the time close allies in the Army of Conquest; indeed, some of their factions are even known to have spoken of a merger.

In 2016, Erdogan began sending Turkish troops into Syria and Iraq, with the intention not of combating IS so much as dislodging the Kurdish factions in the region from control of territory along the Turkish border. But Erdogan's forces have found themselves fighting IS anyway, a reality brought home in brutal fashion in December 2016 with the release of a video showing IS executing Turkish soldiers by burning them alive.

Erdogan's bellicosity on the international scene has come at a heavy price. When he first took the helm as prime minister, his avowed foreign policy was one of "zero problems with the neighbors." Instead of force or heavy-handed tactics, he sought to exert influence in the region using soft power, based on cultural affinities and shared economic interests within the former sphere of influence of the Ottoman Empire. Today, as the foreign policy commentator Piotr Zalewski points out, Turkey has gone from zero problems to zero friends. Erdogan has been forced to back down from his bellicosity toward Israel in order to secure Turkey's right to host part of a lucrative pipeline carrying Israeli natural gas to Eastern Europe. Shooting down the Russian plane over southern Turkey in November 2015 has turned out to be a catastrophic own goal. Not only did the strike fail to protect Turkish-backed Turkic fighters on the ground, it actually provoked Russia to step up its raids against those fighters. Erdogan, usually so careful to preserve his uncompromising image, has had to apologize to Vladimir Putin to head off threatened Russian economic sanctions that would have restricted access to Turkey's second-largest export market. The apology, in turn, infuriated the Islamic State, which regards Russia as one of its most formidable foes. IS expressed its outrage by attacking Istanbul airport in June 2016 with suicide bombers who hailed from Russia and two former Soviet republics. Six months later, in December 2016, a Turkish police officer turned Islamist assassinated the Russian ambassador in Ankara. It is significant that both attacks happened within days of high-level talks between Russia and Turkey about bringing an end to the conflict in Syria.

Turkey's sole remaining friend in the region is Shia Iran. On Syria, to be sure, the two countries remain at odds; Erdogan is as vocal in demanding Assad's ouster as Iran is determined that he should stay. But on almost every other topic, Turkey and Iran now find themselves in agreement. In March 2016, the two countries emerged from talks in Tehran agreeing to work together to "stanch the bloodshed," as Iran's President Rouhani put it. Indeed, with U.S. and EU sanctions on Iran lifted, Turkish-Iranian trade is booming, and Turkey is bidding fair to become the conduit for future Iranian energy exports to Europe. "It is above all in our own countries' interest to strengthen our political dialogue and reduce our differences of opinion to a minimum," Erdogan said the following month, after yet another high-level Turkish-Iranian meeting. "We have to work together to overcome the problems of terrorism and sectarianism and the related humanitarian crises that are shaking our region." He has reportedly even stooped to helping Iran evade international sanctions. This newfound amity can only stoke Arab nervousness, and may engender further poor policy decisions from Riyadh. And the more instability, the more state failure, the more regional confrontation—the more "savagery," in al-Qaeda's terminology—the more this state of affairs will nourish groups like Ahrar al-Sham, the Islamic State, and al-Qaeda's own followers in Syria.

. . .

Support from Turkey and Saudi Arabia has allowed groups like Ahrar al-Sham to prosper, even in the face of setbacks that might have destroyed other militant groups. In January 2014, the Islamic State of Iraq and the Levant killed one of Ahrar's senior commanders in Aleppo. The following month, Abu Khalid al-Suri himself died in a suicide bombing most likely also perpetrated by ISIL, in circumstances which, as we shall see in the next chapter, say much about the constant infighting that has come to typify the Syrian insurgency. Then, in September of the same year, an even bigger disaster befell Ahrar al-Sham: yet another bomb killed at least a dozen of its senior leaders. It was not clear who was responsible; but the act dealt the group a grievous blow. The dead included Hassan Abboud, Ahrar al-Sham's emir and Abu Khalid's comrade-in-arms from their time in Sednaya Prison together. Since that devastating attack, air strikes have claimed the lives of yet more Ahrar commanders. In 2015, Ahrar's willingness to entertain political solutions and its reliance on Turkish support led to a falling-out with al-Nusra. In early 2016, the dispute turned deadly, with the two groups clashing in Idlib Province near the Turkish border. Despite these losses, Ahrar al-Sham has regrouped and battled on, helping to lead an Islamist capture of every town in Idlib province, apparently shooting down at least one Syrian air force jet. Ahrar was even able to overcome its differences with al-Nusra sufficiently to launch a fierce joint assault on regime forces near Abu Khalid's hometown of Aleppo, although the city would later fall to Assad's troops, backed by Russian aerial bombardment.

Ahrar has shown itself adept at forming alliances with other rebel groups—no easy feat in a battleground as fractured as Syria. Ahrar's foreign relations spokesman has likened this process of coalition-building to the "dialogue, then neighborliness, then coexistence, then coordination, then unification" that characterized postwar Europe. In December 2012 and November 2013, it formed coalitions with smaller groups, arrangements that later led to mergers with eight of its allies. In March 2015, Ahrar subsumed yet another militia, the Suqor al-Sham Brigades. The same month it also became a charter member of the Army of Conquest, an alliance of Islamist groups supported by Turkey and Saudi Arabia.

And yet, despite the efforts of the Islamic State, the various Islamist factions, and the secular opposition, the Assad regime still stands. Partly that is because of the opposition's well documented failure to unite against him—a source of deep frustration for the West. But even more so, it is because he enjoys powerful regional backing of his own.

. . .

On the battlefields of Syria and Iraq, one man has become ubiquitous. He can be seen standing on the hoods and flatbeds of trucks, surrounded by fighters who jostle and shush each other to hear and see better. His face lightly frosted with a close-cropped white beard, his dreamy eyes seeming to shine with the recollection of a fond memory, the man addresses his audience in a pillow-soft tenor. But this man is a soldier, through and through. "When the war ends," he has said, "the honest mujahid clasps his hands sorrowfully. We lost, and the martyrs won." He is neither a Syrian nor an Iraqi, and he is certainly no Sunni foreign fighter. He is General Qassem Soleimani, supreme commander of Iran's elite Quds Force. His rapt audiences are made up of Shia fighters nominally independent of the Quds Force, but in reality every bit as much under his command. Not only do these militants sing songs about Soleimani; one group even produced a viral music video of one of those songs featuring militiamen saluting the general's image.

Soleimani hails from a small town in Kerman Province, a tribal area of Iran's southeast. At the start of the 1979 Islamic revolution, he joined the Revolutionary Guards and began his remarkable upward trajectory. In the 1980s, during the war with Saddam Hussein's Iraq, he led the Guards' 41st Division, nicknamed Tharallah—"Vengeance of God"—one of the aliases of Imam Hussein, one of the key figures of Shia Islam, who was killed in Karbala, Iraq, in the year 680. By the end of 1997, he had become commander of the Quds Force, Iran's lethal special forces unit initially formed to bolster pro-Iranian regimes abroad. Soleimani was chosen for the task partly because of his background in Kerman, which had long plagued the regime with ongoing tribal unrest. Within three years, Soleimani had pacified the province. At the same time, Soleimani was put in charge of managing relations with the upstart Taliban movement in neighboring Afghanistan. The general lent his country's support to the opposition Northern Alliance, but he also sought to calm tensions where necessary. When the Taliban executed 25,000 Shia in Mazar-i Sharif, including a group of Iranian diplomats, factions on both sides were hot for war. Iran began massing forces along the Afghan border, but Soleimani stepped in and defused the situation without resort to further violence.

Soleimani has been called the Shadow Commander, and with good reason. His influence can be felt throughout Iranian foreign policy, on which he has long enjoyed the unmediated ear of the Ayatollah Khamenei. During negotiations with the Americans in Baghdad in 2007, at the height of the U.S. counterinsurgency campaign, the Iranian ambassador to Iraq repeatedly excused himself to take orders via cellphone—not from his superiors in the foreign ministry but directly from General Soleimani. The following year, Soleimani sent David Petraeus—then commander of coalition forces in Iraq—a message reading, "General Petraeus, you should be aware that I, Qasem Soleimani, control Iran's policy for Iraq, Syria, Lebanon, Gaza, and Afghanistan." (Legend has it that the American's reply was to the effect, "General Soleimani, go pound sand down a rat hole.")

Few Iranians would dare be so impertinent to the Shadow Commander. At home, Soleimani has become a cult figure, as omnipresent on Iranian state television as he is in the Twitter feeds of Shia militias in Iraq and Syria. One Iranian filmmaker, accepting an award for his work, dedicated the trophy to Soleimani. Some Iranians have suggested that the general run for president, raising fears of a velvet coup by the military. But the place where Soleimani exerts the most feverish devotion remains the battlefield, where his tribal background and special forces training allow him to use sectarianism to military and political advantage.

The general's centrality to the Syrian conflict reflects the Assad regime's decades-long relationship with Iran. During the Iran-Iraq War in the early 1980s, Hafez supported Tehran by shutting down a critical pipeline carrying oil exports out of Iraq. Later, Iran financed Syria's acquisition of a nuclear reactor and a clutch of Scud missiles from North Korea. And in 2003, Supreme Leader Khamenei responded positively to Assad's suggestion that the two regimes collaborate to make life difficult for the United States in Iraq. Today, Iran bankrolls Assad's war effort, providing an estimated $4 billion to $8 billion per year in grants, credits, and military hardware. Just as significantly, Iran has sent proxies and its own regular forces to Syria to fight for the government.

Iran has a number of clear reasons to support Assad. First, there is the religious bond between Alawites and Shia. Iran, the world's most powerful Shia state, views itself as the Shia protector, and one of its main foreign policy goals is to establish a grand alliance of Shia-ruled countries—a category that, thanks to the removal of

Saddam Hussein, now includes Iraq alongside Syria and Lebanon. Secondly, Iran has economic reasons for cultivating Syria and Iraq as allies, not least the fact that it will need their cooperation if it is ever to build a planned overland pipeline to the Mediterranean from the giant South Pars–North Dome gas field on the Persian Gulf. An Iran-to-Lebanon crescent, held together by faith and backed up by petrochemical power, would be a force to be reckoned with. But Iran's biggest concern is maintaining the supply corridor to its cat's-paw in the Israeli-Palestinian conflict, the Lebanese militant group Hezbollah. Shipments directly into Lebanon are not an option because of Israel's naval and air patrols in the region. But thanks to their alliance with Assad, Iranian supply planes have carte blanche to land at Damascus International, where their deadly cargo is loaded onto trucks for transshipment over the mountains to Lebanon. Were the Syrian government to fall into the hands of the country's Sunni majority—which, as at the time of the French Mandate, makes up around three-quarters of its population—those planes would be turned back, and Iran would be left without a card to play in the Middle East's most symbolically significant fight. Moreover, Hezbollah lies at the heart of Iran's wider goal of reclaiming a measure of its former hegemony in the region.

With Iranian funds, training, and weaponry, Hezbollah enjoys tactical and intelligence capacity other factions can only dream of; in the early spring of 2014, for example, having tracked down the bomb makers responsible for suicide attacks in areas of Lebanon under its control, Hezbollah sent an undercover commando detachment deep into rebel-held Syria to find the house where several suspects were staying and reduce it to rubble with the targets inside. Such operations reveal a sophistication in planning and execution not unlike that of the Navy SEALs who took down Osama bin Laden. Hezbollah has undoubtedly changed the balance of the Syrian conflict. At the same time—and in part, no doubt, because of the sheer audacity of its operations—the group has suffered atrocious casualties in

Syria. By the end of 2015, around a quarter of its personnel deployed in the conflict had been killed, representing about 10 percent of the group's entire fighting strength. General Soleimani makes a point of visiting the graves and families of the fallen; in January 2015, he was pictured reading the Koran alone at the flower-scattered tomb of a Hezbollah fighter, Jihad Mughniyah, son of the Hezbollah commander Imad Mugniyah who trained al-Qaeda members in Lebanon in the early 1990s. But Hezbollah is not the only group doing Soleimani's bidding in the region. In mid-2015, Iranian-backed militias from Iraq, Afghanistan, and Pakistan, among other countries, were almost single-handedly fighting Sunni rebels for control of Syria's largest city, Aleppo, with practically no involvement from Assad's own forces. Over the border in Iraq, Iran funds and facilitates Shia militias collectively some twenty thousand strong, under the umbrella command of Qassem Soleimani.

Soleimani's Revolutionary Guard has an active presence of its own in Syria. The Iranian regular and paramilitary forces he commands participate directly in combat, helping to prop up Syrian units plagued by defections. The Iranians have not held back from the thick of the fight, suffering an astronomical toll of casualties. Perhaps as many as two hundred of the two thousand personnel deployed have been reported killed, putting the death rate around three times that suffered by U.S. Marines in the Vietnam War. Among the dead have been several high-ranking commanders, including at least two Revolutionary Guard generals. But Iran's repeated demonstrations of its extraordinary commitment to Assad have purchased the Islamic Republic even greater leverage in Syria, the Middle East, and the wider world. From the perspective of a Sunni extremist, Iran's involvement in the Syrian conflict represents a clear and present military threat; but it also brings a propaganda windfall. As Zarqawi's incessant railing against "rejectionists" and "apostates" during the Iraq War amply demonstrated, sectarian invective can be at least as effective a tool of terrorist recruitment as anti-Western messages. Both types of rhetoric play into the same persecution complex that al-Qaeda and the Islamic State have fostered, heightened, and exploited to such devastating effect. Moreover, the longer the conflict grinds on, the longer the "savagery" lasts—and the greater the opportunity for terrorist exploitation.

From the embers of this regional catastrophe, extremist groups can look forward to a multi-faceted bonanza. They gain the direct or indirect support of governments like those of Saudi Arabia and Turkey, desperate to counter the influence of their adversaries. Massive refugee flows create deep pools of potential recruits, while the ready deployment of sectarianism as a tool of foreign policy helps radicalize those recruits and others from around the world. Meanwhile, instability and the resulting failure of central government creates "zones of savagery" ripe for exploitation. Bin Laden himself could not have imagined a more propitious set of circumstances for al-Qaeda.

CHAPTER 7

THOSE WHO LOOSE AND BIND

Somewhere in the Levantine desert, at an undistinguished spot where the sand stretches to the horizon in all directions, a group of young men in black, wearing tactical vests, gingerly tease back seemingly endless coils of razor wire. One of them addresses the camera filming the scene. "Thanks to God," he says, "we are now on the border between Syria and Iraq. We have brought a bulldozer to take down the barricades to open the route for Muslims. We do not believe in the Sykes-Picot Agreement." A little way beyond the forbidding springs of wire, an earthen berm marks the border itself. As promised, a bulldozer pulls up, diesel smoke chugging from its high-mounted exhausts. It begins barging a path through the tall bank. "We've broken Sykes-Picot!" one of the fighters shouts in triumph. Overhead, black flags flutter from buildings, vehicles, and the hands of jubilant fighters.

Few in the West today have ever heard of the Sykes-Picot Agreement, an Anglo-French treaty that helped give shape to the largely arbitrary boundaries of the modern Middle East. But references to the pact are de rigueur among adherents of the Islamic State; indeed, negating the agreement is central to their ideology. The State's purported caliph, Abu Bakr al-Baghdadi, has promised that his fighters' "blessed march will not stop until we drive the last nail in the coffin of the Sykes-Picot conspiracy." In online videos, fighters display their foreign passports, open to the picture page, before tearing them into pieces. One issue of *Dabiq* the State's English-language online magazine, carries a full-page photograph of U.S., Canadian, British, French, German, and other passports with bullet holes shot through them, lying on the ground among spent shell casings. One of the passport-rippers explains for the benefit of the viewing public: "We will live in one Islamic State. We will spread from the West to the East, and no one but great God will rule us." The destruction of both travel documents and international boundaries is intended to symbolize a rejection of the modern concept of a nation-state, in favor of something else, something explicitly, defiantly premodern: an empire of faith.

· · ·

Despite the opportunities Ayman al-Zawahiri and others perceived in the maelstrom that was the Arab Spring, al-Qaeda's state-building efforts in the years immediately following 2011 met with mixed results. In Yemen, al-Qaeda in the Arabian Peninsula managed to rule over Zinjibar for only three months before the strategic port was wrested away again by a combination of government security forces and Sunni tribes disgruntled by AQAP's harsh interpretation of Sharia. By the summer of 2012, AQAP's proto-state in western Yemen had for all practical purposes collapsed. But in other areas of the country, particularly bin Laden's ancestral desert homeland of Hadhramut, AQAP enjoyed a deeper relationship with tribal groups; and at least on some level, the franchise had learned the importance of currying favor with the locals. So as not to antagonize Yemenis any further, AQAP concentrated its fire on the Yemeni armed forces and tried to avoid civilian casualties, even going so far as to apologize publicly when its fighters killed health workers alongside soldiers in an ambush at a military hospital.

Soon enough, AQAP would be presented with another opportunity to capitalize on chaos in Yemen. In September 2014, the Iranian-backed Houthi rebel group, which had been battling Yemen's government for a decade, seized most of the capital, Sanaa. President Abdu Rabbu Mansour Hadi fled south to the port of Aden, only to be forced out of that city, too, a month later. The following March, an international coalition led by neighboring Saudi Arabia began air strikes against the Houthis with the aim of countering Iranian influence in Yemen. AQAP lost no time in taking advantage of the ensuing turmoil. It quickly overran Mukalla, a city of 500,000 inhabitants, the capital of Hadhramut Province and Yemen's third largest port. In June 2015, AQAP's founder and leader, Nasser al-Wuhayshi, died in a drone strike; but the group's expansion continued. Over the course of 2015, it quadrupled its membership, from one thousand to four thousand fighters; and to judge by photographs from a mass AQAP rally in Mukalla in early 2016, that estimate may actually be on the low end of the scale. In January 2016, AQAP took Houta, twenty miles north of Aden, and the following month it captured four more towns in the space of just one week. By April, the Yemeni government estimated that AQAP had looted $100 million from the central bank of Mukalla and was earning up to $2 million a day from taxes on merchandise transiting the port.

Disturbed by these lightning gains, in April or May 2016 the United States deployed a "very small number" of ground troops to Yemen with the aim of ejecting AQAP from the territory it controlled, especially Mukalla. In the face of Yemeni and Emirati advances, aided by Saudi Arabia and the United States, AQAP did indeed leave Mukalla in early May; but in truth there is little to prevent AQAP's return. Many residents now prefer its rule to that of Yemen's chronically weak, corrupt governing institutions. Strategically, the group has focused on taking long sections of coastline and major highways, allowing it to set up a smuggling network to supply itself and the people living under its rule, which helps keep local populations loyal. Where AQAP governs, it always claims to do so in partnership with local tribes. Its propaganda touts its efforts to keep hospitals open, build bridges, and dig wells—something the Yemeni government rarely did in the rural hinterland, despite the country's degraded infrastructure and protracted drought. As a resident of Mukalla told Reuters, "I prefer that al-Qaeda stay here. . . . The situation is stable, more than any 'free' part of Yemen. The alternative to al-Qaeda is much worse." Meanwhile, AQAP makes little secret of the fact that it sees Yemen as a base for renewed attacks against its international antagonists, particularly in the West.

In North Africa, the Arab Spring presented al-Qaeda in the Islamic Maghreb with a similar opportunity for conquest. In 2012, as turmoil engulfed post-Gaddafi Libya—a country already awash in a tsunami of loose weaponry—AQIM seized an area of northern Mali the size of Turkey. In short order, the group set up training camps for its own operatives and those of other organizations, including Boko Haram, which would notoriously go on to kidnap 276 girls from a school in northeastern Nigeria. During the AQIM occupation of northern Mali, the group's leader, Abdelmalek Droukdal— holed up hundreds of miles away in the Algerian mountains—tried to rein in AQIM's unruly cadres, advising them to avoid alienating local populations and local armed groups, and to be prepared for the inevitable foreign intervention. He explicitly criticized his own commanders for applying Sharia with "extreme speed" to a society that was not used to it, singling out public beatings, the sequestering of women and children, and the destruction of local shrines as activities likely to give rise to local hostility. "Your officials need to control themselves," Droukdal admonished his nominal underlings. To the outside world, moreover, they should "be silent and pretend to be a 'domestic' movement that has its own causes and concerns."

There was no need, Droukdal said, "for you to show that we have an expansionary, jihadi, al-Qaeda, or any other sort of project." Even with these precautions in place, he told them, foreign military intervention was "very probable, perhaps certain. . . . We must not go too far or take risks in our decisions or imagine that this project is a stable Islamic state. It is too early for that."

Around the same time, for good measure, AQAP's Nasser al-Wuhayshi also tried to pass on lessons he had learned from his own fraught experience in governing; his advice was similar to Droukdal's. Had it been heeded, it could have functioned as a timely reality check for a group of militants Droukdal had correctly diagnosed as rampantly overzealous. But AQIM's subfactions, especially in the Sahel, the region of which Mali forms part, had never operated fully under centralized control. Droukdal and Wuhayshi's words fell on deaf ears. In early 2013, French forces routed AQIM and drove its fighters out of most areas of Mali. The group melted away into the desert; but within three years it was back doing what it had always done most effectively: mounting headline-grabbing terrorist attacks. AQIM fighters assaulted hotels in Bamako and Ouagadougou in November 2015 and January 2016, respectively, and in March 2016 carried out shootings at a beach resort in Ivory Coast and a rocket attack on a gas plant in Algeria. Late in 2015, AQIM announced that Mokhtar Belmokhtar's breakaway group, al-Mourabitoun, had rejoined the fold; the Bamako hotel assault was billed their first joint attack.

In Somalia, Kenyan forces had made major advances against the strongholds of another al-Qaeda franchise, al-Shabaab. In October 2012, the Kenyans retook Kismayo, a vital trade hub and a key component in al-Shabaab's financial sustainability. Within a few months, troops from Somalia and the surrounding region had retaken most of the country's major cities, including Mogadishu, eventually confining al-Shabaab to remoter areas. In the years that followed, African Union ground forces and American drone strikes decimated al-Shabaab's second-tier leadership and cadre of military and technical experts. But al-Shabaab remained strong in its core areas, and continued to attract recruits from all over the world, including the United States. By early 2016, the group had, like AQIM, reconstructed its capacity for terrorism, including operations well beyond its rural heartland.

Greek myth tells of an ancient monster with a thicket of serpentine heads. The Hydra, it was called, and legend held that the moment you lopped off one of its heads, two more would grow in its place, making the beast almost impossible to kill. Since 9/11, al-Qaeda has displayed similar resilience. Routed in Afghanistan, it rose again in Iraq, Yemen, Mali, and Somalia. In each of these countries, it has faced severe setbacks; but so far, it has always come back even stronger than before.

. . .

While the fortunes of al-Qaeda's Arabian and African franchises waxed and waned and waxed once more, in Iraq and Syria the situation was developing in a somewhat different direction. Zarqawi's al-Qaeda in Iraq had become the Islamic State of Iraq. It would further mutate into the Islamic State of Iraq and the Levant (ISIL) in April 2013 and simply the Islamic State (IS) in June of the following year. But before either of those name changes, it would have to endure near-death, followed by a stunning resurgence.

Between 2008 and 2010, the Islamic State of Iraq faced a concerted movement to destroy it once and for all. While U.S. surge troops and Sunni Awakening militias took care of the rank and file, coalition special forces moved in to capture or kill the leadership. The anti-ISI campaign came to a head in April 2010 when both the figurehead, Abu Omar, and the power behind the throne, Abu Hamza al-Muhajir, were cornered by U.S. forces in a house in the desert outside of Tikrit. Rather than be arrested, the two blew themselves up with suicide vests; photographs of their bloodied corpses soon began circulating online, touted by ISI as proof positive of their "martyrdom." With hostile forces closing in on all sides, the future for ISI seemed bleak. In one sense, however, these losses would ultimately help strengthen the group, because the raids stripped away the deadwood among its top leadership. Zealots like Muhajir and incompetents like Abu Omar tended to get themselves killed, while the more capable Iraqi middle management—many of them former officers in Saddam Hussein's sprawling security establishment—possessed better survival skills and had a greater ability to blend in with the local population. In time, these well-trained, ruthless men would come to form much of the top leadership in the resurrected Islamic State of Iraq.

When it came to those who were captured, moreover, the coalition developed an unfortunate habit of keeping them together, at a prison called Camp Bucca, which soon became known wryly as the Academy. The main subject of instruction, of course, was jihad. As one ex-inmate, a jihadi who uses the nom de guerre Abu Ahmed, put it years later: "If there was no American prison in Iraq there would be no Islamic State now. Bucca was a factory. It made us all. It built our ideology. . . . [M]any of us were back doing what we did before we were caught. But this time we were doing it better."

At its height, the complex near the Kuwaiti border in southern Iraq housed some 24,000 prisoners. Upon arrival, captured insurgents would immediately recognize their comrades among the detainees. They could not have gathered in such numbers on the outside without attracting undue attention, but in camp these men readily found each other and set about deepening their relationships and learning new skills. One jihadist, who was to become an Islamic State commander, praised Bucca in glowing terms:

> *Camp Bucca was a new service proffered to the mujahidieen, so to speak, by the U.S. government and the White House. It provided them with safety, food, drink, clothing, and housing, as*

well as books. As such, Camp Bucca was an ideal environment for Islamic education. . . . Inmates would immerse themselves in combat doctrine for a year or two, and come out as ticking time-bombs ready to become cannon fodder or stir up conflict. And even those who were remanded into Bucca with no knowledge whatsoever of combat doctrine eventually got acquainted with inmates who would teach them, educate them, and guide them.

Camp Bucca helped forge an unholy partnership between hardcore jihadists and another group of equally ruthless and dangerous men— former members of Saddam Hussein's security apparatus. Saddam maintained one of the world's largest and most lethal fighting forces. At the time of the Gulf War, the Baathist state's military comprised some one million troops. Even after years of cutbacks, in 2003 the Iraqi armed services were still 400,000 strong in a nation of just twenty-six million. Immediately following its invasion, the United States foolishly dissolved this standing army and declared persona non grata any government employee who had been a member of the Baath Party. America thus removed at a stroke the one possible means of maintaining order in postinvasion Iraq. Worse, it pushed Baathists, suddenly unemployed and deeply embittered, straight into the arms of the burgeoning Sunni insurgency. Elements of the former regime cooperated with more radical insurgents from the earliest days of the uprising, reportedly helping Zarqawi to carry out the massive August 2003 bombing at the Imam Ali mosque in Najaf that killed Ayatollah Hakim along with almost 100 other Shia worshippers.

Jihadists and their Baathist counterparts brought complementary attributes to the table. The religious radicals lacked nothing in zeal but possessed little organizational capacity and were for the most part unloved by local Sunnis; the ex-Saddam operatives, on the other hand, suffered from low morale in the wake of successive defeats but had excellent training in fighting and governing, courtesy of the former regime. Together, they made a lethal combination. But the blossoming partnership was more than a marriage of convenience; the two groups shared a common goal of restoring their Sunni sect to the dominant position in Iraq, and both were willing to engage in the most horrific violence and repression to achieve it.

Practically all of the Islamic State's founding fathers passed through Bucca at some point. They included Abu Bakr al-Baghdadi, the "caliph"; Abu Muslim al-Turkmani, his number two; Haji Bakr, a former Baathist colonel and éminence grise who helped Baghdadi to power; Abu Muhammad al-Adnani, the Islamic State's principal spokesman; Abu Ayman al-Iraqi, a senior military strategist; Abu Abdul Rahman al-Bilawi, who planned the operation that seized Mosul, Iraq; Abu Qasim, in charge of foreign fighters and suicide bombers; Abu Luay, a senior security official; Abu Shema, the quartermaster general; Abu Suja, in charge of programs to support the families of dead Islamic State fighters; and many others.

The most senior leader of Zarqawi's original al-Qaeda in Iraq to be imprisoned at Camp Bucca would also go on to help lead the Islamic State. Abu Ali al-Anbari, once a physics teacher in the former al-Qaeda stronghold of Tal Afar, began preaching Salafi jihadism in the 1980s, publishing "dozens" of religious tracts and sermons before finally being hounded out of the country by Saddam's security forces in 1998. Anbari went to Afghanistan to train with al-Qaeda. On his return two years later, he joined Ansar al-Islam, the al-Qaeda–linked group that would go on to shelter Zarqawi in the months before the U.S. invasion. In 2004, he pledged bayat to Zarqawi, who appointed Anbari his deputy and al-Qaeda's emir in the important strategic city of Mosul. Partly because of the connections he made during his two years in Afghanistan, Anbari also served as al-Qaeda in Iraq's liaison to the organization's overall leadership in Khorasan. In February 2006, around the time of the Golden Dome suicide bombing that precipitated the worst sectarian conflict of the Iraq War, Anbari traveled to Pakistan to brief senior leaders on al-Qaeda in Iraq's "progress." He did not meet either bin Laden or Zawahiri face-to-face; but such was the tension between Khorasan and its Iraqi faction at the time that the meetings cannot have been cordial.

After his return to Iraq, the Americans arrested Anbari and imprisoned him at Camp Bucca, where his closeness to Zarqawi would have given him considerable status among jihadis and former regime operatives alike. Following his release in 2012, Anbari would become one of the Islamic State's most capable administrators, with a hand in running its intelligence, finance, and military apparatus, as well as helping to direct overseas terrorist operations. Anbari would also serve as one of the organization's most influential ideologues, delivering sermons detailing the organization's doctrines on topics such as the killing of non-Sunnis and the evils of democracy—sermons eagerly consumed by the Islamic State rank and file in the form of dozens of audio recordings. Anbari's career thus represents continuity all the way from the old al-Qaeda in Afghanistan through the early days of the anti-U.S. insurgency to the reborn Islamic State that would go on to rule millions of Syrians and Iraqis. As one Arabic-language newspaper put it, "Anbari was everything and everybody."

· · ·

Inmates at Camp Bucca wrote names and phone numbers inside the elastic of their underwear, so that when they were released they could recreate the deadly networks they had developed behind bars. On the outside, former Baathists soon became the backbone of the new Islamic State of Iraq. With their governmental, intelligence, and military experience, these men made themselves essential both to ISI's battlefield achievements and to the terror tactics it has deployed against ordinary citizens. In this respect, the Baathists resembled the Egyptians who surrounded bin Laden in the late 1980s and became indispensable to the success of the fledgling al-Qaeda organization. If anything, however, the Baathists were even more ruthless. Today, whenever an Islamic State secret policeman asks a five-year-old child, "What do your parents think of the caliph?" then has his whole family beheaded based on the answer, the Islamic State, wittingly or not, is using tactics of which Saddam Hussein would have been proud.

One of the most capable ex-Baathists in the Islamic State of Iraq hierarchy was Haji Bakr (a nom de guerre). Even among those who knew him well, few were able to pin down his true personality; to meet the demands of any given situation, he was capable of oscillating from affable to psychotic. He had been in Air Force intelligence, and, as with many Iraqi soldiers, when the military was dissolved he joined the ranks of al-Qaeda in Iraq, linking up with Abu Musab al-Zarqawi in the Sunni heartland of Anbar Province. Like the regime he once served, the colonel was far from fundamentalist in religious matters; indeed, some more zealous members of ISI faulted him for going clean-shaven and being lax in religious practice—criticism he eventually sought to assuage by growing a beard and outwardly comporting himself more in accordance with Salafi teachings. But Haji Bakr's military and intelligence expertise was too valuable to ignore, and soon, he began to rise through the ranks of the incipient Islamic State of Iraq. From 2006 to 2008, he was imprisoned at Camp Bucca as well as at the infamous Abu Ghraib prison. After his release, he became a senior military adviser to the two ISI leaders, Abu Omar and Abu Hamza al-Muhajir. One of his favorite tactics for serving his masters' interests was to arrange for their rivals to meet an untimely end, just as Saddam's intelligence services used to do with the late dictator's own enemies. By the time Omar and Muhajir exploded their suicide vests in 2010, Haji Bakr had risen to the top of the Islamic State of Iraq's *shura* council, the body that governed ISI and picked its senior leadership (and still performs those roles in ISI's successor organization, the Islamic State). From that pivotal position, Haji Bakr was able to engineer the accession of Abu Omar's successor as emir. It was still too dangerous for the council to meet face-to-face; instead, like bin Laden and Zawahiri, the members had to communicate by courier. Haji Bakr took full advantage of the fog of war thus created to push his own nominee; he wrote to every member of the council, telling each one that the others had all unanimously decided to support one particular candidate. In the end, all but two members went along with this "consensus," and Haji Bakr's man was elected.

The man thus catapulted to the top of the organization was another Iraqi, an aspiring cleric called Abu Bakr al-Baghdadi. Like his predecessor, Abu Omar, Baghdadi was not actually from Baghdad; he hailed instead from the countryside around the ancient city of Samarra, at the center of the Sunni Triangle, where Zarqawi's 2006 bombing of the golden-domed Askari shrine was to herald a major escalation in sectarian violence. Baghdadi was born into an agricultural family in the early 1970s. Two of his brothers and two uncles served in Saddam's security forces, but like the young Ayman al-Zawahiri twenty years before, as a schoolboy Baghdadi was known as a reticent bookworm, albeit one who excelled at soccer—his skills would later earn him the nickname Maradona, after the Argentine soccer legend. At college in Baghdad, he studied the Sharia and the Koran before going on to obtain a master's in the study of medieval interpretations of the Koran. He joined the Muslim Brotherhood—a banned organization under Saddam—but soon left in dismay, having found that even the Brotherhood was not radical enough for his taste.

According to Baghdadi's official biography, he became a professor at Tikrit University and served as imam at mosques in Samarra, Baghdad, and Fallujah, cofounding an insurgent group called the Army of the Sunnis in the aftermath of the U.S. invasion. This is almost certainly an exaggeration. Unofficial sources place Baghdadi as an assistant prayer leader at a mosque in a poor area of Baghdad and possibly an assistant imam in Fallujah. For the most part, though, Baghdadi was a student. After earning his master's in 1999, he began work on a PhD at an institution then known as Saddam University, but his studies were cut short by his arrest in February 2004. Even this happened by accident; Baghdadi simply happened to be in the wrong place at the wrong time—the house of a friend who was involved in the insurgency and who was the real target of the raid. Baghdadi's Department of Defense file lists his occupation as "Administrative Work (Secretary)." One Pentagon official describes him as having been a "street thug." In fact, he probably did not quite match that description, for there is no evidence that Baghdadi was ever a fighter of any kind; his jihad was clerical, in both senses of the word.

Baghdadi spent most of 2004 in U.S. custody, first at Camp Adder, near Nasirayah, in the Shia south, and then, for about two months, at the Academy, Camp Bucca. Among the other inmates, he gained a reputation for being quiet and withdrawn, although he did occasionally deliver Friday sermons and lecture the inmates on Islamic law. One jihadi colleague said, "I got a feeling from him that he was hiding something inside, a darkness that he did not want to show to other people. . . . He was remote, far from us all." However, this remoteness seems to have afforded Baghdadi an air of impartiality, for the Americans would turn to him to help arbitrate disputes between rival groups of inmates.

In December 2004, the United States released Baghdadi, apparently because he was deemed too "low level" to pose a real threat; his detainee file indicated that there was scant evidence that he was even a part of the insurgency at all prior to his arrest. But if he was not already involved with the insurgency, he soon became so. He seems to have traveled to Syria to complete his PhD, but while there he became involved in preparing jihadi recruits about to make the journey across the border into Iraq. Under Abu Omar, Baghdadi played a role in the group's communications, although precisely what that role was represents yet another subject of biographical dispute. On one end of the scale, he became a trusted confidant to the emir, drafting important correspondence, including Abu Omar's letters to Osama bin Laden, coordinating communications between the Islamic State of Iraq and its "governors" in the field, and eventually ascending to the organization's *shura* council. In another version of events, he was a post office clerk, responsible for receiving, storing, and passing on letters, with no knowledge of the sender or recipient. Whatever Bagh-dadi's precise role, it is clear that, prior to his promotion to the top of the Islamic State of Iraq, practically nobody, inside the organization or out, had any idea who he was.

Yet ironically, Baghdadi's very obscurity helped ensure his safety. Few people knew for certain what he looked like; indeed, only two genuine photographs of him are known to have existed at this time. So secretive was his regime that in high-level meetings even ISI's top military brass would be told only that the emir was in the room, without his being specifically identified. Some senior commanders reportedly assumed that their leader was Zarqawi's old deputy, the administrator and ideologue Abu Ali al-Anbari. In any case, it would be difficult to challenge a man whose very appearance was a mystery; he was, in some sense, the inverse of Saddam Hussein, whose face was known around the world but who was rumored to employ multiple body doubles for security.

For Baghdadi and Haji Bakr, the first order of business was to purge the senior leadership and replace any waverers with their own loyalists. Those who refused to go quietly would simply be murdered. In fact, Haji Bakr—assisted by the ever-present Anbari—quickly created an organization within ISI with the specific task of assassinating prominent people who took issue with his and Baghdadi's leadership—senior internal figures as well as Iraqi tribal and religious leaders.

Thanks to the unparalleled training and networking opportunities afforded by Camp Bucca, continuity in leadership had been assured. As Abu Ahmed, the former inmate, said, "There wasn't a void at all, because so many people had been mentored in prison." To some in ISI, however, Baghdadi's accession as emir, with Haji Bakr pulling his levers in the shadows, was nothing less than a Baathist coup. For these critics, jihadi shills acted merely as a thin veneer on what was in reality an organization now controlled entirely by former Saddam loyalists. One senior operative, who later defected to a rival militia, described Baghdadi's ISI as "the Baath state with beards and

Siwak"—a reference to the traditional toothbrush favored by Salafis. "The Baath killed our people," he wrote. "How can they lead us?" A satirical slogan online corrupted Islamic State's official tagline, "A Caliphate in accordance with Prophetic method," to "A Caliphate in accordance with Baathist method." But Baghdadi and Bakr's merciless handling of opposition, together with the organization's undeniable military achievements under the new regime, have combined to silence most of the doubters.

. . .

The Islamic State of Iraq's first big break under Baghdadi was to come not in its native Iraq but across the border in Syria. By mid-2011, little more than a year after Abu Omar's death, the unrest was rapidly degenerating into a vicious and desperate civil war between Assad and various opposition factions. Baghdadi and Haji Bakr did not want to risk hollowing out ISI by allowing Iraqi fighters to travel over the border. Instead, they formed a task force of non-Iraqis, led by a Syrian, Abu Mohammed al-Julani, to explore opportunities in Syria. To avoid tarnishing its image by open association with foreigners, the new group called itself Jabhat al-Nusra Li Ahl al-Sham, or The Support Front for the People of the Levant. But behind the scenes, in recognition of the Syrian battlefront's centrality, ISI provided al-Nusra with unprecedented support, splitting its own budget fifty-fifty with Julani's group. Around the same time, Assad began his amnesty for dangerous jihadists like Abu Khalid al-Suri; these men, along with hundreds of foreign fighters now pouring into the country, soon helped al-Nusra and Ahrar al-Sham grow into two of the most formidable militant groups in Syria. Haji Bakr's longer-term vision, informed by his experience in Saddam's military, was even grander. He wanted to use the rapidly disintegrating state of Syria as a base to build up ISI for an invasion of Iraq. In late 2012, the colonel relocated himself from Iraq to a town north of Aleppo in order to oversee the plan personally.

In the meantime, ISI was going through a renaissance in Iraq, too. By 2011, the last American combat units had left, and the remainder were in the process of packing up and going home. Iraq's Shia prime minister, Nouri al-Maliki, took their departure as his cue to crack down on his own political enemies, especially Sunnis, and the political system began to fracture along sectarian fault lines that had been kept under wraps for decades. Maliki dishonored Iraq's agreement with the Sunni Awakening militias that had done so much to decimate the Islamic State of Iraq; all he saw in these armed groups were thousands of Sunnis with guns, whom he viewed as a potential threat to his Shia-led administration. Maliki refused to pay their salaries, a move that created further resentment among Sunnis even as it took the pressure off ISI. Desperate to shore up his regime, the prime minister detained hundreds of opponents without charge. Most prominently, he hit members of Vice President Tariq al-Hashimi's security detail with terrorism charges that were widely seen as trumped up; under torture, the bodyguards "confessed" to having participated in terrorist activities under orders from Hashimi. In the midst of this affair, while the last U.S. troops were leaving Iraq, Maliki visited Washington. At the White House, President Obama told the Iraqi prime minister that, as far as the United States was concerned, the Hashimi affair was a purely domestic matter. To Maliki, this was tantamount to a green light. One day after the U.S. drawdown was completed, he issued an arrest warrant for Hashimi, who was eventually sentenced to death and forced to flee the country. In the months that followed, thousands of Sunnis were detained, and hundreds murdered, by Shia militias with links to the prime minister. Corpses littered the streets of Baghdad and other Iraqi cities, reminding many Iraqis of the bloodiest days of the Sunni insurgency. But Maliki was not done yet; in December 2012, his regime reprised the Hashimi affair with a different cast of characters by indicting and apprehending the bodyguards of the Sunni finance minister, Rafi Al-Essawi.

In the face of Maliki's abuses—exacerbated by Iraq's failing economy, rising inflation, and sky-high youth unemployment—protests soon erupted. Enraged, Maliki ordered demonstrators to "terminate" their activities "before we terminate you." In April 2013, in Hawijah, his security forces made good on this open threat by moving against a Sunni protest camp. Television footage shot in the aftermath of the attack showed the bodies of protesters piled up in the streets, including at least one lying dead in a wheelchair. With Sunni anger at fever pitch, Baghdadi and Haji Bakr could hardly have wished for better conditions in which to reboot the Islamic State of Iraq project. They had already begun picking off militants formerly involved in the anti-ISI Sunni Awakening, co-opting some leaders and assassinating those who refused to be converted. In July 2012, he launched a campaign called Breaking the Walls, focused on staging high-profile jail breaks to release remaining ISI members from regime custody; these efforts would culminate a year later with an attack on Abu Ghraib that freed more than five hundred inmates. At the same time, ISI stepped up its efforts to recruit more fighters from abroad. The group began producing slick, high-definition videos depicting the fighting as a sort of real-life, post-apocalyptic Hollywood action movie, complete with explosions and bleeding corpses. Within hours of being posted, these videos would garner thousands of views. In the summer of 2014, the organization took a leaf out of AQAP's book and began publishing *Dabiq*, whose overproduced pages hyped the life-changing power of extreme violence. *Dabiq* has since disappeared from circulation, perhaps as a result of the heavy casualties IS has sustained in defending its territory against Iraqi and Syrian forces. Propaganda across all media glorified gruesome images of the dead who had martyred themselves. The group employed a small army of analysts monitoring traditional and social media channels, and a team of bloggers to document its exploits in various languages. Like many organizations today, the group even outsourced part of its media operation to India, relying on a blogger from Bangalore to disseminate propaganda to more than 17,000 followers via the handle @ShamiWitness. To increase its page views still further, the organization used sophisticated tactics to redirect online traffic to its own content. Between May 2015 and February 2016 alone, Twitter suspended more than 125,000 accounts for supporting terrorism; but IS remained one step ahead by quickly reestablishing closed feeds under new names and deploying specialized software to evade the blocks placed on it by social media sites.

As efficient as online channels may be as a means of disseminating propaganda, when it comes to recruitment, they can at best only prepare the ground. When your goal is to persuade young men to leave the safety of their homes and come to a war zone to fight, nothing beats face-to-face contact. For this reason, IS has seen its greatest successes in a relatively small number of highly concentrated hotbeds of jihadism around the world. For example, eight young men from the Lisleby neighborhood of Fredrikstad, Norway (population 6,000 of a total city population of about 78,000), are known to have traveled to Syria together, following in the footsteps of a charismatic local youth who played soccer in the neighborhood. If Americans joined IS at that rate, there would be half a million of them fighting in Syria today, instead of the few hundred at most who have actually made the trip. Molenbeek, the Brussels neighborhood that was home to many of those who attacked Paris and Brussels in November 2015 and March 2016, respectively, functions in much the same way. Three cities in Tunisia are responsible for over one-third of the huge Tunisian contingent fighting in Syria—around 2,500 fighters out of a total of 7,000 or more. Over the border in Libya, the town of Derna has a history of producing disproportionate numbers of fighters dating back to the Soviet invasion of Afghanistan in the 1980s, a tradition it is continuing today.

Prior to 2014, ISI/ISIL may have had three to four thousand foreign fighters. By January of that year, the figure had risen to more than seven thousand, and by the end of 2015, it may have been as high as thirty-one thousand fighters from more than one hundred different countries, with the figures still on the rise. Moreover, IS has managed to maintain its troop strength despite a death rate of up to ten thousand per year, suggesting that its pipeline of fighters remains formidable.

. . .

Over the course of 2013, the Islamic State of Iraq—renamed the Islamic State of Iraq and the Levant in April 2013—began aggressively conquering territory in both Syria and Iraq. Once again, the Baath-dominated ISIL took its cues from the tactics once employed by Saddam Hussein's regime. In rebel-held communities all across the country, ISIL would first open what appeared to be a religious community center, offering education about Islam. From among the attendees of its courses, recruiters would pick a few particularly fervent young men to inform on their neighbors and spy on any rival rebel groups in the area. These recruits would tell ISIL who the powerful families were locally and dig up dirt on resident notables to be used later for blackmail. In some cases, ISIL had its operatives marry into influential families to garner further intelligence. At the same time, ISIL would begin concentrating its fighters in the area— typically foreigners who would have less compunction about killing or subjugating the natives. When the local faction judged that it had amassed enough manpower and enough leverage with the local population, it would go public and seize the municipal government, violently if necessary. A case in point is Raqqa, Syria's sixth largest city, which was to become the "capital" of the Islamic State. Raqqa first fell to the anti-Assad Syrian rebels in March 2013. Two months later, ISIL began assassinating the rebel leadership of the town, starting with the elected head of the city council. Anyone who opposed ISIL's rule would be murdered; one outspoken ISIL critic was found trussed and executed by gunshot to the head. With these terror tactics, ISIL soon compelled *bayat* from the local tribes, and by January 2014 it was firmly in control of Raqqa. The pattern repeated across northern Syria.

Throughout the rapidly expanding areas under its control, the organization began raking in proceeds from smuggling, seizures of government property, trafficking in looted antiquities, theft from

Shia, Christians, Yazidis, government employees, and anyone else deemed an enemy, extortion (referred to as "taxes"), highway robbery ("tolls"), "repentance fines" extracted from former police officers and soldiers, ransom payments (although it was equally happy to execute hostages for the propaganda value, particularly after other revenue streams kicked in), and, in particular, illicit sales of stolen oil. Backed by a vast criminal oil cartel, ISIL was soon making more money in a week than al-Qaeda ever dreamed of.

· · ·

One morning in January 2014, shortly after ISIL subjugated Raqqa, a detachment of Syrian rebel fighters arrived at Haji Bakr's hideout north of Aleppo. For the sake of anonymity, the colonel had foregone heavy security, so the rebels, acting on a tip from a neighbor, were able to walk right up to his front door more or less unimpeded. When the rebels tried to take him into custody, Bakr, still dressed in his morning pajamas, appeared at the door and sprayed them with bullets from his Kalashnikov. The rebel commander returned fire and shot Haji Bakr dead. To a less sturdy organization, the loss of its shadow leader might have been a critical blow; but Haji Bakr had built ISIL on strong foundations so as to withstand precisely this kind of eventuality. And so, in the wake of his death, there was no discernable letup in the group's rampage across the region; if anything, its conquests seemed to gather steam. In Mosul, with two million inhabitants Iraq's third-largest city, ISIL set up what was in effect a protection racket, passing the city limits under cover of darkness to extract money from residents and businesses before disappearing into the surrounding desert during the day. In June, ISIL fighters attacked the city with suicide car bombs and gunmen in trucks. Initially, they intended only to terrorize the local population, not to take the city. But the U.S.-trained and -equipped Iraqi army simply dissolved, leaving ISIL in control of one of the Middle East's major metropolitan centers. Within days, ISIL had taken Saddam Hussein's hometown of

Tikrit and was threatening to advance on Baghdad. By June 15, ISIL controlled most of Iraq's Sunni-majority provinces—an area comparable in size to Austria or Jordan—and ruled over a population of up to eight million luckless souls.

. . .

Even as the group consolidated its astonishing rise, a factional conflict raged within the group itself. In early 2013, as the organization tightened its grip on the towns and villages of northern Syria, Baghdadi received word that Abu Mohammed al-Julani, the head of the detachment sent to Syria, had been reinforcing his direct contacts with Khorasan and was poised to declare his group, Jabhat al-Nusra, an al-Qaeda affiliate in its own right. Naturally, Baghdadi wanted al-Nusra answering to him, not operating independently as a coequal branch of al-Qaeda. ISI therefore ordered Julani to announce publicly that al-Nusra was subordinate to Baghdadi. Julani and his *shura* council rejected that suggestion. Julani's position was a reasonable one, given the importance of maintaining al-Nusra's credibility among the Syrian population by keeping the al-Qaeda connection under wraps. For precisely that reason, bin Laden had repeatedly warned against using the al-Qaeda brand too liberally. ISI sent some of its commanders to Julani to try to persuade him otherwise, but al-Nusra again rejected their advances and reportedly imprisoned a handful of them.

Abu Ali al-Anbari, the former deputy to Zarqawi, had been close to Julani—so close, in fact, that in correspondence Julani called Anbari "beloved father" and Anbari referred to Julani as "beloved son." Anbari had warned Baghdadi of Julani's intransigence and the likelihood that he would try to split off from ISI, so Baghdadi knew he would have to act decisively to keep al-Nusra in line. He moved to head Julani off at the pass. On April 9, 2013, Baghdadi announced that his organization was changing its official name from the Islamic State of Iraq to the Islamic State of Iraq and the Levant, or ISIL (the Levant being a region encompassing Syria, Jordan, Lebanon, Israel, and parts of some other countries), and that the group called al-Nusra was part and parcel of this binational umbrella organization. Baghdadi explained:

> [W]e assigned al-Julani who is one of our soldiers with a group of our sons and pushed them from Iraq to the Levant to meet with our cells in the Levant and set for them the plans and drew for them the policy of work and supplied them with half of what is in the treasury every month. . . . [The] time has come to declare before the people of the Levant and the whole world that Jabhat al-Nusra is only an expansion for the Islamic State of Iraq and part of it.

To Julani, this was not only unwise from a PR standpoint; it was rewriting history. He was adamant that al-Nusra was, and always had been, an al-Qaeda affiliate in its own right. The very next day, he released his own audio message expressing this view and "renewing" al-Nusra's direct *bayat* to Ayman al-Zawahiri.

This fast-developing feud took the al-Qaeda emir by surprise. Suddenly, Zawahiri faced not one but three critical problems: first, a split between his Iraqi and Syrian branches, just as the rebellions in both countries were reaching a critical stage; second, a very public admission that al-Nusra was part of al-Qaeda, in violation of the longstanding principle that local groups should avoid open association with Khorasan; and finally, an obvious challenge to Zawahiri's own authority and relevance, two commodities of which he was already short. Al-Qaeda's historic opportunity was in danger of being missed altogether. Zawahiri moved quickly to try to minimize the damage. The day after Julani's message came out, Zawahiri wrote to both sides, ordering them to freeze the status quo ante. Six weeks later, he released his final ruling. The edict faulted both sides for failing to consult him before going public; declared that ISIL and al-Nusra were separate entities, each a franchise of al-Qaeda in its own right; admonished the two affiliates to cooperate and share resources; and appointed Baghdadi and Julani as emirs of their respective organizations for a probationary period of one year apiece.

Baghdadi rejected this ruling, publicly accusing Zawahiri of acting contrary to the will of God. His chief spokesman clarified the caliph's objections, denouncing Zawahiri for splitting ISIL up along the despised Sykes-Picot boundary between Iraq and Syria, for encouraging rebellion within the jihad, and for doing the work of the enemy. Baghdadi sent fighters to confiscate al-Nusra's weapons, assassinate its leadership, and poach thousands of men previously loyal to Julani. The defectors represented perhaps as much as 70 percent of al-Nusra's total strength. Julani himself survived this onslaught, however. While ISIL moved to distance itself from al-Qaeda, Julani thickened his group's ties with Khorasan and increased direct communications with central command. In an interview, he told Al Jazeera that Zawahiri had given al-Nusra "a large margin to decide on our own" when it came to the jihad in Syria. It was an assertion unlikely to endear him to Baghdadi, who still considered himself Julani's superior.

As the final piece of his plan to break the stalemate, Zawahiri appointed Abu Khalid al-Suri as his special envoy to the region, with plenary power to resolve disputes between rival militant groups. Zawahiri trusted al-Suri, having known him since the Afghan jihad against the Soviets. When al-Suri examined relations between ISIL and Al-Nusra, he did not like what he saw; he described it as *fitna*, an Arabic word traditionally used to denote severe discord or strife. Al-Suri quickly took sides, issuing public statements denouncing ISIL, accusing it of wantonly destroying Muslim life and of acting as a covert front for foreign intelligence agencies bent on further discrediting the insurgency.

In light of the rapidly widening rift within the jihadi cause, a number of efforts quickly got under way to knit the two sides back together. Zawahiri turned to the capable and well-connected AQAP leader Nasser al-Wuhayshi to mediate. Wuhayshi sent letters to Baghdadi and Julani asking them to state their respective cases. Julani wrote back that ISIL's involvement in Syria risked blowing apart the anti-Assad insurgency and leaving the hated Alawite dictator in power; Baghdadi did not respond at all. In November 2013, Ahrar al-Sham and five other groups aligned with al-Qaeda joined to form the Islamic Front, and issued a call for unity among all groups sharing their goals of ousting Assad and imposing on Syria an extreme Salafi-jihadi conception of Sharia. Neither ISIL nor al-Nusra joined, but the ultimate intention was apparently to bring them in as a means toward reconciliation.

Around the same time, a young Saudi cleric, Sheikh Abdullah al-Muhaysini, arrived in Syria to attempt his own resolution to the dispute. Unlike Abu Khalid al-Suri, Muhaysini's impressive social and religious credentials commanded the reverence of all sides, at least initially. The son of a wealthy family on good terms with the Saudi government, Muhaysini holds a master's degree in Islamic jurisprudence. Before his move to Syria, he preached in a mosque in the sacred city of Mecca and helped raise funds for jihad. From the moment of his arrival in northern Syria in October 2013, Muhaysini began mediating factional disputes, apparently meeting with some early success. In January 2014, Muhaysini published his Umma Initiative, an umbrella proposal for an independent Sharia court to iron out intramural disagreements between the various jihadi groups. There was, he said, "enough room in this arena of jihad for all of us." As an example, Muhaysini pointed to bin Laden and Mullah Omar's efforts to work together—an ironic choice of model, given the hell through which bin Laden's repeated disobedience had put the Taliban, culminating in the Afghan group's removal from power and the near-destruction of bin Laden's own organization.

But Muhaysini himself did not remain neutral for long. Like al-Suri, he developed an intense dislike for ISIL. Perhaps unsurprisingly, ISIL rejected his Umma Initiative out of hand. In February

2014, he publicly denounced ISIL and blamed the group for prolonging the strife. At the same time, he became closer to al-Nusra. Julani took him along on a propaganda tour of Idlib province. It would seem that Muhaysini came close to the battlefront; he apparently sustained a stomach wound from a sniper, and he has been the subject of at least one ISIL assassination attempt. In March 2015, he became chief judge of the then newly established Army of Conquest, the Saudi- and Turkish-backed jihadi coalition that has since made advances across Idlib and Latakia provinces. However, he has apparently not been called upon to resolve disputes between the members of the coalition, signaling that his star may now be on the wane.

Muhaysini may have picked sides early on, but a number of other clerics, including Zarqawi's old mentor Abu Mohammed al-Maqdisi, put forward proposals similar to his Umma Initiative, and Zawahiri himself endorsed the central element of each of these plans, the concept of an independent Sharia court to resolve disputes between militant groups. The Islamic State of Iraq and the Levant rejected them all. One senior ISIL cleric, a onetime protégé of Abu Mohammed al-Maqdisi, penned a tract implying that the formerly revered Maqdisi had gone senile. At a meeting with some of those working to broker a reconciliation between ISIL and al-Nusra, Abu Ali al-Anbari brought a halt to negotiations by saying, "Either we exterminate [al-Nusra] or they exterminate us." Anbari then repeated this formula three times, imbuing it, in the minds of his fundamentalist audience, with the significance of a solemn oath.

ISIL wanted unity, but only on condition that everybody submit to its rule; Baghdadi said as much in an audio statement in January 2014. ISIL, Baghdadi reasoned, was no longer any old insurgent group; it was a real, sovereign state, and as such could deal with any disputes in its own courts. Thus the root of the problem became clear: ISIL genuinely believed its own propaganda. It felt itself to be a real governing entity, and therefore superior to any mere jihadi organization, including its parent group, al-Qaeda.

. . .

Finally, on February 3, 2014, utterly exasperated with Baghdadi's intransigence, Zawahiri publicly disowned the Islamic State of Iraq and the Levant. ISIL, he said, was "not an affiliate with the al-Qaeda group and has no organizational relationship with it." Al-Qaeda was "not responsible for their actions." It was the first time al-Qaeda had publicly discarded one of its own affiliates. Zawahiri would later say in an interview that it was better to have ten decent followers than "scores of thousands making the *umma* hate them, their deeds, and their behaviors." True as that might be, al-Qaeda now faced the nightmare scenario it had been so eager to avoid ever since it had linked up with Zarqawi almost a decade before: it was left with no meaningful presence in Iraq, now once again the epicenter of global jihad. Meanwhile, in Syria, the war of words between ISIL and al-Nusra had by now escalated into a war of bombs and bullets, centered around Aleppo. In December 2013, ISIL kidnapped and later executed a senior al-Nusra fighter. The next month, it killed a commander from Abu Khalid al-Suri's group, Ahrar al-Sham. Then, on February 23, around three weeks after Zawahiri kicked Baghdadi to the curb, five ISIL fighters stormed Ahrar al-Sham's headquarters in Aleppo and opened fire before detonating a suicide bomb. Al-Suri was the main target, and he was killed in the assault, blown apart along with a number of other senior comrades. Zawahiri issued a video eulogy for his personal representative, featuring the al-Qaeda leader's voice dubbed over pictures of al-Suri and other respected jihadi figures. The video opened with a clip of Mahmud, bin Laden's late aide, saying, "God prefers to see the destruction of the whole universe rather than the spilling of Muslim blood," before cutting to footage of Abu Khalid al-Suri walking with bin Laden in Afghanistan. On the soundtrack, Zawahiri can be heard offering congratulations for the martyrdom of Abu Khalid and condolences for "this blind *fitna* that has befallen the Levant . . . for the sake of ignorance and ambition and aggression and greed for power," a situation Zawahiri compares to the bloody-mindedness that led to the assassinations of the third and fourth caliphs, Uthman and Ali, and in the twentieth century to the collapse of the Algerian insurgency under the weight of its own excesses. Abu Khalid, Zawahiri says, was killed "treacherously" by "extremist fools" and "ignorants" who would soon face "moral death." All Muslims must reject them. Not once does he mention by name either Baghdadi or his organization. But it is quite clear whom he means.

Ideologically, the running battles between Khorasan and ISIL went right back to the tensions between Zawahiri and Zarqawi, expressed most clearly in their 2005 exchange of letters. While every al-Qaeda affiliate ultimately wanted to see the advent of a renewed caliphate covering the whole Islamic world and governing according to their concept of Sharia, not every jihadi agreed on how this should be achieved—or how soon. Zawahiri, following bin Laden, favored achieving the goal gradually. To them, an Islamic state—phase three of the *Management of Savagery* plan—could never be sustainable until a majority of its citizens could be convinced that it was the right way to govern. Indeed, building such public support was the essence of phase two. During phases one and two, there is no state or caliphate, so holding onto land for its own sake is not of prime importance. If a strong enemy arises, therefore, there need be no shame in pulling out and preserving your own strength to fight another day. Thus, at the end of April 2016, al-Qaeda in the Arabian Peninsula pulled out of the Yemeni city of Mukalla in Hadhramut Province in the face of advances by Yemeni and allied troops. In a public statement, AQAP said that it withdrew in order to save civilians from further violence and "to fight our enemy as we want, not as they want." For the Islamic State, such reasoning is meaningless. In the overheated minds of Baghdadi and his followers, the jihad has already reached phase three—the establishment of the caliphate. As an established sovereign entity, it is the duty of the caliphate to defend its borders and fight for every inch of its territory, which is exactly what the Islamic State is doing, at enormous cost in blood and treasure. What is more, in phase three there is no longer any room for building public support; anyone who opposes the caliphate deserves death. So, to be clear, it is not the case that al-Qaeda and the Islamic State are working from different blueprints. Both sides still follow *The Management of Savagery*. But they have very different views on how far the plan has advanced. That, rather than any fundamental doctrinal difference, is why the behavior of these two groups diverges so markedly.

Beyond the *Management of Savagery*'s three phases, however, orthodox al-Qaeda dogma also holds that there can be only one Islamic Emirate, with one supreme Commander of the Faithful at its apex. Currently, the emirate is the Taliban and the commander is the Taliban's leader; bin Laden gave *bayat* to Mullah Omar as such, and Zawahiri continued the tradition by pledging allegiance both to Mullah Omar and to his successors, Mullah Mansour and Hibatullah Akhundzada. There is no room for a "caliphate-in-addition." To underline this point, Zawahiri renewed his *bayat* to Mullah Omar, affirmed that "al-Qaeda and its branches everywhere are soldiers in his army," and released a video of bin Laden in which the sheikh says: "Our *bayat* to the Commander of the Faithful is a supreme *bayat*. It is founded on Koranic proof-texts and prophetic hadith. . . . It is incumbent upon every Muslim to affirm in his heart that he has given *bayat* to the Commander of the Faithful, Mullah Omar. This is the supreme *bayat*."

For Baghdadi, this line of thinking was beside the point. As far as he was concerned, the Taliban had failed; they had lost control over their territory in 2001, and an emirate without land was no emirate at all—an argument that might soon be used against ISIL itself. ISIL not only possessed territory; it was the heartland of the original caliphates, and ISIL was governing it in accordance with its iron-fisted conception of Sharia. In other words, ISIL believed it had a chance to establish something far greater than Taliban-controlled Afghanistan had ever been, and Baghdadi was going to grasp that opportunity whether Zawahiri liked it or not. Men like Baghdadi and Bakr—like their prototype, Abu Musab al-Zarqawi—could not care less about consensus building; as far as they were concerned, citizens would either submit to ISIL's rule or they would be killed. Thus, Khorasan and ISIL, with their competing absolutist positions, had reached an impasse; it was increasingly clear that, contrary to Muhaysini's conciliatory dicta, this jihad was not big enough for both of them.

. . .

It had long been apparent that ISIL was heading toward declaring itself a caliphate—an empire with a self-proclaimed mandate to rule over all Muslims on earth. Such a system of government had been the norm for much of the Middle Ages, and in theory right down to the dissolution of the Ottoman Empire at the end of the First World War. But a caliphate had to be governed by a caliph. Certain qualifications deemed necessary in ISIL's extreme Salafi-jihadi philosophy could not be earned by any old book-smart farm boy from Samarra. Notably, the caliph had to descend from the Prophet Muhammad's own tribe, the Quraysh. So ISIL commissioned a Bahraini scholar, Turki Binali, to construct a genealogy for the would-be supreme ruler.

Turki Binali could be described as the Islamic State's answer to Abdullah al-Muhaysini, al-Nusra and the Army of Conquest's charismatic young Saudi religious leader. With his youthful looks, half-rim glasses, and long, bushy beard, Binali might appear indistinguishable from his millennial contemporaries on the streets of Brooklyn or Portland, were it not for his traditional clerical garb and the pistol he carries by his side. The Islamic extremism expert Cole Bunzel describes Binali as "the Islamic State's most prominent and prolific resident scholar," a description made all the more striking by the fact that Binali was only twenty-eight years old when he began his career as the Islamic State's highest-profile scholarly apologist. The scion of a well-connected family in Bahrain, Binali trained under Zarqawi's old mentor, the venerable Jordanian Salafi-jihadi cleric Abu Mohammed al-Maqdisi. Maqdisi appointed the precocious Binali, at the age of just twenty-five, to his personal Sharia council. In April 2013, still in his twenties, Binali responded to Baghdadi's proclamation of the Islamic State of Iraq and the Levant with a tract called "Extend Your Hands to Give *Bayat* to Baghdadi." In it, he wrote, "We ask God for the day to come when we will see our Sheikh seated upon the throne of the caliphate." Three months later, Binali published his tendentious genealogy of Baghdadi, in which he claims that he descends from the Quraysh through Hussein, son of the Prophet's cousin and son-in-law Ali—ironically, two of the central figures of Shia Islam, both of whose shrines had been attacked by Zarqawi's suicide bombers.

In March 2014, ISIL itself floated the idea of a caliphate by seeding through its social media channels the rather clunky hashtag, "#We_Demand_Sheikh_Al-Baghdadi_Declare_The_Caliphate." A few weeks later, Binali published another essay, this time dealing with the characteristics required of the caliphate itself. He argued that it need not possess all the attributes of powerful historical caliphates such as the Abbasid, which, at least in theory, exercised political power over all Muslims in the world. Instead, Binali wrote, a caliphate needed only "power, authority, and control of [some amount of] territory." It need not hold sway over all Muslim lands; as Binali observed, many of the early caliphs—indeed, the Prophet himself—controlled less territory than ISIL did. Nor, contrary to the interpretations of some scholars, did all Muslims need to have a say in picking the caliph. In other words, in Binali's view, all the building blocks for a caliphate were already in place.

Finally, on June 29, 2014—the first full day of Ramadan—the organization's chief spokesperson, Abu Mohammed al-Adnani, announced the return of the caliphate, "a hope that flutters in the heart of every mujahid." Adnani went on to make clear what, in his view, this meant for the world's Muslims: "[W]ith this declaration of the caliphate, it is incumbent upon all Muslims to pledge allegiance to the caliph. . . . The legality of all emirates, groups, states, and organizations becomes null by the expansion of the caliph's authority and arrival of its troops to their areas." With this announcement, ISIL became simply IS—the Islamic State.

One week later, on July 4, the man who now called himself Caliph Ibrahim, Abu Bakr al-Baghdadi, suddenly stepped out of the shadows and up a flight of stone stairs to the pulpit of the Al-Nuri Mosque in Mosul. The venue, exquisitely filigreed with Arabic calligraphy, was an auspicious choice, underlining the Islamic State's confident grip of the newly conquered city while simultaneously connecting Baghdadi to the illustrious caliphs of the past. Huddled around the ruins of Nineveh, a city more ancient even than written language, Mosul has figured prominently in caliphates dating back almost to the dawn of Islam. The mosque itself, with its distinctive leaning minaret, was built on the order of Nur ad-Din Zangi, the medieval ruler venerated by Zarqawi. It was completed around 1173, making it almost an exact contemporary of England's Canterbury Cathedral. Baghdadi carried on the theme of stability and continuity in his own choice of wardrobe, sporting a black robe and a black turban, in imitation of the Abbasid caliphs who ruled Iraq from the eighth to the thirteenth century, and of the Prophet at his conquest of Mecca in AD 629. As a student of Koranic elocution, he spoke elegant, classical Arabic in a clear, level tone, betraying no trace of anxiety. The actual content of the speech consisted mostly of platitudes about Ramadan and the importance of doing jihad. But one passage stood out as a statement of the terms upon which Baghdadi intended to govern, framed in explicitly Koranic language:

I have been appointed your governor, yet I am not the best among you, nor am I better than you. If you see that I am right, assist me, and if you see that I err, advise me and set me back on the right track. Obey me as long as I obey Allah, but if I disobey Allah, you are not obliged to obey me. I shall not promise you what kings and rulers promise their subjects—a life of luxury, tranquillity, security, and comfort. I shall promise you what Allah promised his believing servants . . . that he will make them rulers on the land, as he made those before them rulers.

For a debut public address, it was an audacious performance—one that drew immediate comparisons to Mullah Omar's 1996 appearance in Kandahar in which he stood on a rooftop, donned the so-called cloak of the Prophet, and called himself Commander of the Faithful. But just behind the high-definition cameras, the more mundane details of the scene told a different story. First, the ordinary congregants present had not come voluntarily; they had been ordered into the mosque by Islamic State operatives. Guards armed with assault weapons kept them in their seats until the caliph was done speaking. In the mosque's gallery, veiled women sat weeping, stifling their tears for fear of retribution. Even more striking was the absence, at this supposedly world-shaking event, of any important figures from beyond the narrow confines of the IS hierarchy. Just about the only people there to witness the speech in person, aside from the ordinary worshippers quaking in fear, were the same cadre of Baathist ex-Iraqi army officers who had been with Baghdadi all along. There were no prominent imams, no revered scholars, no tribal leaders from any of the vast territory controlled by IS in both Syria and Iraq. Indeed, many of these people would publicly decry the speech within days of its publication. But this performance was not for them; it was for jihadis from around the world just like Baghdadi and his Baathist minders—extremists looking for a winning side, no matter how vicious it might be.

. . .

By the time of the Mosul takeover, the Islamic State had become a highly organized governing entity. Its structure bears striking similarity to that of the old al-Qaeda as it existed in Kandahar before 9/11. Centrally, it is presided over by a *shura* council, a Sharia council, and subordinate committees covering Security and Intelligence, Military Affairs, Provincial Affairs, Finance, and Media. The *shura* council, to all intents and purposes Baghdadi's cabinet, consists of between nine and eleven members, predominantly if not exclusively Iraqis—many of them ex-Baathists. Their responsibility is to see that the caliph's orders are carried out. In parallel, the six-member Sharia council functions like a jihadi version of the Supreme Court, making sure all branches of government function in accordance with the Islamic State's myopic reading of Sharia law, enforcing its decisions through a Sharia police force and religious courts. Meanwhile, the Security and Intelligence Council, established by Haji Bakr, is responsible for keeping Baghdadi safe and in power, primarily by rooting out plots against him and liquidating potential rivals in time-honored Baathist style. This pattern of government is repeated, fractal-like, in each of Islamic State's eighteen provinces across Syria and Iraq, and again within those provinces at more local levels. When it comes to its war machine, IS devolves a great deal of authority to commanders in the field, making for a nimble force, capable of fighting on multiple fronts at once. Tribal affairs departments are tasked with reaching out to the powerful tribes, winning or coercing their loyalty. But despite these complex governing structures, the big decisions at the top remain the preserve of a shadowy elite behind the scenes, referred to, appropriately enough, by the medieval Arabic term for the people who selected caliphs—and deposed them, often violently—*ahl al-hall wa al-aqd,* or "those who loose and bind." Similar phrases are found in Jewish literature and in the New Testament. In Islam, the words carry the sense of ultimate power, both to allow something to be done (to loose) and to forbid it from being done (to bind). It will surprise nobody to learn that, in the Islamic State, the men who "loose and bind," like so many of the group's most powerful figures, are predominantly former servants of Saddam.

Islamic State's governing style, too, reflects its hybrid origins: harsh *takfiri* religious laws, enforced with Baathist ruthlessness. Stores and businesses of all kinds must close five times a day for prayers. Practically anything remotely enjoyable—including a picnic in the park—is banned, as either a waste of time and money or—much worse—an opportunity to mix with those of the opposite sex. For the same reason, it is a crime for women to appear in public without a male chaperone. At all times, women must cover their bodies literally down to the tips of their fingers; even female doctors have to wear veils and thick black gloves while operating on patients—who must be female. IS patrols, a frequent sight on city streets, have been known to arrest and beat up café owners for allowing women to eat in their establishments without veils. Men have a dress code to follow, too, albeit nowhere near as strict; for example, the hems of their pants must be above the ankle length, supposedly because the Prophet never let his garments touch the ground.

Many crimes and their punishments bear a striking similarity to those used in the middle ages, the era from which the Islamic State draws much of its extreme interpretation of Sharia. Thus, for example, blasphemy, homosexuality, and adultery are punishable by death, while slander and drinking alcohol attract a sentence of eighty lashes, and sex before marriage can earn each partner 100 lashes and exile for a year (although, given the harshness of life under IS, many might see the latter as a reward). For many crimes, public flogging is seen as the "minimum punishment." Homosexuals and male adulterers are thrown from tall towers. Female adulterers are stoned to death. Certain criminals, such as bandits who commit murder, are often crucified, usually after being shot or beheaded. In many cities under IS control, including the capital, Raqqa, severed heads can be found impaled on railings, with plaques listing their owners' alleged crimes. Some prisoners, like the captured Jordanian pilot Moath al-Kasasbeh, have been burned alive, and pictures of their charred remains distributed as a warning to others—or an inducement to attract violent young men to the ranks of Islamic State's armies. Clerics like Turki Binali have justified these practices on the basis of laws enforced in the medieval caliphates; but whereas medieval practice imposed a heavy burden of proof for carrying out such punishments, sometimes requiring testimony from up to eight witnesses, it is unlikely that the Islamic State bothers with such niceties.

In dealing with opposition, the State takes its cue from Saddam Hussein, deploying a web of secret police and informants to watch its citizens' every move. Like Saddam, the Assads, and a host of other dictators it claims to despise, IS has little compunction about massacring peaceful protesters or executing thousands of political opponents. Reports have surfaced of IS assassins slipping over the border into Turkey to kidnap and behead exiled opposition figures. With the advent of U.S. air strikes, the group has reportedly become even more suspicious as it races to unmask those who may be passing intelligence to the Americans. Predictably, the State's repression has a sharp ethnic and sectarian edge. It has murdered thousands of Shia, Yazidis, and members of Sunni tribes who refused to collaborate. The pages of *Dabiq* glorify the demolition of Shia mosques and shrines, some of which had survived centuries of warfare only to succumb to Islamic State's dynamite. The brutality does not end with those the State considers its enemies; women and girls, some as young as thirteen, have been forced into sexual slavery or marriages to IS fighters. In areas where Iraqi forces have made advances, the State has used families as human shields, executing civilians who attempt to flee.

At the same time, IS has worked to cultivate an image as a real government providing genuine services. It has wisely retained municipal employees with the specialist knowledge necessary to keep the power on, the schools open (albeit with a revised curriculum), the water and buses running, and the trash off the streets. Despite its professed contempt for the existing frontiers, the State has made sure to curry favor with locals by putting Iraqis in charge in Iraq and Syrians in Syria. Its propaganda shows operatives distributing food to orphans, repairing roads and electrical infrastructure, cleaning the streets, providing cancer treatment to children, and operating nursing homes for older residents. It brands its healthcare system, Islamic State Health Service, with a logo similar to that of the United Kingdom's National Health Service, and provides "statistics" to document the quality and widespread availability of healthcare in the caliphate. IS provides an education, albeit one mostly geared toward ensuring the State's longevity by indoctrinating the next generation. IS schools use fundamentalist textbooks—in many cases, the same ones children learn from in Saudi Arabia, often printed out from Saudi government websites. For many children, secular subjects such as chemistry have been eliminated to make way for yet more hours of Islamic studies. At least one Mosul family risked reprisals by pulling their child from school, "as we preferred that he had no education at all than the one IS is promoting." More disturbingly still, the State also coaxes children into its cult of terror and death, encouraging them to inform on their parents, training them with automatic weapons, and forcing them to watch or carry out executions.

Even leaving aside the constant danger of punishment for a host of misdemeanors, daily life under the Islamic State is grim. Massive depopulation and hermetic isolation from the outside world have caused local economies to collapse and led to hyperinflation in the cost of essential everyday goods. The State's efforts to rein in the ill effects with price controls have apparently failed. In fall 2014, it announced that it would soon start minting its own solid gold currency, in imitation of the caliphates of old, although the *Dabiq* article touting this development betrayed a poor grasp of modern economics, referring, for example, to gold and other metals as having an "intrinsic value." It is telling that, as eager as IS has been to publicize the supposed benefits of life in the caliphate, it cracks down hard on anyone who attempts to show the outside world a more balanced picture of their day-to-day reality; for example, it has made filming in public with a cellphone camera a capital offense.

. IS has thus succeeded partly by following bin Laden's advice on state building and partly by doing the opposite. On the one hand, it has made a real attempt to govern and win favor from certain local populations. On the other hand, its brutality toward perceived transgressors has gone much further than any of its al-Qaeda forebears—and that is saying a lot. The Islamic State has elevated murder from a tactic to an end in itself—a vital part of its ideology, which the *New Yorker*'s Dexter Filkins calls "bloodlust" and a form of "psychosis." Ultimately, however, this very brutality puts a hard limit on the amount of genuine local support IS has been able to muster, a flaw that leaves the door open for the Islamic State's own eventual downfall. When the tide turns decisively against IS, few who have lived under its oppressive reign will shed a tear.

・ ・ ・

By the second quarter of 2016, it had become clear that the Islamic State was on a downward trajectory in its heartland of Syria and Iraq. Over the course of the previous year, it had lost around 40 percent of its territory. Ramadi in Iraq and ancient Palmyra in Syria were back in government hands—the latter an important symbolic defeat, thanks largely to Russian, Iranian, and Hezbollah support. The State's red-bearded Chechen defense minister and key propagandist, Omar al-Shishani, had been killed, as had his two predecessors as head of the military council, the ex-Baathists Abu Mohannad al-Sweidawi and Abu Abdul Rahman al-Bilawi. Baghdadi himself was reportedly wounded in an airstrike in March 2015, seriously enough that the leadership passed to others while he recuperated. More gravely still, in March 2016, Abu Ali al-Anbari, the Islamic State's most senior link to Zarqawi, was killed resisting capture in a U.S. special forces raid inside Syria. The following August, IS acknowledged the death of its loudest and most effective spokesper-son, Mohammed al-Adnani.

IS has responded to the downturn in its fortunes by lashing out at the countries engaged in air strikes against its positions, most spectacularly by blowing a Russian airliner out of the sky shortly after takeoff from Sharm el-Sheikh, Egypt, and by using gunmen and suicide bombers to attack nightspots in Paris and transport hubs in Brussels and Istanbul. Collectively, those three attacks killed more than four hundred people. As IS continues to lose its ability to win real military victories, it will increasingly look to strike soft tar-gets. As shocking as these bombings and shootings have been, they have done little to stanch the hemorrhaging of Islamic State terri-tory; on the contrary, the Paris atrocities prompted France to step up its air strikes and bring forward the deployment of its flagship, the nuclear aircraft carrier *Charles De Gaulle*, to the eastern Mediterranean.

But IS has a backup plan. Just like al-Qaeda after 9/11, it has cul-tivated a network of affiliates in various parts of the world. As a self-described "state," IS refers to these affiliates as "provinces." Thus, in November 2014—three months after the start of U.S. air strikes—Baghdadi announced:

> *O Muslims, rejoice, for we bring you good news of the announce-ment of the Islamic State's expansion to new lands: to Saudi Ara-bia and Yemen, and to Egypt, Libya, and Algeria. We announce the acceptance of the* bayat *of those who gave us* bayat *from among our brothers in those lands, the voiding of the names of the organizations in them, their declaration as new provinces of the Islamic State, and the appointment of governors over them.*

To be sure, Baghdadi's announcement was, at least at the time, not quite as momentous as the caliph made out. The Libyan "provinces" were in reality confined to one small town and one neighborhood of the city of Sirte. The Algerian group was no more than a tiny splinter of AQIM, whose leadership promptly and publicly rejected IS, as did that of its sister organization, AQAP. Only the Sinai group, Ansar Beit al-Maqdis, had any independent existence worth mentioning prior to the announcement; significantly, this was the organization that, a year later, would destroy the Russian airliner. But the other provinces would soon gain in strength, the same way IS itself did: by identifying and exploiting power vacuums.

In Libya, following Gaddafi's death in October 2011, two rival governments battled for control: the internationally recognized House of Representatives in the east, centered around Tobruk, and the Islamist-linked General National Congress in the west, with its hub in Tripoli. Each side enjoyed the support of its own coterie of heavily armed tribal militias, creating an effective stalemate with a demarcation line running down the middle of the country. On the border between the two zones of control lay Sirte, Gaddafi's home town, held until 2015 by Ansar al-Sharia in Libya, the armed group that assassinated Ambassador Christopher Stevens and several other Americans in Benghazi in September 2012. In May 2015, Islamic State fighters captured Sirte with the help of defectors from Ansar al-Sharia and proceeded to set up a government there based upon the IS regime in Iraq and Syria. The Libyan branch's methods proved no less brutal than those of its parent organization. Three months after taking control, IS put down a rebellion by the Ferjan tribe and executed fifty-seven of its members—twelve of them by public beheading and crucifixion. The group has also decapitated dozens of Coptic Christians, a community that has lived in Libya since before the dawn of Islam, and released videos of some of the murders. Strategically, Islamic State's aim is to seize as much of Libya's oil and gas infrastructure as possible in an attempt to create an illicit petro-state of the kind that keeps its comrades in business in Syria and Iraq. In the months prior to his death, Abu Ali al-Anbari, one of the Islamic State's top administrators, was dispatched to Libya to firm up relations with the IS faction there. As of spring 2016, the group had extended its territory dozens of miles along the coast to the east and west of Sirte and was battling for control of the strategic petrochemical ports of Sidra and Ras Lanuf. Beyond its beachhead on the Gulf of Sidra, IS fought rival militias for dominance in Libya's second city of Benghazi and maintained training camps in the country's western coastal region, from which it launched its attacks in neighboring Tunisia—notably against the jihadi recruitment hotbed of Ben Gardane, the town that Zarqawi had once wished was next door to Fallujah.

On March 20, 2015, IS carried out its first suicide bombing in Yemen, killing 142 people at two Shia mosques in Sanaa. Since then, the local IS faction has continued to assault Yemen's Shia minority, evidently hoping to foster the kind of sectarian bloodshed that opened doors for IS in Syria and Iraq—a project undoubtedly boosted by the involvement of Saudi Arabia and Iran on opposite sides of Yemen's ongoing civil war. IS has not yet claimed territory in Yemen beyond training camps, but unlike AQAP, the IS Yemen franchise is not even trying to govern—merely to create chaos. In this, it appears to be succeeding. In December 2015, it assassinated the governor of Aden Province, then attempted to kill his successor the following month. Two months after that, it carried out a gun assault on a nursing home run by Mother Teresa's Missionaries of Charity—an attack so vile and cowardly that even al-Qaeda quickly condemned it.

In Afghanistan and Pakistan, the market for extremist groups remains vibrant but highly saturated, with many armed factions competing for attention; still, even there, IS has made inroads. It is recruiting especially effectively among discontented urban young men in Pakistan's overcrowded cities, where unemployment is high. In 2015, IS declared the Islamic State of Khorasan, or ISK, the latest of its provinces. ISK, in turn, has set up training camps in eastern

Afghanistan, and possibly also one in the tribal regions of Pakistan. As in other IS provinces, ISK has focused on attacking the local Shia minority. It also fights with the Afghan Taliban in Paktika Province, across the border from Pakistan's lawless Waziristan region.

The process of peeling off splinter groups from factions aligned with al-Qaeda continues. At times, al-Shabaab, al-Qaeda's Somali faction, has seemed close to switching its allegiance to IS, but it has so far resisted calls to do so. IS has also signed up some groups al-Qaeda regarded as indefensibly violent, such as Boko Haram, a Nigerian terror outfit that waged a long and unsuccessful campaign for admittance to al-Qaeda before turning to IS. Al-Qaeda's aversion to Boko Haram arose partly from a deep-seated racism toward sub-Saharan Africans; but it was partly also an effort to avoid getting dragged into a local conflict with little relevance to the global jihad, and to shield the organization from pollution by a group whose methods were considered purely vicious. The Islamic State, in its drive for additional provinces, is apparently more willing to overlook these details. On the other hand, northern Nigeria may yet prove fertile ground for jihad, with its poisonous combination of porous borders, corruption, tribalism, and some of the world's worst healthcare and education.

In Southeast Asia, the Islamic State has attracted the *bayat* of the Abu Sayyaf group—once an ally of al-Qaeda—based in the southern Philippines. Abu Sayyaf has already started beheading Western hostages and Filipino soldiers. Like many of the areas outside Syria and Iraq where the Islamic State has established a foothold, Abu Sayyaf's home region is poor, remote, and lacking in effective government control, hampering the Philippine military's attempts to eradicate the group. *Takfiri* jihad in Southeast Asia has the potential to be particularly incendiary, given the prevalence of non-Muslims, whom *takfiris* like the Islamic State regard as legitimate targets.

By the end of 2015, some thirty-four militant groups had sworn formal allegiance to IS, and a further ten had pledged their support.

It would be wrong to presume that all these groups are equally dangerous. Many are nothing more than criminal gangs, rather than full-fledged terrorist organizations. Some are tiny; indeed, smaller groups have a disproportionate incentive to pledge bayyat to IS, in order to gain the publicity, donations, and recruits they so badly need. Nevertheless, some of these groups represent the thin end of a sectarian wedge that may yet topple governments across the Middle East and beyond. IS, like al-Qaeda before it, has also proved lethally adept at inspiring lone wolf attackers within Western countries. "If you can kill a disbelieving American or European . . . or an Australian, or a Canadian, or any other disbeliever from the disbelievers waging war, including the citizens of the countries that entered into a coalition against the Islamic State, then . . . kill him in any manner," the IS spokesperson al-Adnani said in September 2014. "Smash his head with a rock, or slaughter him with a knife, or run him over with your car, or throw him down from a high place, or choke him, or poison him." Subsequent truck attacks in Nice, Berlin, and elsewhere have shown how effective such messages can be. Even if IS is defeated in Syria and Iraq, therefore, it looks likely to lead a long and vicious afterlife.

CHAPTER 8

STEADFAST SONS

The foothills of the Spin Ghar mountain range, two dozen miles due south of Jalalabad in the borderland between Afghanistan and Pakistan, were once home to hundreds of olive plantations. For tens of thousands of acres, the farms clustered along the banks of the Nangarhar Canal, a monumental hydroelectric irrigation project completed in the 1960s, when Afghanistan was safe and liberal enough to form a regular stop on the hippie trail from Europe to India and the Far East. By the turn of the new millennium, however, more than twenty years of continuous warfare had almost destroyed the canal's capacity to pump life-giving water to the groves, all but killing off what had once been a flourishing business.

One day in the fall of 2001, with yet another foreign invasion brewing just beyond the horizon, a father sat with three of his young sons in the shade of one of the few remaining olive trees. Together, they performed a simple ceremony of farewell. To each of the three boys, the father gave a *misbaha*—a set of prayer beads symbolizing the ninety-nine names of God in classical Arabic. "It was as if we pulled out our livers and left them there," one of the sons was to recall. Then the father took his leave and disappeared into the mountains, heading for a familiar redoubt known as the Black Cave or, in the local Pashto language, Tora Bora.

Hamza bin Laden, who received a rosary that day, was to spend most of the next decade in captivity. Behind bars, he was to grow up, receive his education, marry, become a parent twice over. But still Hamza missed his own father deeply. "How many times, from the depths of my heart, I wished to be beside you," Hamza wrote to Osama in 2009. "I remember every smile that you smiled at me, every word that you spoke to me, and every look that you gave me." Hamza grew up with a fervor for jihad and a determination to follow in the footsteps of his illustrious father. Toward the end of his life, as we have seen, bin Laden began grooming Hamza for leadership. He made plans for Hamza to join him in Abbottabad. For a while, the portents seemed encouraging; Umm Khalid, who was with her husband in Abbottabad, told Hamza of a "very good" dream she had in which "you were conducting Adhan [the Muslim call to prayer] from atop a very high building, in the same voice in which you said, 'Stay strong my father, for heaven awaits us and victory is ours if God permits'"—a reference to the poem that Hamza recited during his brother Mohammed's wedding in 2000. In the end, Hamza and bin Laden never saw each other again. But fourteen years after their farewell under the olive tree, and four years after his father's death, Hamza's return to the jihadi stage, along with several of his father's most trusted and competent lieutenants, would portend a bin Ladenist resurgence. Today, even as the Islamic State slowly dwindles, its parent organization, al-Qaeda, is making a comeback.

· · ·

In the months after 9/11 and the fall of the Taliban, a parade of bin Laden family members and high-ranking al-Qaeda figures made their way to the Shia stronghold of Iran. At first blush, that may seem a surprising destination for some of the world's most fervent Sunni extremists—men who pepper their public utterances with slurs calling Shia Muslims "rejectionists" and "apostates." But in the wake of the awful attacks on New York and Washington, the Islamic Republic seemed like the best of a narrowing range of bad options, primarily because it was the one place in the Muslim world where America's military and law enforcement writ would not run. The Iranian authorities, for their part, simply deported most of the al-Qaeda members they captured. But they held onto a handful of high-value detainees, to use as bargaining chips in hostage negotiations and other sticky situations. Among these valuable hostages were bin Laden relatives like Hamza and his mother, as well as *shura* council members like Abu Khair al-Masri, the head of the Political Committee, Abu Mohammed al-Masri, master of al-Qaeda's training camps, and, of course, the old tactician Saif al-Adel. Today, more than fifteen years after 9/11, these three men—Saif, Abu Khair, and Abu Mohammed—are the top al-Qaeda operatives not in American custody, apart from al-Qaeda's leader, Ayman al-Zawahiri.

The protean status of these al-Qaeda grandees during their long Iranian captivity is in many ways a reflection of the paradoxical relationship that developed between Sunni al-Qaeda and the world's foremost Shia power. On an ideological level, the two sides despised each other, and for this reason their attempts to work together never quite came to fruition, as Saif al-Adel, for one, was painfully aware. Moreover, Tehran had long counted bin Laden's Afghan allies, the Taliban, among its more troublesome regional irritants. On the other hand, Iran had at least two reasons to hold out the possibility of better conditions or even freedom. First, al-Qaeda or its associated groups would from time to time get hold of Iranian diplomats as hostages, and Tehran would need bargaining chips to set them free. Secondly, Iran and al-Qaeda shared common enemies in the shape of the Great Satan, America, and its top Arab ally, Saudi Arabia. Assad, the ayatollahs' protégé in Damascus, had helped Sunni jihadists throw sand in America's gears; perhaps Iran might try something similar.

It was therefore in Tehran's interests to keep the senior al-Qaeda militants alive and well until such time as they proved useful, either as leverage or as attack dogs. Thus, while al-Qaeda frequently bemoaned the imprisonment of its people in Iran in the same breath as that of their comrades more firmly incarcerated at Guantánamo Bay or black sites, the U.S. State Department simultaneously complained repeatedly that "Iran remained unwilling to bring to justice senior Al-Qaeda members it continued to detain, and refused to publicly identify those senior members in its custody. Iran previously allowed al-Qaeda facilitators to operate a core facilitation pipeline through Iran since at least 2009, enabling al-Qaeda to move funds and fighters to South Asia and Syria."

The Iranian authorities reportedly permitted Mahmud, the factotum, to serve as al-Qaeda's "emissary" to Iran, and facilitated his travel back and forth across the border from Pakistan. Thus the status of the al-Qaeda "prisoners" tended to vary with the degree of leverage their organization enjoyed.

. . .

Immediately following their arrest in Shiraz in April 2003, Saif, Abu Khair, and Abu Mohammed found themselves hauled off to Tehran and jailed for around twenty months in the dungeons of a building belonging to Iran's feared intelligence apparatus. They were held incommunicado and without charge; but they were neither mistreated nor even formally interrogated. Around the beginning of 2005, they were moved to a spacious military compound with an apartment complex, a soccer field, and a mosque, adjacent to a training camp for one of the many Shia militant groups on Tehran's payroll. Their families were allowed to join them, although at least one fellow detainee suspected that this was no more than a ruse to allow the Iranians to keep tabs on potentially troublesome family members. A few months later, Saif, Abu Khair, and Abu Mohammed were moved again, to an apartment block in a different part of the same military base. The Iranian authorities had split the al-Qaeda detainees into four groups, one of which comprised most of the senior leaders as well as members of the bin Laden family, including Hamza and his mother. Their new apartments, however, proved cramped, dingy, and unsanitary, to the point where some residents began to show signs of mental and physical illness. In mid-2008, the detainees staged a protest; the authorities broke up the demonstration and beat all the prisoners, including the women. Nevertheless, about a year later, the detainees and their families were moved once again, to a third area on the base, a walled-off section containing neat, recently refurbished houses, each with its own yard. But this was still a prison, after all. The houses stood surrounded by three layers of fences, of which the innermost was capped with razor wire and surveillance cameras.

The prisoners remained restive. In fact, many considered this sedentary, secluded life even further beneath their dignity than the squalor of their previous accommodations; for these hardy mujahideen, the sense of suburban comfort only heightened their humiliation. One of them told his captors he would sooner be extradited to Israel than spend any more time in the gilded cage the Iranians had prepared for them. In March 2010, the prisoners staged what one detainee later described as "a huge act of disturbance." This time, masked, black-clad Iranian troops were ordered in to storm the compound. The soldiers beat the men and some of the children, and hauled the senior detainees off to solitary confinement for 101 days.

The detainees' ability to communicate with the outside world seems to have varied tremendously over time. At first, they were held, as one U.S. official put it, "under virtual house arrest, not able to do much of anything." Phone calls to family members were strictly limited. But the strictures gradually loosened, just as the detainees' living conditions slowly improved. The Iranian authorities eventually set up a system whereby minders could send emails on behalf of their wards, and each week permitted one prisoner to browse the web, although full internet access was not allowed. And there were other ways of communicating with the outside. Saif al-Adel's father-in-law, Mustafa Hamid, who was held in Iran under looser conditions, visited the main group of detainees every few months. With his greater liberty, Hamid was in a position to serve as courier; indeed, this may be how Saif was able to publish his column on security and intelligence in the AQAP house magazine *Muskar al-Battar*. Other detainees managed to escape and bring manuscripts with them, like bin Laden's daughter Iman, who smuggled out the text of Abu Ghaith's *Twenty Guidelines on the Path of Jihad*—a book highly critical of Zarqawi's violence against civilians in Iraq—and eventually had it published, with a foreword by another detainee, the former al-Qaeda religious leader Abu Hafs al-Mauritani.

Despite their restlessness, the detainees managed to create behind bars elements of their own miniature society. The men of the compound came together five times a day for prayers and conversation at the mosque. Requests to allow the children to attend school apparently went unmet; but Hamza's mother, who is well educated, urged her son to pursue learning as best he could, and a group of senior detainees took it upon themselves to educate him in Koranic study, Islamic jurisprudence, and the hadith. While still in custody, Hamza married a daughter of Abu Mohammed al-Masri and became a father twice over.

· · ·

Al-Qaeda lobbied hard for the release of its top men, and by 2010, the group had acquired a bargaining chip of its own. Two years previously, Pakistani tribal elements had kidnapped an Iranian diplomat and sold him as a hostage to al-Qaeda. Through the Haqqani Network—one of the armed groups that protects al-Qaeda's Waziristan hub—a prisoner swap was arranged. On August 10, Hamza bin Laden was freed along with his mother, wife, and children, and headed for Mahmud and his private army in Waziristan. Umm Hamza eventually joined her husband in Abbottabad, but security concerns would delay Hamza's own long-sought reunion with his father until it was too late.

Around the same time as Hamza, Saif Al-Adel was also released. He, too, made for Pakistan, and as we have seen, was in position to serve as interim emir on bin Laden's death, amassing pledges of loyalty for the sheikh's permanent successor, Ayman al-Zawahiri. Unlike Hamza, however, Saif later went back to Iran. We do not know the reason for sure. One of his wives apparently had stayed behind with their children, giving him a personal incentive to return (and perhaps affording the Iranians some leverage to coax him back); but it is also possible that Zawahiri sent him on a mission—to Syria, Iraq, or Yemen, for example—that required him to pass through the Islamic Republic on his way. Saif had served in the capacity of an emissary before and would do so again within a few years; perhaps he was arrested in transit. Whatever the case, by the end of 2011 he was back in Iran with his fellow *shura* council members, Abu Khair and Abu Mohammed. Around the end of 2011, the Iranian authorities reportedly offered all three their freedom if they would return to their home country of Egypt. Each of them refused. This was prudent: Even with Mubarak gone and the Muslim Brotherhood ascendant, Egypt was not a safe place for marked men. At least in Iran they were allowed to live with their families; in Egypt they might very well face execution, as the Iranians were no doubt aware. As things stood, it would be another almost four years before the *shura* council three would taste real freedom.

. . .

Over the course of 2013 and 2014, as the dispute between Julani and Baghdadi widened into a full-scale blood feud between Khorasan and the Islamic State, it seemed that at least some of the dire predictions about Ayman al-Zawahiri's leadership were coming true. The Egyptian may have inherited Osama bin Laden's portfolio and job title; but from his grave under the Indian Ocean, the sheikh could pass on neither his innate aura of command nor his historical relevance to the global jihad. At the height of the feud, in July 2014, Zawahiri renewed his own and al-Qaeda's *bayat* to Mullah Omar, the Taliban leader. At the time, it seemed a smart symbolic move to underline the illegitimacy of Baghdadi's claim to supremacy. A year later, however, it emerged that Mullah Omar had actually succumbed to tuberculosis in April 2013; either way, Zawahiri and al-Qaeda had pledged allegiance to a man who had been dead for fifteen months. This looked bad for Zawahiri; either he had known Omar was dead and sworn fealty to a cadaver—a grave transgression in al-Qaeda's Salafi-jihadi version of Islam—or he had not known at all and was therefore too far out of the loop to call himself a true emir. The gaffe provoked ridicule from some jihadists, dismay from others. At a time when Zawahiri was already struggling to show his relevance in the age of the Islamic State, it seemed to confirm the worst fears about his leadership.

We will never know whether Baghdadi and the Islamic State would have been able to defy bin Laden the way they did Zawahiri; but we can say with some assurance that bin Laden, with his charisma and compelling personal narrative, would have proven a tougher opponent. For Zawahiri, there was a limit to how far he could take things. The nuclear option would be to declare Baghdadi an apostate, which would amount to a jihadi death sentence; but the likely absence of any consequences for Baghdadi as a result would only further expose the weakness of Zawahiri's command.

But Zawahiri does not stand alone at the prow of al-Qaeda; indeed, his crew has recently grown significantly stronger. In an audio message recorded in May or June 2015, Zawahiri triumphantly introduced a man he called "a lion from the den of al-Qaeda." After four years of silence following his father's death, Hamza bin Laden's voice could be heard once again; and his words remained faithful to al-Qaeda's message. He praised the leaders of AQAP, AQIM, and al-Nusra, insulted President Obama as "the black chief of [a] criminal gang," lauded the attacks on Fort Hood and the Boston Marathon, and called for jihadis to "[t]ake the battlefield from Kabul, Baghdad, and Gaza to Washington, London, Paris, and Tel Aviv." The implication was clear: Hamza, the sheikh's son, is being prepared for leadership. Bin Laden's legacy lives. Even Islamic State supporters widely claim to be followers of "bin Laden's al-Qaeda," as distinct from "Zawahiri's al-Qaeda." If the Islamic State were once again stateless, and a bin Laden were once again at the head of al-Qaeda, IS jihadists might return to the fold—and to the global form of jihad originally advocated by Hamza's revered father. If ever a chance existed to reunify al-Qaeda with its own wayward progeny, Hamza embodies that chance. Nor is al-Qaeda unique among jihadi groups in seeking to promote the progeny of an esteemed former leader; under Hibatullah Akhundzada, the Taliban has brought in Mullah Mohammad Yaqoob, son of the group's founder, Mullah Omar, as one of Akhundzada's two deputies.

As is traditional in al-Qaeda propaganda messages, Hamza in his 2015 statement also called for the release of imprisoned al-Qaeda members, singling out in particular the "sheikhs" whom he credits with his education while in captivity, including the Shura big three— Abu Khair al-Masri, Saif al-Adel, and Abu Mohammed al-Masri. "May God release them all," Hamza entreated. In short order, his prayer seemed to be answered. AQAP, in the midst of its Yemeni ascendancy, had been targeting Iranian interests. In December 2014, it bombed the Iranian ambassador's residence in Sanaa, and the following month it shot dead an Iranian diplomat who resisted a kidnapping attempt. The group had also successfully taken two Iranian diplomats alive. Sometime in 2015, it swapped them for al-Qaeda's three top leaders in Iran, who made their way to a hero's welcome in Waziristan.

The returning trio brought back with them a combined century of experience in jihad. Abu Khair, an expert in explosives, had led al-Qaeda's Political Committee—serving, in effect, as the group's foreign minister—and had sheltered Osama bin Laden in Kabul in the days after 9/11. Before joining al-Qaeda, he had been a member of the governing council of Egyptian Islamic Jihad, so he was close to Zawahiri, too. Abu Mohammed had once been in charge of al-Qaeda's training arm and had worked with Saif al-Adel to train Somali militants in the early 1990s and plan the 1998 East Africa embassy bombings. American intelligence officials have called him al-Qaeda's "most experienced and capable operational planner not in U.S. or allied custody." And then there is Saif al-Adel, whose long career has included serving in the Egyptian armed forces, helping to found al-Qaeda, precipitating the Black Hawk Down incident in Somalia, acting as a mentor to Abu Musab al-Zarqawi, serving as al-Qaeda's head of security, with intimate involvement in virtually all the organization's terrorist attacks up to and including 9/11, and, at the time of his arrest, working to procure nuclear weapons. All three men were closely involved in al-Qaeda's first major blow against the United States, the embassy bombings of 1998. All three were on the *shura* council on September 11, 2001. And after a long absence, all three are now back in harness.

Of the three senior returnees from Iran, Saif may be the most dangerous. Regardless of what he may or may not do, the contents of his brain alone rank as one of al-Qaeda's most potent weapons. Indeed, Khorasan has tried to bring his knowledge to a wider jihadi audience—and in so doing, reintroduce Saif himself as a leader—through a series of essays on strategy and tactics published under his name. "With someone like Saif al-Adel," the former jihadist Noman Benotman has said, "You don't even need him to be active himself. What he has in his head is enough." Some reports have placed him in Syria, and indeed his military expertise would make him a considerable asset in that conflict; but his movements have so far not been confirmed.

Saif's release comes at a time when al-Qaeda's main global affiliates, AQIM, AQAP, and the bin Ladenist faction in Syria, are going strong, bolstered by the ongoing turmoil in Syria, Yemen, and Libya. They have resisted the blandishments of the Islamic State, although IS has been able to shave off a few fighters here and there. AQAP's new leader, its former military chief Qasim al-Raymi, is an al-Qaeda stalwart. He trained in Afghanistan before 9/11 and went on to plot bombings at multiple foreign embassies in Sanaa. In 2006, Raymi was one of those who broke out of prison alongside the late Nasser al-Wuhayshi, an event that has acquired almost mythical significance in al-Qaeda. Within days of Wuhayshi's death in mid-2015, Raymi had reaffirmed the group's *bayat* to Zawahiri in gushing terms, calling the Egyptian "the eminent sheikh" and "the beloved father." AQAP remains al-Qaeda's most dangerous franchise, largely because of its success in taking advantage of the chaos created by Saudi Arabia's ill-starred intervention in Yemen's civil war.

In response to the Islamic State's harvest of *bayats* from around the world, Zawahiri has even announced the formation of a brand-new affiliate. Al-Qaeda in the Indian Subcontinent, led by a former commander in the Pakistani Taliban, aims to unify Sunni extremist jihadis across the region and "rescue" Muslims living in Bangladesh, Myanmar, Assam, Gujarat, and Kashmir. The new group has already claimed responsibility for a series of public murders of secular political commentators in Bangladesh.

Meanwhile, al-Qaeda's Waziristani nerve center, Khorasan, continues to enjoy the protection of the Pakistani Taliban and the powerful Haqqani Network, which has ties to the Pakistani security services. Successive Taliban leaders have lavished praise on al-Qaeda in general and Zawahiri in particular. Shortly after Mullah Omar's death was announced in July 2015, Zawahiri pledged allegiance to his successor, Mullah Mansour. When Mansour himself died, in a May 2016 drone strike, Zawahiri was again quick to pledge allegiance to the new Taliban leader, Hibatullah Akhundzada.

On May 9, 2016, one day after Zawahiri issued his latest call for unity among the jihadi groups fighting in Syria, al-Qaeda posted a second audio message from Hamza bin Laden. Entitled "Jerusalem Is but a Bride Whose Dowry Is Our Blood," the statement reiterated Zawahiri's plea for unity and urged jihadis to think of the Syrian conflict as a springboard to the "liberation" of Palestine. "The road to liberating Palestine," he said, "is today much shorter compared to before the blessed Syrian revolution." And as in his previous message, he encouraged "lone wolf" attacks on Jews and Jewish interests around the world. Clearly, Hamza bin Laden is being prepared for leadership.

. . .

Analyze the fortunes of jihadi groups for long enough, and you begin to see a clear pattern. The Taliban, for example, began as an insurgent group, one of many to emerge from the wreckage of Afghanistan's civil war. It conquered some territory for itself and became a proto-state. Then 9/11 happened, the United States invaded, and the Taliban, whose support in most parts of Afghanistan was feeble enough to begin with, lost its grip on government. But it did not go away. Instead, it morphed again, this time from a proto-state into a terrorist group, responsible for a long string of bloody attacks across Afghanistan and Pakistan. Over the ensuing decade, the Taliban has used violence to promote itself once again into an insurgency. As of this writing, it controls a number of provinces of Afghanistan and is vying for control of several more.

Al-Qaeda, of course, began as a terrorist group. Its early experiments in governing in places like Somalia, Mali, and Yemen having failed, it fell back on terrorism. Now, in the long aftermath of the Arab Spring, it is fighting insurgencies in a number of countries—most notably Yemen and Syria—but has wisely held back from attempting to govern before it has built the requisite public support. The Islamic State's history is somewhat different. It grew out of the

Iraqi insurgency against the United States before officially joining al-Qaeda. After years of setbacks following Zarqawi's death, the Islamic State of Iraq found itself demoted to mere terrorism, albeit of a particularly bloody and divisive kind. But since the beginning of the war in Syria, it has rapidly cycled through insurgency once more to become a proto-state—a caliphate, in its own terminology. Now, as it faces steady decline in Iraq and Syria, the Islamic State is fighting an insurgency in Libya and has shown its enduring capacity to commit terrorism around the world. Indeed, IS seems to know that its role is changing, as evidenced by messages such as al-Adnani's May 2016 call for lone wolf attacks.

The stages in this jihadi life cycle—terrorism, insurgency, proto-state—can be mapped roughly onto the three phases outlined in *The Management of Savagery*: creating chaos, capitalizing on it, and finally establishing a state. No doubt the author of that volume never intended his phases to be thought of as cyclic; but this ability to morph from form to form goes some way to explaining the terrible endurance of jihadi groups like al-Qaeda. More urgently for present purposes, if the Islamic State is in the process of regressing to a stateless terrorist group without territory to govern, its dispute with al-Qaeda over the status of the "caliphate" becomes moot, and a reunion becomes ideologically possible for both groups—all the more so with Hamza, rather than Zawahiri, running the show.

For twenty years, the global body politic has been infected with a virulent disease. The name of this malady is bin Ladenism, and the self-proclaimed Islamic State is merely its most recent symptom. As its impetuous behavior makes clear, IS thinks and acts exclusively in the short term. It succeeded in conquering large swatches of Iraq and Syria because, at first, nobody tried particularly hard to stop it. Within weeks of the advent of American air strikes, it became clear that IS had already reached its high-water mark. As presently conceived, it lacks a long-term future, although some of its members can no doubt look forward to long careers in terrorism. By contrast, many powerful interests have been trying for a long time to destroy al-Qaeda, and the group has outflanked them all. Indeed, since 9/11, it has actually increased its membership and its geographic reach. This new, stateless al-Qaeda possesses distinct advantages over the Islamic State. Its decentralized structure makes it almost impossible to pin down; like a B-movie vampire, try to drive a stake through its heart and it transforms into a thousand bats and flies somewhere else. Contrast this with the Islamic State, now forced to defend its self-styled caliphate at high cost. When the world eventually summons the will to rid itself of this criminal movement, it knows where to find it. Not so with al-Qaeda, whose subgroups stretch out in a loose band across the breadth of two continents, and whose sympathizers pepper the globe. The organization's fanatic patience, its insistence on playing the long game, has made it far more resilient than anyone expected.

For today's al-Qaeda, there is little profit in antagonizing the West with spectacular terrorist attacks. Instead, its strategy for the present involves building up resources and territory in places like Syria, Yemen, and North Africa while the world is distracted by the Syria conflict. When the Islamic State finally crumbles, however, the spotlight will return to al-Qaeda. At that point, they will strike, and strike hard. With bin Laden's filial heir and ideological successors firmly back in the fold, and the group's affiliates making territorial gains in Yemen and elsewhere, al-Qaeda once again has the means and the opportunity to attack. All it waits for is the right time.

CONCLUSION

SLAYING THE HYDRA

> *So [Hercules] called for help on Iolaus [his charioteer]
> who, by setting fire to a piece of the neighboring wood
> and burning the roots of the [Hydra's] heads with the
> brands, prevented them from sprouting. Having thus got
> the better of the sprouting heads, [Hercules] chopped off
> the immortal head, and buried it, and put a heavy rock
> on it, beside the road that leads through Lerna to Elaeus.*
>
> —PSEUDO-APOLLODORUS, *THE LIBRARY*,
> BOOK 2, CHAPTER 5

On the surface, it seemed I had a fair amount in
common with the man sitting across the table from me. We were
around the same age, both Arabs by birth, both Muslims, both well
read in the scripture and literature of our faith. We had both been
trained in counterinterrogation techniques, as his deft deflections of
my questions made clear. Beyond that, our biographies diverged to
such an extent that only in cosmological terms could we be said to

live on the same planet. I was an FBI Special Agent, while Abu Jandal had once been the trusted bodyguard of Osama bin Laden. Needless to say, Jandal held rigid views on Islam, on America, and on the relationship between the two. He lectured me at length on each of these topics, and I let him talk. Then, a few days into our interview, I brought him a simple history, in Arabic, of the United States. Jandal was amazed; this self-described revolutionary had no inkling that America—the main enemy in bin Ladenist demonology—had itself been born in revolution. To him, it was simply some abstract place—like Hell, perhaps. Along with Israel, the United States was, for Abu Jandal, the epicenter of all evil.

It was now about a week after 9/11. Jandal had heard about the attacks, but only in the most general terms. I brought in a magazine, pointed to the horrific pictures of people throwing themselves out of the burning twin towers. "Bin Laden did this," I said. Jandal scoffed. The photos, he said, looked like something out of a Hollywood action movie. Even if they were real, he insisted, the attacks must be the work of the perfidious Israelis. "The sheikh is not that crazy," he said. But he no longer seemed convinced by his own words.

. . .

In its final report on the events of September 11, 2001, the 9/11 Commission wrote:

> The history, culture, and body of beliefs from which Bin Ladin shapes and spreads his message are largely unknown to many Americans. Seizing on symbols of Islam's past greatness, he promises to restore pride to people who consider themselves the victims of successive foreign masters. He uses cultural and religious allusions to the Holy Koran and some of its interpreters. He appeals to people disoriented by cyclonic change as they confront modernity and globalization. His rhetoric selectively draws from multiple sources—Islam, history, and the region's political

and economic malaise.... Thus our strategy must match our means to two ends: dismantling the al Qaeda network and, in the long term, prevailing over the ideology that contributes to Islamist terrorism.

Since 9/11, and particularly since the Arab Spring, the threat has evolved. This book has chronicled that evolution and highlighted some of the important personalities who represent change or, conversely, continuity in the al-Qaeda movement. From this history, I draw several conclusions.

First, al-Qaeda and its progeny are remarkably resilient. In 1989, bin Laden left Afghanistan in disgrace when his rash miscalculation at the Battle of Jalalabad led to the deaths of thousands of Arab fighters. Seven years later, he was ejected from Sudan under international pressure. In 2001, after the U.S. invasion of Afghanistan, bin Laden and Zawahiri went on the run, while Saif al-Adel and other senior figures languished in an Iranian prison. Each time, al-Qaeda has seemed doomed to fail but has actually recovered and come back stronger. Instead of imploding after 9/11, it mutated to fit the new reality, becoming a series of franchises across North and East Africa and the Arab world, governed by an umbrella organization based in northern Pakistan. This new model has not only survived its founder's death; it has expanded its membership exponentially. As expected, Ayman al-Zawhiri, struggling under his reputation as an interloper, has not proved a charismatic leader. Most notably, he was unable to keep the Islamic State in the fold (although it is by no means clear that bin Laden would have done any better in this regard). On the other hand, under Zawahiri's leadership the remaining franchises have regenerated their capacity to carry out deadly terrorist attacks. Al-Qaeda in the Arabian Peninsula has held and governed territory in Yemen. Meanwhile, al-Qaeda's overall membership has grown exponentially, and the organization has successfully faced down challenges from the Islamic State and its international "provinces."

The Islamic State offers a parallel object lesson in the durability of terrorist groups. It seemed on the brink of collapse in 2007 and 2008—its senior leadership either dead, in hiding, or in prison. But the group's supply of capable leaders—many of them former Saddam operatives—coupled with the Iraqi government's mishandling of Sunni unrest and the power of the Islamic State's message to attract fresh recruits, ensured its survival. It rose to even greater prominence in 2014 when it set itself up as the government of large areas of northern Iraq and northeastern Syria. By the middle of 2016, the Islamic State was once again in decline; but the growing strength of its "provinces," particularly in Libya, suggests that, like al-Qaeda before it, the Islamic State may be poised to evolve into a multinational umbrella group with a number of franchises. That evolution, together with the impending elevation of Hamza bin Laden to a place of power within al-Qaeda, may yet open the door for a reunification between al-Qaeda and the Islamic State.

Second, sectarianism has become a central feature of conflicts in the Middle East, and this will remain the case for the foreseeable future. Between 2003 and 2006, the Jordanian terrorist Abu Musab al-Zarqawi, acting under the al-Qaeda banner but against the orders of his nominal superiors, turned al-Qaeda in Iraq into a machine for murdering Shia Muslims as well as fighting the United States, and thereby bequeathed Iraq a sectarian bloodbath that continues to this day. Zarqawi did not invent the concept of sectarianism, which has figured in Middle East power struggles since the ayatollahs took power in Iran in 1979; but its importance has grown with Iraq's transition to a Shia-led government, the Iranian-Saudi proxy wars in Syria and Yemen, and, of course, the rebirth of Zarqawi's movement as today's Islamic State. Sectarian hatred was never an explicit part of bin Laden's agenda—his mother, after all, is an Alawite, a member of the same Shia sect as Bashar al-Assad—but violence against Shia Muslims and their cultural symbols has proved a potent recruiting tool for the Islamic State, as well as its Iranian-backed opponents.

We should not expect governments or nonstate groups in the region to abandon sectarianism anytime soon.

Third, the Arab Spring has shifted al-Qaeda's calculus. In the months before bin Laden's death, the uprisings dissolved his monomaniacal focus on defeating the United States. To bin Laden, the wave of state failure sweeping the region in the first half of 2011 appeared to represent the chaos predicted in *The Management of Savagery.* If that was true, bin Laden reasoned, it was time to move to the next stage: building trust among local populations. Thus, holding territory and providing government services are now as much a part of the agenda of al-Qaeda franchises as are acts of terrorism against "apostate" Arab governments; and on both aspects of this agenda, al-Qaeda in the Arabian Peninsula is in the lead. Unlike the Islamic State, however, al-Qaeda still does not believe the time has come to proclaim a restored caliphate; hence the disagreement, often bloody, over whether IS constitutes a "state" in the true sense of the word.

Fourth, the war in Syria has exposed the true nature of the struggle underlying the rise of al-Qaeda and the Islamic State. The conflict is a rebuke to the world view put forward in books like Samuel Huntington's 1996 *The Clash of Civilizations,* which envisage an epic conflict between cultures ("Western," "Islamic," "Orthodox," and so on), to replace the Cold War's confrontation between democratic and Communist economic and political systems. After 9/11, some commentators seized upon this theory to explain what was going on. But one glance at the complicated lattice of strife enmeshing the contemporary Middle East is enough to suggest that, if anything, the world has reverted to the norm of *intra*civilizational conflict. Sunnis fight Shia, Persians battle Arabs, Turks struggle with Kurds, and on down to the tribal, communal, and even neighborhood level. All of the major combatants are Muslim; for all their military might, outside powers like the United States and the Russian Federation can at best only marginally affect the outcome.

As we struggle to make sense of the multiplicity of state and nonstate actors vying for control in the modern Middle East, we must be able to answer a question the 9/11 Commission asked itself over a decade ago: "Who is the enemy?" The Commission began its answer in this way:

> *The enemy is not just "terrorism." It is the threat posed specifically by Islamist terrorism. . . . The enemy goes beyond al Qaeda to include the radical ideological movement, inspired in part by al Qaeda, that has spawned other terrorist groups and violence.*

Today, we need a subtler approach—one informed by a deep understanding of jihadi ideology and the personalities who attempt to carry it out. The term "Islamist terrorism" is not nuanced enough for the times we live in. Indeed, the Islamist movement has always been a fragmented one. If we look to the al-Qaeda literature, we find a five-part typology of Sunni Islamist organizations. First, al-Qaeda's own creed, the global Salafi-jihadi movement. Second, the "Sahwa" Salafism popular in Saudi Arabia, which also seeks to implement a Salafi understanding of Sharia, but gradually and through peaceful means. Third, the Muslim Brotherhood, the international group of which Egypt's former president, Mohammed Morsi, is a leading member. Fourth, the political Islam of the late Hassan al-Turabi, according to which Sudan has been governed since 1989. And finally, the "popular jihad" practiced by groups like Hamas, which piggybacks onto preexisting secular political struggles like the one between Israel and the Palestinians. For al-Qaeda, all these substrains are susceptible to secularism, "heresy," and political compromise, with one exception: the Salafi-jihadi movement of which al-Qaeda forms a prominent part. Today, with the split between al-Qaeda and the Islamic State, we are witnessing a clash within the Salafi-jihadi strain itself, a division not about the end goal—both sides believe in a restored caliphate—but how quickly to get there. This, then, is the enemy with which this book has been concerned: not Islam, not "radical Islam," not even

jihadism, but *Salafi*-jihadism, especially in its two major contemporary manifestations, al-Qaeda and the Islamic State.

. . .

In seeking solutions to this problem, the United States has tended
to turn to its intelligence and law enforcement apparatus and, even
more readily, to its armed forces. It is easy to see why. The American
military is one of the most formidable war-winning machines in history. We should not be afraid to use it to stop terrorists from exploiting the vacuums created by state failure. In such circumstances,
covert intelligence gathering, Special Forces raids, drone strikes, and
training of local security services are all vital tools. But being in possession of the world's best hammer, as President Obama memorably
put it in an address to the cadets at West Point, we must be careful
not to see every problem as a nail. Instead, when confronted with the
kind of societal collapse that fosters terrorism, we must be crystal-
clear on exactly what the job of the military is: to hold back the bad
guys, and by so doing provide time and space in which to build the
institutions necessary for lasting peace. To actually craft such institutions, you need to use all the tools of diplomatic, political, and economic support at your disposal. Right now, unfortunately, our plans
never seem to look beyond the military phase. And so, in places like
Afghanistan and Iraq, we have gotten ourselves into a vicious cycle:
invade, occupy, withdraw, repeat. Imagine if, in Europe after World
War II, there had been no Marshall Plan, and after defeating Hitler
and Mussolini the United States had simply occupied the continent.
Europeans would rightly have seen America not as an ally but as a
hostile power, and history would have been very different. Fortunately, the United States did not behave in that way. Instead, through
the Marshall Plan, we worked hard to rebuild the shattered societies,
economies, institutions, and infrastructure left behind by six years of
war. We should bear that in mind today when we encounter societies
afflicted by the cancer of jihadism.

Under our current approach, it seems that, no matter how many times we defeat al-Qaeda on the field of battle, it keeps coming back to life stronger than before. Hercules faced a similar test when he fought the Lernaean Hydra. After a few rounds of lopping off heads, he realized that the sword alone would not get the job done. So he called for help, not from another mythological hero like himself, but from his humble charioteer, who wielded a brand to cauterize the neck and prevent another head from sprouting. Al-Qaeda's "neck," the attribute that, more than any other, allows it to keep growing new heads ad infinitum, is its narrative: the message it uses to attract new recruits from all over the world. When I heard the news of bin Laden's death, I was determined that the United States should not assume that al-Qaeda was finished. I wrote:

> *Investigations, intelligence and military successes are only half the battle. The other half is in the arena of ideas, and countering the rhetoric and methods that extremists use to recruit. We can keep killing and arresting terrorists, but if new ones are recruited, our war will never end.*

For more than two generations, al-Qaeda has successfully peddled the view that the West is engaged in a "war against Islam" with the active connivance of client rulers in capitals around the Muslim world. This opinion is by no means confined to a handful of extremists. On the contrary, millions of Muslims around the world believe that the West is deliberately suppressing their religion and stifling political change in order to keep repressive secular governments in power. Unfortunately, almost nothing is being done to counter this impression, giving jihadis free rein to exploit the misconception for their own ends. Indeed, the United States has fueled the narrative by invading Iraq—apparently fulfilling Salafi-jihadi prophesies that tell of an apocalyptic battle for Mesopotamia—by imprisoning hundreds without charge at Guantánamo Bay, by mocking Islamic taboos in order to humiliate prisoners at Abu Ghraib, by failing to avoid civilian casualties from air strikes, by doing little to end repressive sectarianism in Syria and Iraq, and in myriad other ways. The West's inability (or unwillingness) to defeat the Islamic State provides further grist for our enemy's propaganda mill. In theory, the United States stands at the head of a coalition of over sixty nations ranged against the Islamic State. In practice, most of these make no contribution, or only a token contribution, to the fight; but of course that does not stop the Islamic State from claiming that it has stood up to America and its dozens of global allies, something IS propagandists are able to hold up as evidence that they are invincible, that God is on their side, that the apocalypse is on the way, and on and on.

Groups like the Islamic State and al-Qaeda imprison potential recruits in ideological echo chambers in which every new piece of information is interpreted as evidence supporting jihadi messages: If IS suffers a defeat, it must be because of Shia treachery; if it wins a victory, that is evidence of God's favor. It becomes almost impossible for the truth to reach these recruits; thus, despite the repulsiveness of their politics and the weakness of their theology, the extremists' false promise of history-making adventure comes through loud and clear, while competing messages are barely heard at all. Fundamentally, people need to feel that they are in control of their destinies, that they are part of a broader whole, and that their lives matter. What is on offer in the depressed cities and neighborhoods from which the Islamic State draws most of its recruits—be they in the Muslim world or the West—is just the opposite: a life of mediocrity, isolation, and tedium. So it is no surprise that, in its propaganda videos, the Islamic State goes out of its way to depict its recruits as enjoying action, excitement, and comradeship.

How can we begin to counter such messages? How do we cauterize the wounds from which extremism grows? First, we must expose the basic hypocrisy of a movement that claims to be the arbiter of true Islamic piety yet routinely bombs mosques—including, in 2016, the second-holiest in the world, the Prophet's Mosque in Medina, a site visited by millions of Muslim pilgrims every year, particularly during the month of Ramadan, when the Islamic State chose to strike. While we are laying bare the lies, we must craft a true story to drown out the false ones terrorists tell. It is not a question of trying to match jihadi claims tit for tat with bare denials, but of creating an entirely new narrative—ideally one with even greater appeal, because it is based not on lies and despair but on truth and hope.

Such a story has the potential to push thousands of young off the treadmill of radicalization before it carries them into the jihadi echo chamber. But the narrative will only succeed if it is tailored, like that of the terrorists, not just from country to country but down to the level of different groups and communities. The reasons people join groups like al-Qaeda and the Islamic State vary radically from country to country. In some African nations, for example, economic reasons factor highly, alongside ethnic and familial motives. Security officials in Singapore found users of extremist websites especially drawn to the idea of taking up arms to "protect" fellow Muslims. Elsewhere, the touchstone might be sectarianism, ethnic chauvinism, or tribal rivalries. Counterstrategies need to be similarly focused; boilerplate messages about how "killing is un-Islamic" or "the West is not at war with Islam" are too vague and too easily dismissed.

The identity of the messenger is equally critical. People are likely to dismiss messages they see as coming from the West or from a distrusted local government, and often with good reason. Where terrorists recruit using religious ideology, scholars and clerics are the ones best placed to deliver a counternarrative. Scholars from Singapore's Religious Rehabilitation Group play a critical role in countering extremist narratives by, among other things, emphasizing the importance of moderation in Islamic practice. Similarly, when extremists target would-be recruits through local or tribal grievances, community leaders should head up the response. Rehabilitated former terrorists, where they exist, have the credibility to debunk the idea that terrorism is an honorable and exciting lifestyle, as they have done to great effect as part of the UK's strategy in Northern Ireland.

While each group and situation is unique, counternarrative approaches that have worked elsewhere can be adapted and tailored to new challenges. Germany is working to rehabilitate and reintegrate returnees from Syria using techniques devised to deal with repentant neo-Nazis. The Netherlands initially developed its program to respond to the jihadi extremist Hofstad Network, but Dutch authorities have successfully applied a similar approach to countering other extremists, including right-wing Islamophobes. These particular programs may or may not achieve results right away; but at the very least they represent a step in the right direction.

If you want to inoculate a population permanently against the disease of extremist ideology, you need to give them the tools of critical thinking to resist false narratives and identify true ones. As we saw earlier, a striking dearth of educational opportunity, and the resultant paucity of critical thinking skills, makes many Arab countries fertile ground for extremist groups, whose leaders spout dogma and demand almost blind obedience to orders. In the absence of the healthy skepticism we in the West take for granted, recruiters are able to distort religion and twist the truth into a set of outlandish conspiracy theories. Thus institutions of learning form a frequent jihadi target. The nickname of the Nigerian terrorist group Boko Haram literally means "Western education is forbidden," and indeed that describes a key pillar of its cause. But Boko Haram is hardly unique on this front. Both al-Shabaab and the Taliban have been known to target universities. In October 2012, nine months before Boko Haram killed more than forty people, mostly students, during an attack on a school in Yobe State, the Pakistani Taliban tried to murder fifteen-year-old Malala Yousafzai, a prominent campaigner for education for girls like herself, by shooting her in the head. Why? Because the Taliban knows that the biggest long-term threat to its existence is neither planes nor tanks but teachers and books. In the end, it is education and critical thinking that will truly blow the doors off the Taliban's backward ideology. If we want to tackle bin Ladenism, therefore, we could do worse than to bankroll the building of schools and the training of teachers.

Those who commit themselves to jihad rarely turn from that path voluntarily; but we must leave the door open for those who do, not least because of their value in terms of delivering a convincing counternarrative. Those who repent must be appropriately punished for their actions, of course; but wherever possible they should also have a chance at rehabilitation. Over the last decade, Singapore, Indonesia, Saudi Arabia, and Malaysia have realized some measure of success in operating official rehabilitation programs that take a long view of what is, after all, a long-standing challenge. These initiatives are not free of problems, of course. But what each of these countries has ultimately understood is that successful rehabilitation efforts take time. We in the West, with our proclivity for quick political fixes, stand to learn a lot.

Rehabilitation programs must be made to work before it is too late. Someday, probably sooner rather than later, the fighting in Syria will end, and when that happens, some twelve thousand foreign fighters, their combat skills honed in the ranks of the Islamic State, al-Nusra, Ahrar al-Sham, and any number of other militant groups, will begin pouring out of the Levant. Some will simply move on to whatever they regard as the next Syria, be it Libya, Yemen, or elsewhere; but many will return home, some of them planning to bring the fight with them, others brutalized and traumatized by the death and maiming and disease and anarchy they have witnessed. War has always taken a psychological toll on its combatants; but to treat a person as a hardened terrorist solely because he fought in Syria is to further dehumanize him. Such an approach can only reinforce the bin Ladenist creed that Muslims everywhere are under violent attack and have a duty to respond in kind. By contrast, helping them to readjust, working to rehabilitate them, equipping them with alternative narratives and with the critical thinking skills necessary to spot a false story is not only the right thing to do; it is also the prudent thing to do. The more the United States can be involved in that effort, the more it will be seen as the guarantor of peace in the Middle East and around the world, instead of what it has so long been: the bringer of practically perpetual conflict.

What is decidedly *not* needed is the sort of bureaucratic entanglement that too often stands out as a Washington hallmark. The United States has been working on developing a Countering Violent Extremism program, but it has needlessly spread the domestic portfolio across a range of agencies, from the Department of Education to the FBI, muddling strategy and hog-tying operations. The resulting inertia is a tragic waste; this form of leverage is far too valuable to wither on some administrative vine. The fact is, these programs have been proven to work, even in some of the toughest and most hate-filled places on earth. The first year of a new presidency can be fertile ground for reshaping policy; I hope that the Trump administration will take to heart the lessons we have learned, at great cost in both blood and treasure, about the necessity of countering terrorist ideology.

. . .

All too often, the debate about jihadism becomes clouded by the fact that jihadists have co-opted the language of Islam to justify their crimes; I hope that in the course of this book I have shown that there is nothing Islamic about terrorism. To underline the point, let me close with a personal example from a Western, English-speaking society that is overcoming decades of terrorism and sectarian strife— Northern Ireland.

Several years ago, I arrived in Belfast just ahead of the annual Protestant Orange walk, a controversial sectarian parade that sometimes passes through or near predominantly Catholic neighborhoods. I was being driven down what turned out to be part of the parade route in a Protestant part of town when I saw a huge pile of wood stacked in an open area, protected by security guards.

"What's up?" I asked my driver.

"Oh," he said. "That's the bonfire."

"And the guards?"

"They're making sure no one from the other side sneaks in and lights it beforehand."

"So, they have the walk . . ."

"Yes," he cut in. "They march, then they light the fire, and then they burn the effigy of the pope."

"The pope?" I asked in amazement. This was back during Benedict XVI's reign. "The pope is German!"

"Ah," my driver answered, without missing a beat. "But he's Catholic, isn't he?"

A few days later, still in Belfast, I met with a Catholic whom I will call John. He told me that he had grown up wanting to be a British soldier. Then the Troubles started. He watched his home torched. He heard his mother being called a "Catholic whore" by the soldiers manning checkpoints dotted all over his small part of the world. Instead of a British soldier, he became an IRA fighter, and a ruthless one at that. John had done more than his share of killing, and of prison time. In 1981, he took part in the infamous hunger strike in protest against the treatment of IRA prisoners as ordinary criminals rather than combatants. Decades later, John still couched his story in sectarian terms: Protestant this, Catholic that. I'd heard similar things many times, not only in my counterterrorism work but growing up in the Middle East: Sunni this, people would say, Shia that; Christian this, Alawite that; Druze this, Jew that. Finally, out of the blue, I asked John a simple question: "Do you believe in God?" The question caught him off guard. He chewed on it for a while before answering. "I don't want to insult you or anyone else in this room," he said finally. "But, you know, God is a stupid idea."

If he were being honest, would Khalid Sheikh Mohammed, the architect of 9/11, have said the same thing? KSM purported to be a faithful Muslim, but his trips to Filipino brothels are well documented. Mohammed Atta pounded shots of vodka before boarding American Airlines Flight 11 on September 11, 2001; in the preceding weeks, his fellow hijackers had been spotted enjoying the services of lap dancers. Abu Musab al-Zarqawi, the founder of what became al-Qaeda in Iraq and eventually the Islamic State, was a drug-dealing thug who graduated to ordering suicide bombers to attack weddings and mosques. Perhaps Zarqawi, KSM, and the 9/11 hijackers would not go so far as to say that God is a stupid idea; but in their lives they certainly showed little enough respect for what they profess to regard as the Almighty's commandments. So what exactly motivates people like John and KSM, if not religious fervor? We know some of the answers: nationalism; tribalism; sectarianism. Old wounds that never seem to heal. You cannot pray or kill your way out of a bind like that. But you can try to find a new path and forge a new under-standing. Since the mid-1990s, Northern Ireland has taken great strides down that path; with the right strategy, and a bit of luck, the Muslim world can, too.

Those who kill on behalf of al-Qaeda and other violent Salafi-jihadi groups are brutal men who have caused bloodshed and chaos and suffering almost beyond belief. Some of them, like Ayman al-Zawahiri and Saif al-Adel, possess a demonic intelligence. But they are not geniuses. Believe me, I have interrogated enough of them to know. Among them, you will not find an Einstein—or a Kissinger. Put four in one room and they will state fifty different opinions, pro-nounce twenty fatwas, and wind up hating one another. If you know who they are and how they are connected, and if you understand the forces that drive them, you can begin to anticipate their next move and, in the long run, start to undermine their appeal. If nothing else, I hope this book has contributed in some small measure to that pro-cess of understanding.

ACKNOWLEDGMENTS

No book on this scale could be published at all without the hard work of dozens of dedicated individuals. Constraints of space and memory prevent me from mentioning everyone who contributed, but I trust they know the depth of my gratitude.

First and foremost, I must thank my collaborator throughout this project, A. J. Wilson, without whose intellect, persistence, and way with words this book would simply never have seen the light of day. His wife, Rachel Madan, deserves special mention for her forbearance through the long hours A.J. spent helping me make this book the best it could be.

At the Soufan Group, I am privileged to work every day alongside a staff of truly remarkable individuals. Each of them deserves my gratitude, but particular credit must go to Patrick Skinner, Richard Barrett, Martin Reardon, Michael Masters, Heidi Fink, Anita Waddell, Tim Rhein, and Sydney Black.

For their guidance over the course of this project, my thanks to Lawrence Wright, Howard Means, Umej Singh Bhatia, and Daniel Freedman. Their generous advice, backed by their decades of experience, infinitely strengthened the final product. I'd also like to thank Jeff Nussbaum and the team at West Wing Writers for their support throughout the writing process.

Keeping abreast of developments on the ground in the Middle East can often prove extremely difficult, and I could not do so without the frequent assistance of my sources in Iraq, Syria, and elsewhere. Although for obvious reasons I cannot name them here, I will be forever in their debt.

Special thanks must go to my agent, Andrew Wylie, without whom this book would never have made it off the ground; to my editor, Janet Byrne, who vastly improved the finished manuscript with her usual combination of skill and tenacity; and to Starling Lawrence and his all-star team at Norton—Sarah Bolling, Kyle Radler, Don Rifkin, and Nancy Palmquist—who believed in this project and gave their all to make it a success. Many of these individuals worked with me previously on *The Black Banners*; once again, they wowed me with their dedication and professionalism.

But above all, thanks to my wife, Heather, who continues to inspire me daily. My work may have become less challenging since my retirement from government service, but there has been no letup in my relentless schedule. It takes a very special person to accept this in a spouse year in and year out; luckily, Heather is such a person.

NOTES

SOURCES CITED THROUGHOUT THIS BOOK

General Accounts of al-Qaeda's Development, 1988–present: Lawrence Wright, *The Looming Tower: Al-Qaeda and the Road to 9/11* (New York: Alfred A. Knopf, 2006), Kindle edition; National Commission on Terrorist Attacks Upon the United States, "The 9/11 Commission Report," July 22, 2004, http://govinfo.library.unt.edu/911/report/911Report.pdf; Nasser al-Bahri (aka Abu Jandal) with Georges Malbrunot, *Guarding Bin Laden: My Life in al-Qaeda* (London: Thin Man Press, 2013), Kindle edition; Najwa bin Laden, Omar bin Laden, and Jean Sasson, *Growing Up bin Laden: Osama's Wife and Son Take Us Inside Their Secret World* (New York: St. Martin's Press, 2009); Ali H. Soufan, *The Black Banners*, with Daniel Freedman (New York: W. W. Norton, 2011); *United States v. Usama bin Laden et al.* (U.S. District Court, Southern District of New York, S(7) 98 Cr. 1023), indictment, trial transcript, and exhibits, http://cryptome.org/usa-v-ubl-dt.htm.

Statements by bin Laden, Zarqawi, Zawahiri, and Other Key Figures: Foreign Broadcast Information Service (FBIS), "Compilation of Usama Bin Laden Statements, 1994–January 2004," https://fas.org/irp/world/para/ubl-fbis.pdf; David Aaron, ed., *In Their Own Words: Voices of Jihad* (Washington, DC: RAND Corporation, 2008).

Bin Laden's Correspondence in Hiding, 2001–2011: Selections from documents recovered from the bin Laden compound have been declassified and published: Office of the Director of National Intelligence, "Bin Laden's Book-

shelf," n.d., https://www.dni.gov/index.php/resources/bin-laden-bookshelf.
Hereinafter BLB.

INTRODUCTION: FRIENDS AND ENEMIES

Expansion of al-Qaeda and the Islamic State since 2011: Bill Roggio and
    Thomas Joscelyn, "Al Qaeda Has Not Been Neutralized," *Long War
    Journal*, November 20, 2015, http://www.longwarjournal.org/archives
    /2015/11/al-qaeda-has-not-been-neutralized.php; Stephen Snyder, "ISIS and
    al-Qaeda Squabble Like Schoolboys," PRI's *The World*, November 9, 2015,
    http://www.pri.org/stories/2015-11-09/isis-and-al-qaeda-squabble
    -schoolboys; Priyanka Boghani, "ISIS Is in Afghanistan, but Who Are They
    Really?" *Frontline*, November 17, 2015, http://www.pbs.org/wgbh/frontline
    /article/isis-is-in-afghanistan-but-who-are-they-really/; The Soufan Group,
    "Foreign Fighters: An Updated Assessment of the Flow of Foreign Fighters
    into Syria and Iraq," December, 2015, http://soufangroup.com/wp-content
    /uploads/2015/12/TSG_ForeignFightersUpdate3.pdf.

 xiv "absolute jubilation throughout government": Brian Stelter, "How the
    bin Laden Announcement Leaked Out," *New York Times*, May 1, 2011,
    http://mediadecoder.blogs.nytimes.com/2011/05/01/how-the-osama-
    announcement-leaked-out/.

 xv "[W]e cannot rest": Ali H. Soufan, "The End of the Jihadist Dream," *New
    York Times*, May 2, 2011, http://www.nytimes.com/2011/05/03/opinion
    /03Soufan.html.

 xvii "not as easy . . . on the corner": Mark Duell, "Muslim Fanatics Who
    Recruited British Jihadists to 'Five-Star' War in Syria Now Say They Are
    Fed Up of Tourists Who Think They Can Just 'Grow a Beard and Grab a
    Gun'," *Daily Mail*, February 18, 2014, http://www.dailymail.co.uk/news
    /article-2561903/Fighting-Syria-harder-growing-big-beard-grabbing-
    gun-warns-British-fanatic.html.

 xviii "It's hard to conceive": Peter Slevin and Dana Priest, "Wolfowitz Concedes
    Iraq Errors," *Washington Post*, July 24, 2003, http://www.washington
    post.com/wp-dyn/articles/A37468-2003Jul23.html.

 xviii "If there is a one percent chance": Dan Froomkin, "The Cheney Suprem-
    acy," *Washington Post*, June 19, 2006, http://www.washingtonpost.com
    /wp-dyn/content/blog/2006/06/19/BL2006061900578.html.

CHAPTER 1: THE SNAKE WITH BROKEN TEETH

Sohaib Athar: Harry McCracken, "SXSW: The Man Who Live-Tweeted
    the Bin Laden Raid," *Time*, March 11, 2012, http://techland.time.com

/2012/03/11/sxsw-the-man-who-live-tweeted-the-bin-laden-raid/; Declan McCullagh, "Sohaib Athar on Twitter Fame after bin Laden Raid," CNET, May 4, 2011, http://www.cnet.com/news/sohaib-athar-on-twitter -fame-after-bin-laden-raid-q-a/.

Abbottabad and the bin Laden Mansion: Abbottabad Commission, "Final Report," January 4, 2013, http://www.aljazeera.com/indepth/spotlight /binladenfiles/2013/07/201378143927822246.html; Jeremy Bernstein, "That 'Sweet Abbottabad Air'," *New York Review of Books*, May 5, 2011, http://www.nybooks.com/blogs/nyrblog/2011/may/05/sweet-abbottabad -air/; BBC News, "Bali Bomb-Maker Umar Patek Jailed for 20 years," June 21, 2012, http://www.bbc.com/news/world-asia-18529829; Barton Gellman, Julie Tate, and Ashkan Soltani, "In NSA-Intercepted Data, Those Not Targeted Far Outnumber the Foreigners Who Are," *Washington Post*, July 5, 2014, https://www.washingtonpost.com/world/national -security/in-nsa-intercepted-data-those-not-targeted-far-outnumber-the -foreigners-who-are/2014/07/05/8139adf8-045a-11e4-8572-4b1b969b6322 _story.html; Tim Lister, "Abbottabad—The Military Town Where bin Laden Hid in Plain Sight," CNN, May 2, 2011, http://www.cnn.com /2011/WORLD/asiapcf/05/02/bin.laden.abbottabad/; "Plan Showing Pro- posed Double Storey House to Be Built at Garga Cantt. Area, Abbottabad," *BBC News*, n.d., http://news.bbc.co.uk/2/shared/bsp/hi/pdfs/09_05_2011 _plans.pdf; Associated Press, "Pakistani Property Records Give New Insights into bin Laden," *Times-Picayune*, May 4, 2011, http://www.nola. com/politics/index.ssf/2011/05/pakistani_property_records_giv.html.

Bin Laden's Daily Life in Hiding: Abbottabad Commission report; Asad Hashim, "The Bin Ladens' Life on the Run," Al Jazeera, July 8, 2013, http://www .aljazeera.com/indepth/features/2013/07/2013781444498188.html; Mat- thew Cole and Nick Schifrin, "Courier Hid Osama Bin Laden Well," ABC News, May 4, 2011, http://abcnews.go.com/Blotter/courier-hid-osama-bin -laden/story?id=13528409; Rob Crilly, "Osama bin Laden's '2004 House in Pakistan' Back on the Market," *Telegraph*, March 9, 2012, http://www .telegraph.co.uk/news/worldnews/al-qaeda/9133690/Osama-bin-Ladens -2004-house-in-Pakistan-back-on-the-market.html; Carlotta Gall, "U.S. Still Waits for Access to Bin Laden Widows," *New York Times*, May 10, 2011, http://www.nytimes.com/2011/05/11/world/asia/11pakistan.html; Declan Walsh, "In Hiding, Bin Laden Had Four Children and Five Houses," *New York Times*, March 29, 2012, http://www.nytimes.com/2012/03/30 /world/asia/on-run-bin-laden-had-4-children-and-5-houses-a-wife-says .html; Elisabeth Bumiller, Carlotta Gall, and Salman Masood, "Bin Laden's Secret Life in a Diminished World," *New York Times*, May 7, 2011, http:// www.nytimes.com/2011/05/08/world/asia/08binladen.html.

U.S. Efforts to Trace bin Laden and the Navy SEAL Raid: Abbottabad Commission report, paragraphs 31–43, 706; Mark Bowden, "The Death of Osama bin Laden: How the U.S. Finally Got its Man," *Guardian*, October 12, 2012, https://www.theguardian.com/world/2012/oct/12/death-osama-bin-laden-us; Nicholas Schmidle, "Getting bin Laden: What Happened That Night in Abbottabad," *New Yorker*, August 8, 2011, http://www.newyorker.com/magazine/2011/08/08/getting-bin-laden; Bob Woodward, "Death of Osama bin Laden: Phone Call Pointed U.S. to Compound—and to 'the Pacer'," *Washington Post*, May 6, 2011, https://www.washingtonpost.com/world/national-security/death-of-osama-bin-laden-phone-call-pointed-us-to-compound--and-to-the-pacer/2011/05/06/AFnSVaCG_story.html; *60 Minutes*, "SEAL's First-Hand Account of bin Laden Killing," CBS News, September 24, 2012, http://www.cbsnews.com/news/seals-first-hand-account-of-bin-laden-killing/; Phil Bronstein, "The Shooter," *Esquire*, February 11, 2013, http://www.esquire.com/news-politics/a26351/man-who-shot-osama-bin-laden-0313/; Reuters, "Osama bin Laden Compound in Abbottabad in Pictures," *Guardian*, May 4, 2011, https://www.theguardian.com/world/gallery/2011/may/04/osama-bin-laden-compound.

12 "God has not made a disease . . . old age": Abu Dawud, *Sunan Abu Dawud*, trans. Ahmad Hasan, ninth century CE, http://www.usc.edu/org/cmje/religious-texts/hadith/abudawud/028-sat.php#028.3846, Bk. 28, No. 3846.

13 "Computer science": "Letter dtd 07 August 2010," BLB.

14 "commanders . . . grow up": "Summary on Situation in Afghanistan and Pakistan," BLB; "Letter to Shaykh Abu Abdallah dtd 17 July 2010," ibid.

14 "good men . . . carry the burden": "Letter to Shaykh Abu Abdallah dtd 17 July 2010," BLB.

14 "to be safe . . . incrementally": ibid.

15 "The harm . . . have been leveled": CBS News, "Hi-Tech Drones Aid Terror Hunt," July 10, 2009, http://www.cbsnews.com/videos/hi-tech-drones-aid-terror-hunt/.

16 "You should wash them": "Letter to Shaykh Mahmud 26 September 2010," BLB.

16 "Please send me the résumés": "Letter dtd 07 August 2010," BLB.

17 "Perhaps a job": "Letter to Shaykh Mahmud," BLB.

17 "How can we correspond": "Gist of conversation Oct 11," BLB.

17 "Couriers are the only way": ibid.

17 "Security procedures . . . no room for mistakes": "Letter to Shaykh Mahmud," BLB.

17 "change his lifestyle . . . whom he is to avoid": "Letter dtd 18 JUL 2010," trans. Ali H. Soufan, BLB.

18 an article in the *New York Times*: Matthew Rosenberg, "CIA Cash Ended Up in Coffers of Al Qaeda," *New York Times*, March 14, 2015, http://www.nytimes.com/2015/03/15/world/asia/cia-funds-found-their -way-into-al-qaeda-coffers.html.

19 "an American channel": Reuters, "Bin Laden Eyed 9/11 Anniversary Media Blitz," *Newsweek*, March 1, 2016, http://www.newsweek.com/ osama-bin-laden-septemder-11-anniversary-432192.

19 "One year . . . keep me posted": "Letter dtd 07 August 2010," BLB.

19 "a passion for reading": "Letter to Uthman," BLB.

19 "It is a known fact . . . extreme importance": ibid.

20 "nominate a qualified brother": "Letter dtd 07 August 2010," BLB.

20 "pious and patient . . . knowledge": "Letter to Uthman," BLB.

21 "By fighting the local enemy": "Letter Addressed to Atiyah," BLB.

21 "It is unlawful . . . burn in Hell forever": N.J. Dawood, trans., The Koran, 5th rev. ed. (London: Penguin, 1990), 4:92–93.

23 "we want the maximum number": "Letter dtd 07 August 2010," BLB.

23 "a truce . . . Saudi Arabia": "Letter dtd 18 JUL 2010," trans. Ali H. Soufan, BLB.

25 "Ben Ali, tell Mubarak": Jeffrey Fleishman and Amro Hassan, "Will Revolt in Tunisia Inspire Others?" *Los Angeles Times*, January 16, 2011, http:// articles.latimes.com/2011/jan/16/world/la-fg-tunisia-arab-world-20110116.

25 "This is the most important point in our history": "Letter to Shaykh Mahmud," BLB.

26 "These gigantic events . . . rule of the caliphate": "Letter from UBL to Atiyah," BLB.

26 "Though the majahideen . . . We must really mobilize": ibid.

26 "tell the people . . . let them pick the fruit": "Afghani Opportunity," BLB.

27 "We should talk . . . ordered us to implement": "Letter to Shaykh Mahmud," BLB.

27 "the first enemy of the people": "Afghani Opportunity," BLB.

28 "The fragmentation in the region . . . little influence in the matter": ibid.

28 "You should work": "Letter to Shaykh Mahmud," BLB.

28 "the rest of the brothers . . . full mobilization": ibid.

29 she was only sixteen years old: Al-Bahri, *Guarding Bin Laden*, chap. 16, loc. 2322

30 "losing too much time": "Letter dtd 16 December 2007," BLB.

30 "I hope you will consider it completely cancelled": "Letter to Um Abd-al-Rahman dtd 26 April 2011," BLB.

30 "We have been through . . . from good to better": ibid.

30 "maintain equality . . . impartially": Dawood, trans., The Koran, 4:3, 4:129.

31 "fill our hearts with joy": "Undated Letter 3," BLB.

32 "the Iranians are not to be trusted": ibid.

33 "the mujahideen legions . . . to serve you": "Letter from Hamzah to father dtd July 2009," BLB.

34 "He is very sweet . . . the son of 'someone' ": "Letter dtd November 24 2010," BLB.

34 "Saad died": "Letter dtd November 24 2010," BLB.

34 "We pray": "Undated Letter 3," BLB.

36 "Good news . . . Praise God!": "Letter from Abu Abdullah to his mother 2," BLB.

36 "trusted in God for his protection": Abbottabad Commission report, paragraph 47.

36 "If you had twenty-five eighteen-year-olds": Elisabeth Bumiller, Carlotta Gall, and Salman Masood, "Bin Laden's Secret Life in a Diminished World," *New York Times*, May 7, 2011, http://www.nytimes.com /2011/05/08/world/asia/08binladen.html.

37 "They are getting exhausted . . . another place": "Undated Letter 3," BLB.

37 "As far as I am concerned . . . very generous to me": ibid.

37 "the facts prove": "Letter to Shaykh Mahmud," BLB.

37 "We consider . . . begun to be seen": "Letter to Um Abid al-Rahman," BLB.

41 "mowing the lawn": Schmidle, "Getting bin Laden."

CHAPTER 2: ALLEGIANCE

General: Ari Weisfuse, "Negotiating Oblivion: Sayf al Adl: Al Qaeda's Top Operative" (Senior Thesis, Brandeis University, 2014), http://bir.brandeis .edu/bitstream/handle/10192/27590/WeisfuseThesis2014.pdf;NellyLahoud, "Beware of Imitators: Al-Qaida through the Lens of Its Confidential Secretary," June 4, 2012, https://www.ctc.usma.edu/posts/beware-of-imitators -al-qaida-through-the-lens-of-its-confidential-secretary.

Importance of *Bayat* **in al-Qaeda:** *U.S. v. Bin Laden*, trial transcript; Al-Bahri, *Guarding Bin Laden*, chap. 11; author's personal interview with Ali Omran in prison in Jakarta, Indonesia, 2009.

Saif's Personality and Leadership Style: Mohamed Fadel Fahmy, "Egyptian Comrades Remember Reported Leader of al Qaeda," CNN, May 20, 2011, http://www.cnn.com/2011/WORLD/meast/05/20/al.qaeda.succession /index.html; Al-Bahri, *Guarding Bin Laden*, chap. 11; Bin Laden et al., *Growing Up bin Laden*, chap. 15.

Saif's Life before Jihad: Asharq al-Awsat, "Will the Real Saif al-Adel Please Stand Up?" March 1, 2012, http://english.aawsat.com/2012/03/article 55243015; Ali Zalat, "Al-Masri Al-Youm Visits the Home of the Acting al-Qaeda Leader in Shibin al-Kawm: Family Adamant about His Death; Denies Ties to al-Qaeda," trans. Ali H. Soufan, *Al-Masri al-Youm*, May 23, 2011, http://today.almasryalyoum.com/printerfriendly .aspx?ArticleID=297777; Ali Zalat, "The 'Real' Saif al-Adel: Believed Dead by Brother, 'Held in Iran' by Brother-In-Law," trans. Ali H. Soufan, *Al-Masri al-Youm*, February 29, 2012, http://www.almasryalyoum.com /news/details/164179.

Ibrahim Makkawi: Asharq al-Awsat, "Will the Real Saif al-Adel Please Stand Up?" March 1, 2012, http://english.aawsat.com/2012/03/article 55243015; Paisley Dodds (Associated Press), "Mistaken ID in FBI Most-Wanted Profile?" NBC News, June 29, 2011, http://www.nbcnews.com /id/43584343/#.VmShZuOfoXA.

Afghanistan, 1987–1992: Mustafa Hamid and Leah Farrall, *The Arabs at War in Afghanistan* (London: Hurst, 2015); Mustafa Hamid, "A Mother's Deep Sorrow," *The Airport 90*, trans. Combaing Terrorism Center at West Point, n.d., https://www.ctc.usma.edu/posts/a-mothers-deep-sorrowthe-airport-project-english-translation-2; Fahmy, "Egyptian Comrades"; Lahoud, "Beware of Imitators."

Sudan and Somalia, 1992–1996: Clint Watts, Jacob Shapiro, and Vahid Brown, "Al-Qaida's (Mis)Adventures in the Horn of Africa," July 2, 2007, https://www.ctc.usma.edu/posts/al-qaidas-misadventures-in-the-horn -of-africa; Thomas Joscelyn, "Iran's Proxy War Against America," Claremont Institute, October 1, 2007, 31–33, 42–44; Combating Terrorism Center at West Point, trans., "The Five Letters to the African Corps" (AFGP-2002-600053), https://www.ctc.usma.edu/posts/five-letters-to-the-africa -corps-english-translation-2; Omar al-Sumali, Report on activities in Somalia (AFGP-2002-600113), trans., Combating Terrorism Center at West Point, https://www.ctc.usma.edu/posts/a-short-report-on-the-trip-from-nairobi-english-translation-2; United States Army, *United States Forces, Somalia After Action Report and Historical Overview: The United States Army in Somalia, 1992–1994* (Washington, DC: Center of Military History, United States Army, 2003), http://www.history .army.mil/html/documents/somalia/SomaliaAAR.pdf; Lahoud, "Beware of Imitators"; J. M. Berger, "The Alleged 1994 Assassination Attempt on Osama bin Laden: Declassified State Department Cable Adds Color to Little Known Sudan Incident," *IntelWire*, August 12, 2007, http:// intelwire.egoplex.com/2007_08_12_exclusives.html.

Yemen, 1995: Gabriel Koehler-Derrick, ed., "A False Foundation? AQAP, Tribes and Ungoverned Spaces in Yemen," October 2, 2011, https://www.ctc.usma.edu//posts/a-false-foundation-aqap-tribes-and-ungoverned-spaces-in-yemen; Wright, *Looming Tower*, chap. 7; 9/11 Commission Report, 59–60, 145, 489.

Flight from Khartoum to Jalalabad, May 18, 1996: The facts as presented here are drawn from the firsthand account of bin Laden's son, Omar (Bin Laden et al., *Growing Up bin Laden*, 139–142). The 9/11 Commission reported that the bin Laden plane refueled in the United Arab Emirates (9/11 Commission Report, 63, 469). However, this information was based on an interrogation of Khalid Sheikh Mohammed, who was not on the flight, nor indeed even a member of al-Qaeda at the time. Moreover, by 1996, Sudan had become an international pariah, having been designated a state sponsor of terrorism. This makes it less likely that a Sudanese government plane would have chosen to call in the United Arab Emirates, a U.S. ally. Iran, on the other hand, was at that time one of the few countries with which Sudan had a cordial relationship. For these reasons, I have chosen to present Omar bin Laden's account in the text.

Afghanistan, 1996–2001: Al-Bahri, *Guarding Bin Laden*, chaps. 6–11; Lahoud, "Beware of Imitators"; Bin Laden et al., *Growing Up bin Laden*, chaps. 14–15; Kevin Bell, "Usama bin Ladin's 'Father Sheikh': Yunus Khalis and the Return of al-Qaida's Leadership to Afghanistan," May 14, 2013, https://www.ctc.usma.edu/posts/usama-bin-ladens-father-sheikh-yunus-khalis-and-the-return-of-al-qaidas-leadership-to-afghanistan; Vahid Brown, "The Façade of Allegiance: Bin Ladin's Dubious Pledge to Mullah Omar," *CTC Sentinel*, January 13, 2010, https://www.ctc.usma.edu/posts/the-facade-of-allegiance-bin-ladin%E2%80%99s-dubious-pledge-to-mullah-omar; Wright, *Looming Tower*, chaps. 6–7; Hamid and Farrell, *Arabs At War*; *United States v. Salim Ahmed Hamdan* (Military Commission, Guantánamo Bay, Cuba), Official Authenticated Transcript, June 4, 2007–August 7, 2008; Sunday Times, "Focus: Chilling Message of the 9/11 Pilots," October 1, 2006, http://www.thesundaytimes.co.uk/sto/news/focus/article174598.ece.

44 "Sister . . . child crying?": Abbottabad Commission report, paragraph 43.

44 "Congratulations to the Islamic *umma*": "Al-Qaeda Statement on bin Laden's Death," Al Jazeera, May 6, 2011, http://www.aljazeera.com/news/middleeast/2011/05/201156203329911287.html.

45 "voice message": ibid.

46 "swear before God": Al-Bahri, *Guarding Bin Laden*, chap. 11, loc. 1798.

47 Saif al-Adel is number eight: *U.S. v. Bin Laden*, Government Exhibit

2201A-T, https://www.justsecurity.org/wp-content/uploads/2015/01/Gov
-exhibit.pdf.

48 "highly educated": Fahmy, "Egyptian Comrades."

48 "shrewd diplomat": Lahoud, "Beware of Imitators," 20n45.

48 "caustic tongue": Al-Bahri, *Guarding Bin Laden*, chap. 16, loc. 2379; chap. 7, loc. 1010.

50 "generation of amateurs . . . war of the goats": Asharq al-Awsat, "Real Saif al-Adel."

50 "Makkawi hates al-Qaeda": Dodds, "Mistaken ID."

50 "short fused . . . dangerously unbalanced": Wright, *Looming Tower*, chap. 6, loc. 2394.

52 "was never part of any jihad organization": Fahmy, "Egyptian Comrades."

54 "an organized Islamic faction . . . make His religion victorious": Minutes of a meeting of al-Qaeda held in August or September of 1988, in J. M. Berger, ed., *Beatings & Bureaucracy: The Founding Memos of al-Qaeda* (Online: Intelwire Press, 2012), Kindle edition, loc. 202.

56 "narrow Asian eyes . . . full of energy": Hamid, "A Mother's Deep Sorrow," 18–19 (modified translation).

56 "The war in Afghanistan . . . other parts of the world": *U.S. v. Bin Laden*, trial transcript, day 12, page 1642.

57 "What you are trying to do . . . it is Sudan!": Wright, *Looming Tower*, chap. 8, loc. 3038.

57 "an important al-Qaeda leader": *U.S. v. Bin Laden*, trial transcript, day 2, pages 244–245; day 12, page 1642.

59 "When you entered Somalia": "Five Letters to the African Corps."

59 "A lot of bullets . . . out of Somalia": Omar al-Sumali, Report, 4–5.

60 "He which hath": Mark Bowden, *Black Hawk Down: A Story of Modern War* (New York: Grove Press, 2010), Kindle edition, loc. 5725.

61 "The Somali experience": "Five Letters to the African Corps," 12.

61 "a successful Islamic arsenal . . . retreats on the flanks": ibid.

61 "stupid": Hamid and Farrell, *Arabs At War*, 190–191.

62 "clear evidence . . . Arabian Peninsula": Koehler-Derrick, ed., "False Foundation," 24.

68 "There is little I can do after they reach you": Bell, "Usama bin Ladin's 'Father Sheikh'," 39.

68 "We do not say": ibid, 60–61.

69 "Our protection to you": Al-Bahri, *Guarding bin Laden*, chap. 10, loc. 1774.

70 "We will fight him with faith": Wright, *Looming Tower*, chap. 7, loc. 2913.

70 "save Kuwait . . . all time": Bin Laden et al., *Growing Up bin Laden*, 158.

71 "agent . . . American enemy": FBIS, "Compilation," 18–19.

71 "The Brothers from the Northern Group": Soufan, *Black Banners*, 62–66; Hamid and Farrell, *Arabs At War*, 222–225.

72 "beat[ing] them into submission": Al-Bahri, *Guarding Bin Laden*, chap. 7, loc. 877.

75 "Al-Qaeda does not want to be accused": Al-Bahri, *Guarding Bin Laden*, chap. 11, loc. 1832–1880.

75 "It is not permissible . . . guarantee their safety": Peter Arnett, interview with Osama bin Laden, CNN, March 1997.

75 "Fix the car . . . on the move soon": *U.S. v. Hamdan*, transcript, 2140, 2145.

76 "Preventive measures . . . bomb us soon": Al-Bahri, *Guarding Bin Laden*, chap. 10, loc. 1660.

76 "[t]he first act": Weisfuse, "Negotiating Oblivion," 51.

76 "culture of revenge": Al-Bahri, *Guarding Bin Laden*, chap. 9, loc. 1160.

76 "If one day . . . end up in prison": ibid., Introduction, loc. 139.

77 a speech at the wedding of his son: Douglas Frantz and David Rohde, "How bin Laden and Taliban Forged Jihad Ties," *New York Times*, November 22, 2001, http://www.nytimes.com/2001/11/22/international /asia/22TALI.html; *New York Times*, "Bin Laden Shown on TV Tape Smiling at his Son's Wedding," January 11, 2001, http://www.nytimes .com/2001/01/11/world/bin-laden-shown-on-tv-tape-smiling-at-his-son -s-wedding.html.

77 "al-Qaeda would be absorbed": Al-Bahri, *Guarding Bin Laden*, chap. 12, loc. 1966.

77 "constrained by circumstances": ibid.

78 "The season is coming": 9/11 Commission Report, 175.

79 "conduct their affairs": Dawood, trans., The Koran, 42:38.

81 "Al-Shiba . . . May God help us": Soufan, *Black Banners*, 322.

81 "We are like mountains of stone": FBIS, "Compilation," 135–136.

82 "Bin Laden wanted the United States to attack": 9/11 Commission Report, 191.

CHAPTER 3: THE DISASTER

Genesis of the "Planes Operation": Wright, *Looming Tower*, chaps. 6, 9; Thomas Joscelyn, "AQAP Publishes Insider's Account of 9/11 Plot," *Long War Journal*, February 10, 2016, http://www.longwarjournal.org /archives/2016/02/aqap-publishes-insid-story-of-911-attacks.php;   9/11

Commission Report, 145–150, 251–252; Hamid and Farrell, *Arabs At War*, chap. 11; Vahid Brown, "Cracks in the Foundation: Leadership Schisms in al-Qaida from 1989–2006," January 2, 2007, https://www.ctc.usma .edu/posts/cracks-in-the-foundation-leadership-schisms-in-al-qaida -from-1989-2006; Weisfuse, "Negotiating Oblivion."

Assassination of Ahmed Shah Massoud: Thomas Harding, "Blast Survivor Tells of Massoud Assassination," *Telegraph*, October 26, 2001, http:// www.telegraph.co.uk/news/worldnews/asia/afghanistan/1360632/Blast -survivor-tells-of-Massoud-assassination.html; Wright, *Looming Tower*, chap. 19.

Saif's Defense of Kandahar: Ben Venzke and Aimee Ibrahim, eds., "Al-Qaeda's Advice for Mujahideen in Iraq: Lessons Learned in Afghanistan," IntelCenter, April 14, 2003; Al Jazeera, "The Secret Diaries of Abu Zubaydah," http://projects.aljazeera.com/2013/abu-zubaydah/index.html; Asharq al-Awsat, "Al-Qaida Member Recalls U.S. Bombardment, Accuses Taliban of Betrayal," October 29, 2003; *Frontline*, "The Fall of Kandahar," n.d., http:// www.pbs.org/wgbh/pages/frontline/shows/campaign/ground/kandahar .html; Hamid and Farrell, *Arabs At War*, chap. 11.

Murder of Daniel Pearl: Asra Q. Nomani, *The Truth Left Behind: Inside the Kidnapping and Murder of Daniel Pearl* (Washington, DC: Center for Public Integrity, 2011); *New York Times*, "The Guantánamo Docket: Khalid Sheikh Mohammed: JTF-GTMO Assessment," December 8, 2006, http://projects.nytimes.com/guantanamo/detainees/10024-khalid-shaikh-mohammed.

Flight to Iran: Federal Bureau of Investigation, Record of Interview with Sulayman Abu Ghayth, March 6, 2011, http://kronosadvisory.com/Kronos_ US_v_Sulaiman_Abu_Ghayth_Motion_In_Limine_12Mar2014.pdf, paragraph 11, hereinafter Ghaith interview; "Letter dtd 13 Oct 2010," BLB; Leah Farrall, "Interview with a Taliban Insider: Iran's Game in Afghanistan," *Atlantic*, November 14, 2011, http://www.theatlantic .com/international/archive/2011/11/interview-with-a-taliban-insider -irans-game-in-afghanistan/248294/.

83 The guesthouse is clean . . . "Thanks be to God," he says: Transcript of Bin Laden Videotape," NPR, December 13, 2001, http://www.npr.org/ news/specials/response/investigation/011213.binladen.transcript.html.

84 Colonel Ibrahim Makkawi . . . had mused: Wright, *Looming Tower*, chap. 6, loc. 2394; chap. 9, loc. 3293

85 "computer and media projects": 9/11 Commission Report, 145–150; Hamid and Farrell, *Arabs At War*, 216.

89 "seemed least affected": Al-Bahri, *Guarding Bin Laden*, chap. 20, loc. 2938.

89 "The problem is not how to start the war": Hamid and Farrell, *Arabs At War*, 280.

90 "I will make it happen . . . by myself": Weisfuse, "Negotiating Oblivion," 59.

90 "If someone opposes him . . . no advice nor anything": Letter from Saif al-Adel to Khalid Sheikh Mohammed, June 13, 2002.

91 "If the Japanese had seen . . . marketing advertisements": Venzke and Ibrahim, "Al-Qaeda's Advice," 23–24.

91 "An operation . . . evacuating this compound": Soufan, *Black Banners*, 344.

93 "Those young men . . . everywhere else in the world": "Transcript of Bin Laden Videotape," http://www.npr.org/news/specials/response /investigation/011213.binladen.transcript.html.

94 "Get in your truck . . . Go": reconstructed from author's personal research and interviews.

95 "a stormy campaign": Venzke and Ibrahim, "Al-Qaeda's Advice," 18–19.

97 "Your children . . . God willing": Asharq al-Awsat, "Al-Qaida Member Recalls U.S. Bombardment"; Weisfuse, "Negotiating Oblivion," 62–63; Zubaydah Diaries, November 20, 2001.

98 "Airplanes came from every direction": Venzke and Ibrahim, "Al-Qaeda's Advice," 28–29.

99 "harvesting the souls of the enemy": ibid., 30–32.

101 "He was a really good player . . . Sharp and fast": Fahmy, "Egyptian Comrades."

102 "If you can obtain such a weapon . . . no price is too high to pay": Reconstructed based on the memoirs of George Tenet, then the Director of Central Intelligence. George Tenet, *At the Center of the Storm: My Years at the CIA* (New York: HarperCollins, 2007), Kindle edition, loc. 4438.

104 "These people . . . if we want him": Nomani, *The Truth Left Behind*, 42.

105 "Today we are experiencing one setback after another": Letter from Saif al-Adel to Khalid Sheikh Mohammed, June 13, 2002 (modified translation).

105 "pushes you . . . *come from Abu Abdullah*": ibid. (italics added).

106 "joy . . . the beginning of the end": Middle East Media Research Institute, "Special Dispatch No. 313: Terror in America: Al-Jazeera Interview with Top Al-Qaida Leader Abu Hafs 'The Mauritanian'," December 14, 2001, http://www.memri.org/report/en/0/0/0/0/0/0/568.htm.

106 "heroes . . . youth of the *umma*": Venzke and Ibrahim, "Al-Qaeda's Advice," 22.

106 "Hamza the Qatari . . . blood covering his body": ibid., 32.

107 "If they harm you . . . run away": Weisfuse, "Negotiating Oblivion," 66; Dawood, trans., The Koran, 3:112.

107 "not fit for combat . . . Islam once more": Venzke and Ibrahim, "Al-Qaeda's Advice," 17–20, 27, 34.

107 "We do not, by the will of God, doubt the final defeat": ibid., 34.

107 "the Euphrates lays bare a mountain of gold": William McCants, *The ISIS Apocalypse: The History, Strategy and Doomsday Vision of the Islamic State* (New York: St. Martin's Press, 2015), Kindle edition, appendix 1, loc. 2804.

CHAPTER 4: THE EMIR OF THE STRANGERS

General: Nimrod Raphaeli, "Inquiry and Analysis Series Report No. 231: The Sheikh of the Slaughterers: Abu Musab Al-Zarqawi and the Al-Qaeda Connection," Middle East Media Research Institute, July 1, 2005, http://www.memri.org/report/en/print1406.htm; Mary Anne Weaver, "The Short, Violent Life of Abu Musab al-Zarqawi," *Atlantic*, June 8, 2006, http://www.theatlantic.com/magazine/archive/2006/07/the-short-violent-life-of-abu-musab-al-zarqawi/304983/; Bruce Riedel, *The Search for Al-Qaeda: Its Leadership, Ideology, and Future* (Washington, DC: Brookings Institution Press, 2008), Kindle edition, chap. 5; Gary Gambill, "Abu Musab al-Zarqawi: A Biographical Sketch," *Jamestown Foundation Terrorism Monitor* 3, issue 24; Jeffrey Gettleman, "Abu Musab al-Zarqawi Lived a Brief, Shadowy Life Replete With Contradictions," *New York Times*, June 9, 2006, http://www.nytimes.com/2006/06/09/world/middleeast/09zarqawi.html; McCants, *ISIS Apocalypse*, chap. 5; Nir Rosen, "Iraq's Jordanian Jihadis," *New York Times*, February 19, 2006, http://www.nytimes.com/2006/02/19/magazine/iraq.html.

Zarqawi's Early Life, 1967–1999: Middle East Media Research Institute, "Special Dispatch No. 84: Al-Hayat Inquiry: The City of Al-Zarqaa in Jordan— Breeding Ground of Jordan's Salafi Jihad Movement," January 17, 2005, http://www.memri.org/report/en/print1298.htm; Joas Wagemakers, "Abu Muhammad al-Maqdisi: A Counter-Terrorism Asset?" *CTC Sentinel* 1, issue 6, https://www.ctc.usma.edu/posts/abu-muhammad-al-maqdisi-a-counter-terrorism-asset.

Afghanistan, 1999–2001: "Jihadist Biography of the Slaughtering Leader Abu Musab al-Zarqawi, by Saif al-Adl, the Military Commander of Qaidat al-Jihad," posted in an al-Qaeda online forum, June 20, 2009, http://triceratops.brynmawr.edu/dspace/bitstream/handle/10066/5092/ZAR20090817.pdf. Note that, despite the attribution to Saif al-Adel, the authorship of this biography is hotly disputed.

Saddam Hussein's State Sponsorship of Terrorism: Judith S. Yaphe, "Statement to the National Commission on Terrorist Attacks upon the United States,"

July 9, 2003, http://www.9-11commission.gov/hearings/hearing3/witness
_yaphe.htm; Senate Intelligence Committee, "Report on Postwar Find-
ings about Iraq's WMD Programs and Links to Terrorism and How
They Compare with Prewar Assessments," September 8, 2006, hereinafter Senate Intelligence Committee report; Council on Foreign Relations,
"Terrorism Havens: Iraq," December 1, 2005, http://www.cfr.org/iraq
/terrorism-havens-iraq/p9513.

Development of al-Qaeda in Iraq: Craig Whitlock, "Zarqawi Building His Own
Terror Network," *Washington Post*, October 3, 2004; M.J. Kirdar, "Al
Qaeda in Iraq," Center for Strategic and International Studies, June 2011;
Cole Bunzel, "From Paper State to Caliphate: The Ideology of the Islamic
State," Brookings Institution, March 2015, http://www.brookings.edu/~/
media/research/files/papers/2015/03/ideology-of-islamic-state-bunzel
/the-ideology-of-the-islamic-state.pdf; Stanford University, "Mapping
Militant Organizations: Ansar al-Islam," July 3, 2016, http://web.stanford
.edu/group/mappingmilitants/cgi-bin/groups/view/13; Martin Chulov,
"ISIS: The Inside Story," *Guardian*, December 11, 2014, http://www.the
guardian.com/world/2014/dec/11/-sp-isis-the-inside-story; Bryan Price,
Dan Milton, Muhammad al-Ubaydi, and Nelly Lahoud, "The Group That
Calls Itself a State: Understanding the Evolution and Challenges of the
Islamic State," Combating Terrorism Center at West Point, December 16,
2014, https://www.ctc.usma.edu/posts/the-group-that-calls-itself-a-state
-understanding-the-evolution-and-challenges-of-the-islamic-state; Joseph
Felter and Brian Fishman, "Al-Qaida's Foreign Fighters in Iraq: A First Look
at the Sinjar Records," Combating Terrorism Center at West Point, 2008,
https://www.voltairenet.org/IMG/pdf/Al_Qa_ida_s_Foreign_Fighters
_in_Iraq-_A_First_Look_at_the_Sinjar_Records.pdf; McCants, *ISIS
Apocalypse*, chap. 1.

Relations with al-Qaeda Central: Jeffrey Pool, trans., "Zarqawi's Pledge of
Allegiance to al-Qaeda: From Muaskar al-Battar, Issue 21," *Jamestown
Foundation Terrorism Monitor* 3, issue 24; Gordon Corera, "Unraveling Zarqawi's al-Qaeda Connection," *Jamestown Foundation Terrorism
Monitor* 3, issue 24; Council on Foreign Relations (CFR), "Letter from
Abu Musab al-Zarqawi to Osama bin Laden," February 1, 2004, http://
www.cfr.org/iraq/letter-abu-musab-al-zarqawi-osama-bin-laden/p9863,
hereinafter Zarqawi–Bin Laden letter; *United States v. Abd al Hadi
al-Iraqi* (Military Commission, Guantánamo Bay) Charges and Speci-
fication, February 10, 2014, http://www.mc.mil/Portals/0/pdfs/alIraqi
/Hadi%20Al%20Iraqi%20Referred%20Charge%20Sheet.pdf, count 55;
Combating Terrorism Center at West Point, trans., Letter from Ayman

al-Zawahiri to Abu Musab al-Zarqawi, July 9, 2005, https://www.ctc
.usma.edu/posts/zawahiris-letter-to-zarqawi-english-translation-2,
hereinafter Zawahiri-Zarqawi letter; Combating Terrorism Center at West
Point, trans., Letter from Atiyah Abd al-Rahman [a.k.a. Mahmud] to Abu
Musab al-Zarqawi, ca. December 2005, https://www.ctc.usma.edu/posts
/atiyahs-letter-to-zarqawi-english-translation-2, hereinafter Mahmud
-Zarqawi letter.

Fallujah: Bill Roggio, "Zarqawi's Fallujah," *Long War Journal*, November 15,
2004, http://www.longwarjournal.org/archives/2004/11/zarqawis_falluj
.php; Hannah Allam, "The Iraqi Who Ran Fallujah Rebels' Real Leader
Was Local, May Say," *Philadelphia Inquirer*, November 24, 2004, http://
articles.philly.com/2004-11-24/news/25380120_1_fallujah-insurgents-
insurgent-control-zarqawi; Associated Press, "Two Locals Were Core
of Fallujah Insurgency," NBC News, November 24, 2004, http://www
.nbcnews.com/id/6578062/ns/world_news-mideast_n_africa/t/two
-locals-were-core-fallujah-insurgency/#.VqZ6PVMrLI0.

Tal Afar: George Packer, "The Lesson of Tal Afar," *New Yorker*, April 10,
2006, http://www.newyorker.com/magazine/2006/04/10/the-lesson-of
-tal-afar; Lara Logan and Daniel Schorn, "Tal Afar: Al-Qaeda's Town,"
CBS News, March 10, 2006, http://www.cbsnews.com/news/tal-afar-al
-qaedas-town/.

Tracking Down and Killing Zarqawi: Sean D. Naylor, "Closing In On
Zarqawi," *Army Times*, May 8, 2006, http://abcnews.go.com/images
/WNT/Army_Times.pdf; Peter Grier and Faye Bowers, "U.S. At Least
Seizes Zarqawi's Laptop," *Christian Science Monitor*, April 27, 2005,
http://www.csmonitor.com/2005/0427/p03s01-woiq.html; "Letter to Special Committee of al-Jihad's Qaida of the Mujahidin Affairs in Iraq and
to the Ansar al-Sunnah Army," BLB; ABC News, "Pressure Grows on al
Qaeda in Iraq," January 30, 2006, http://abcnews.go.com/International
/story?id=1557349; Sabrina Tavernise and Dexter Filkins, "Local Insurgents Tell of Clashes with Al Qaeda's Forces in Iraq," *New York Times*,
January 12, 2006, http://www.nytimes.com/2006/01/12/international
/middleeast/12insurgent.html; Georg Mascolo, Holger Stark, and Bern-
hard Zand, "Zarqawi's Death: A Terrorist Is Finally Brought to Account,"
Der Spiegel, June 12, 2006, http://www.spiegel.de/international/spiegel
/zarqawi-s-death-a-terrorist-is-finally-brought-to-account-a-420861.
html; Mark Bowden, "The Ploy," *Atlantic*, May 2007, http://www.the
atlantic.com/magazine/archive/2007/05/the-ploy/305773/; John F. Burns,
"U.S. Strike Hits Insurgent at Safehouse," *New York Times*, June 8, 2006,
http://www.nytimes.com/2006/06/08/world/middleeast/08cnd-iraq

.html; Dexter Filkins and John F. Burns, "At Site of Attack on Zarqawi, All That's Left Are Questions," *New York Times*, June 11, 2006, http://www.nytimes.com/2006/06/11/world/middleeast/11scene.html; BBC News, "Zarqawi'DiedofBlastInjuries," June 12, 2006, http://news.bbc.co.uk/2/hi/middle_east/5072104.stm.

109 "I was expected to inform": Gambill, "Biographical Sketch."

110 "As far as I know": Antonio Ferrari, "Interview with His Majesty King Abdullah II," *Corriere della Sera*, September 27, 2004, http://www.kingabdullah.jo/index.php/en_US/interviews/view/id/307.html.

111 a cavalier disregard for education: United Nations Development Program, "Human Development Data for the Arab States: Mean Years of Schooling (of Adults Over 25)," 1980–2011, http://www.arab-hdr.org/data/indicators/2012-24.aspx; Ikram al-Yacoub, "Sum of All Fears: Arabs Read an Average of 6 Minutes a Year, Study Reveals," *Al Arabiya News*, July 14, 2012, http://www.alarabiya.net/articles/2012/07/14/226290.html; Middle East Monitor, "ALECSO Report: 97 Million Illiterates in Arab Countries," February 10, 2014, https://www.middleeastmonitor.com/20140210-alecso-report-97-million-illiterates-in-arab-countries/; United Nations Development Program, "Arab Human Development Report 2003: Building a Knowledge Society," http://www.arab-hdr.org/publications/other/ahdr/ahdr2003e.pdf, 67.

116 "an ordinary guy . . . dangerous situations": Weaver, "Short, Violent Life."

118 "Zarqawi was the muscle": ibid.

118 "Jail was very good . . . proselytize": Rosen, "Iraq's Jordanian Jihadis."

119 "When I heard Zarqawi speak": ibid.

120 "loathing at first sight": Weaver, "Short, Violent Life."

121 "council of infidels": Rosen, "Iraq's Jordanian Jihadis."

121 "Shiites should be executed": Weaver, "Short, Violent Life."

122 "Herat was the beginning": ibid.

123 "refused to march": Gambill, "Biographical Sketch."

123 "open several new battlefronts": "Jihadist Biography."

124 "prepare for confrontations": ibid.

125 "did not add up": Senate Intelligence Committee repart, 334–346.

126 "If we cannot defeat the Americans": Sami Kleib, *Al-Assad between Departure and the Approach of Destruction: The Syrian War in Secret Documents* (Beirut: Dar al-Farabi, 2016), trans. Ali H. Soufan.

126 "90 percent": Agence France-Presse, "Maliki Blames Syria for Attacks, Assad Denies Claim," France 24, September 4, 2009, http://www.france24.com/en/20090901-maliki-blames-syria-attacks-assad-denies-claim-.

129 "There are serving U.S. flag-rank officers": Senate Armed Services Committee, "Inquiry in the Treatment of Detainees in U.S. Custody: Report," November 20, 2008, xii.

129 "Crusade . . . ethnic groups": FBIS, "Compilation," 247–251.

130 "There is no doubt": Aaron, ed., *In Their Own Words*, 107.

130 "The shedding of Muslim blood . . . killing some Muslims": ibid., 103–104.

130 "blood will be spilled": Zarqawi–Bin Laden letter.

131 "[W]ar has ups and downs": Aaron, ed., *In Their Own Words*, 194.

132 "rejectionists . . . rancor toward the Sunnis": Zarqawi–Bin Laden letter.

132 "Why is it permissible": Riedel, *The Search for Al-Qaeda*, chap. 5, loc. 1928.

133 "[A]fter one year of jihad": Raphaeli, "Sheikh of the Slaughterers" (quoting Abu Anas al-Shami).

135 "If Ben Gardane had been located next to Fallujah": The Soufan Group, "TSG IntelBrief: The International Hotbeds of the Islamic State," July 22, 2015, http://soufangroup.com/tsg-intelbrief-the-international-hotbeds-of-the-islamic-state/.

135 "waging jihad with my brothers": Bunzel, "From Paper State to Caliphate," 15.

136 "heroic operations": BBC News, "Children Massacred by Iraq Bombs," September 30, 2004, http://news.bbc.co.uk/2/hi/middle_east/3702710.stm.

136 "[T]he dignity of the Muslim men and women . . . slaughtered in this way": Dexter Filkins, "The Struggle for Iraq: Revenge Killing," *New York Times*, May 12, 2004, http://www.nytimes.com/2004/05/12/world/struggle-for-iraq-revenge-killing-iraq-tape-shows-decapitation-american.html.

137 "We used to start": Aaron, ed., *In Their Own Words*, 107.

137 "evidence of God's justice": Magdi Abdelhadi, "Controversial Preacher with 'Star Status'," BBC News, July 7, 2004, http://news.bbc.co.uk/2/hi/uk_news/3874893.stm.

138 an article entitled "Al-Zarqawi—Aid and Advice": Middle East Media Research Institute, "Al-Hayat Inquiry," http://www.memri.org/report/en/print1298.htm.

138 "[T]he gates of heaven are open . . . their reins": Raphaeli, "Sheikh of the Slaughterers."

138 "My nation, the nation of the sword and the pen": ibid.

139 Zarqawi's naked sectarianism alienated many Iraqi Sunnis: Michael Lipka, "The Sunni-Shia Divide: Where They Live, What They Believe and How They View Each Other," Pew Research Center, June 18, 2014, http://www.pewresearch.org/fact-tank/2014/06/18/the-sunni-shia-divide-where

-they-live-what-they-believe-and-how-they-view-each-other/; Pew Research Center, "The World's Muslims: Unity and Diversity," August 9, 2012, http://www.pewforum.org/2012/08/09/the-worlds-muslims-unity-and-diversity -executive-summary/.

139 "expertise or experience . . . safety and victory are incompatible": Zarqawi– Bin Laden letter.

139 "the head of the pyramid": Whitlock, "Zarqawi Building His Own Terror Network."

140 "compared to the enormity . . . throats of the mujahideen": Zarqawi–Bin Laden letter.

140 "The unhurried observer . . . hands of these people": ibid.

141 "God's religion . . . their paradise": ibid.

141 "This is our vision": ibid.

142 "Hold fast to the rope of God . . . guidance of prophethood": Jeffrey Pool, trans., "Zarqawi's Pledge of Allegiance to al-Qaeda: From Muaskar al-Battar, Issue 21," *Jamestown Foundation Terrorism Monitor* 3, issue 24, 4–6.

143 "The warrior commander": "Osama Bin Laden to the Iraqi People: It Is Forbidden to Participate in Iraqi and PA Elections," Middle East Media Research Institute, December 30, 2004, http://www.memri.org/report /en/0/0/0/0/0/0/0/1286.htm.

144 "man is deified": Aaron, ed., *In Their Own Words*, 145–147.

146 "[p]ray for the healing": Raphaeli, "Sheikh of the Slaughterers."

147 "[m]y wounds were light . . . to a commander": ibid.

148 "The jihad in Iraq": Zawahiri-Zarqawi letter.

148 "avoid any action . . . kill the captives by bullet": ibid.

149 "Even if our Sunni brothers . . . become entangled": Aaron, ed., *In Their Own Words*, 243.

149 "if the jihad fighter": ibid., 92.

149 "a new arrow . . . commendable": ibid., 93.

150 "armed camps": Packer, "The Lesson of Tal Afar."

150 "Martyrdom operations": Aaron, ed., *In Their Own Words*, 246.

150 "all-out warfare . . . no mercy": ibid., 246.

151 "dangerous . . . because he is a Shiite": ibid., 246–247.

151 "We do not understand": ibid., 247.

152 "Everything was white at our wedding . . . red because of the blood": Jo Meek, "Couple Remember Wedding Bombing," BBC News, March 2, 2006, http://news.bbc.co.uk/2/hi/4766726.stm.

152 "coward . . . burn in Hell": BBC News, "Zarqawi 'Defends Jordan Attacks'," November 18, 2005, http://news.bbc.co.uk/2/hi/middle_east

/4450590.stm; CNN, "Voice on Tape: Jordanians Not Targeted," November 18, 2005, http://www.cnn.com/2005/WORLD/meast/11/18/zarqawi .jordan/.

153 "centers for waging war . . . Safeway, etc.": Aaron, ed., *In Their Own Words*, 261.

153 "furious": Weaver, "Short, Violent Life."

153 "commanders of the global jihad": Aaron, ed., *In Their Own Words*, 261.

153 "perilous and ruinous . . . I am not joking": Mahmud-Zarqawi letter.

154 "win them over . . . leave the path of excuses": ibid.

154 "[A]nyone who commits tyranny": ibid.

155 One veteran jihadi would later claim: BBC News, "Zarqawi 'Not Leading Iraq Unrest'," April 3, 2006, http://news.bbc.co.uk/2/hi/middle_ east/4872236.stm (quoting Huthaifa Azzam).

155 "the starting point . . . an Islamic emirate": Bunzel, "From Paper State to Caliphate," 16.

155 "stand[ing] as a stumbling block": Price et al., "Group That Calls Itself A State," 20.

156 "The tribes are fed up": ABC News, "Pressure Grows on al Qaeda in Iraq," January 30, 2006, http://abcnews.go.com/International/story?id=1557349; Tavernise and Filkins, "Local Insurgents," http://www.nytimes.com/2006 /01/12/international/middleeast/12insurgent.html.

158 "That's one dead son of a bitch": Bowden, "The Ploy."

158 "The Wedding of the Martyr": Gettleman, "Brief, Shadowy Life," http://www.nytimes.com/2006/06/09/world/middleeast/09zarqawi. html; John Murphy, "In Jordan, Praise and Condemnation," *Baltimore Sun*, June 9, 2006, http://articles.baltimoresun.com/2006-06-09/news /0606090304_1_nom-de-guerre-abu-jordanian.

158 "dark-eyed companions": Dawood, trans., The Koran, 56:22–23.

158 "may God burn him in hell": Murphy, "Praise and Condemnation."

158 "deeply saddened . . . future generations": CNN, "On Tape, bin Laden mourns al-Zarqawi's Death," June 30, 2006, http://edition.cnn.com /2006/WORLD/meast/06/30/binladen.tape/index.html.

159 "There is no such thing as Zarqawism": Bowden, "The Ploy."

159 "We had killed Zarqawi too late": Sean Naylor, "Inside the Pentagon's Manhunting Machine," *Atlantic*, August 28, 2015, http://www .theatlantic.com/international/archive/2015/08/jsoc-manhunt-special -operations-pentagon/402652/.

159 "The path that [Zarqawi] trod . . . does not stop": Aaron Y. Zelin, "Al-Furqan Media Presents a New Audio Message from the Islamic State of Iraq's Shaykh Abu Bakr al-Hussayni al-Qurayshi al-Baghdadi:

'Announcement of the Islamic State of Iraq and al-Sham'," *Jihadology*, April 9, 2013, http://jihadology.net/2013/04/09/al-furqan-media-presents -a-new-audio-message-from-the-islamic-state-of-iraqs-shaykh-abu-bakr-al -%E1%B8%A5ussayni-al-qurayshi-al-baghdadi-announcement-of-the -islamic-state-of-iraq-an/.

160   "This is the story of the whole war . . . where this notion comes from": Bowden, "The Ploy."

CHAPTER 5: DOCTOR, WISE MAN, TEACHER, TRAITOR

General: Lawrence Wright, "The Man Behind bin Laden: How an Egyptian Doctor Became a Master of Terror," *New Yorker*, September 16, 2002; Ayman al-Zawahiri, Knights Under the Prophet's Banner 2nd ed., Asharq al-Awsat, trans., (Online: As-Sahab Media Production, 2010), https:// azelin.files.wordpress.com/2010/11/6759609-knights-under-the-prophet-banner.pdf; Nimrod Raphaeli, "Ayman al-Zawahiri," *Terrorism and Political Violence* 14, no. 4; Wright, *Looming Tower*, chaps. 2, 6, 9, 13; *U.S. v. Hamdan*, transcript.

Zawahiri's Abortive Journey to Russia, 1996: Andrew Higgins and Alan Cullison, "Saga of Dr. Zawahiri Sheds Light on the Roots of al Qaeda Terror," *Wall Street Journal*, July 2, 2002, http://www.wsj.com/articles /SB1025558570331929960.

EIJ–Al-Qaeda merger: *U.S. v. Bin Laden*, trial transcript, day 37, pages 5369– 5370; 9/11 Commission Report, 69.

Al-Qaeda ideology: William McCants, trans., *The Management of Savagery: The Most Critical Stage through Which the Umma Will Pass* (Boston: John M. Olin Institute for Strategic Studies, May 23, 2006); SITE Intelligence Group, "Abu Musab al-Suri's Military Theory of Jihad," *Insite Blog*, ca. December 2010, http://news.siteintelgroup.com/blog/index.php /about-us/21-jihad/21-suri-a-mili; Lawrence Wright, "The Master Plan," *New Yorker*, September 11, 2006, http://www.newyorker.com/magazine /2006/09/11/the-master-plan; McCants, *ISIS Apocalypse*, chap. 4.

Decline of al-Qaeda in Iraq: McCants, *ISIS Apocalypse*, chaps. 1–2; Bunzel, "From Paper State to Caliphate"; Bill Roggio, Daveed Gartenstein-Ross, and Tony Badran, "Intercepted Letters from al-Qaeda Leaders Shed Light on State of Network in Iraq," Foundation for Defense of Democracies, September 12, 2008, http://www.defenddemocracy.org /media-hit/intercepted-letters-from-al-qaeda-leaders-shed-light-on-state -of-network-in/; Price et al., "Group That Calls Itself A State."

AQAP and Anwar al-Awlaki: The Soufan Group, "TSG IntelBrief: Profiling al-Qaeda in the Arabian Peninsula Part 1," August 14, 2013, http://

soufangroup.com/tsg-intelbrief-profiling-al-qaeda-in-the-arabian-peninsula-part-1/; The Soufan Group, "TSG IntelBrief: Profiling al-Qaeda in the Arabian Peninsula Part 2," August 15, 2013, http://soufangroup.com/tsg-intelbrief-profiling-al-qaeda-in-the-arabian-peninsula-part-2/; Jere van Dyk, "Who Were the 4 U.S. Citizens Killed in Drone Strikes?" CBS News, May 23, 2013, http://www.cbsnews.com/news/who-were-the-4-us-citizens-killed-in-drone-strikes/; Scott Shane, "The Lessons of Anwar al-Awlaki," *New York Times Magazine*, August 27, 2015, http://www.nytimes.com/2015/08/30/magazine/the-lessons-of-anwar-al-awlaki.html; Scott Shane, "The Anwar al-Awlaki File: From American Citizen to Imam to Terrorist to Drone Killing," National Security Archive, September 15, 2015, http://nsarchive.gwu.edu/NSAEBB/NSAEBB 529-Anwar-al-Awlaki-File/; McCants, *ISIS Apocalypse*, chaps. 2–3; Combating Terrorism Center at West Point, trans., "Letter to Nasir al-Wuhayshi," 2010, https://www.ctc.usma.edu/posts/letter-to-nasir-al-wuhayshi-english-translation-2.

Al-Shabaab: Jonathan Masters and Mohammed Aly Sergie, "Al-Shabab," Council on Foreign Relations, March 13, 2015, http://www.cfr.org/somalia/al-shabab/p18650; National Counterterrorism Center (NCTC), "Counterterrorism Guide: Al-Shabaab," n.d., http://www.nctc.gov/site/groups/al_shabaab.html; Bill Roggio and Thomas Joscelyn, "Shabaab Formally Joins al Qaeda," *Long War Journal*, February 9, 2012, http://www.longwarjournal.org/archives/2012/02/shabaab_formally_joi.php; Carla E. Humud et al., "Al Qaeda-Affiliated Groups: Middle East and Africa," Congressional Research Service, October 10, 2014, https://fas.org/sgp/crs/mideast/R43756.pdf; "Letter dtd 13 Oct 2010," BLB.

Al-Qaeda in the Islamic Maghreb: The Soufan Group, "TSG IntelBrief: AQIM: The Threat to Western Interests in Africa and Beyond," October 10, 2012, http://soufangroup.com/tsg-intelbrief-aqim-the-threat-to-western-interests-in-africa-and-beyond/; Humud et al., "Al Qaeda-Affiliated Groups: Middle East and Africa."

Zawahiri Becomes Emir: Al-Bahri, *Guarding Bin Laden*, chaps. 20–21.

161 "We have become an idea": Lahoud, "Beware of Imitators," 109.

161 "al-Qaeda is a message": Humud, et al., "Al Qaeda-Affiliated Groups: Middle East and Africa", 1 (quoting al-Sahab interview).

162 "There is no solution without jihad . . . all other methods": Aaron, ed., *In Their Own Words*, 71.

162 "If I fall . . . bargains market?": Zawahiri, *Knights*, 36.

162 "a legacy of despair": Aaron, ed., *In Their Own Words*, 71.

163 "Brother, push ahead": Raphaeli, "Zawahiri."

163 "Regardless of the method": Zawahiri, *Knights*, 58.

164 "something missing . . . you cannot be its leader": Wright, "Man Behind bin Laden," 68.

164 "inhumane . . . a genius": ibid., 60.

165 "let the genie out of the bottle": ibid., 63.

167 "I saw this [trip]": Zawahiri, *Knights*, 7–9.

168 "Do they want us to shoot up the streets": Wright, "Man Behind bin Laden," 68.

168 "The treadmill of torture": Zawahiri, *Knights*, 20.

168 "Islamic state and Islamic society . . . until the victory of Islam": Enemy of Injustice, "الكبرى الجهاد قضية في الظو امر ي أيمن الشيخ من افـعة 1981," You-Tube, April 4, 2015, https://www.youtube.com/watch?v=YB0BDAyHaJg; Wright, "Man Behind bin Laden," 62.

169 "As of now . . . wanted by the Americans and the Jews": Zawahiri, *Knights*, 10–11.

171 "the emir cannot be a blind man . . . the emir cannot be a prisoner": Wright, *Looming Tower*, chap. 2, loc. 1071.

172 "the transformation of the United States": Zawahiri, *Knights*, 27–34, 52–59.

172 "He who owns my food": Soufan, *Black Banners*, 111.

173 "The unintended death": Zawahiri, *Knights*, 29.

174 "Terrorism is the enemy of God": Wright, *Looming Tower*, chap. 9.

174 "left the embassy's ruined building": Zawahiri, *Knights*, 12.

175 "[a]ll we did was to apply God's Sharia": Wright, *Looming Tower*, chap. 13, locs. 3968–3988.

176 "a disaster that almost destroyed the group": Higgins and Cullison, "Saga of Dr. Zawahiri."

177 "All these crimes and sins": World Islamic Front, "Statement: Jihad Against Jews and Crusaders," February 23, 1998, http://fas.org/irp/world /para/docs/980223-fatwa.htm.

177 "the forces of the disbelievers . . . their own homes and bodies": Zawahiri, *Knights*, 5.

178 "expected some members . . . pillar of our success": Higgins and Cullison, "Saga of Dr. Zawahiri."

178 "We must admit . . . during the periods of siege": Zawahiri, *Knights*, 31–33.

179 "his family is with him": "Letter to Shaykh Abu Abdallah dtd 17 July 2010," BLB.

179 "an Islamist coalition": Zawahiri, *Knights*, 61.

179 "Tracking down the Americans and the Jews": ibid., 63.

180 "in the heart of the Arab region . . . heart of the Islamic world": ibid., 60–66.

181 "I can't share this with you": Soufan, *Black Banners*, 99.

185 "the professor of the mujahideen": McCants, *ISIS Apocalypse*, chap. 4, loc. 1488.

185 "The Islamic movement . . . the greatest power, America": ibid., locs. 1507–1518.

187 "nothing but a regular militant": Abu Ahmed, "The Hidden Truth about al-Baghdadi's State," Ali H. Soufan, trans., published in a series of posts on social media channels, ca. 2014.

188 "We are an arrow . . . where you wish": McCants, *ISIS Apocalypse*, chap. 1, locs. 256–281; Bunzel, "From Paper State to Caliphate," 20–22.

189 "very dangerous": Bill Roggio, Daveed Gartenstein-Ross, and Tony Badran, "Intercepted Letters from al-Qaeda Leaders Shed Light on State of Network in Iraq," Foundation for Defense of Democracies, September 12, 2008, http://www.defenddemocracy.org/media-hit/intercepted -letters-from-al-qaeda-leaders-shed-light-on-state-of-network-in/, 5.

189 "any day": McCants, *ISIS Apocalypse*, chap. 2, loc. 532.

189 "totally isolated": Roggio et al., "Intercepted Letters."

190 "Where is this Islamic State": Bunzel, "From Paper State to Caliphate," 22.

190 "Some of Our Fundamentals . . . political process": ibid., 38–41.

190 "would carry your shoes": McCants, *ISIS Apocalypse*, chap. 2, loc. 588.

191 "an extraordinary crisis": "Analysis of the State of ISI," n.d., https://www .ctc.usma.edu/posts/analysis-of-the-state-of-isi-english-translation-2.

191 "the malice has increased . . . stabbed in the back": Osama bin Laden, "A Message to Our People in Iraq," October 2007, http://thesis.haverford .edu/dspace/bitstream/handle/10066/4656/OBL20071023.pdf.

193 "an easy spoil": Rukmini Callimachi, "Yemen Terror Boss Left Blueprint for Waging Jihad," *Associated Press*, August 9, 2013, http://bigstory .ap.org/article/yemen-terror-boss-left-blueprint-waging-jihad.

194 "If you want Sanaa . . . high deficit": Letter to Wuhayshi.

195 one tribal elder reported: Robert F. Worth, "Is Yemen the Next Afghanistan?" *New York Times Magazine*, July 6, 2010, http://www.nytimes .com/2010/07/11/magazine/11Yemen-t.html.

197 "connect the Horn of Africa jihad": Masters and Sergie, "Al-Shabab," http://www.cfr.org/somalia/al-shabab/p18650.

197 "victory or martyrdom": Andrea Elliott, "A Call to Jihad, Answered in America," *New York Times*, July 11, 2009, http://www.nytimes .com/2009/07/12/us/12somalis.html.

198 "to be compassionate . . . use against us": "Letter dtd 13 Oct 2010," BLB.

200 "I tell our brothers in al-Qaeda": Jason Burke, "Al-Qaida in the Midst

of Fierce Succession Battle," *Guardian*, May 18, 2011, http://www
.theguardian.com/world/2011/may/18/al-qaida-succession-battle-saif-al
-adel-acting-leader.

200 "mother al-Qaeda . . . collaborators": Vahid Brown, "Sayf al-Adl and
al-Qaida's Historical Leadership," *Jihadica*, May 18, 2011, http://www
.jihadica.com/sayf-al-adl-and-al-qaidas-historical-leadership/.

200 "We await your instructions": UPI, "Somalia Islamists Vow Loyalty to
Zawahiri," June 21, 2011, http://www.upi.com/Top_News/Special/2011
/06/21/Somalia-Islamists-vow-loyalty-to-Zawahiri/23491308676873/.

201 "[o]ur war against the Zionist Crusaders": Matthew Cole and Rym Mom-
taz, "Al Qaeda Leader in Yemen Pledges Allegiance to Zawahiri," *ABC
News*, July 26, 2011, http://abcnews.go.com/Blotter/al-qaeda-leader
-yemen-pledges-allegiance-zawahiri/story?id=14164884.

202 "Bin Laden was a born leader": Al-Bahri, *Guarding Bin Laden*, chap. 21,
3150.

203 "change the face of history": Humud et al., "Al Qaeda-Affiliated Groups:
Middle East and Africa," 40.

CHAPTER 6: THE SYRIAN WARS

General: The Soufan Group, "Foreign Fighters Update"; The Soufan Group,
"TSG IntelBrief: The Logic of Foreign Fighters as Suicide Bombers,"
October 23, 2014, http://soufangroup.com/tsg-intelbrief-the-logic-of
-foreign-fighters-as-suicide-bombers/; The Soufan Group, "TSG IntelBrief:
Sending Soldiers to Syria," February 9, 2016, http://soufangroup.com/tsg-
intelbrief-sending-soldiers-to-syria/; The Soufan Group, "TSG IntelBrief:
A Regional Showdown in Syria," February 17, 2016, http://soufangroup
.com/tsg-intelbrief-a-regional-showdown-in-syria/.

Abu Khalid al-Suri: Aron Lund, "Who and What Was Abu Khalid al-Suri
Part 1," Carnegie Endowment for International Peace, February 24,
2014, http://carnegieendowment.org/syriaincrisis/?fa=54618; Aron Lund,
"Who and What Was Abu Khalid al-Suri Part 2," Carnegie Endowment
for International Peace, February 25, 2014, http://carnegieendowment
.org/syriaincrisis/?fa=54634; Thomas Joscelyn, "Syrian Rebel Leader Was
bin Laden's Courier, Now Zawahiri's Representative," *Long War Journal*,
December 17, 2013, http://www.longwarjournal.org/archives/2013/12/aq
_courier_rebel_leader_zawahiri.php; Markaz Sham, trans., "Eulogy of
Abu Khalid al-Suri By Dr. Zawahiri," April 5, 2014, https://justpaste.it
/ez9c; Thomas Joscelyn, "Al Qaeda's Chief Representative in Syria Killed
in Suicide Attack," *Long War Journal*, February 23, 2014, http://www

.longwarjournal.org/archives/2014/02/zawahiris_chief_repr.php; Richard Spencer, "Four Jihadists, One Prison: All Released by Assad and All now Dead," *Telegraph*, May 11, 2016, http://s.telegraph.co.uk/graphics/projects /isis-jihad-syria-assad-islamic/; U.S. Department of the Treasury, "Treasury Designates al-Qaida Supporters in Qatar and Yemen," December 18, 2013, https://www.treasury.gov/press-center/press-releases/Pages/jl2249.aspx.

Hama uprising, 1982: Deborah Amos, "30 Years Later, Photos Emerge from Killings in Syria," NPR, February 2, 2012, http://www.npr.org /2012/02/01/146235292/30-years-later-photos-emerge-from-killings-in -syria; Azmat Khan, "On 30th Anniversary of Hama Massacre, Syrian Troops Lock Down City," *Frontline*, February 2, 2012, http://www.pbs.org /wgbh/frontline/article/on-30th-anniversary-of-hama-massacre-syrian -troops-lock-down-city/; David Kenner, "Massacre City," *Foreign Policy*, August 5, 2011, http://foreignpolicy.com/2011/08/05/massacre-city-2/.

Bashar Al-Assad: Kleib, *Al-Assad*; BBC News, "Syrian President Bashar al-Assad: Facing Down Rebellion," October 21, 2015, http://www.bbc.com /news/10338256.

Ahrar al-Sham: Stanford University, "Mapping Militant Organizations: Ahrar al-Sham," July 14, 2016, http://web.stanford.edu/group/mapping militants/cgi-bin/groups/view/523; Kim Sengupta, "Turkey and Saudi Arabia Alarm the West by Backing Islamist Extremists the Americans Had Bombed in Syria," *Independent*, May 12, 2015, http://www.independent. co.uk/news/world/middle-east/syria-crisis-turkey-and-saudi-arabia-shock -western-countries-by-supporting-anti-assad-jihadists-10242747.html; Sam Heller, "How Ahrar al-Sham Has Come to Define the Kaleido- scope of the Syrian Civil War," *War on the Rocks*, June 6, 2016, http:// warontherocks.com/2016/06/how-ahrar-al-sham-has-come-to-define-the -kaleidoscope-of-the-syrian-civil-war/; Robert S. Ford and Ali El Yassir, "Yes, Talk with Syria's Ahrar al-Sham," Middle East Institute, July 15, 2015, http://www.mei.edu/content/at/yes-talk-syria%E2%80%99s-ahrar -al-sham.

Prince Mohammed bin Nayyif and Prince Mohammed bin Salman: Robert Windrem, "Royal Pains: Two Princes Vie for Power in Saudi Arabia, Make a Mess," NBC News, January 23, 2016, http://www.nbcnews .com/news/world/royal-pains-two-princes-vie-power-saudi-arabia- make-mess-n502271; Ben Hubbard, "Suicide Bombings Hit 3 Cities in Saudi Arabia, One Near a Holy Site," *New York Times*, July 4, 2016, http://www.nytimes.com/2016/07/05/world/middleeast/saudi-arabia -us-consulate-kuwait.html; The Soufan Group, "TSG IntelBrief: Saudi Arabia Fights the Islamic State at Home," July 20, 2015, http://soufan

group.com/tsg-intelbrief-saudi-arabia-fights-the-islamic-state-at-home/;
David D. Kirkpatrick, "Surprising Saudi Rises as a Prince Among Princes,"
New York Times, June 6, 2015, http://www.nytimes.com/2015/06/07/
world/middleeast/surprising-saudi-rises-as-a-prince-among-princes.html;
Patrick Cockburn, "Prince Mohammed bin Salman: Naïve, Arrogant
Saudi Prince Is Playing with Fire," *Independent*, January 9, 2016, http://
www.independent.co.uk/news/world/middle-east/prince-mohammed
-bin-salman-naive-arrogant-saudi-prince-is-playing-with-fire-a6804481.
html; Sengupta, "Turkey and Saudi Arabia Alarm the West"; Economist, "Saudi Arabia: Young Prince in a Hurry," January 9, 2016, http://
www.economist.com/news/briefing/21685467-muhammad-bin-salman
-gambles-intervention-abroad-and-radical-economic-change-home.
Recep Tayyip Erdogan: BBC News, "Recep Tayyip Erdogan: Turkey's
Ruthless President," July 21, 2016, http://www.bbc.com/news/world-
europe-13746679; The Soufan Group, "TSG IntelBrief: Turkey in the
Aftermath of a Failed Coup," July 21, 2016, http://soufangroup.com
/tsg-intelbrief-turkey-in-the-aftermath-of-a-failed-coup/; Jonathan Broder,
"The End of Turkey's Double Game with ISIS?" *Newsweek*, December 5,
2015, http://www.newsweek.com/2015/12/25/end-turkeys-double-game
-isis-401606.html; Sengupta, "Turkey and Saudi Arabia Alarm the West."
Qassem Soleimani: Stahlgewitter Syrien, "A New Video of Iranian Quds
Force Commander General Qasem Suleimani Visiting Troops in
Syria," YouTube, February 9, 2016, https://www.youtube.com/watch
?v=fvP8hDomhhU; Ali Shehab, *Soleimani*, documentary film, 2015;
Bozorgmehr Sharafedin, "General Qasem Soleimani: Iran's Rising Star,"
BBC News, March 6, 2015, http://www.bbc.com/news/world-middle-east
-27883162; Ali Mamouri, "The Enigma of Qasem Soleimani and His Role
in Iraq," trans. Anthony Goode, *Al-Monitor*, October 13, 2013, http://
www.al-monitor.com/pulse/hi/originals/2013/10/the-enigma-behind
-qassem-suleimani.html; The Soufan Group, "TSG IntelBrief: Iran's Forces
in Syria," November 24, 2015, http://soufangroup.com/tsg-intelbrief
-irans-forces-in-syria/; The Soufan Group, "TSG IntelBrief: Iran's Role in a
Syrian Endgame," October 2, 2015, http://soufangroup.com/tsg-intelbrief
-irans-role-in-a-syrian-endgame/.
205 "Now the Arabs have found their voice": Al Jazeera, "Zawahiri Vows
to Continue al-Qaeda's Jihad," June 8, 2011, http://www.aljazeera.com
/news/asia/2011/06/201168125353986730.html.
207 "Freedom is not achieved . . . No other way.": "Message for general
Islamic nation," BLB.
210 "[m]y brother and friend": Joscelyn, "Syrian Rebel Leader."

211 "Homs 2011 = Hama 1982, but slowly, slowly": Amos, "30 Years Later."

211 bin Laden's chief courier in Europe: Associated Press, "Spanish Judge Indicts Osama bin Laden, 34 Others for Terrorism," *USA Today*, September 17, 2003, http://usatoday30.usatoday.com/news/world/2003-09-17 -spain-alqaeda_x.htm.

213 "an international emergency law": Kleib, *Al-Assad.*

214 "an overhaul of the Arab and Islamic world": *Newsweek*, "Periscope: Beyond Baghdad," August 18, 2002, http://www.newsweek.com/periscope -144087.

215 "We are the only leaders in the region": Kleib, *Al-Assad.*

217 "There is neither a secret nor a public link . . . al-Qaeda": Lund, "Abu Khalid al-Suri Part 1."

217 "He was to me": Sham, trans., "Eulogy of al-Suri."

220 "an impulsive policy of intervention": Cockburn, "Prince Mohammed bin Salman: Naïve, Arrogant Saudi Prince."

220 "Democracy is like a tram": Steven A. Cook, "Keep Calm, Erdogan," *Foreign Affairs*, June 3, 2013, https://www.foreignaffairs.com/articles /turkey/2013-06-03/keep-calm-erdogan.

221 one in three Turks believed the outlandish theory: Mehul Srivastava and Laura Pitel, "Turkey Conspiracy Theories Proliferate as Fog of War Recedes," *Financial Times*, July 19, 2016, http://www.ft.com/cms /s/0/044f7ed8-4dbb-11e6-88c5-db83e98a590a.html.

221 "The mosques are our barracks": BBC News, "Turkey's Ruthless President."

222 "tyranny . . . state terrorism": Soner Cagaptay and Marc J. Sievers, "Turkey and Egypt's Great Game in the Middle East," Washington Institute for Near East Policy, March 8, 2015, http://www.washingtoninstitute.org /policy-analysis/view/turkey-and-egypts-great-game-in-the-middle-east.

224 from zero problems to zero friends: Piotr Zalewski, "How Turkey Went from Zero Problems to Zero Friends," *Foreign Policy*, August 22, 2013, http://foreignpolicy.com/2013/08/22/how-turkey-went-from-zero-problems-to-zero-friends/.

224 "stanch the bloodshed": Ayla Jean Yackley and Bozorgmehr Sharafedin, "Rivals Turkey and Iran Seek to 'Manage Differences'," Reuters, March 5, 2016, http://www.reuters.com/article/us-iran-turkey-visit-idUSKCN 0W70DB.

224 "It is above all . . . shaking our region": Mert Ozkan, "Turkey Urges Cooperation with Iran to Fight Terrorism, Sectarian Strife," Reuters, April 16, 2016, http://uk.reuters.com/article/uk-turkey-iran-erdogan-idUKKCN 0XD0M4.

225 reportedly even stooped to helping Iran evade international sanctions: Con

Coughlin, "Turkey and China 'Helping Iran Evade UN Sanctions," *Telegraph*, February 19, 2012, http://www.telegraph.co.uk/news/worldnews /middleeast/iran/9091736/Turkey-and-China-helping-Iran-evade-UN -sanctions.html; Jamie Dettmer, "Turkey and Iran Accused of Oil -For-Cash Sanctions Scheme," *Daily Beast*, December 28, 2013, http:// www.thedailybeast.com/articles/2013/12/28/turkey-and-iran-accused -of-oil-for-cash-sanctions-scheme.html.

226 "dialogue, then neighborliness": Aron Lund, "Islamist Mergers in Syria: Ahrar al-Sham Swallows Suqour al-Sham," Carnegie Endowment for International Peace, March 23, 2015, http://carnegieendowment.org/syria incrisis/?fa=59471.

226 "When the war ends . . . the martryrs won": Ali Shehab, *Soleimani*.

228 "General Petraeus . . . go pound sand down a rat hole": Dan Lamothe, "Animosity between David Petraeus and Iranian Commander, Qasem Soleimani, Still on Display," *Washington Post*, March 20, 2015, https:// www.washingtonpost.com/news/checkpoint/wp/2015/03/20/animosity -between-david-petraeus-and-iranian-commander-qassem-soleimani -still-on-display/.

CHAPTER 7: THOSE WHO LOOSE AND BIND

General: McCants, *ISIS Apocalypse*, chaps. 4–6; Al Mayadeen, *In Search of Baghdadi*, television documentary, trans. Ali H. Soufan; Clarion Project, "The Islamic State's (ISIS, ISIL) Magazine," http://www.clarionproject .org/news/islamic-state-isis-isil-propaganda-magazine-dabiq, hereinafter *Dabiq*; Chulov, "Inside Story"; Barrett, *The Islamic State*; Price et al., "Group That Calls Itself A State"; Bunzel, "From Paper State to Caliphate"; *Frontline*, "The Rise of ISIS," television documentary, October 28, 2014, http://www.pbs.org/wgbh/frontline/film/rise-of-isis/.

Al-Qaeda in the Arabian Peninsula: Yara Bayoumy, Noah Browning, and Mohammed Ghobari, "How Saudi Arabia's War in Yemen Has Made al Qaeda Stronger—and Richer," Reuters, April 8, 2016, http://www .reuters.com/investigates/special-report/yemen-aqap/; TSG, "AQAP Parts 1 and 2"; McCants, *ISIS Apocalypse*, chap. 3; The Soufan Group, "TSG IntelBrief: Capitalizing on Chaos in Yemen," February 19, 2016, http:// soufangroup.com/tsg-intelbrief-capitalizing-on-chaos-in-yemen/; Alessandria Masi, "Al Qaeda Winning Hearts and Minds over ISIS in Yemen with Social Services," *International Business Times*, April 7, 2016, http://www .ibtimes.com/al-qaeda-winning-hearts-minds-over-isis-yemen-social -services-2346835; The Soufan Group, "TSG IntelBrief: The Quadrupling of Al-Qaeda in Yemen," June 6, 2016, http://soufangroup.com/tsg-intelbrief -the-quadrupling-of-al-qaeda-in-yemen/.

Al-Qaeda in the Islamic Maghreb: Associated Press, trans., "Mali: Al-Qaeda's Sahara Playbook," n.d., http://hosted.ap.org/specials/interactives/_inter national/_pdfs/al-qaida-manifesto.pdf; Callimachi, "Yemen Terror Boss."

Al-Shabaab: Jeffrey Gettleman, "Despite Several Blows to Shabab, Worries Persist about Their Resilience," *New York Times*, April 5, 2016, http:// www.nytimes.com/2016/04/06/world/africa/shabab-somalia-african -union.html.

Camp Bucca: The Soufan Group, "TSG IntelBrief: From Bucca to Kobani: The Hybrid Ideology of the Islamic State," October 24, 2014, http:// soufangroup.com/tsg-intelbrief-from-bucca-to-kobani-the-hybrid -ideology-of-the-islamic-state/; *Frontline*, "Who Runs the Islamic State?" October 28, 2014, http://www.pbs.org/wgbh/frontline/article/who-runs -the-islamic-state/.

Abu Ali al-Anbari: Jack Moore, "ISIS Replace Injured Leader Baghdadi with Former Physics Teacher," *Newsweek*, April 22, 2015, http://www .newsweek.com/isis-replace-injured-leader-baghdadi-former-physics -teacher-324082; Michael Weiss and Hassan Hassan, "Everything We Knew about this ISIS Mastermind Was Wrong," *Daily Beast*, April 15, 2016, http://www.thedailybeast.com/articles/2016/04/15/everything-we -knew-about-this-isis-mastermind-was-wrong.html; Kyle Orton, "Obituary: Abd al-Rahman Mustafa al-Qaduli (Abu Alaa al-Afri)," *The Syrian Inti- fada*, March 25, 2016, https://kyleorton1991.wordpress.com/2016/03/25/ obituary-abd-ar-rahman-mustafa-al-qaduli-abu-ala-al-afri/; U.S. Dep- artment of the Treasury, "Treasury Designates al-Qaida Leaders in Syria," May 14, 2014, https://www.treasury.gov/press-center/press-releases/Pages/ jl2396.aspx; U.S. Department of State, "Rewards for Justice: Reward Offers for Information on Islamic State of Iraq and the Levant (ISIL) Ter- rorists," May 5, 2015, http://www.state.gov/r/pa/prs/ps/2015/05/241912 .htm; W.J. Hennigan and Brian Bennett, "Raid That Killed an Islamic State Leader Marks a Shift in U.S. Strategy," *Los Angeles Times*, March 25, 2016, http://www.latimes.com/world/middleeast/la-fg-isis-leader -raid-syria-20160325-story.html; Radwan Mortada, "Abu Ali al-Anbari Died As He Lived: The Most Powerful Man in the Islamic State," Ali Soufan, trans., *Al Akhbar*, May 5, 2016, http://www.al-akhbar.com/ node/257334.

Haji Bakr: Christoph Reuter, "The Terror Strategist: Secret Files Reveal the Structure of Islamic State," *Der Spiegel*, April 18, 2015, http://www .spiegel.de/international/world/islamic-state-files-show-structure-of

-islamist-terror-group-a-1029274.html; Radwan Mortada, "Al-Qaeda Leaks: Baghdadi and Golani Fight Over the Levant Emirate," *Al Akhbar*, January 10, 2014, http://english.al-akhbar.com/node/18186.

Abu Bakr al-Baghdadi: Aaron Y. Zelin, "Abu Bakr al-Baghdadi: Islamic State's Driving Force," BBC News, July 31, 2014, http://www.bbc.com/news /world-middle-east-28560449; Abu Ahmed, "The Hidden Truth"; Hunter Walker, "Here Is the Army's Declassified Iraq Prison File on the Leader of ISIS," *Business Insider*, February 18, 2015, http://www.businessinsider.com /abu-bakr-al-baghdadi-declassified-iraq-prison-file-2015-2; Tim Arango and Eric Schmitt, "U.S. Actions in Iraq Fueled Rise of a Rebel," *New York Times*, August 10, 2014, http://www.nytimes.com/2014/08/11/world/middle east/us-actions-in-iraq-fueled-rise-of-a-rebel.html.

Islamic State Recruitment: The Soufan Group, "TSG IntelBrief: The Offline Allure of the Islamic State," February 8, 2016, http://soufangroup.com /tsg-intelbrief-the-offline-allure-of-the-islamic-state/; TSG, "Foreign Fighters Update"; Patricia Zengerle and Mark Hosenball, "U.S. Spy Chiefs Say Number of Foreign Militants in Syria Rises," Reuters, January 29, 2014, http://www.reuters.com/article/us-usa-security-syria-idUSBREA0S1 XL20140129; The Soufan Group, "TSG IntelBrief: Strangling the Islamic State of Foreign Fighters," August 3, 2015, http://soufangroup.com/tsg -intelbrief-strangling-the-islamic-state-of-foreign-fighters/.

Dispute with al-Nusra and Creation of ISIL: Thomas Joscelyn, "Al Nus-rah Front Leader Renews Allegiance to al Qaeda, Rejects New Name," *Long War Journal*, April 10, 2013, http://www.longwarjournal.org/ archives/2013/04/al_nusrah_front_lead.php; Abu Bakr al-Baghdadi, "Give Good News to the Believers," audio message, April 9, 2013, https:// azelin.files.wordpress.com/2013/04/shaykh-abc5ab-bakr-al-e1b8a5 ussaync4ab-al-qurayshc4ab-al-baghdc481dc4ab-e2809cannouncement -of-the-islamic-state-of-iraq-and-al-shc481m22-en.pdf; Thomas Joscelyn, "Analysis: Zawahiri's Letter to al Qaeda Branches in Syria, Iraq," *Long War Journal*, June 10, 2013, http://www.longwarjournal.org/archives /2013/06/analysis_alleged_let.php; Mortada, "Al-Qaeda Leaks"; Bill Roggio and Linsa Lundquist, "Islamic Front Endorses Jihad, Says, 'The Muhajireen Are Our Brothers," *Long War Journal*, November 28, 2013, http://www.longwarjournal.org/archives/2013/11/islamic_front_endors. php; Karen DeYoung, "Al-Qaeda Leader Zawahiri Seeks to End Infight-ing Among Syrian Militants," *Washington Post*, January 23, 2014, https://www.washingtonpost.com/world/national-security/al-qaeda -leader-zawahiri-seeks-to-end-infighting-among-syrian-radicals/2014 /01/23/05c80874-8451-11e3-8099-9181471f7aaf_story.html.

Abdullah al-Muhaysini: Thomas Joscelyn, "Popular Saudi Cleric Endorses Islamic Front, Calls for Cooperation with al Qaeda," *Long War Journal*, December 14, 2013, http://www.longwarjournal.org/archives/2013/12/popular_saudi_sheikh.php; Thomas Joscelyn, "Saudi Cleric's Reconciliation Initiative for Jihadists Draws Wide Support, then a Rejection," *Long War Journal*, January 27, 2014, http://www.longwarjournal.org/archives/2014/01/saudi_clerics_reconc.php; Abdullah Suleiman Ali, "Abdullah al-Muhaysini: From Pledging Allegiance to al-Saud to Leading Jihad in Syria," trans. Ali H. Soufan, *As-Safir*, November 13, 2015, http://assafir.com/Article/1/456416; Waleed Rikab, "Abdallah al-Muhaysini, a Pivotal Figure in the Islamist Insurgency in Syria," *Syria Comment*, October 7, 2015, http://www.joshualandis.com/blog/abdallah-al-muhaysini-a-pivotal-figure-in-the-islamist-insurgency-in-syria-by-%EF%BB%BFwaleed-rikab/.

Al-Qaeda's Break with ISIL: Thomas Joscelyn, "Al Qaeda's General Command Disowns the Islamic State of Iraq and the Sham," *Long War Journal*, February 3, 2014, http://www.longwarjournal.org/archives/2014/02/al_qaedas_general_co.php; Liz Sly, "Al-Qaeda Disavows Any Ties with Radical Islamist ISIS Group in Syria, Iraq," *Washington Post*, February 3, 2014, https://www.washingtonpost.com/world/middle_east/al-qaeda-disavows-any-ties-with-radical-islamist-isis-group-in-syria-iraq/2014/02/03/2c9afc3a-8cef-11e3-98ab-fe5228217bd1_story.html; Thomas Joscelyn, "Zawahiri Eulogizes al Qaeda's Slain Syrian Representative," *Long War Journal*, April 4, 2014, http://www.longwarjournal.org/archives/2014/04/zawahiri_eulogizes_a.php; Sham, trans., "Eulogy of Abu Khalid al-Suri"; The Soufan Group, "TSG IntelBrief: Al-Qaeda-ISIS Split: Tactics over Strategy," February 6, 2014, http://soufangroup.com/tsg-intelbrief-al-qaeda-isis-split-tactics-over-strategy/.

Turki Binali: Cole Bunzel, "The Caliphate's Scholar-in-Arms," *Jihadica*, July 9, 2014, http://www.jihadica.com/the-caliphate%E2%80%99s-scholar-in-arms/; Associated Press, "The Millennial ISIS Preacher Radicalizing the Next Generation of Jihadis," *New York Post*, January 28, 2015, http://nypost.com/2015/01/28/meet-isiss-30-year-old-preacher-of-bloody-rampages/.

Establishment of the "Caliphate": Al Arabiya, "ISIS Abu Bakr al-Baghdadi First Friday Sermon As So-Called 'Caliph'," July 5, 2014, http://english.alarabiya.net/en/webtv/reports/2014/07/07/ISIS-Abu-Bakr-al-Baghdidi-first-Friday-sermon-as-so-called-Caliph-.html; Alissa J. Rubin, "Militant Leader in Rare Appearance in Iraq," *New York Times*, July 5, 2014, http://www.nytimes.com/2014/07/06/world/asia/iraq-abu-bakr-al-baghdadi-sermon-video.html.

Islamic State's Governing Methods: Suhaib Anjarini, "The Islamic State: From Baghdadi the Founder to Baghdadi the 'Caliph'," *Al Akhbar,* July 10, 2014, http://english.al-akhbar.com/node/20599; BBC News, "Inside Mosul: What's Life Like under Islamic State?" June 9, 2015, http://www.bbc.com/news/world-middle-east-32831854; Sarah Birke, "How ISIS Rules," *New York Review of Books,* February 5, 2015, http://www.nybooks.com/articles/2015/02/05/how-isis-rules/; Mike Thomson, "Inside 'Islamic State': A Raqqa Diary," BBC News, March 5, 2016, http://www.bbc.com/news/magazine-35728424; Rori Donaghy and Mary Atkinson, "Crime and Punishment: Islamic State vs. Saudi Arabia," *Middle East Eye,* January 20, 2015, http://www.middleeasteye.net/news/crime-and-punishment-islamic-state-vs-saudi-arabia-1588245666; United Nations High Commissioner for Human Rights (UNHCR), "UN Commission of Inquiry: Syrian Victims Reveal ISIS's Calculated Use of Brutality and Indoctrination," November 14, 2014, http://www.ohchr.org/EN/NewsEvents/Pages/DisplayNews.aspx; Mustafa Salim, "Radmadi Residents Describe Their Nightmare Escape from Islamic State," *Washington Post,* December 31, 2015, https://www.washingtonpost.com/world/middle_east/ramadi-residents-describe-their-nightmare-escape-from-islamic-state/2015/12/31/c0671ec8-ae6a-11e5-b281-43c0b56f61fa_story.html.

Islamic State's "Provinces": The Soufan Group, "TSG IntelBrief: What's Next for the Islamic State?" March 31, 2016, http://soufangroup.com/tsg-intelbrief-whats-next-for-the-islamic-state/; Daniel L. Byman, "ISIS Goes Global: Fight the Islamic State by Targeting Its Affiliates," Brookings Institution, http://www.brookings.edu/blogs/markaz/posts/2016/02/17-islamic-state-affiliates-byman; The Soufan Group, "Libya, Extremism, and the Consequences of Collapse," January 27, 2016, http://soufangroup.com/libya-extremism-and-the-consequences-of-collapse/; Paul Cruikshank et al., "ISIS Comes to Libya," CNN, November 18, 2014, http://www.cnn.com/2014/11/18/world/isis-libya/; The Soufan Group, "TSG IntelBrief: The Islamic State's Savagery in Yemen," March 10, 2016, http://soufangroup.com/tsg-intelbrief-the-islamic-states-savagery-in-yemen/; TSG, "Capitalizing on Chaos"; The Soufan Group, "TSG IntelBrief, The Islamic State's Prospects in Pakistan," April 4, 2016, http://soufangroup.com/tsg-intelbrief-the-islamic-states-prospects-in-pakistan/; Bill Roggio and Caleb Weiss, "Islamic State Joins Others in Training Children for Jihad in Afghanistan," *Long War Journal,* January 28, 2016, http://www.longwarjournal.org/archives/2016/01/islamic-state-joins-others-in-training-children-for-jihad-in-afghanistan.php; The Soufan Group, "TSG IntelBrief: The Islamic State's Horrors in Afghanistan,"

November 12, 2015, http://soufangroup.com/tsg-intelbrief-the-islamic
-states-horrors-in-afghanistan/; Bill Roggio, "Taliban, Islamic State Clash
in Eastern Afghanistan," *Long War Journal*, February 13, 2016, http://
www.longwarjournal.org/archives/2016/02/taliban-islamic-state-clash-
in-eastern-afghanistan.php; BBC News, "Islamic State 'Accepts' Boko
Haram's Allegiance Pledge," March 13, 2015, http://www.bbc.com/news
/world-africa-31862992; The Soufan Group, "TSG IntelBrief: The Islamic
State Eyes Southeast Asia," April 27, 2016, http://soufangroup.com
/tsg-intelbrief-the-islamic-state-eyes-southeast-asia/; The Soufan Group,
"TSG IntelBrief: The Philippines Battles Abu Sayyaf," April 13, 2016,
http://soufangroup.com/tsg-intelbrief-the-philippines-battle-abu-sayyaf/.

233 "Thanks to God . . . We've broken Sykes-Picot!": VICE News, "Bull-
dozing the Border Between Iraq and Syria: The Islamic State," YouTube,
August 13, 2014, https://www.youtube.com/watch?v=TxX_ThjtXOw.

234 "blessed march will not stop": *Dabiq* 5, 33.

234 fighters display their foreign passports: McCants, *ISIS Apocalypse*, chap.
6, loc. 2264; *Dabiq* 10, 38.

234 "We will live in one Islamic State": McCants, *ISIS Apocalypse*, chap. 6,
loc. 2264.

236 "I prefer that al-Qaeda stay here": Bayoumy et al., "Saudi Arabia's War in
Yemen."

236 "extreme speed . . . It is too early for that": AP, trans., "Al-Qaeda's Sahara
Playbook."

239 "martyrdom": Chulov, "Inside Story"; Bill Roggio, "U.S. and Iraqi
Forces Kill al Masri and Baghdadi, al Qaeda in Iraq's Top Two Leaders," *Long War Journal*, April 19, 2010, http://www.longwarjournal.org
/archives/2010/04/al_qaeda_in_iraqs_to.php.

239 "If there was no American prison in Iraq": Chulov, "Inside Story."

239 "Camp Bucca was a new service": Al Mayadeen, *In Search of Baghdadi.*

240 in 2003 the Iraqi armed services were still 400,000 strong: Sharon Otter-
man, "Iraq's Prewar Military Capabilities," Council on Foreign Relations, April 24, 2003, http://www.cfr.org/iraq/iraq-iraqs-prewar-military
-capabilities/p7695.

242 "Anbari was everything and everybody": Mortada, "Abu Ali al-Anbari
Died As He Lived," http://www.al-akhbar.com/node/257334.

245 "Administrative Work (Secretary)": Walker, "Declassified Iraq Prison
File."

245 "street thug": Arango and Schmitt, "Rise of a Rebel."

245 "I got a feeling from him": Chulov, "Inside Story."

246 "There wasn't a void": ibid.

246 "the Baath state with beards . . . How can they lead us?": Abu Ahmed, "The Hidden Truth."

247 "A Caliphate in accordance with Baathist method": McCants, *ISIS Apocalypse*, chap. 6, loc. 2210.

249 "terminate . . . before we terminate you": Price et al., "Group That Calls Itself A State," 22–23.

253 "beloved father . . . beloved son": Mortada, "Abu Ali al-Anbari Died As He Lived."

254 "[W]e assigned al-Julani who is one of our soldiers": Baghdadi, "Give Good News."

254 his own audio message: Thomas Joscelyn, "Al Nusrah Front Leader Renews Allegiance to al Qaeda, Rejects New Name," *Long War Journal*, April 10, 2013, http://www.longwarjournal.org/archives/2013/04/al _nusrah_front_lead.php.

255 "a large margin to decide on our own": Thomas Joscelyn, "Al Qaeda Head Addresses Infighting in Syria," *Long War Journal*, January 23, 2014, http://www.longwarjournal.org/archives/2014/01/al_qaeda_head _addres.php.

256 "enough room in this arena of jihad for all of us": Joscelyn, "Popular Saudi Cleric."

257 a tract implying that the formerly revered Maqdisi had gone senile: Bunzel, "The Caliphate's Scholar-in-Arms."

257 "Either we exterminate [al-Nusra] or they exterminate us": Mortada, "Abu Ali al-Anbari Died As He Lived."

258 "not an affiliate . . . not responsible for their actions": Thomas Joscelyn, "Al Qaeda's General Command Disowns the Islamic State of Iraq and the Sham," *Long War Journal*, February 3, 2014, http://www.long warjournal.org/archives/2014/02/al_qaedas_general_co.php; Liz Sly, "Al-Qaeda Disavows Any Ties with Radical Islamist ISIS Group in Syria, Iraq," *Washington Post*, February 3, 2014, https://www.washingtonpost .com/world/middle_east/al-qaeda-disavows-any-ties-with-radical-islamist -isis-group-in-syria-iraq/2014/02/03/2c9afc3a-8cef-11e3-98ab-fe5228217 bd1_story.html.

258 "scores of thousands": Humud et al., "Al Qaeda-Affiliated Groups: Middle East and Africa."

258 "God prefers to see the destruction of the whole universe . . . moral death": Sham, trans., "Eulogy of al-Suri."

259 "to fight our enemy as we want, not as they want": Joscelyn, "AQAP Says It Withdrew from Mukalla to Protect Residents."

260 "al-Qaeda and its branches . . . This is the supreme *bayat*": Bunzel, "From Paper State to Caliphate," 32–34.

261 "the Islamic State's most prominent . . . throne of the caliphate": Bunzel, "The Caliphate's Scholar-in-Arms."

262 "#We_Demand_Sheikh_Al-Baghdadi_Declare_The_Caliphate": Aaron Y. Zelin, "ISIS Is Dead, Long Live the Islamic State," Washington Institute for Near East Policy, June 30, 2014, http://www.washingtoninstitute .org/policy-analysis/view/isis-is-dead-long-live-the-islamic-state.

262 "power, authority, and control of [some amount of] territory": McCants, *ISIS Apocalypse*, chap. 5, loc. 2040.

262 "a hope that flutters . . . arrival of its troops to their areas": Zelin, "ISIS is Dead."

263 "I have been appointed your governor": Al Arabiya, "ISIS Abu Bakr al-Baghdadi First Friday Sermon."

265 "those who loose and bind": Reuter, "Terror Strategist."

268 "as we preferred that he had no education at all": BBC News, "Inside Mosul."

268 "intrinsic value": *Dabiq* 5, 18.

269 "bloodlust . . . psychosis": *Frontline*, "Rise of ISIS."

270 "O Muslims, rejoice": Bunzel, "From Paper State to Caliphate," 42; *Dabiq* 5, 22–33.

274 "If you can kill . . . or poison him": Yara Bayoumi, "ISIS Urges More Attacks on Western 'Disbelievers,' " September 22, 2014, http://www .independent.co.uk/news/world/middle-east/isis-urges-more-attacks -on-western-disbelievers-9749512.html.

CHAPTER 8: STEADFAST SONS

Captivity in Iran: Farrall, "Interview with a Taliban Insider"; Ghaith interview; "Letter dtd 13 Oct 2010," BLB; Robert Windrem, "Al-Qaida Finds Safe Haven in Iran," NBC News, June 24, 2005, http://www.nbcnews .com/id/8330976/#.VmNxqeOfoXA; Tenet, *At the Center of the Storm*; "Letter from Hamzah to father dtd July 2009," BLB.

Hamza's Release: "Letter from Hamzah to father dtd July 2009," BLB; "Letter to Um Abid al-Rahman," BLB; "Letter dtd 5 April 2011," BLB.

Saif's Release: Thomas Joscelyn, "Senior al Qaeda Leaders Reportedly Released from Custody in Iran," *Long War Journal*, September 18, 2015, http:// www.longwarjournal.org/archives/2015/09/senior-al-qaeda-leaders -reportedly-released-from-iran.php; Thomas Joscelyn, "Al Qaeda Insider

Returns to Twitter, Discusses Group's Global Leadership," Foundation for Defense of Democracies, March 16, 2016, http://www.defenddemocracy .org/media-hit/thomas-joscelyn-al-qaeda-insider-returns-to-twitter-discusses -groups-global-leadership/; Yassin Musharbash, "Saif al-Adel Back in Waziristan: A Top Terrorist Returns to al-Qaida Fold," *Der Spiegel*, October 25, 2010, http://www.spiegel.de/international/world/saif-al-adel-back -in-waziristan-a-top-terrorist-returns-to-al-qaida-fold-a-725181.html; J.J. Green, "Mysterious al-Qaida Figure Emerges in Syria," WTOP, November 5, 2015, http://wtop.com/national-security/2015/11/mysterious-al-qaida -figure-emerges-in-syria/.

The Taliban: Thomas Joscelyn, "New AQAP Leader Renews Allegiance to the 'Beloved Father,' Ayman al Zawahiri," *Long War Journal*, July 9, 2015, http://www.longwarjournal.org/archives/2015/07/new-aqap-leader -renews-allegiance-to-the-beloved-father-ayman-al-zawahiri.php; Bill Roggio and Thomas Joscelyn, "New Taliban Emir Accepts al Qaeda's Oath of Allegiance," *Long War Journal*, August 14, 2014, http:// www.longwarjournal.org/archives/2015/08/new-taliban-emir-accepts- al-qaedas-oath-of-allegiance.php; Sarah Almukhtar and Karen Yourish, "More Than 14 Years After U.S. Invasion, the Taliban Control Large Parts of Afghanistan," *New York Times*, April 19, 2016, http://www.nytimes.com /interactive/2015/09/29/world/asia/afghanistan-taliban-maps.html.

Al-Qaeda in the Indian Subcontinent: Ellen Barry, "Al Qaeda Opens New Branch on Indian Subcontinent," *New York Times*, September 4, 2014, http://www.nytimes.com/2014/09/05/world/asia/al-qaeda-announces- new-branch-on-indian-subcontinent.html.

275   once home to hundreds of olive plantations: Hijratullah Ekhtyar, "Afghan Olive Farms Waiting for Water," Institute for War and Peace Reporting, January 25, 2012, https://iwpr.net/global-voices/afghan-olive-farms-waiting -water.

275   "It was as if we pulled out our livers": "Letter from Hamzah to father dtd July 2009," BLB.

276   "How many times . . . every look that you gave me": ibid.

276   "you were conducting Adhan . . . if God permits": "Letter from Abu Abdullah to his mother," trans. Ali H. Soufan, BLB.

278   "Iran remained unwilling": U.S. Department of State, "Country Reports on Terrorism for 2014," April 2015, http://www.state.gov/j/ct/rls/crt /2014/239410.htm, chap. 3. It should be noted, in this connection, that the United States has never publicly identified all the detainees held at Guantánamo Bay. Comprehensive lists of their names are based in part upon leaked documents: see, for example, *New York Times*, "The Guantánamo Docket," n.d., http://projects.nytimes.com/guantanamo/about.

278 "emissary": Thomas Joscelyn, "Treasury Targets Iran's 'Secret Deal' with al Qaeda," *Long War Journal*, July 28, 2011, http://www.longwarjournal .org/archives/2011/07/treasury_targets_ira_1.php.

279 "a huge act of disturbance": "Letter dtd 13 Oct 2010," BLB.

279 "under virtual house arrest": Windrem, "Al-Qaida Finds Safe Haven."

282 "a lion from the den . . . Washington, London, Paris, and Tel Aviv": Thomas Joscelyn, "Analysis: Osama bin Laden's Son Praises al Qaeda's Branches in New Message," *Long War Journal*, August 17, 2015, http://www.longwarjournal.org/archives/2015/08/osama-bin-ladens-son -praises-alqaeda-branches-in-new-message.php; CNN, "Osama bin Laden's Son Urges Attacks on the West," August 14, 2015, http://www.cnn .com/videos/us/2015/08/14/osama-bin-laden-son-hamza-bin-laden-todd -dnt-tsr.cnn/video/playlists/osama-bin-laden/.

283 "sheikhs . . . May God release them all": Joscelyn, "Osama bin Laden's Son Praises al Qaeda's Branches."

284 Abu Mohammed: *U.S. v. Bin Laden*, indictment, counts 16–17, 37–38; *U.S. v. Bin Laden*, trial transcript, day 8, page 1127; day 11, pages 1544–1547.

284 "most experienced and capable": Joscelyn, "Senior al Qaeda Leaders Reportedly Released."

284 "With someone like Saif al-Adel . . . his head is enough": Musharbash, "Saif al-Adel Back in Waziristan."

285 "the eminent sheikh . . . the beloved father": Joscelyn, "New AQAP Leader Renews Allegiance."

285 "rescue": Barry, "Al Qaeda Opens New Branch on Indian Subcontinent."

286 "Jerusalem Is but a Bride . . . blessed Syrian revolution": Thomas Joscelyn, "Osama bin Laden's Son Says Jihad in Syria Key to 'Liberate Palestine,'" *Long War Journal,* May 9, 2016, http://www.longwarjournal .org/archives/2016/05/osama-bin-ladens-son-says-jihad-in-syria-key-to -liberating-palestine.php; VICE News, "Osama bin Laden's Son Hamza Calls for Jihadi Unity in Syria," May 10, 2016, https://news.vice.com /article/osama-bin-ladens-son-hamza-calls-for-jihadi-unity-al-qaeda.

CONCLUSION: SLAYING THE HYDRA

290 "The history, culture and body of beliefs": 9/11 Commission Report, Executive Summary.

294 "The enemy is not just 'terrorism' ": ibid.

296 "Investigations, intelligence and military successes": Soufan, "End of the Jihadist Dream."

INDEX

Abbasids, 113–14, 187, 263
Abbott, James, 6
Abbottabad, 5–44, 47, 208, 276, 281
Abboud, Hassan, 216, 225
Abdullah, King of Saudi Arabia, 35, 219
Abdullah II, King of Jordan, 110, 113,
    119–20, 141
Abdulmutallab, Omar Farouk, 20
Abraham Lincoln, USS, 108
Absi, Abu Atheer al-, 212
Abu Abdul Rahman, 30, 91
Abu Ahmed (nom de guerre), 239, 246
Abu Bakr Naji (pseud.), 27–28, 184–86,
    189, 190, 207–9, 259, 260, 287,
    293
Abu Ghaith, 280
Abu Ghraib prison, 108, 129, 136, 243,
    249, 296–97
Abu Jahl, 25
Abu Jandal ("The Father of Death"), 75,
    77–78, 81, 89, 289–90
Abu Luay, 241
Abu Qasim, 241
Abu Qatada, 116
Abu Sayyaf, 273
Abu Shema, 241
Abu Suja, 241
Abu Zubaydah, 101
Achille Lauro hijacking (1985), 125
Addis Ababa, 174
Addison's disease, 170

Adel, Saif al- (Mohammed Salahuddin
    Zeidan), xvii, 14, 47–108, 121, 123,
    127, 196, 199–200, 211, 277, 278–80,
    281, 283, 284–85, 291
Aden, 79, 235, 272
Adhan (call to prayer), 276
Adnani, Abu Mohammed al-, 127, 159,
    241, 262–63, 269–70, 274, 287
adultery, 221, 266
Afghanistan, 230, 241, 242, 260–61,
    272–73
  government of, 17–18, 97, 98, 230, 241,
    242, 260–61, 272–73
  Soviet invasion of, xiv, xvi, 4, 8, 11, 30,
    32, 39, 49, 50, 53–56, 80, 81, 86, 89,
    103, 116, 120, 149, 166, 169, 171,
    218, 250, 255
  Taliban rule in, xvi, 2, 67–69, 74–78,
    86–100, 106–7, 120–21, 134, 143,
    148, 179, 181, 191, 197 199, 227,
    256, 260–61, 273, 276, 277, 282,
    285, 299–300
  U.S. occupation of, 20, 69–70, 75–76,
    123–24, 125, 148, 179, 192, 227,
    228, 238, 275–76, 286, 291
Africa, xvi, 16, 22, 23, 25, 26, 58, 76,
    195–99, 200, 206–7, 236, 237–38,
    273, 288, 291
African Union, 197, 237–38
ahl al-hall wa al-aqd ("those who loose
    and bind"), 264–65

Ahrar al-Sham (Free Men of the Levant), 216, 217–18, 220, 223, 225–26, 247, 256, 258, 300

Air Force, U.S., 100

airliner hijackings, 72–73, 81, 83–84, 93, 302–3

see also September 11th attacks (2001)

Akhundzada, Hibatullah, 260, 283, 285

AKP (Turkish political party), 221

al-Abdali complex, 153

Alawites, 213, 228, 256, 292, 302

Ali and Uthman (caliphs), 133, 137, 259, 262

Allah, 264

Allawi, Ayad, 143

al-Azhar University, 166

Albania, 163

al-Bunyan al-Marsous (The Solid Edifice), 116

alcohol prohibition, 221, 266

Aleppo, 212, 222, 225, 226, 230, 247, 252, 258

Alexander the Great, xii

al-Falah mosque, 115–16

Algeria, 27, 178, 185, 198–99, 206, 208, 237, 258, 270

Algiers, 198

Al Hayat, 149

Al Jazeera, 19, 24, 28, 37, 106, 149, 152, 180, 205, 207, 255

al-Masoum neighborhood of Zarqa, 114, 115–16

al-Mourabitoun, 237

al-Muqtafi, Caliph, 114

Al-Nuri Mosque, 263

al-Nusra, 121, 154, 183, 217, 219, 220, 223, 225–26, 247, 254–55, 257, 258, 261, 283, 300

al-Qaeda:

affiliates and network of, 16, 79–80, 121–22, 155, 161, 181–83, 191–94, 198, 200–201, 203, 216, 219, 238, 242, 254–59, 270, 271–73, 288, 291, 293

arrests and imprisonments for, 6–7, 9, 12, 14, 17, 26, 29, 31, 54, 64–65, 76, 101, 102–4, 106, 109–10, 124, 128, 138, 142, 145–46, 156–57, 169, 172–80, 191, 193, 238–39, 242–45, 278–81, 296

audio messages of, 129, 130, 143, 144–45, 147, 190, 191, 242, 254, 258, 282–83, 286

bounties offered for, 12–13, 48

cells of, 51, 55, 58, 76, 78–82, 102–3, 126–27, 130–31, 165, 166–68, 174, 175, 176, 178, 179–83, 196, 212, 219, 254

couriers for, 11–12, 17, 91, 147, 203, 211, 243–46

decentralization of, 182–83, 197–98, 200

doctrines of, 27–28, 183–86, 189, 190, 207–9, 225, 231, 242, 249, 259, 260, 268–69, 287, 290–94

External Operations Committee of, 80

factions of, 54, 56, 62, 77–78, 137–38, 196, 215–16, 223, 226, 237, 242–43, 247, 251, 253, 256, 272–73, 281–82, 285

fixers for, 6–7, 35, 122, 176, 181, 211

funding for, 9, 16, 88, 140, 151, 170, 172, 217, 219, 235, 252

leadership of, xiii–xvi, 15–16, 45, 187–90, 199–202, 243–46, 269–70, 276–80, 286, 287, 291–92; *see also specific leaders*

media coverage for, 104, 141–42, 149, 152–53, 158, 181, 216

membership of, xvi, 12, 14–18, 19, 23–24, 29, 33, 45–47, 54, 63, 72, 74, 77, 79–81, 93, 101–4, 107, 118–19, 125–26, 155–56, 175, 182–83, 189, 191–92, 200–202, 211–17, 230, 235, 244–45, 276–80, 287–88, 291

"Planes Operation" of, 85, 89–90, 93, 95, 101, 179, 211; *see also* September 11th attacks (2001)

Political Committee of, 284

propaganda from, xvi, xvii, 18–19, 33, 52, 80, 81–82, 88, 123, 124, 136–39, 142–43, 158–59, 183–85, 189, 194, 230–31, 236, 249–50, 252, 257, 267–69, 283, 296–97

public support for, 104–5, 137–39, 147–48, 152–53, 173–74, 183–85, 190, 195, 198, 217, 234–35, 259, 261, 267–68, 286, 293

recruitment by, 13–15, 93, 121–22, 126, 128, 138–40, 147, 181–82, 191, 201, 214, 230–31, 245, 249–50, 251, 272, 297–303

reintegration program of, 14–15

resurgence of, xvii–xviii, 183, 196, 238–39, 275–77, 282–90, 295–96, 300

safe houses, 8–10, 15, 76–77, 92, 101–3, 105, 147, 157–58

"savagery" as tactic of, 27–28, 184–86, 189, 190, 207–9, 225, 231, 259,

260, 268–69, 287, 293; *see also*
    Management of Savagery: The Most
    Critical Stage Through Which the
    Umma Will Pass, The (Abu Bakr Naji)
  Security Committee of, 80
  territory controlled by, 195, 216–17,
    234–35, 236, 251, 257, 259, 260–61,
    266–73, 286–88, 292
  as "The Base," 3, 183
  training camps of, 20, 55–60, 63, 68,
    72–73, 79, 81, 88, 90–91, 121–22, 128,
    181, 187, 211, 236, 272–73, 277, 284
  U.S. as target of, 19–21, 75, 85–90,
    181–82, 185, 192, 203; *see also*
    specific attacks
  see also specific affiliate organizations
    and members
al-Qaeda al-Askaria (Military Base), 54
al-Qaeda in Iraq, 16, 108, 110, 142–43,
  146–60, 241, 292, 303
al-Qaeda in the Arabian Peninsula
  (AQAP), xv, 16, 23, 44, 65, 183,
  191–201, 202, 203, 234–36, 237,
  249, 255–56, 259–60, 271, 272, 280,
  283, 285, 292, 293
al-Qaeda in the Indian Subcontinent, 285
al-Qaeda in the Islamic Maghreb (AQIM),
  xv, 16, 23, 44, 198–201, 203, 236–
  38, 271, 283, 285
al-Qaedat al-Jihad (Base of Jihad), 79–80
Al Quds Al Arabi, 19
al-Ruseifah refugee camp, 114, 115
al-Sahab (the Cloud), 18
al-Sahwa (awakening), 156
al-Sawwaqa prison, 110
al-Shabaab (Harakat al Shabaab al-
    Mujahidin), xv, 16, 62, 196–98,
    200–201, 203, 237–38, 273, 299
al-Shiba (the Old Men), 81
al-tibb al-nabawi (traditional "prophet"
    medicine), 11–12, 166
al-Wafa al-Igatha al-Islamia, 96–97
"Al-Zarqawi—Aid and Advice" (Maqdisi),
    138
Al-Zarqawi: The Second Generation of Al-
    Qaeda (Hussein), 185–86
American Airlines Flight 11 hijacking
    (2001), 302–3
American Airlines Flight 77 hijacking
    (2001), 193
AMISOM, 197, 203
Amman, 78–79, 114, 119–20, 130–31,
    152–54

Amman bombings (2005), 152–54
amnesties, 115, 119–20, 215–16, 247
Anbari, Abu Ali al-, 241–42, 253–54, 257,
    269, 271–72
Anbar Province, 145, 146–47, 156, 190, 243
Ankara, 221
  assassination of Russian ambassador in
    (2016), 224
Ansar al-Islam, 124, 125–26, 128
Ansar al-Sharia (Partisans of Islamic Law),
    183, 195
Ansar al-Sharia in Libya, 271
Ansar al-Sunna, 156
Ansar Beit al-Maqdis, 271
Antioch, Prince of, 113–14
Apache helicopter gunships, 95, 150
apostates, 1–2, 21–23, 73, 117, 171, 177–
    78, 185–86, 190, 230–31, 276–77, 293
Aqaba, 152
Arabian Peninsula, xv, 3, 70–72, 114, 153,
    177, 199, 201, 217, 293
Arabic language, 69, 263–64, 275
Arab League, 164
Arab Liberation Front, 125
Arab nationalism, 22, 51, 165, 205–7, 208
Arab Spring, xv, 24–28, 33, 36, 44–45,
    181, 186, 195, 199, 205–6, 211, 213,
    234, 236, 286, 291, 293
Arab Thought Foundation, 111–12
Arafat, Yasser, 115
Army of Conquest, 220, 223, 226, 257, 261
Army of the Sunnis, 244
Army Rangers, U.S., 146
Arnett, Peter, 75
asas (foundation of the faith), 3
Ashari theology, 148
Assad, Bashar al-, 25, 45, 126, 127, 151,
    185, 209–10, 212–15, 218, 223,
    224–25, 226, 228, 230, 247, 251,
    256, 267, 277–78, 292
Assad, Bassel al-, 212–13
Assad, Hafez al-, 185, 211, 228–29, 267
assassinations, 2–3, 10, 55, 64, 70, 72, 73,
    74, 86–87, 92–93, 131, 132–33, 156,
    168–69, 170, 173, 174, 182, 192, 200,
    218, 219, 224, 246, 249, 251, 257,
    258–59, 267, 271, 272
Assassins (Persian religious order), 2–3,
    10, 182
Associated Press, 223
Association of Muslim Scholars, 137, 144,
    150–51
Aswan Dam, 51

Athar, Sohaib, 5–6, 7, 246
Athens, xii
Atta, Mohammed, 302–3
Awlaki, Anwar al-, 17, 192–94, 202
"Axis of Evil," 214
Azerbaijan, 175–76
Azzam, Abdullah, 116, 166, 171

B-52 bombers, 99
Baath Party, 124, 126–27, 135, 210, 213,
    214, 240, 241, 242–43, 246–47, 251,
    264, 265–66, 269
Baghdad, 108, 126, 127, 131–36, 156, 209,
    214–15, 220, 244, 253
Baghdad bombings (2009), 127
Baghdadi, Abu Bakr al-, xvii, 154, 159–60,
    187–90, 200, 218, 234, 241, 243–56,
    258, 259, 260–64, 270–71, 281–82
Baghdadi, Abu Omar al-, 155, 200, 218,
    238–39, 243, 244, 245, 247, 285
Bahrain, 25, 208, 262
Balad Airbase, 158
Bali nightclub bombing (2002), 6–7, 46
Balkan conflict, 66
Baluchistan, 35, 101
Bamako hotel attack (2015), 199
Bandar bin Sultan, Prince of Saudi Arabia,
    219
Bangalore, 249
Bangladesh, 285
Bani Hassan tribe, 114
Baqral-Hakim, Ayatollah Mohammed,
    133, 240
bayat (oath of allegiance), xiv, 45–47,
    71–72, 77–79, 96, 121, 122–23, 127,
    134, 140, 142–43, 159, 183, 188, 189,
    196, 199–200, 241, 251, 254, 256,
    260, 270, 273–74, 282, 285
Bayat Al-Imam (Allegiance to the Imam),
    109, 117–18
BBC, 24
Bedouin tribes, 114
Begin, Menachem, 167
beheadings, 104, 108, 110, 113–14, 135,
    136–37, 144, 148, 150, 190, 195,
    242–43, 266, 271, 273
Beirut, 2, 87–88
Beirut barracks bombing (1983), 87–88
Bekaa Valley, 57
Belfast, 301–2
Belgium, 59–60, 92, 112, 250
Belmokhtar, Mokhtar, 198, 203, 237
Ben Ali, Zine el-Abidine, 24–25, 206

Benedict XVI, Pope, 302
Ben Gardane, 134–35, 272
Benghazi, 271, 272
Benghazi attack (2012), 271
Benotman, Noman, 284
Berg, Nick, 136
Berlin Christmas market attack (2016),
    xvi, 274
Beyoncé, 24
Bible, 82, 265
Bilawi, Abu Abdul Rahman al-, 241, 269
Bilis Qooqaani, 60
Binali, Turki, 261–62, 267
bin Laden, Hamza, 14, 31–35, 44,
    275–76, 277, 279, 280–83, 286, 287,
    288, 292
bin Laden, Hussein, 41
bin Laden, Iman, 280
bin Laden, Khairia, 33
bin Laden, Khalid, 9–10, 29–31, 37, 39,
    40, 44, 91
bin Laden, Maryam and Sumayia, 38, 39
bin Laden, Mohammed, 276
bin Laden, Omar, 66, 67, 314*n*
bin Laden, Osama:
    Abbottabad raid against, 5–7 12–13,
        35–44, 47, 208, 276, 281
    Abbottabad residence of, 5–44, 47, 208,
        276, 281
    in Afghanistan, 8, 10, 39, 64, 67–69,
        76–77, 87, 89, 106, 192, 275–76, 291,
        314*n*
    assassination attempts against, 64, 70,
        73, 74, 87, 92
    bayat to Mullah Omar given by, 46–47,
        77–78, 188, 189, 256, 260, 282
    bodyguards of, 8, 47, 64, 73, 75, 76,
        77–78, 81, 92, 169–70, 202, 289–90
    burial of, 43–44
    death of, 37–41, 43–44, 194, 199, 202,
        205, 229, 281, 293, 296
    dreams of, 35–36
    family of, 9–10, 11, 17, 36, 69; *see also*
        specific family members
    "Geronimo" as designation for, 39,
        40–41
    in Haripur, 9, 10
    health of, 11–12, 37, 80, 166, 170
    intelligence on, 5–7, 12–13, 35–44, 64,
        94
    in Jalalabad, 54–55, 56, 67–68, 73, 92,
        116, 170, 275, 291, 314*n*
    in Kabul, 14, 76–77, 284

in Kandahar, 10–11, 47
leadership of, xiii–xiv, xv, 10–11, 201–2,
231, 241, 269, 282, 314*n*
legacy of (bin Ladenism), xviii, 183, 196,
276, 282–83, 285, 287–90, 295–96, 300
manhunt for, 12–13, 94
media coverage of, 37, 69, 75
Saudi background of, 31, 55, 65–66, 69,
70–71, 191
security measures for, 8–11, 47, 64, 73,
75, 76, 77–78, 81, 92, 169–70, 202,
289–90
in Sudan, 65, 70, 314*n*
in Swat, 8–9, 10, 12
as "The Pacer," 12
in Tora Bora, 8, 10, 64, 67, 68–69, 87,
89, 106, 192, 275–76
U.S. opposed by, 19–21, 75, 85–90,
181–82, 185, 192
bin Laden, Saad, 34, 41, 44
bin Laden, Uthman, 92
bin Rashid al-Baghdadi, Abdullah, 155
black banners, 71, 107–8, 136, 189
Black Banners (Soufan), xvii
Black Guard, 73
Black Hawk helicopters, 39, 44, 54, 60–61,
95, 146, 196, 284
blackmail, 251
Black September (1970), 115
Blackwater Security Consulting, 134
blasphemy, 266
blood feuds, 281–82
BM-12 rocket launcher, 30, 91, 99
Boko Haram, 2, 236, 273, 299
Bolton, John R., 214
Bonn Conference (2001), 99
Bosnian War, 66, 70, 71, 83
Boston Marathon bombings (2013), 193,
194, 283
Bouazizi, Mohamed, 24–25
Bourguiba, Habib, 206, 207
Breaking the Walls, 249
British Empire, 178, 209, 233–34
Brussels, xvi, 92, 94, 112, 212, 250, 270
Brussels bombings (2016), xvi, 92, 212,
250, 270
Bunzel, Cole, 261
Bush, George H. W., 59
Bush, George W., 94, 108, 128, 129, 213–14

C-4 explosive charges, 40
C-130 Hercules transportation aircraft, 95,
98, 100

Caesar, Julius, xii
Cairo, 164–65
Cairo University, 164, 165
Caliphate, 21, 26, 27, 36, 89, 132–33,
137, 142, 159, 185–87, 199, 208,
247, 259–60, 261, 262–65, 267, 268,
287–88, 293, 294
caliphs, xvii, 4, 21, 45, 77, 113–14,
186–87, 241, 242–43, 259, 262–64,
265, 270
Call of the Global Islamic Resistance, The
(al-Suri), 184–85, 186, 210
Camp Adder, 245
Camp Bucca, 119, 212, 239–47
Camp Chapman attack (2009), 199
Camp David Accords (1978), 52
Canterbury Cathedral, 263
Carter, Jimmy, 167
Catholics, 301–2, 303
Cato the Younger, xii
Caucasus Emirate, 199
CBS (U.S. news organization), 19
cellphones, 13, 14, 227, 269
Central Intelligence Agency (CIA), 12, 36,
84–85, 116, 124, 125, 128, 166, 199,
211–12, 214
Charles de Gaulle, 270
Chattanooga shootings (2015), 193
Chechnya, 66, 70, 114–15, 120, 175–76,
199
Cheney, Dick, xviii
children, 11, 17, 29, 242–43, 268
Chinook helicopters, 43
Christians, 2, 22, 52, 190, 209, 251–52,
271, 272, 301–2, 303
Cicero, Marcus Tullius, xii
Clash of Civilizations, The (Huntington),
293
clerics, 21–22, 137, 144, 148–51, 155–56,
164–65, 261–62, 267
Clinton, Bill, 61, 67, 88
Cold War, xi–xii, 3–4, 54, 61, 293
Cole, USS, attack on (2000), xiii, 77, 82,
192
"Commander of the Faithful," 186–87,
260, 264
Communism, 53, 56, 149, 169
Coptic Christians, 52, 271
Corriere della Sera, 110, 113
Countering Violent Extremism program,
301
Creed of Abraham, The (Maqdisi), 117
crucifixions, 266, 271

cruise missiles, 34, 69, 76, 87, 88, 95, 96–97
Crusades, 2, 113–14, 129, 153, 178, 201
Culture of the Silencers, 156

Dabiq, 159, 234, 249, 267, 268
"daisy cutter" bombs, 100
Damascus, 126, 127, 177, 214, 220, 229
Damascus International Airport, 126, 229
Daraa, 25
Dayton Accords (1995), 66
Defense Department, U.S., 245
Delian League, xii
Delta Force, 26, 146, 158
democracy, 3–4, 144–45, 205–6, 207, 208, 220–21, 242
Democracy Is a Religion (Maqdisi), 145
Derna, 250
Dhuluiya, 151
dictatorships, 25, 206–7, 212–13, 220–25, 267
"dirty bombs," 74
Djibouti, 197
Doctor Zhivago (Pasternak), 48–49
drones, 13, 14, 15, 146, 193, 202, 203, 235, 237–38, 285, 295
Droukdal, Abdelmalek, 198, 236–37
Druze, 209, 302
Dudayev, Dzhokhar, 66

East Africa embassy bombings (Nairobi and dar es Salaam) (1998), 14, 26, 48, 55, 58, 69, 76, 78, 85, 88, 92, 94, 116, 163, 196, 284
Echo of Battles, 194
economic sanctions, 224–25
education, 111–13, 251, 267, 268, 297–303
Education Department, U.S., 301
Egypt, xv, xvi, 25, 27, 45, 48–53, 64, 84, 113, 119, 139, 141, 164–76, 201, 202, 206, 208, 242, 270, 281, 294
EgyptAir Flight 990 disaster (1999), 90
Egyptian Army, 165–66
Egyptian embassy bombing (Islamabad) (1995), 174
Egyptian Islamic Jihad (EIJ), 45, 51, 52, 58, 79–80, 105–6, 165–76, 187, 200, 284
Eid al-Fitr, 81
Eisenhower, Dwight D., 206
elections, U.S.:
of 2000, 82, 88
of 2008, 215
of 2016, 301

"Elephant" (tank), 91, 99
Emir of the Strangers, 155
emirs, 216, 243, 246, 260
Emwazi, Mohammed ("Jihadi John"), 212
End of Days, 185–86, 189, 296–97
"End of History, The?" (Fukuyama), 3–4
English language, 168, 193
Erdogan, Recep Tayyip, 220–25
Essawi, Rafi Al-, 248
Ethiopia, 196
Europe, xii, xvii, 132, 197, 224, 295
European Union (EU), xvii, 224
"Executive Presidency" (Turkish political concept), 221
"Extend Your Hands to Give Bayat to Baghdadi" (Binali), 262
extortion, 190, 252

F-15 fighters, 65–66
F-16 fighters, 157–58, 222
Fahd, King of Saudi Arabia, 71
Fahdawi, Khalid Sulaiman al-, 156
Faisalabad, 101
Fallujah, 108, 127, 134, 135, 136–40, 144, 146, 150, 152, 156, 244, 272
Farjul Islam Mosque, 51–52
Faruq training camp, 55, 91, 97, 211
Fatimid al-Azhar mosque, 164
fatwas, 1, 21–22, 69, 177–78, 303
Fazul, Harun, 55, 67, 68, 76, 196, 200, 201–2
Federal Bureau of Investigation (FBI), xii–xiii, 26, 49, 128, 182, 193, 289–90, 301
Federally Administered Tribal Areas (FATA), Pakistan, 6
Ferjan tribe (Libya), 271
Fighting Vanguard, 210–11
Filkins, Dexter, 269
Finsbury Park Mosque, 116
fitna (discord), 255, 258–59
flogging, 266
Foley, Laurence, 131
foreign fighters, xvii, 53, 62–63, 70–72, 76–77, 81, 86–87, 96, 99, 100, 102, 103, 121–27, 134–35, 138–44, 149, 155–56, 218, 222–23, 226, 241, 247–251, 267, 291
Fort Hood shootings (2009), 193, 283
41st Division (Tharallah, "Vengeance of God"), Iranian, 227
France, 178, 199, 229, 233–34, 237, 270
Fredrikstad, 250

Freedom Flotilla, 24, 222
Free Syrian Army, 217, 219–20
French Mandate, 229
Fukuyama, Francis, 3–4

Gadahn, Adam, 18, 19
Gaddafi, Muammar, 15, 24, 236, 271
Gaddafi, Muatassim, 24
Gamaa al-Islamiya (GI), 170–71, 174, 176, 177
Garrison, William F., 60–61
Gaza, 24, 222, 228
General Electric (GE), 135
General National Congress, 271
Germany, 111, 123, 124, 220, 299
Ghab Valley, 219–20
Global Islamic Media Front, 153
Golden Mosque bombing (2006), 154–55, 159, 241
Great Britain, xvi, 38, 116, 178, 209, 233–34, 268, 299, 301–2
Greece, xii, 111–12, 238
Guantánamo Bay detention camp, 63, 64–65, 103–4, 129, 136, 278, 296–97
Gulf Arabs, xv, 70–72, 201, 217, 293
Gulf War (1990–1991), 56, 57, 62, 69–71, 116–17, 240

Habib, Khalid al-, 15
Hadhramut Province, 234–35, 259
Hadi, Abdu Rabbu Mansour, 235, 260, 285
Hadid, Omar, 135
hadiths, 12, 107–8, 157, 260, 280
Hage, Wadi al-, 116
Haji Bakr (nom de guerre), 241, 243–44, 246, 247, 249, 252, 261, 265
Hama, 211
Hamas, 66–67, 294
Hamdan, Salim Ahmed, 75–76
Hamid, Mustafa, 55–56, 59, 61, 89, 95, 102, 103, 280
Hamididdin, Imam Ahmad Bin Yahya, 51
Hamza the Qatari, 106
Haqqani Network, 280–81, 285
Harakat al Shabaab al-Mujahidin (al-Shabaab), xv, 16, 62, 196–98, 200–201, 203, 237–38, 273, 299
haram (forbidden), 46, 299
Haripur, 9, 10
Hashemite monarchy (Jordan), 118, 119–20, 121, 131
Hashimi, Tariq Al-, 248

Hashimiyah Square, 153
hashishin (assassins), 2–3
Hawijah, 249
Hekmatyar, Gulbuddin, 124
Helwan Steelworks, 51
Henry V (Shakespeare), 60–61
Herat, 95, 98, 102, 121–22, 123, 128, 153
Hercules, 296
Hezbollah, 57, 84, 220, 229, 230, 269
Hibhib, 157–58, 159
hijab (head scarf), 3
Hijra (Muhammad's journey), 10, 181
Hind helicopter gunships, 54
Hitler, Adolf, 295
Hofstad Network, 299
Holy Land, 2
homosexuality, 266
Homs, 211
Horn of Africa, 200
hostages, 16, 17–18, 72, 129, 203, 236, 252, 277, 280–81, 283
house arrest, 279–80
House of Representatives (Libyan group), 271
House of Saud, 2, 65, 70–71
Houta, 235
Houthis, 51, 235
hunger strikes, 302
Huntington, Samuel, 293
Hussein (caliph), 227, 262
Hussein, Fouad, 185–86
Hussein, King of Jordan, 109–10, 115, 116, 119, 127–28
Hussein, Saddam, xviii, 56, 62, 69–71, 108, 116, 119, 124, 127–28, 129, 134, 146, 212, 214–15, 228–29, 239–53, 266, 267, 292
Hydra, vii, 238, 296

Ibn Taymiyyah, 21–22, 141, 149, 173
Idlib, 177, 216–17, 220, 225–26, 257
ijtihad (independent thinking), 3
Imam Ali Mosque, 133
Imam Ali Mosque bombing (2003), 133, 240
imams, 151, 164, 193, 244
Incirlik Air Base, 222
Independent (UK newspaper), 19
India, 60, 249, 285
Indian Ocean, 44
Indonesia, 199, 300
infidels, 1–2, 117, 118, 121, 130, 138, 141, 185–86

Inspire (publication of al-Qaeda in the
        Arabian Peninsula), 194, 197
intifada, Palestinian, 86, 125, 172
Iran, 14–15, 27, 31–34, 41–42, 78, 101,
        124, 149, 167–68, 205, 213, 214–15,
        220–30, 269, 272, 276–84, 292, 314n
Iranian Revolutionary Guard, 78, 101,
        227, 230
Iran-Iraq War (1980–1988), 228
Iraq:
    constitution of, 151
    corruption in, 112, 190, 207, 213, 235–
        36, 273
    elections in (2005), 144–45
    government of, 135, 144–45, 151
    insurgency in, 133–36, 155, 187–91,
        217, 227–28, 238–49, 252–53, 257,
        286–87, 297–303
    political instability in, 206, 219, 223, 230,
        238, 272, 274, 280, 281, 292, 297
    U.S. counterinsurgency measures in,
        227–28, 297–303
    U.S. invasion and occupation of, 20,
        107–8, 124–29, 133, 185–86, 214,
        230, 240, 248, 296
    U.S. troop surge in, 191, 238
Iraqi, Abdul Hadi al-, 147
Iraqi, Abu Ayman al-, 241
Iraqi Governing Council, 135
Iraqi National Assembly, 144–45
Iraq War (2003–2011), 20, 107–8, 124–29,
        133, 185–86, 214, 230, 240, 248, 296
Irish Republican Army (IRA), 302
Isawi, Hamza al-, 156
Islamabad, 9, 50, 174
Islambouli, Khalid, 168
Islamic Courts Union (ICU), 196–97
Islamic Front, 256
Islamic fundamentalism, 1–3, 21–23,
        26, 52, 64, 68, 72, 73, 77, 113–23,
        134–35, 141–45, 148, 164–69, 171,
        190–91, 197–98, 205–8, 216–21,
        236–43, 256–69, 273, 282, 290–303
Islamic Jihad of Yemen, 62–63, 178
Islamic State (IS), xvi, xviii, 21, 22, 45, 92,
        110–14, 119, 127 134–35, 180–86,
        198, 199, 209–10 222, 223, 230–37,
        255–57, 259–62, 272, 274, 276, 281–
        82, 285, 286–88, 292–97, 300; *see
        also* Islamic State of Iraq (ISI); Islamic
        State of Iraq and the Levant (ISIL)
Islamic State Health Service, 268
Islamic State of Iraq (ISI), 36, 150, 155,

159–60, 162, 186–91, 195, 200, 208,
        219, 238–46, 250, 251, 253–54, 287;
        see also Islamic State (IS); Islamic
        State of Iraq and the Levant (ISIL)
Islamic State of Iraq and the Levant (ISIL),
        121, 210, 225, 238, 250, 251, 252,
        253–55, 256–61, 262, 263; *see also*
        Islamic State (IS); Islamic State of Iraq
        (ISI)
Islamic State of Khorasan (ISK), 272–73
Islamophobia, 299
Israel, 24, 49, 51, 52, 58, 66–67, 71, 78,
        86, 116, 120, 125, 145, 148, 152, 165,
        167, 177, 179–80, 198–99, 222, 224,
        229, 254, 279, 286, 290, 294
Istanbul, xvi, 220, 270
Istanbul airport attack (2016), 270
Istanbul nightclub attack (2017), xvi, 2
Ivory Coast, 237

Jabhat al-Nusra, 177, 210, 216, 253
Jabhat al-Nusra Li Ahl al-Sham (Support
        Front for the People of the Levant), 247
Jabhat Fateh al-Sham (Levantine Conquest
        Front), 183, 220
Jahiliyyah (Days of Ignorance), 3
Jaji, Battle of, 39, 53, 87, 89
Jalalabad, 54–55, 56, 67–68, 73, 92, 116,
        170, 275, 291, 314n
Jamma Islamiya, 46
Jeddah, 31, 55, 65–66
Jerusalem, 182, 286
"Jerusalem Is but a Bride Whose Dowry Is
        Our Blood" (H. bin Laden), 286
Jews, 2, 22, 70, 130, 153, 179–80, 190,
        265, 286, 302, *see also* Judaism
jihad and jihadists, 6–37, 44, 47, 70–72,
        124–25, 143, 147, 153, 162–65, 169,
        171–72, 176–200, 203, 207–23,
        230–31, 236–50, 255–64, 271–74,
        282–87, 290–303
Jihad and Reform Front, 156
"John" (Belfast Catholic), 302, 303
Jordan, 74, 78–79, 109–10, 113, 114–22,
        130–31, 139, 140, 141, 152–54, 158,
        206, 254
Judaism, 265; *see also* Jews
Julani, Abu Mohammed al-, 247, 253,
        254–56, 257, 281–82
Jund al-Sham (Soldiers of the Levant), 122

Kaambooni training camp, 59–60
Kabul, xiii, 71, 72, 92, 94, 95, 98, 106, 134

kafirs (unbelievers), 22, 43, 89–90
Kakul Military Academy, 6
Kalashnikov AK-47 assault rifle, 29, 38, 53, 65, 87, 91
Kampala, 197
Kandahar, 10–11, 47, 67, 79–81, 91, 92, 94–100, 103, 107, 120, 121–22, 142, 176, 264, 265
Kandahar airport, 92, 97, 99
Kandahar Religious Institute, 98–99
Karachi, 8, 72–73
Karbala, 133, 227
Karzai, Hamid, 18, 97, 99
Kasasbeh, Moath al-, 266–67
Katyusha rocket launchers, 152
Kenya, 197, 237
Kerman Province, 227
Kertchou, L'Houssaine, 55
Khaldan training camp, 55–56, 128
Khamenei, Ayatollah Ali, 126, 215, 228
Khan, Genghis, 21–22
Khan, Samir, 194
Khanaqin, 151
Kharijites, 21, 137
Khartoum, 31, 57, 58, 59–60, 63, 64, 172, 174–75, 314*n*
khat (drug), 197
Khatib, Hamza al-, 45
khatibs (preachers), 156
Khomeini, Ayatollah Ruhollah, 167–68
Khorasan, 71, 107–8, 182, 187, 188, 189, 191, 199, 203, 241–42, 253, 254, 255, 259, 261, 272–73, 284, 285
Khost Province, 199
Khyber Pass, 179
Khyber tribes, 35
kidnappings, 16, 17–18, 72, 129, 203, 236, 252, 277, 280–81, 283
Kismayo, 197, 237
Knights Under the Prophet's Banner (Zawahiri), 167
Koran, 21, 30–31, 69, 79, 90, 106, 107, 113, 118, 135, 142, 230, 244, 260, 263–64, 280, 290
Kosovo, 66
Kufa mosque, 21, 43
kunya (nickname), 29, 33, 187
Kurdistan, 125–26, 128, 145
Kurdistan Alliance, 145
Kurds, 125–26, 128, 144, 145, 222, 223, 293
Kuwait, xvi, 7–8, 56, 62, 63, 69–71, 85, 117, 214, 239

Kuwaiti, Abrar al- (Abrar Saeed Ahmed), 8–9, 10, 11, 32, 36–37, 40
Kuwaiti, Ibrahim al- (Ibrahim Saeed Ahmed) (Mohammed Arshad Naqab Khan, pseud.), 7–10, 11, 13, 32, 36–37, 40

Latakia, 216–17, 257
Lebanon, 57–58, 66–67, 84, 87–88, 206, 220, 223, 228, 229, 254
Levant, 22, 66–67, 78, 121, 122, 178, 253–54, 258, 300
Lewinsky, Monica, 88
Libi, Abu Laith al-, 15, 26, 28–29
Libi, Ibn al-Sheikh al-, 128
Library, The (Pseudo-Apollodorus), vii, 289
Libya, xvi–xvii, 15, 24, 44, 153, 199, 205, 208, 236, 250, 251, 270, 271–72, 285, 287, 300
Libyan Islamic Fighting Group, 13–14, 50, 153
Lisleby neighborhood of Fredrikstad, 250
literacy, 111–13
London bombings (2005), 2, 182–83
lone wolf attacks, 274, 286, 287
Los Angeles Airport bombing plot (2000), 79
Louis XIV, King of France, 206

Madrid bombings (2004), 2, 182–83
Maghreb, 72, 181
Mahdi (Islamic Messiah), 189
"Mahmud" (Atiyah Abd-al-Rahman), 13–14, 16, 17, 19, 20–21, 23, 24, 25, 27, 28, 31, 32, 33, 35, 37, 41, 46, 153–55, 179, 202, 258, 278, 281
Majlis al-Shura (consultative council), 79
Makkawi, Mohammed Ibrahim, 49–50, 84
Malaysia, 300
Mali, 199, 236–37, 238, 286
Maliki, Nuri al-, 126–27, 186, 248–49
Management of Savagery: The Most Critical Stage Through Which the Umma Will Pass, The (Abu Bakr Naji), 27–28, 184–86, 189, 190, 207–9, 259, 260, 287, 293
Maqdisi, Abu Mohammed al-, 117–18, 119, 137–38, 145, 149, 151, 152, 257, 262
Marines, U.S., 59, 63, 144, 206, 230
Marka, 197

Maronites, 209
Marshall Plan, 295
"martyrdom brigades," 93, 129–30, 150, 153
Marx, Karl, 114
Masri, Abu Hafs al-, 48, 66, 68, 80, 82, 95–96, 103, 116
Masri, Abu Khair al-, 14, 80–81, 101–2, 103, 105–6, 277, 278–80, 281, 283, 284
Masri, Abu Mohammed al-, 14, 33, 74–75, 81, 82, 100, 101–2, 103, 105–6, 277, 278–80, 281, 283, 284
Masri, Said al-, 15, 80
Massoud, Ahmed Shah, 86–87, 92–93
Matthew, Gospel of, 82
Mauritani, Abu Hafs al-, 80, 90, 106, 280
Mauritani, Younis al-, 202
Mauritania, 198–99
Mazar-i-Sharif, 95, 227
McChrystal, Stanley, 159
Mecca, 10, 52, 65, 133, 218, 256, 263
Medina, 10, 133, 218, 297–98
Mes Aynak training camp, 72
Mesopotamia, 126, 132–33, 153, 296–97
Middle East, xvi, 23, 26, 107–13, 138, 163, 172, 199, 205–9, 220, 229, 230, 233–34, 274, 292, 293–303
military coups, 221
militias, 62, 216–17, 226–28, 230, 246–47, 255, 271–72
Millennium bomb plots (2000), 79, 101, 120, 152
misbaha (prayer beads), 275–76
Misrata, 13
Missionaries of Charity, 272
Mogadishu, 54, 58–61, 63, 64, 70, 88, 95, 196, 237, 284
Mohammed, Khalid Sheikh (KSM), 8, 9, 12, 15, 29, 63, 72–73, 85, 88–89, 93, 96, 101, 102, 104–5, 116, 211, 302, 303, 314n
Mohammed bin Nayyif, Crown Prince of Saudi Arabia, 218–19
Mohammed bin Salman, Crown Prince of Saudi Arabia, 219
Molenbeek neighborhood of Brussels, 92, 112, 250
money laundering, 17–18
Mongols, 21–22, 141, 173
Mora, Alberto, 129
Morocco, 205, 206
Morsi, Mohammed, 222, 294

Moses, 145
mosques, 21, 51–52, 73, 115–16, 133, 149, 151, 164, 171, 193, 218, 219, 221, 240, 244, 256, 263, 264, 272, 280, 297–98
Mosul, 114, 222, 241, 252, 265, 268
Mother Teresa, 272
Mubarak, Hosni, xv, 25, 33, 49, 50, 119, 141, 169, 171, 174, 201, 281
Mughniyah, Jihad, 230
Mugniyah, Imad, 57–58, 230
Muhajir, Abu Hamza al-, 187–88, 189, 190, 238–39, 243
Muhammad, 4, 10, 25, 38, 45, 46, 62, 67, 70, 157, 171, 187, 218, 261, 263–64, 266
Muhaysini, Sheikh Abdullah al-, 256–57, 261
mujahideen, 8, 26–27, 33, 39, 53–56, 83, 103, 116, 140, 148, 154, 185, 196, 226, 239–40, 262–63
Mujahideen Shura Council, 156, 159–60
Mukalla, 235, 236, 259
murtadeen (apostates), 22
Musharraf, Pervez, 6
Muskar al-Battar, 280
Muslim Brotherhood, 49, 115, 140, 163, 165, 166, 185, 210–11, 222, 244, 281, 294
Mussolini, Benito, 295

Najibullah, Mohammed, 54–55, 68
Nangarhar Canal, 275
Nasirayah, 245
Nasser, Gamal Abdel, 22, 51, 165, 207
National Health Service (NHS) (UK), 268
National Interest (U.S. magazine), 3
National Islamic Front (NIF), 56–57
Navy, U.S., xiv, 39–40, 152, 229
neo-Nazis, 299
Netherlands, 299
"new jihadi highway," 222–23
New Testament, 265
New Yorker, 20
New York Times, xiv, xv, 18, 156
Nice, Bastille Day attack in (2016), 2, 274
Niger, 199
Nigeria, 2, 236, 273
9/11 Commission, xviii, 82, 290–91, 294, 314n
Nineveh, 263
nisbah (toponym), 8
North Africa, xvi, 23, 206–7, 236, 288, 291

North Atlantic Treaty Organization (NATO), 103, 222
Northern Alliance, 69, 72, 73, 86–87, 92–93, 95, 98–99, 103, 107, 121, 123, 227
Northern Group, 71–72
Northern Ireland, 299, 301–2, 303
North Korea, 228
Northwest Airlines bombing attempt (2009), 20
Northwest Airlines Flight 253 bombing attempt (2009), 194
Nouakchott bombing (2009), 198–99
nuclear weapons, xviii, 102, 127–28, 228, 284

Obama, Barack, xiv, 17, 20, 215, 219, 248, 295
Office of Mujahideen Services, 116
oil and gas reserves, 112, 223, 224, 228, 229, 252, 271, 272
Omar, Mullah Mohammed, 14, 46–47, 67, 69, 77–78, 86, 92, 97–98, 99, 153, 188, 189, 256, 260, 264, 282, 283, 285
Omran, Ali, 46
O'Neill, John, xii–xiii, xiv
One Percent Doctrine, xviii
Operation Infinite Reach, 88
Operation Restore Hope, 59–60, 63
Organization of African Unity (OAU), 174
Orthodox Christians, 209
Ottoman Empire, 132, 209, 224, 261
Ouagadougou attacks (2016), 237

Pakistan, 5–44, 46, 69, 71, 90, 100–105, 120, 147, 164, 166, 169, 171, 174, 189, 199, 201–2, 211, 230, 241–42, 272–73, 275, 278, 280–81, 285, 286, 291, 299–300
Pakistani Taliban (Tehrik-i Taliban Pakistan), 199, 201, 285, 299–300
Paktika Province, 273
Palestine Liberation Organization (PLO), 115
Palestinians, 24, 66, 78, 86, 114, 115, 116–17, 125, 137, 153, 172, 177, 222, 229, 286, 294
Palmyra, 269
pan-Arabism, 51, 205–7
Paris attacks (2015), xvi, xvii, 92, 111, 212, 250, 270
Pashto language, 276

Pashtun tribe, 7, 11, 67, 69, 97
Pasternak, Boris, 48–49
Patek, Umar, 6–7
peacekeeping forces, 196, 197
Pearl, Daniel, 8, 104
Peloponnesian War, xii
Peres, Shimon, 222
Persian Empire, xii, 71
Peshawar, 117, 120, 122, 166–70
Petraeus, David, 6, 227–28
Philippines, 199, 273
"Planes Operation," 85, 89–90, 93, 95, 101, 179, 211
police forces, 68, 150, 168, 219, 242–43, 265–66, 267
polygamy, 30–31
"popular jihad," 294
Powell, Colin, 127–28, 129
pressure-cooker bombs, 194
prisoner swaps, 280–81
Prophet's Mosque bombing (2016), 218, 297–98
prostitution, 193, 302
"protection taxes," 190, 252
Protestants, 301–2, 303
Pseudo-Apollodorus, vii, 289
Puntland, 197
purdah (female seclusion), 11
Putin, Vladimir, 224

Qaedat al-Jihad fi Bilad al-Rafidayn (The Base of Jihad in the Land of Two Rivers), *see* al-Qaeda in Iraq
Qaim, 146–47
Qamari, Issam al-, 167, 168
Qaradawi, Yusuf al-, 137
Qatar, 207
Qosi, Ibrahim, 64–65
Quds Force, 78, 94, 226–27
Quraysh tribe, 261, 262
Quso, Fahd al-, 192
Qutb, Sayyid, 22, 163, 164, 165, 169

Raddatz, Martha, xiv
Radisson Hotel attack plot, Amman (2000), 78–79; *see also* Millennium bomb plots 2000
Rahman, Sheikh Omar Abul al-("The Blind Sheikh"), 157–58, 170–71
Ramadan, 36, 81, 84, 96–97, 98, 262, 263, 298
Ramadi, 146, 156, 189, 269
Raqqa, 251–52, 266

Rashidun Caliphate, 208
Ras Lanuf, 272
Rawalpindi, 9, 101, 102
Raymi, Qasim al-, 285
Red Army, 166
Reed, Jack (U.S. senator), 36
refugees, 114, 115, 116–17, 166, 169, 231
rehabilitation programs, 298–300
religious police, 68, 266–67
Religious Rehabilitation Group
    (Singapore), 298–99
"Republic of al-Zarqawi," 134, 137, 138;
    see also Fallujah
Reuters (news organization), 236
ricin, 128
Riyadh, 65, 225
Roman Empire, 184
Rouhani, Hassan, 224
RQ-7 Shadow reconnaissance drone, 146
Ruseifah, 114–15
Russia, xvi, xvii, 70, 102, 175–76, 209, 222,
    223, 224, 226, 269, 270, 271, 293
Russian airliner bombing, Egypt (2015),
    xvi
Russian military plane shootdown, Turkey
    (2015), 223, 270, 271

Saadi, Abdul Alim al-, 156
Sabar, Khairia (Umm Hamza), 31–34, 37,
    41, 279, 280–81
Sabar, Siham (Umm Khalid), 29–30, 31,
    276
Sabbah, Hassan-i, 2, 4, 10, 182; see also
    Assassins
Sadat, Anwar, xv, 52, 165, 167, 168–69, 170
Saddah, Amal al-(Umm Ibrahim), 29, 38,
    39, 40, 41, 43, 44
Saddam University, 244
Sahel, 237
Sahwa Salafism, 294
St. Luke's Church (Abbottabad), 6
Saladin, 113
Salafist Group for Preaching and Combat,
    198
Salafist movement, 114, 117, 148, 198,
    205–6, 241, 243, 256, 261–62, 282,
    294–97, 303
Salahuddin code system, 74
Saleh, Ali Abdullah, 23, 62
Salman bin Abdelaziz, King of Saudi
    Arabia, 219
Salvation from Hell (Egyptian military
    group), 50

Samarra, 154–55, 159, 241, 244
Samir the Najdi, 106
Sanaa, xiii, 23, 193, 194–95, 196, 235,
    272, 283, 285
Sanaa embassy bombing (2008), 194, 196
San Diego, 193
Saudi Arabia, xiv, xvi, 2, 23, 28, 35, 52–
    53, 56, 62, 64, 69, 70, 102–3, 116,
    117, 140, 151, 164, 182, 191, 194,
    208, 217–18, 235 , 256, 257, 268,
    270, 272, 277, 294, 300
Saudi National Guardsmen, 64
Sawt al-Jihad, 184
Schwarzkopf, H. Norman, 70
Scud missiles, 228
SEALs, xiv, 39–40, 229
sectarian violence, 58, 132–33, 137–42,
    148–51, 159, 186, 216, 217, 225, 228,
    230–31, 240, 241, 248, 253, 267,
    272–73, 276–78, 292–93, 298, 301–2
Sednaya Prison, 211–12, 215–16, 225
Seljuks, 3
Senate Armed Services Committee, 129
September 11th attacks (2001), xiii, xvi,
    xviii, 2–25, 29–35, 45, 48, 57, 63,
    72, 81–95, 101, 106, 116, 123, 128,
    161, 170, 179, 181, 182, 185, 193,
    199, 211, 213–14, 238, 265, 276, 277,
    284–94, 302–3, 314n
Serbia, 83
"Shadow Commander," 227–28; see also
    Soleimani Qassem
Shahzad, Mohammed Tahir, 6–7
Shakespeare, William, 60–61
shalwar kameez (Pashtun dress), 11, 120
@ShamiWitness, 249
Shamraiz (farmer), 10
Shangla, 8
Sharia, 21–22, 34, 117, 120–21, 130, 137,
    175, 178, 184, 190, 197–98, 234,
    236, 244, 245, 256, 257, 259, 260–
    61, 262, 294
Sharm el-Sheikh, 270
Sheikh, Omar, 104
sheikhs, 155–56, 170–71
Sherzai, Gul Agha, 97, 98, 99
"Shia Crescent," 140–41
Shia Muslims, 51, 57, 58, 66, 108, 110,
    113, 121, 132, 135, 139, 140–45,
    148–56, 159, 186, 190, 191, 209,
    220, 223–29, 240, 245, 248, 251–52,
    262, 267, 272–73, 276–78, 292, 293,
    297, 302

Shibam tourist attacks (2009), 196
Shibin al-Kawm, 51, 53
Shiraz (region of Iran), 66, 101–3, 278
Shishani, Omar al-, 269
"shock and awe" tactics, 108, 214–15
shura council, 47, 79, 81, 90, 104, 105–6, 147, 172, 179, 199–200, 201, 243–44, 245, 253, 265, 277, 281, 284
Sidqi, Atef, 173
Sidra, 272
Sindi, Abdullah al- (Umar Siddque Kathio Azmarai), 35
Singapore, 298, 300
Sirte, 270–71, 272
Sisi, Abdel Fattah al-, 222
Sistan Basin, 66
Sistani, Ayatollah Ali al-, 144, 145
siwak (toothbrush), 246–47
Six-Day War, 51, 165
smuggling, 251–52
socialism, 51, 62
social media, 138, 194, 249–50, 262, 298
Soleimani, Qassem, 226–28, 230
solitary confinement, 279
Somalia, 16, 47–48, 54, 58–62, 63, 64, 70, 88, 95, 103, 181, 195–98, 200, 237–38, 273, 284, 286
"Some of Our Fundamentals," 190
Southeast Asia, 273, 278
South Pars–North Dome gas field, 229
Soviet Union, xiv, xvi, 3–4, 8, 11, 30, 32, 39, 49, 50, 53–56, 71, 80, 81, 86, 89, 103, 116, 120, 149, 166, 169, 171, 218, 250, 255
Sparta, xii
Spin Ghar, 275
State Department, U.S., 278
State Security Court, Jordanian, 109–10
Stevens, Christopher, 271
Stinger missiles, 54
stonings, 190, 195, 197, 266
Strela-2 surface-to-air missiles, 91
sub-Saharan Africans, 273
Sudan, 56–57, 58, 63, 65, 88, 125, 172, 174–75, 291, 314*n*
suhur (predawn breakfast during Ramadan), 96–97
suicide bombings, xv, 2–3, 46, 127, 129, 135–36, 137, 149–54, 156, 162, 163, 174, 188, 197, 215, 218, 219, 222, 224, 225, 241, 243, 252, 258, 262, 270, 272
sujud (bowing to the floor), 162

Sunni Awakening, 156, 189–90, 238, 248
Sunni Muslims, 21, 51, 57, 58, 66, 110, 113, 124, 125–26, 132–33, 134, 137–45, 148–56, 159, 167, 174, 186, 189–91, 209, 213, 218, 222, 226, 229, 230, 234, 238–44, 248–49, 253, 267, 276–78, 292, 293, 294, 302
Sunni Triangle, 134, 244
Sun Tsu, xviii
Supreme Court, U.S., 82, 88
Suqor al-Sham Brigades, 226
Surah Al-Fath, 43
Suri, Abu Khalid al- (Mohammed Bahaiah), 210–11, 215–16, 217, 220, 225, 226, 247, 255, 256, 258–59
Suri, Abu Musab al-, 121, 181, 184–85, 186, 190, 210–11
Swat, 8–9, 10, 12
Sweidawi, Abu Mohammad al-, 269
Sykes-Picot Agreement (1916), 172, 233–34, 255
Syria, xvi, 25, 31, 44–45, 51, 65, 70, 72, 111, 126, 154, 173, 177, 183, 186, 205–31, 238, 242, 245, 247, 250–55, 268, 272, 274, 278, 281–88, 292, 293, 297, 299, 314

Taha, Rifai Ahmad, 177
Tajikistan, 71
takfiris (Islamic radicals), 22–23, 64, 73, 141–42, 171, 266, 273
Tal Afar, 150, 241
Talib, Ali Ibn Ali, 21, 132–33
Taliban, xvi, 2, 67–69, 74–78, 86–100, 106–7, 120–21, 134, 143, 148, 179, 181, 191, 197 199, 227, 256, 260–61, 273, 276, 277, 282, 285, 299–300
Tanta, 164
Tarnak Farm, 73–76, 81, 82, 90–91, 94
Tartusi, Abu Basir al-, 151
Tawhid wal Jihad (Monotheism and Jihad), 122–23, 124, 136, 140, 142, 144–45, 159
Tehran, 228, 278–80
Tel Aviv, 179
terrorists:
  air strikes targeted against, 146–47, 157–58, 162–63, 177, 193, 197, 202, 225, 235, 267, 269–72, 285, 287, 295, 297
  civilian casualties from, 21, 75, 88–89, 116, 119, 130, 135, 137–39, 146, 150–54, 173–74, 280, 296–97

terrorists (*continued*)
as detainees, 128–29, 215, 239–47, 277–80, 314*n*
executions carried out by, 174–75, 197–98, 223, 266–69, 281
as foreign fighters, xvii, 53, 62–63, 70–72, 76–77, 81, 86–87, 96, 99, 100, 102, 103, 121–27, 134–35, 138–44, 149, 155–56, 218, 222–23, 226, 241, 247–251, 267, 291
global, 17, 19–23, 44, 47, 70–72, 124–25, 143, 147, 153, 163, 171–72, 177–78, 181–86, 191, 193–94, 196, 198–99, 200, 203, 217, 258, 273–74, 282, 284–85, 290–97
hostages and kidnappings of, 16, 17–18, 72, 129, 203, 236, 252, 277, 280–81, 283
intelligence on, xviii, 74, 78–79, 102–3, 111, 115, 120, 121–22, 128–29, 156–58, 174, 203, 220, 255, 277–80, 284, 295
interrogations of, 211–12, 215, 314*n*
as Islamic fundamentalists, 1–3, 21–23, 26, 52, 64, 68, 72, 73, 77, 113–23, 134–35, 141–45, 148, 164–69, 171, 190–91, 197–98, 205–8, 216–21, 236–43, 256–69, 273, 282, 290–303
lone wolf attacks by, 274, 286, 287
martyrdom ideology of, 17, 41, 44, 76, 87, 90, 93, 106–7, 129–33, 150, 153, 162–63, 226, 238–39, 258–59
militias of, 62, 216–17, 226–28, 230, 246–47, 255, 271–72
Muslim victims of, 21, 116, 119, 130, 135, 137–39, 150–54, 173–74, 280
organizations of, 219, 237–38, 287, 293–94; *see also specific organizations*
in prisons, 108, 118–19, 128–29, 168–71, 211–12, 215–16, 225, 239–47, 277–81, 285, 296–97
sectarian violence by, 58, 132–33, 137–42, 148–51, 159, 186, 216, 217, 225, 228, 230–31, 240, 241, 248, 253, 267, 272–73, 276–78, 292–93, 298, 301–2
secular regimes attacked by, 22–23, 24, 25, 111–12, 117, 121, 140–41, 177–78, 181–82, 183, 190, 205–7, 212–13, 217, 220–25, 226, 267, 281, 293, 294
suicide bombings of, xv, 2–3, 46, 127, 129, 135–36, 137, 149–54, 156, 162, 163, 174, 188, 197, 215, 218, 219, 222, 224, 225, 241, 243, 252, 258, 262, 270, 272
"Syrian pipeline" for, 126–27, 138, 139, 151
videos recorded by, xvii, 81–82, 136–37, 148, 155, 157, 175, 234, 223, 249, 258, 271

Tigantourine natural gas complex, 203
Tikrit, 238–39, 244, 252–53
Tikrit University, 244
Time, 94
Tobruk, 271
Tora Bora, 8, 10, 64, 67, 68–69, 87, 89, 106, 192, 275–76
torture, 128–29, 168–69, 248
"tourism Jihad," 54, 93
TOW anti-tank missiles, 219–20
Townshend, Pete, 207
Toyota pickup trucks, 91
tribal groups, 1, 35, 58–59, 62, 114, 154, 155–56, 179, 190–91, 195, 198, 199, 207, 234, 236, 246, 251, 261, 262, 264, 265, 267, 271, 273, 280, 293, 298
Tripoli, 15
Troubles (Northern Ireland), 301–2, 303
Trump, Donald, 301
Tsarnaev, Dzhokhar and Tamerlan, 194
Tunisia, 24–25, 26, 134–35, 206, 207, 218, 250, 272
Turabi, Hassan al-, 294
Turkey, xvi, 114, 123, 124, 209, 217–18, 220–25, 226, 231, 257, 267, 270
Turkmani, Abu Muslim al-, 241
Turkmens, 150, 224, 293
TWA Flight 847 hijacking (1985), 84
Twenty Guidelines on the Path of Jihad (Abu Ghaith), 280
Twitter, 249–50

Uganda, 197
ulama (clerics), 151
umma (Islamic nation), 25, 33, 44, 106, 184, 207–8, 256–57, 258
Umm Abdul Rahman, 30
Umma Initiative, 256–57
unemployment, 112–13
United Arab Emirates (UAE), 69, 235, 314*n*
United Iraqi Alliance, 144, 145
United Nations, 59–60, 64, 68, 103, 121, 127–28, 129, 131–32, 196, 198, 213–14

United Nations Security Council, 127–28, 129, 213–14

United Nations Security Council Resolution 1373, 213–14

United States:
as al-Qaeda target, 19–21, 75, 85–90, 181–82, 185, 192, 203; *see also specific attacks*
global influence of, xi–xii, 3–4, 87
intelligence operation of, 128–29
Middle East policies of, 26, 107–8, 163, 209, 216, 296–97
oil supplies of, 107–8
public opinion in, 64, 82, 87–88, 94, 127–29, 215
special forces of, 26, 92, 97, 99, 100, 157, 192, 269, 295

Urdu language, 32

U.S. Agency for International Development (USAID), 131

U.S. Joint Special Operations Command, 12

Uzbekistan, 199

veils, 190, 264, 266

Vieira de Mello, Sérgio, 108, 131–32

Vietnam War, 20, 54, 61, 89, 230

Wahhabism, 148

Wall Street Journal, 8, 104

warlords, 67, 68–69, 113

Waziristan, 6–7, 13, 16, 19, 28, 31, 33, 35, 44, 90, 100–101, 154, 179, 199, 202, 273, 280–81, 283, 285

weapons of mass destruction (WMDs), xviii, 127–29, 131, 214, 284

Welfare Party (Turkey), 221

Wells, H. G., 113

West Bank, 116–17

Western civilization, 2, 3–4, 72–73, 163, 182, 183–86, 193–94, 197, 226, 230–31, 234, 236, 293, 296–303

Westgate Mall attack, Nairobi (2013), 203

White Palace, 221

Whitewater Development Corp., 67

WikiLeaks, 24

Wolfowitz, Paul, xviii

women, xviii, 11, 29, 68, 112, 134, 150, 190, 236, 264, 266, 267, 279, 299

World Trade Center bombing (1993), 55, 63–64, 84–85, 88

Wuhayshi, Nasser al-, 90, 192, 193–95, 201, 203, 235, 237, 255–56, 285

Yaqoob, Mullah Mohammad, 283

Yasa, 21–22

Yathrib, 10

Yazidis, 251–52, 267

Yemen, xiii, xvi, 23, 26–27, 44, 47–51, 62–65, 79, 82, 181, 192–95, 201–208, 219, 220, 234–35, 238, 259, 270, 272, 281, 285– 288, 292, 300

Yobe State, 299

Yom Kippur War (1973), 50, 172

Yousafzai, Malala, 299

Yousef, Ramzi, 55, 63–64, 84–85

Yugoslavia, 117

Yusufiyah, 57

Zaidan, Ahmad, 18, 19

zakat (charity), 9

Zalewski, Piotr, 224

Zangi, Nur ad-Din, 113–14, 148, 263

Zarqa, 110, 114–17, 118, 158

Zarqawi, Abu Musab al-, xvii, 4, 23, 75, 78, 95, 96, 104, 108, 109–60, 161, 185–88, 206, 214, 217, 230–31, 241–44, 253, 257, 258, 261, 263, 269, 272, 280, 284, 287, 292, 303

Zarqawism, 158–60

Zawahiri, Ayman al-, xv, xvii, 11–19, 28, 45–52, 79–80, 90, 92, 104, 119, 130, 140–41, 147–54, 160–68, 170, 176–79, 187, 199–201, 208, 210, 211, 234, 241, 243, 254–61, 277, 281–87, 291

Zhou Enlai, 84

Zinjibar, 195, 234

Zurmat, 100